VEDA RECITATION IN VĀRĀṆASĪ

VEDA RECITATION IN VĀRĀṆASĪ

WAYNE HOWARD

MOTILAL BANARSIDASS
Delhi Varanasi Patna Madras

Head Office: Bungalow Road, Delhi 110 007
Branches: Chowk, Varanasi 221 001
Ashok Rajpath, Patna 800 004
6 Appar Swamy Koil Street, Mylapore,
Madras 600 004

First Edition: Delhi, 1986

ISBN: 81-208-0071-0

Printed in India by Jainendra Prakash Jain at Shri Jainendra Press,
A-45 Naraina, Phase I, New Delhi 110 028 and published by
Narendra Prakash Jain for Motilal Banarsidass, Delhi 110 007.

CONTENTS

List of Illustrations viii
List of Tables viii
Preface ix
Key to Divisions of Vedic Texts xi

Introduction to Vārāṇasī's Vedic Heritage 1
The Imprint of the *Aśvamedha* 1
Dakṣiṇī Paṇḍits 5
Recent *Śrauta* Rituals 10

I. ṚGVEDA AND ATHARVAVEDA

The Source of Ṛgveda in Vārāṇasī 21
Accentuation 23
Forms of Ṛgvedic Recitation 25
Euphonic Combination (*Sandhi*) 27
Recitations 30
Ṛgveda 1.1.1-9 31
Ṛgveda 1.2.1-9 33
Ṛgveda 1.3.1-12 46
Ṛgveda 9.45.1-6 54
Ṛgveda 2.12.1 56
Analysis 75
Udātta 75
Anudātta 78
Svarita 81
Pracaya 84
Conclusions 86
Udātta 86
Anudātta 88
Svarita 89
Pracaya 92
General Remarks 93
Atharvaveda 109

II. YAJURVEDA

Geography of the White Yajus, with Relation to Vārāṇasī 115

The Mādhyandina School : Recitations 121
Jaṭā 124
Kramamālā 124
Puṣpamālā 131
Pañcasandhi 133
Śikhā 136
Rekhā 138
Dhvaja 141
Daṇḍa 142
Ratha 148

The Mādhyandina School : Analysis 151
Outline of Tone Usage 151
Accent 163
Initiality 165
Finality 166
Parigraha Analysis 167
Hiatus 167
Visarga 168
Ghuṃ 168
Conjuncts 168
Final Consonants 169
Successive Short Syllables 169
Protracted Syllables 169

Other Mādhyandina Recitations 170
Fragment from a Mixed *Vikṛti* 170
The *Puruṣa* Hymn 173

General Characteristics of Mādhyandina Yajurveda 190

Other Yajurvedic Recitations 191
The Taittirīyas 191
The Kāṇvas 192

III. SĀMAVEDA

Saṃhitā of the Kauthuma School 199

Vārāṇasī As the Center of Kauthuma Tradition 202

The Sāmaveda Community in Vārāṇasī 207

The Numeral Notation 214

Transcriptions of Selected *Sāmans* 225
- *Śyena* (Grāmageyagāna 73.1) 229
- *Pāṣṭhauha* I (Grāmageyagāna 192.1) 233
- *Pāṣṭhauha* II (Grāmageyagāna 192.2) 233
- *Dhurāsākamaśva* (Grāmageyagāna 193.1) 233
- *Gaurīvita* (Grāmageyagāna 318.1) 236
- *Tārkṣyasāman* I (Grāmageyagāna 332.1) 236
- *Tārkṣyasāman* II (Grāmageyagāna 332.2) 249
- *Indrasya Tāta* (Grāmageyagāna 333.1) 249
- *Ātīṣādīya* (Grāmageyagāna 572.6) 257
- *Loman* (Grāmageyagāna 582.1) 260
- *Rathantara* (Āraṇyakagāna 49.1) 260
- *Setuṣāman* (Āraṇyakagāna 57.1) 263
- *Āmahīyava* (Ūhagāna 1.1.1) 277
- *Vāmadevya* (Ūhagāna 1.1.5) 281
- *Rathantara* (Ūhyagāna 1.1.1) 282
- *Bhakāra-Rathantara* (on Ūhyagāna 1.1.1) 286

Analysis 295
- Comments on Motive Distribution 295
- *Prakṛti* 1 298
- Rules for Singing *Prakṛti* 1 303
- *Prakṛti* 2 305
- Rules for Singing *Prakṛti* 2 309
- *Prakṛti* 3 312
- Rules for Singing *Prakṛti* 3 313
- *Prakṛti* 4 315
- Rules for Singing *Prakṛti* 4 316
- *Prakṛti* 5 318
- Rules for Singing *Prakṛti* 5 320
- Sequences 323
- Duration 333

The *Gāyatra* 341

Gallery of Vedic Paṇḍits (*Vārāṇasī*) 347

Bibliography 359

Notes 365

Index 385

LIST OF ILLUSTRATIONS

1. Map: Twelve Sites of Recent *Śrauta* Rituals 16
2. Śrī Dr. Śrīkṛṣṇa Vāman Dev (Ṛgvedī) 347
3. Śrī Dr. Viśvanāth Vāman Dev (Ṛgvedī) 348
4. Śrī Anant Rām Puṇtāmbekar (Ṛgvedī) 349
5. Śrī S. Śrīnivās Dīkṣit (Kṛṣṇa Yajurvedī) 350
6. Śrī Rājārām Bhaṭ Nirmale (Śukla Yajurvedī) 351
7. Śrī Dr. Gajānan Śāstrī Musalgā̃vkar (Śukla Yajurvedī) 352
8. Śrī Lakṣmīkānt Śāstrī Khaṇaṅg (Śukla Yajurvedī) 353
9. Śrī Agniṣvātt Śāstrī Agnihotrī (Sāmavedī) 354
10. Śrī Nārāyaṇ Śaṅkar Tripāṭhī (Sāmavedī) 355
11. Śrī P. Kṛṣṇamūrti Śrauti (Sāmavedī) 356
12. Śrī Rāmcandra Śāstrī Raṭāṭe (Atharvavedī, Ṛgvedī) 357
13. Śrī Nārāyaṇ Śāstrī Raṭāṭe (Atharvavedī, Ṛgvedī) 358

LIST OF TABLES

1. Incidence of Initiality 166
2. Incidence of Finality 167
3. Kauthuma Saṃhitā 201
4. Motive Distribution in Sixteen *Sāmans* 299

PREFACE

The principal focus of this study is on a syllable-by-syllable analysis of the most characteristic styles of Veda recitation in Vārāṇasī (Banāras, Kāśī), the main Vedic center in North India. This is the second book resulting from fifteen months of field research (September, 1970 to December, 1971) made possible by a Fulbright-Hays Scholarship. Major contributors to the success of the visit to India have already been presented in my *Sāmavedic Chant* (New Haven and London, 1977). I will not repeat that long list of names here but will state that great assistance in Vārāṇasī itself was given by Dr. Prem Lata Sharma (Musicology Department, Banāras Hindu University). Direct help was obtained from a large number of Vedic reciters and chanters; acknowledgement of their contributions is made at various places in the present work. Prof. Jan Gonda (Utrecht), Prof. George Cardona (Pennsylvania), and Prof. Sumitra M. Katre (San Jose) have been generous and constructive with their advice on translations, phonetics, and other topics. I deeply appreciate also the aid of Prof. Rama Nath Sharma (Hawaii), whose insightful comments could not, unfortunately, be included due to press of time. I should especially mention the helpful services of Martha Irby (Mitchell Memorial Library, Mississippi State University), who assisted me in obtaining books and articles, and the Greenwood-Leflore Public Library (Greenwood, Mississippi), whose microfilm readers were made available to me. I am particularly grateful to Motilal Banarsidass for agreeing to undertake publication and to the American Musicological Society, which has sponsored the work by awarding a subvention. Last but not least, I should thank my parents, who have helped me throughout.

The four Vedas (Ṛg, Yajur, Sāma, Atharva) are not "books" in the usual sense, though within the past hundred years each Veda has appeared in several printed editions. They are comprised rather of tonally accented verses and hypnotic, abstruse melodies whose proper realizations demand oral instead of visual transmission. They are robbed of their essence when transferred to paper, for without the human element the innumerable nuances and fine intonations — inseparable and necessary components of all four compilations — are lost completely. The ultimate authority in Vedic matters is never the printed page but rather the few members of the Brāhmaṇa caste who are today keeping the centuries-old traditions alive. However, the Vedas are approaching a point in history which will determine whether they survive or slip into extinction. They have shown remarkable vigor and perseverance in the past—thriving under potentially destructive political, economic, and religious upheaval—but whether they can withstand the accelerated rate of social change in the twentieth century is a formidable question which leaves their future in grave doubt.

I came to India with the purpose of recording and documenting as much as I could from as many different Vedic reciters as possible. As a music historian my principal concern was Sāmaveda, the Veda of notated melodies, but I was able to record many examples from the other three collections as well. By the time I left India I had on tape specimens from over a hundred reciters and chanters. The bulk of my recordings was made in South India; but some interesting discoveries were made also in the North, where Vedic traditions have not been as well researched and defined. In order to fill this lacuna, the following survey is devoted to the most important Vedic center in North India—the holy city Vārāṇasī. This ancient and mysterious pilgrimage place was headquarters for the greater part of my tour. Here I was able not only to determine which Vedas and *śākhā*s (schools or recensions of the Vedas) are to be found within the city limits but also to tape-record productions of some of the most highly respected Vaidikas (Vedic chanters).

This study deals only with the principal Vedic collections, the *saṃhitā*s, and not with the later *brāhmaṇa*s (exegeses on proper sacrificial conduct), *āraṇyaka*s (philosophical forest texts), and *upaniṣad*s (mystical collections forming the foundation of the Vedānta philosophy). Many of these auxiliary texts are also recited (one paṇḍit, for instance, knows by memory all eight *brāhmaṇa*s of the Kauthuma Sāmaveda); however, descriptions of these recitations are beyond the compass of the present effort. Among other texts to which reference is made are the *śrautasūtra*s, collections of short aphorisms which supplement the *brāhmaṇa*s.

Most terms are briefly defined on their first appearance in the book. The glossary of my *Sāmavedic Chant* may be consulted for a fuller explanation of many terms relating to the Vedas and Vedic ritual, especially to the Sāmaveda.

The musical transcriptions employ sharps and flats above the notes to show intonations in those directions. A diagonal line between tones indicates a glide; a wavy line shows natural vocal vibrato; a comma shows where breath is taken. The equivalence of the first note of a transcription to the actual pitch is given, as are metronomic readings for all examples.

INTRODUCTION TO VĀRĀṆASĪ'S VEDIC HERITAGE

The Imprint of the Aśvamedha

Ancient Vārāṇasī was the capital of the kingdom of Kāśi, which is first mentioned in connection with Veda recitation by the Śatapatha-Brāhmaṇa. Here we read that King Dhṛtarāṣṭra of Kāśi had undertaken a performance of the horse sacrifice (aśvamedha). This is "the most imposing and best known of the Vedic rituals, the highest manifestation of the royal authority, a demonstration of triumph indulged in by the victorious king."[1] The aśvamedha lasts three days with preliminaries extending as long as two years. Performed always by a king, it is a soma sacrifice, at which the central events are libations of the liquid of the soma plant; but in this particular ritual other important sacrifices occur as well. The sacrificial horse, accompanied by four hundred young men, is released and allowed to roam freely for a year. The soma libations take place after the horse returns. On the second day of soma pressing the animal is subjected to various ritual acts, including the attachment of 101 pearls to its mane and tail. Then a huge offering, involving as many as 602 animals, is held; but only domestic animals are actually sacrificed. After this the horse is strangled and later dismembered. His blood and that of other animals is offered in oblation. At the conclusion of the rite twenty-one sterile cows are sacrificed. The honoraria given the officiating priests are distributed over three days and consist, among other things, of the king's four wives or else their four hundred attendants.[2] The Śatapatha-Brāhmaṇa[3] reveals that Dhṛtarāṣṭra's white sacrificial horse was seized, in its tenth month of wandering by Śatānīka Sātrājita, whose kingdom it had entered. Sātrājita the performed his own aśvamedha, of the type known as govinata. The residents of Kāśi, deprived of the benefits of the ritual, for the time being even gave up the keeping of sacrificial fires.

Subsequent aśvamedha rituals have given their name to the famous tīrth (holy place) in Vārāṇasī known as Daśāśvamedh ("Ten Horse-Sacrifices"). Located on the Gaṅgā (Ganges), it marks the site where the Bhāraśivas, a ruling dynasty, took ceremonial baths at the completion of ten aśvamedha observances near the end of the second century, A.D.[4] The Vārāṇasī riverfront is of course nothing but a series of ghāṭs, bathing places reached by descending flights of steps, located one after the other from the confluence of the Varṇā (Varaṇā, Barṇā) River at the northern edge of the city to the Assī confluence at the southern boundary. According to Kuber Nath Sukul,[5] the original Daśāśvamedh tīrth (the Prayāg tīrth) is situated at the present Rājendra Prasād Ghāṭ (formerly Ghoṛā Ghāṭ: "Ghoṛā" = "Horse"). James Prinsep's map "The City of Bunarus," dated 1822, refers simply to a "Pryag Ghât," located slightly to the north of Daśāśvamedh Ghāṭ.[6] Sukul maintains that a stone horse commemorating the ten aśvamedhas was standing at Ghoṛā Ghāṭ up to the end of the eighteenth century but was removed, perhaps to save it from the flood waters. Some people assert that the stone horse situated near the Saṅkaṭ Mocan Mandir ("Mandir" = "Temple") is the identical sculpture.[7]

Another series of horse sacrifices is described in the Kāśī-Khaṇḍa (the legendary history of Vārāṇasī forming part of the Skanda-Purāṇa), which attributes the performance of ten aśvamedhas to the god Brahmā. As recounted by M. A. Sherring,[8] the god Śiva had not had word of Vārāṇasī for some time, even though he had dispatched several persons to inquire of its condition. In frustration he finally called upon Brahmā and urged him to find some way to rid the city of its successful ruler, Rājā Divodās, who had usurped even the power of the gods. Brahmā traveled to Vārāṇasī on a goose, set up residence, and transformed himself into an old Brāhmaṇ. He then secured an audience with the Rājā, who received him with the kindest hospitality and went so far as to ask what wish he would have fulfilled. It occurred to Brahmā that if Divodās were led to commit even the smallest sin, he would be compelled to hand the city back to the gods and to take his departure. Therefore Brahmā requested that the king supply the necessary materials for the complicated aśvamedha sacrifice--he was convinced that some small error would arise in its preparation. Divodās told him to take supplies not for one ritual but for ten. When these materials were brought to Brahmā, who was seated on the Gaṅgā bank, he discovered that not even the smallest mistake had been committed. The ten aśvamedhas were solemnized, after which Brahmā designated Daśāśvamedh a pilgrimage place equal in importance to Prayāg (Allāhābād). If a Hindu were unable to journey to Prayāg at the time of the melā (festival), he would receive merit at Daśāśvamedh equal to that obtained by bathing at the confluence of the Gaṅgā and Yamunā. Realizing that his mission to Vārāṇasī had ended in failure, Brahmā became reluctant to confront Śiva with the bad news. Like Śiva's previous messengers, he too became powerfully attracted to the city and decided to remain there until Śiva came to him.[9]

Brahmā's sacrifices are said to have occurred where the Ahilyābāī Ghāṭ is presently located. The sanctity of the spot has secured its inclusion in the pañc-tīrth, five revered places of pilgrimage on the riverfront. In addition to the Ahilyābāī Daśāśvamedh, the remaining four tīrths are the following: (1) the Lolārk Well in the Bhadainī Mohalla at Tulsī Dās Ghāṭ, near the Assī confluence; (2) the Maṇikarṇikākuṇḍ at Maṇikarṇikā Ghāṭ; (3) the Pañc-Nad, confluence of "five rivers"[10] at Pañcgaṅgā Ghāṭ; (4) the confluence of the Varṇā with the Gaṅgā, near Rāj Ghāṭ. Today the most important of the five is considered to be Maṇikarṇikā, not Daśāśvamedh. Maṇikarṇikā's attraction has arisen from a story in the Kāśī-Khaṇḍa. As summarized by E. B. Havell,[11] the well (kuṇḍ) there was dug by the god Viṣṇu with his discus, then filled with sweat from his own body. Śiva approached and found Viṣṇu practicing austerities on the tank's north side. Śiva looked into the well, which shone with the brilliance of a hundred million suns. He was filled with such wonder that he proclaimed the greatness of Viṣṇu and asked that he might grant any wish. The god's reply was that Śiva should always live in Vārāṇasī with him. Śiva's body shook with happiness, and an earring, maṇikarṇikā, fell into the well. He then declared that henceforth the well would be called by that name and anointed it the most hallowed place of pilgrimage.[12] The holiness of the place has made it the focal point of the famous pañc-kos (or pañc-kroś) pilgrimage, according to which Vārāṇasī is circumambulated on a fixed route which is never farther than five kos (about ten miles) from the Maṇikarṇikākuṇḍ.[13]

Though somewhat eclipsed by the tīrths associated with purāṇic legend, the Bharaśiva daśāśvamedha has given its name to the Daśāśvamedh Ghāṭ, situated near the center of the city. It is here that tourists embark on boat rides that traverse Vārāṇasī from one end to the other. Compared to the age of the city, all of the ghāṭs are of relatively recent construction. Sukul tells us[14] that the site for Daśāśvamedh Ghāṭ was purchased in 1735 and the ghāṭ constructed soon afterwards by the Mahārāṣṭrian Bājī Rāo Peśvā. In this regard "it would be thus observed that most of the Ghats, which constitute the pride of Varanasi, were built in the eighteenth and nineteenth centuries and that the

Maharashtras had the lion's share in this building programme, which beautified the city's river-front."[15] As will presently be seen, the Mahārāṣṭrians have contributed heavily over the centuries to the city's cultural advancement. One further association of the Daśāśvamedh is its use to designate a particular ward of the city, discussed in all its aspects in the geography of R. L. Singh.[16]

In summary, aśvamedha sacrifices were held in Vārāṇasī at least through the early centuries of the Christian era and have indirectly left a permanent mark on the religious culture of the city. Of subsequent centuries we know little, although Svāmī Maheśānand Giri has informed me that there are yet a few Vedic paṇḍits who have kept up their portions of the ritual and would be able to perform it were they summoned. That such a royal festival would be anachronistic in modern India, where the mahārājās have lost all their former power, goes without saying. But the remarkable perseverance of some of the rare forms of Veda recitation is dramatically underscored by the apparently hopeless circumstances under which they thrive. There was, unfortunately, not sufficient time to establish the identity of the Vaidikas (Vedic scholars) in question (and of course the possibility exists that the whole story was based on mere rumor). Manifestation of the Vedas in their sacrificial forms has deteriorated to such a degree that a performance of even the simplest soma ritual, the agniṣṭoma, is today a rare event in North India.

Dakṣiṇī Paṇḍits

From the Bhāraśiva aśvamedhas to the sixteenth century our knowledge of the Vedic situation in Vārāṇasī is spotty at best. It may be assumed that Vedic learning flourished during the Gupta period (fourth to seventh centuries, A.D.), for the Rāj Ghāṭ excavations have turned up seals referring to caraṇas

(Vedic schools) of the Ṛgveda, Black Yajurveda, and Sāmaveda. In addition there were caturvidyā- and traividyā-caraṇas for the teaching of four and three Vedas, respectively.[17] It is a safe assumption that interest in Vedic lore and the performance of Vedic sacrifices continued during subsequent centuries, with intermittent interruptions. Aberrations in the transmittance of traditional Hindu learning were felt most keenly during the periods of Muslim invasion and rule. The ascendancies of Firoz Tughlak (1351-1388), Sikandar Lodī (1489-1517), and the infamous Aurangzeb (1658-1707) were particularly devastating for the city.

In 1868 the following assessment was made of the Vārāṇasī Vedic situation by Sherring:

> At the present moment, I have been given to understand that not twenty families of Brahmans in all Benares are devoted to the study of the Vedas and that, of those which engage in this peculiar [!] study, there is not one indigenous to Benares, but all are of the Bhaṭṭ Brahmans from Gujerât. I cannot, however, vouch for the absolute truth of this statement, although I believe it is quite true that the study of the Vedas has very much fallen off in Benares.[18]

Although Sherring is not quite accurate in assigning Gujarāt as the sole source of Vedic tradition (however heavily it has contributed, especially with regard to the Sāmaveda), he is perfectly correct in pointing to the proliferation of Brāhmaṇs who hail from some other part of India.

The great majority of the Brāhmaṇs are dakṣiṇī ("southern") paṇḍits; but it must be kept in mind that in the North this term is used to encompass also the Mahārāṣṭrians and therefore does not refer solely to the Dravidian Brāhmaṇs, to whose names the suffix Draviḍ is frequently attached. Though biographies of Indian scholars are extremely rare, an important work, the

Gādhivaṃśānucarita ("History of the Gādhi Family") of Śaṅkara Bhaṭṭa, has come down to us; its contents are elucidated in an article by Mahāmahopādhyāya Haraprasād Śāstrī entitled "Dakshini Pandits at Benares."[17]

We are informed that the colony of southern paṇḍits at Vārāṇasī was established by a Mahārāṣṭrian Ṛgvedī, Nārāyaṇa Bhaṭṭa (Śaṅkara's father). Nārāyaṇa's father, Rāmeśvara, achieved fame through his teaching at Pratiṣṭhāna, on the Godāvarī. Nārāyaṇa was born in March, 1514, while his father was on a pilgrimage to Dvārakā. Eight years later, in 1522, the family moved to Vārāṇasī. A second son was born during the journey and a third later on in the city itself. Apparently Rāmeśvara was quite old when he reached Vārāṇasī, so the work of organizing the southern Brāhmaṇs fell to Nārāyaṇa. It is said that paṇḍits from all over the country looked upon him as their patron. He wrote a number of works, including the Tristhalī-Setu (which concerns the three pilgrimage cities Gayā, Vārāṇasī, and Prayāg), a Prayogaratna, and several other works in various fields. After his death the mantle fell to his second son, Śaṅkara, the author of the Gādhi history. Among his disciples were Mallāri Bhaṭṭa and Bhaṭṭoji Dīkṣita, who wrote the Siddhānta-Kaumudī, a work on Sanskrit grammar popular even today. Śaṅkara's successor was Vidyānidhi Kavīndra, a saṃnyāsī (hermit; the fourth stage in the life of a Brāhmaṇ) from another family who was awarded the title Sarvavidyānidhāna by the Mughul emperor Shāh Jahān (1628-1658). Kavīndra was the head of Vārāṇasī's paṇḍits around the middle of the seventeenth century. He was followed by Gāgā (Viśveśvara) Bhaṭṭa, great grandson of Nārāyaṇa Bhaṭṭa. Gāgā Bhaṭṭa performed the inauguration ceremony (abhiṣeka) of the Marāṭhā chieftain Śivājī (1627-1680). The line of authority then passed on to Nāgojī Bhaṭṭa, who was supported by the Rājā of Pratāpgaṛh in Oudh. Nāgojī died around 1775 and was succeeded by his pupil Vaidyanātha Pāyaguṇḍe.

Haraprasād Śāstrī[20] lists seven *dakṣiṇī* families who have been in the forefront of Hindu society in Vārāṇasī during the past four hundred years:

1. the Śeṣa family.
2. the Dharmādhikārī family, who came to Vārāṇasī about the same time as the Gādhis.
3. the Gādhi or Bhaṭṭa family.
4. the Bhāradvāja family, which included Mahāmahopādhyāya Dāmodara Śāstrī of Vārāṇasī and Mahāmahopādhyāya Govinda Śāstrī of the Calcutta Sanskrit College.
5. the Pāyaguṇḍe family.
6. the Caturdhara or Caudharī family.
7. the Puntamkar (Puṇtāmbekar?) family.

This résumé of southern influence would be incomplete without reference to Vārāṇasī's *vedapāṭhaśālās* (Vedic schools), all of which were established or operated by *dakṣiṇī* paṇḍits. Students of the Veda were taught either by individual scholars in their own homes or else in the *pāṭhaśālās*, where a greater number could be accommodated. According to Sukul,[21] the oldest of these institutions was that of Dinkar Anna Jośī, who came from the South on foot and set up a school in his own home, in the vicinity of Śītalā Ghāṭ (just northeast of Brahmā Ghāṭ). He chose as his successor Bāl Dīkṣit Kāle, who kept up the school's high standards. Among the products of the *pāṭhaśālā* were Rāmcandra Bhaṭṭ Raṭāṭe, Bābūbhaṭṭ Randohkar, Vināyak Dīkṣit Pañcgā̃vkar, Cunnī Lāl Dāve, Vīreśvar Bhaṭṭ Randohkar, Rām Kṛṣṇa Phadke, Triambak Dīkṣit Bhaṭṭ, Viṣṇupādhye Gūrjar, Somnāth Dīkṣit Kāle, and Rājārām Bhaṭṭ Paṭvardhan.

Another *pāṭhaśālā* was founded at Brahmā Ghāṭ by Vināyak Bhaṭṭ Ḍoṅgre. Sukul[22] writes that after Ḍoṅgre's death the reins were passed to Bhikkam Bhaṭṭ Paṭvardhan, who moved the school to his own place of residence on Hāthīgalī and then handed it over to his son Bābāguru. The galaxy of prominent Vaidikas[23] produced by this institution include Son Bhaṭṭ Achaval, Bhik Bhaṭṭ Nanal, Kāśīnāth Hardikar, Viśvanāth Dev, Morbhaṭṭ Dhekāre, Bālkṛṣṇa Sapre, Anant (alias Bābāguru) Paṭvardhan, Dattu Dīkṣit Pañcgāvkar, Mukund Devassthale, Gaṇapati Pitre, Bābū Pādhye Kelkar, Raghunāth Bhaṭṭ Kelkar.

Other pāṭhaśālās[24] were run by Rājārām Kṣlekar, Śrīkṛṣṇa Deoghar, Bālkṛṣṇa Nene, Bābū Dīkṣit Yagyavaru, Candraśekhar Draviḍ, Gaṇeś Bāpaṭ, and Somnāth Bāpaṭ.

Several of Vārāṇasī's Sanskrit colleges and universities, all heavily influenced by dakṣiṇī Brāhmaṇs, deserve special mention. The Sanskrit University (Vārāṇaseya Saṃskṛta Viśvavidyālaya) was founded in 1791 by Jonathan Duncan of the East India Company. It was first called the Sanskrit Pāṭhaśālā, then the Government Sanskrit College, and finally (in 1958) the Sanskrit University. Writing in 1912, Haraprasād Śāstrī[25] states that when the college was first established in 1791 "the Dakshiṇī Brāhmaṇas were its principal professors," and "even at the present moment the Dakshiṇī element preponderates in the staff of that College." Still today the dakṣiṇī influence exerts itself in the form of such eminent figures as Dr. Śrīkṛṣṇa Vāman Dev, one of India's great Ṛgvedīs and member of a prominent Mahārāṣṭrian family. He studied Ṛgveda under Vināyak Dīkṣit Jośī.

Another leading institution is the Sāṅgaveda Vidyālaya, founded and kept up at Rām Ghāṭ by the late Vallabharām Sāligrām Mehtā.[26] The name most often mentioned in connection with this college is that of Rājeśvar Śāstrī Draviḍ, a Yajurvedī, who was its head for many years and who has been awarded the Padma Bhūṣaṇ decoration by the Government of India. He was the first Sanskritist to be so honored. The present writer was fortunate enough to briefly make his acquaintance in a forest, south of Rāmnagar on the east bank of the Gaṅgā, where he was living as a saṃnyāsī. The intermediary who introduced us was so touched by the simple and austere existence of this great figure that he was moved to tears. Many of the Vedic paṇḍits recorded by the present writer are graduates of the Sāṅgaveda Vidyālaya and offer ample testimony to its vitality.

Last but not least among the institutions of higher learning is the Sanskrit College (Saṃskṛta Mahāvidyālaya) of Banāras Hindu University, founded in 1916 through the efforts of Paṇḍit Madan Mohan Mālvīya. The dakṣiṇī influence is felt here as well: the chairman of the Vedic Department has been Prof. A. M. Rāmnāth Dīkṣit, a Tamil Brāhmaṇ and one of India's foremost Sāmavedīs.

A sizable community of Tamil-speaking Aiyar and Aiyaṅgār Brāhmaṇs from South India inhabit the area around Hanumān Ghāṭ in the Bhelupura ward of the city. They have come to Vārāṇasī for various reasons. Some arrived on pilgrimages and then decided to remain permanently; others were brought by immigrants from their own states to assist with the occasional domestic ceremonies. Although most acquire some fluency in Hindī, it is understandable that the immigrants tend to congregate in communities in order that their native tongue, with which they are most comfortable, can be used instead of the less familiar "national language." This trait likewise is true for other ethnic groups. The Beṅgālī population, for instance, has settled chiefly around Kedār Ghāṭ, on which is located the Kedāreśvara Temple, a shrine of special significance to them. The Mahārāṣṭrians are to be found in great numbers near the Durgā Ghāṭ in Cauk, an old section of the city with narrow, winding lanes.

Recent Śrauta Rituals

Apart from the previously mentioned facts concerning early celebrations of the aśvamedha, our knowledge of Vedic ritual in Vārāṇasī from that period to the nineteenth century is almost a complete blank. Although sacrifices must have been held more or less regularly over the centuries, they were not documented (perhaps because of the traditional aversion to writing in general and to histories--especially descriptions of specific śrauta performances--in particular). These śrauta rituals, which draw upon the Vedas and are hence based upon divine revelation (śruti, a "hearing"), are one of two ways in which the Vedas are manifested, the other being svādhyāya or simply repetition of the Veda to one's own self. Therefore in the rituals the Vedas are put to practical "use" (prayoga) and here appear in secret forms known only to certain qualified priests.

The principal śrauta rituals are the soma sacrifices (somayāgas), which exist in seven varieties (saṃsthās) known as agniṣṭoma, atyagniṣṭoma, ukthya, ṣoḍaśin, vājapeya, atirātra, and aptoryāma. Sometimes independent rites are performed along with the somayāgas. The most impressive of these is the agnicayana, the "piling (of bricks for an altar) of fire." The usual shape of the fire altar is that of a bird with outstretched wings.[27]

These and other śrauta rituals require a sacrificer (yajamāna) who is an āhitāgni or agnihotrī. This is a Brāhmaṇ who maintains three sacred fires, gārhapatya, āhavanīya, and dakṣiṇāgni. Each day of his life the agnihotrī offers, twice daily, an oblation of milk to the Vedic fire god, Agni--thus performing the agnihotra ("Oblation to Agni"), the simplest of the śrauta sacrifices.[28]

A valuable service to Vedic scholars interested in the śrauta traditions has been performed by Vārāṇasī's great Ṛgvedī Dr. Viśvanāth Vāman Dev, younger brother of Dr. Śrīkṛṣṇa Vāman Dev (referred to already in regard to the Sanskrit University). Viśvanāth Dev has unearthed information on nineteen śrautayāgas held during the nineteenth and twentieth centuries and has published his findings in a Vārāṇasī Hindī-language newspaper.[29] A copy of that article has been made available to me by Śrī Viśvanāth himself, who has graciously given me permission to quote from its contents. Moreover, he has provided additional information, including a map (reproduced below) showing the twelve locations of the sacrifices.

The nineteen yāgas are now described in the order followed by Viśvanāth Dev. I am told that only the last seven sacrifices belong to the twentieth century. The name of the sacrificer (yajamāna, in each instance of course an āhitāgni) of each ritual is given plus any available information concerning him. Also specified are the places of performance, the year of observance (where known), the type of sacrifice, and (in a few instances) the names of officiating priests. The list is followed by a map on page 16 showing the sacrificial sites (indicated by numbers, the key to which appears on the same page.

1. The earliest śrauta ritual still remembered was held in the nineteenth century (exact date unknown) and performed by Vāman Dīkṣit Pāṭhak, a dakṣiṇī Brāhmaṇ belonging to the Mādhyandina school of White Yajurveda. Viśvanāth Vāman Dev does not mention the site of this sacrifice, but it may have been held at Assī Ghāṭ: Vāman Dev refers to two yāgas at this spot, and one cannot be accounted for otherwise.

2. In 1856 an agnicayana was performed by Namaskāre, a dakṣiṇī Śukla Yajurvedī. It was held in the courtyard of the Reṇukā Devī Mandir, near the Durgā Mandir (the so-called "Monkey Temple") on Durgākuṇḍ.

3. The next ritual (date uncertain) was an agniṣṭoma performed by Har Dīkṣit Kāle, a dakṣiṇī Ṛgvedī. Its location was the Baṅgālī Bāṟā, near Viśveśvara Gañj, where the Saṇḍjī Bāgh is presently situated. Four of the nineteen śrautayāgas listed here were solemnized at the Baṅgālī Bāṟā, the most of any locality.

4. Around 1886 an agniṣṭoma was performed by a Ṛgvedī, Pāṇḍuraṅg Dīkṣit Bhaṭ at the Rāj Mandir on Brahmā Ghāṭ (in between Pañcgaṅgā Ghāṭ and Gāi Ghāṭ). Today the Kāśī Vyāyāmśālā (Athletic Hall) is situated there.

5. In 1891 Vināyak Śāstrī Gāḍgīl, a dakṣiṇī Ṛgvedī from Gwālior, celebrated a sarvapṛṣṭha-aptoryāma at Bhairo Bāvṛī on Bhairavnāth, at the site of the present Kāśī Gośālā. It is in the vicinity of Kāl Bhairav Mandir, behind the chief police station (Kotvālī). The Bhairo Bāvṛī is recorded in the municipal records.

6. Next in the series is an agniṣṭoma performed by Bāl Śāstrī Ranāḍe, a dakṣiṇī Kṛṣṇa Yajurvedī who belonged to the Satyāṣāḍha-Śrauta-Sūtra. He was awarded the title Bālasarasvatī for his outstanding knowledge in several fields at a very young age. The yāga was held on Brahmā Ghāṭ.

7. In 1898 Sadāśiv Dīkṣit Jāvjī Bhaṭṭ, a dakṣiṇī White Yajurvedī of the Mādhyandina school, celebrated an agniṣṭoma at Satī Cabūtarā in Sukhlāl Sāhu Phāṭak (near the Viśvanāth Mandir), in the vicinity of Kuñj Galī. At present the Lacchī Rām Dharmśālā is located there. The hotṛ (chief Ṛgveda priest) for the sacrifice was Raghunāth Gavodkar, who followed the Āśvalāyana-Śrauta-Sūtra.

8-9. Then two yāgas, an atyagniṣṭoma and an aptoryāma with agnicayana, were performed by Nepāl's Rājguru, Śiromaṇi Śāstrī Nepālī of Kathmandu, at Rām Kaṭorā and adjacent Bauliyā Bāgh, near the Sanskrit University. The expense of the aptoryāma ran to 200,000 rupees.

10. Vārāṇasī's famous nobleman Rājā Muṃśī Mādho Lāl used his own wealth to sponsor an agniṣṭoma performed by Son Dīkṣit Kāle, a dakṣiṇī Ṛgvedī. An agnihotra-vrata-grahaṇa took place along with the soma ritual. The place of sacrifice was Muṃśī Mādho Lāl's palace at Bhūlanpur village, located at the junction

of The Mall and Grand Trunk Road on the way to Allāhābād Road.

11. A dakṣiṇī Ṛgvedī, Bhikojī Pant Śeṣ, performed an agniṣṭoma in the courtyard of the Durgā Devī Mandir, near the Sumer Mandir at Rāmnagar (a town on the east bank of the Gaṅgā, slightly southeast of Vārāṇasī). Concerning this temple Havell has the following remarks:

> In design and sculptured decoration the temple of Durgâ, at Ramnagar, on the side of the river opposite to Benares, is a very good example of modern Indian architecture. It was commenced by Raja Chêt Singh in the last half of the eighteenth century, and finished about 1850. Chêt Singh also constructed a fine bathing tank at Ramnagar, which is frequented by large crowds in the month of Magh (January-February). Vedavyâs, the reputed compiler of the Vedas, is said to have appointed Ramnagar to be a place of pilgrimage in that month, so that those who performed it might be relieved of the penalty of being re-incarnated as asses, which they would otherwise incur if they happened to die on this side of the river.[30]

12. Another agniṣṭoma at Baṅgālī Bāṛā was performed by Sadāśiv Śāstrī Soman, a dakṣiṇī Ṛgvedī.

13. This was followed by yet another agniṣṭoma at the same place, where Yajñeśvar Dīkṣit Mahābaleśvarkar, a dakṣiṇī Ṛgvedī, was the sacrificer. It was held early in the twentieth century.

14. Hanumān Ghāṭ, near Hariścandra Ghāṭ, was the site of an agniṣṭoma performed by Puruṣottam Śāstrī Draviḍ, a Kṛṣṇa Yajurveda dakṣiṇī Brāhmaṇ belonging to the Āpastamba-Śrauta-Sūtra.

15. Sītal Pāṇḍey, a Saryūpārīṇ Brāhmaṇ of the Mādhyandina school of White Yajurveda, performed another agniṣṭoma at Baṅgālī Bāṛā.

16. In 1921 an agniṣṭoma was performed by Raghunāthjī, a Gauṛ Brāhmaṇ and a Mādhyandina Yajurvedī, at Assī Ghāṭ. Here one of the Yajurveda priests was Lakṣmīnāth Pāṭhak Saptarṣi (Kātyāyana-Śrauta-Sūtra), while Lakṣmaṇjī Gaṇorkar (Āśvalāyana-Śrauta-Sūtra) served as hotṛ.

17. A Gauṛ Sārasvata White Yajurvedī, Gaṅgādharjī, performed an agniṣṭoma at Sapt Sāgar (Bulānālā), near Town Hall and the Kāśī Devī Mandir.

18. Śaśibhūṣaṇ, a Saryūpārīṇ Brāhmaṇ, was the sacrificer for another agniṣṭoma at the same place. The adhvaryu (chief Yajurveda priest) was Ātmārām Bharvāśilkar, the hotṛ Sītārām Dīkṣit Citlai (Āśvalāyana-Sūtra).

19. The most recent sacrifice, an agniṣṭoma, was held April 25-30, 1966, at the Rājā of Kāśī Temple, Śivālā Ghāṭ. It was performed by Ṛṣiśaṅkar Tripāṭhī, a Gujarāti Śrīmālī Brāhmaṇ belonging to the Kauthuma school of Sāmaveda. The organizer of this yāga was Viśvanāth Vāman Dev.

While it was not possible at this point to furnish names of all priests who functioned in the Vedic rituals, Viśvanāth Dev has assembled for me a list of Vārāṇasī Brāhmaṇs, living and deceased, who fulfilled the roles of hotṛ (Ṛgveda), adhvaryu (Yajurveda), and udgātṛ (Sāmaveda) in recent memory. The Sāmaveda listing includes only living Brāhmaṇs.

a. Hotṛ

1. Śrīkṛṣṇa Vāman Dev
2. Viśvanāth Vāman Dev
3. Anant Rām Puṇtāmbekar
4. Sītārām Dīkṣit Purohit, deceased
5. Kṛṣṇa Dīkṣit Mahadkar, deceased
6. Govindācārya, deceased
7. Bhikojī Pant Śeṣ, deceased
8. Gopālkṛṣṇa Bhaṭṭ, deceased

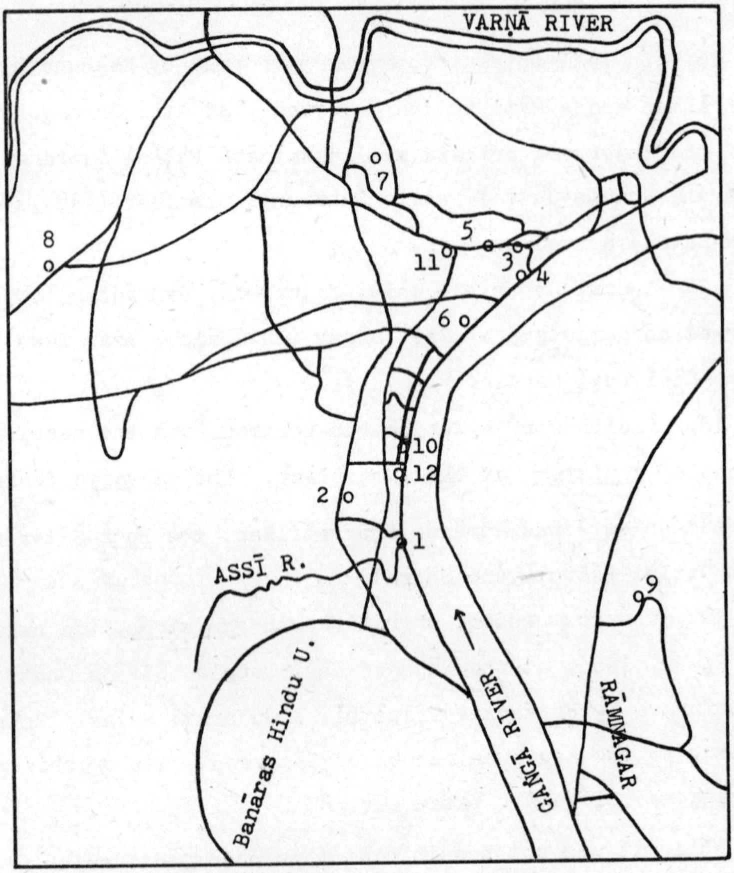

Fig. 1. Twelve sites of recent *śrauta* rituals

KEY

1. Assī Ghāṭ
2. Reṇukā Devī Mandir, near Durgā Mandir
3. Baṅgālī Bāṟā, near Gāi Ghāṭ
4. Rāj Mandir, on Brahmā Ghāṭ
5. Bhairo Bāvṟī, near Kāl Bhairav Mandir
6. Satī Cabūtarā, near Viśvanāth Mandir
7. Rām Kaṭorā and adjacent Bauliyā Bāgh, near the Vārāṇaseya Saṃskṛta Viśvavidyālaya
8. Palace of Muṃśī Mādho Lāl at Bhūlanpur Village
9. Durgā Devī Mandir at Rāmnagar
10. Hanumān Ghāṭ
11. Sapt Sāgar (Bulānālā), near Kāśī Devī Mandir
12. Rājā of Kāśī Mandir, Śivālā Ghāṭ

9. Lakṣmaṇ Gaṇorkar, deceased
10. Raghunāth Gaṇorkar, deceased

b. <u>Adhvaryu</u>

1. Sokhārām Dīkṣit Dāūjī Bhaṭṭ
2. Śrīkṛṣṇa Godse
3. Śiv Rām Tripāṭhī
4. Gaṇeś Dīkṣit Bāpaṭ
5. Maṅgaleśvar Bādal
6. Lakṣmīkānt Dīkṣit
7. Gajānan Godse
8. Vāmanācārya, deceased
9. Somnāth Pāṭhak Saptarṣi, deceased
10. Ātmārām Vāśīmkar, deceased
11. Gaṇeś Dīkṣit Dāūjī Bhaṭṭ, deceased
12. Lakṣmīnāth Pāṭhak Saptarṣi (Agnihotrī), deceased
13. Bhiku Dīkṣit Lele (Agnihotrī), deceased

c. <u>Udgātṛ</u>

1. Ṛṣiśaṅkar Tripāṭhī (Agnihotrī)
2. Śiv Rām Tripāṭhī
3. Devkṛṣṇa Tripāṭhī
4. Nandkṛṣṇa Tripāṭhī
5. Śiv Datt Tripāṭhī
6. Gaṇeś Bhaṭ Bāpaṭ
7. Kāśīnāth Bāpaṭ
8. Cintāmaṇi Pāḷande
9. Nārāyaṇ Dātār

Presumably some of the above have performed outside the city,[31] although all were, or are presently, residents of Vārāṇasī.

All <u>agnihotrīs</u> do not become <u>yajamānas</u> of <u>soma</u> and other sacrifices, so an enumeration of these <u>āhitāgni</u> Brāhmaṇs finds many names not referred to previously. The list is made possible through the kindness of Dr. C. G. Kashikar and Dr. Asko Parpola. Dr. Kashikar compiled the list while preparing the article "Śrauta Traditions in Recent Times," co-authored with Dr. Parpola.[32] The listing does not include Brāhmans who have given up the keeping of sacred fires. Inclusion is alphabetical; additional information concerning the __āhitāgni__ is given where available.

1. Gaṇeś Śāstrī Bettigiri (20th century)
2. Bhavanilāljī (Śāṅkhāyana-Śrauta-Sūtra of Ṛgveda, 20th century)
3. Bholānāth (20th century)
4. Devnāth (20th century)
5. Ratanjī Dīkṣit (Śāṅkhāyana-Śrauta-Sūtra, 20th century)
6. Subrahmaṇya Śāstrī Draviḍ (Āpastamba-Śrauta-Sūtra of Black Yajurveda, 20th century)
7. Hariśaṅkar Rām Dalpatrām Dvivedī (Śrīmālī Brāhmaṇ, 20th century)
8. Bāl Dīkṣit Jośī (early 20th century)
9. Bāl Dīkṣit Kāle (early 20th century)
10. Bālkṛṣṇa Śāstrī Kelkar (early 20th century)
11. Tatya Kelkar (early 20th century)
12. Bhikojī Dīkṣit Lele (Satyāṣāḍha-Śrauta-Sūtra of Black Yajurveda, early 20th century)
13. Mannujī (20th century)
14. Vāyunandan Miśra (20th century)
15. Śrīdhar Bhaṭṭ Pañcgāvkar (20th century)
16. Prabhudattjī (20th century)
17. Āb Dīkṣit Purohit (Ṛgvedī, early 20th century)
18. Bāl Śāstrī Raṅgappa (20th century)
19. Rāmcandra Śrīkṛṣṇa Raṭāṭe (Ṛgvedī, 20th century)
20. Gaṇeś Vyaṅkaṭeśa Sahasrabuddhe (19th century)
21. Vyaṅkaṭeśa Sahasrabuddhe (19th century)
22. Lakṣmīnāth Pāṭhak Saptarṣi (20th century)

23. Kṛṣṇapant Śāstrī (20th century)

24. M. M. Vaṃśidhar Śāstrī (Beṅgālī, 20th century)

25. Viṣṇu Śāstrī Sāthe (early 20th century)

26. Siddhnāth (20th century)

27. Gaṅgādhar Śāstrī Thatte (Satyāṣāḍha-Śrauta-Sūtra, 20th century)

28. Bāl Dīkṣit Toro (20th century)

29. Rāmeśvar Bhaṭṭ Vāze (early 20th century)

30. M. M. Vināyak Śāstrī Vetal (20th century)

I

ṚGVEDA AND ATHARVAVEDA

The Source of Ṛgveda in Vārāṇasī

Three types of Ṛgvedic recitation exist in India: (1) that of Brāhmaṇs with ancestral roots in Mahārāṣṭra, (2) that of Tamil Brāhmaṇs in South India, and (3) that of Nambudiri Brāhmaṇs in South India (Kerala State). By far the most representative of Vārāṇasī are the Mahārāṣṭrian paṇḍits. Fewer in numbers are Tamil reciters, and not a single Nambudiri proponent of any Veda resides in the city.[1]

As noted in the Introduction, the Mahārāṣṭrians have exerted enormous intellectual influence on Vārāṇasī since at least as early as 1522, when Rāmeśvara Bhaṭṭa came to the city. The business of organizing the Mahārāṣṭra colony there fell to his son Nārāyaṇa, who laid the groundwork for the burgeoning achievements of this community during the next four hundred years. This family belonged to the Viśvāmitra gotra and to the Ṛgveda; therefore this Veda, more than any other, has come to be associated in Vārāṇasī with the Mahārāṣṭrians. It is no accident that today the three Brāhmaṇs qualified to serve as hotṛ in the Vedic sacrifices--Śrīkṛṣṇa Vāman Dev, Viśvanāth Vāman Dev, Anant Rām Puṇtāmbekar--hail from Mahārāṣṭrian families. They and apparently most Ṛgvedīs from this state belong to the Śākala school and the Āśvalāyana-Śrauta-Sūtra.

Just how long Ṛgveda has been connected with Mahārāṣṭra is not known. The epigraphy[3] dealing with the northern Āśvalāyanas is found to the east and north: (1) at Barrakpur, Bengal, during the Sena dynasty; (2) around Jodhpur, Rājasthān, eighth century; and (3) in Māndhātā, Mālva (Madhya Pradesh), twelfth century. Southern inscriptions are more numerous: (1) in the Tirunelvēli region, Tamilnāḍ, sixteenth and seventeenth centuries; (2) in the Godāvarī District, fifteenth century; (3) at Kāñcīpura, Tamilnāḍ, seventeenth century; (4) at Tañjāvūr, Tamilnāḍ, during the Pallava dynasty; and (5) in the North Arcot District, Tamilnāḍ, fourteenth century. The past and present (up to 1957) situation of the Vedas in Mahārāṣṭra has been summed up by Dr. V. Raghavan, who journeyed there in the 1950's as a member of the Sanskrit Commission:

> The Mahārāṣṭrians had contributed in the past to the strengthening of the Vedic traditions of Banaras, Āndhra and Tamilnad, particularly during the ascendancy of the Marātha power and the times of the Peshwas when Mahārāṣṭrian Pandits spread themselves all over the country. Also Poona itself attracted Vedic scholars from other parts and especially from Karṇāṭaka. . . . Today there were some Ṛgveda and Kṛṣṇayajurveda current and were taught in the Pāṭhaśālās of Mahārāṣṭra. . . . The Veda pāṭhaśālā of Poona had published an interesting book giving the photographs, biography and qualifications of about 115 Vedic scholars of Mahārāṣtra. Life in Mahārāṣtra was getting rapidly secularised even in respect of marriages and a few years back, the Brahman Sabhā of Bombay organised a session for the chanting of whole Vedas purely as a measure to help the Vedic Pandits and to keep alive their tradition. In Poona, they had the Veda-śāstrottejaka Sabhā, the Mīmāmsā Kāryālaya and the Veda

pāṭhaśālā which were endeavouring to keep up the interest in Svādhyāya.[4]

It may be assumed that since Raghavan's visit the Vedic situation has deteriorated even further. Possibly some paṇḍits presently residing there have had their Vedic training in Vārāṇasī and not locally.

First steps in the study of the important Ṛgveda tradition in Mahārāṣṭra were taken in 1952-53, when recordings were made in Rājasthān by W. S. Allen and in Bombay by J. E. B. Gray. Gray took some additional recordings in 1957 and 1958 from another Mahārāṣṭrian and a year later presented the results of his study in an important article entitled "An Analysis of Ṛgvedic Recitation."[5] The seven-year lapse between the date of the first recording and the appearance of Gray's analysis was due to "the manner in which these . . . . reciters chanted, [which] appeared to run so far counter to the generally accepted notions in the West concerning the nature of the Vedic accentual pattern that their evidence was simply 'filed'."[6] Gray expanded on his findings shortly afterward, taking into account the practices of Nambudiri Ṛgvedīs.[7] There would be no necessity to return to the Mahārāṣṭrian mode of recitation were the testimonials of all paṇḍits the same. However, the recordings made in 1971 by the present writer are so far different from Gray's descriptions of Mahārāṣṭrian Ṛgveda that additional documentation is required. Furthermore, Gray's conclusions on the nature of the Vedic accent will be reexamined in the light of more recent research. Before dealing with the recitations themselves, it is appropriate to review the Vedic accents, the method of accentuation, and the forms which the recitations assume.

Accentuation

The principal Vedic texts, primarily the saṃhitās but also some brāhmaṇas, are accented.[8] The accents revolve around the *udātta* ("raised"), the main accent, the position of which is pre-determined by the exigencies of grammar. The function of the *anudātta* ("not raised") is to introduce an *udātta*, whereas the *svarita* ("intoned") accomplishes a transition from the *udātta* to an accentless syllable. The series of syllables without accent which often follow the *svarita* are termed *pracaya* ("multitude"), although the accentless syllable immediately preceding the *udātta* is always the *anudātta*. Two or more *udāttas* may occur consecutively. Moreover, a non-*udātta* syllable appearing between two *udāttas* is *anudātta*, not *svarita*. The Ṛgveda does not mark *udātta* and *pracaya*, although in transliteration it is customary to designate the *udātta* by the acute sign (´)--not to be confused with the manner of transliterating the palatal sibilant (*ś*). The *anudātta* is indicated by a horizontal stroke beneath a syllable, the *svarita* by a vertical stroke above. The first verse of the second *sūkta* ("hymn") of the Ṛgveda--in praise of the Wind God, Vāyu--is now quoted in order to illustrate the points just presented (U = *udātta*, A = *anudātta*, S = *svarita*, P = *pracaya*):[9]

vā́yav ā́ yāhi darśatemé sómā áraṃkṛtāḥ /
U A U S P P P A U U A U S P P

tḗṣaṃ pāhi śrudhī́ hávaṃ //
U S P P A U U S

Sometimes two or more accentless syllables occur at the beginning of a verse; in this instance all are designated by the *anudātta* sign. However, in actuality only the last of these is a true *anudātta*; the preceding syllables are *pracaya* or *sarvānudātta* ("completely accentless") syllables which are often rendered in a special manner in recitation. For example, the word *codayitrī*, when appearing in initial position (see Ṛgveda 1.3.11), can be accentually analyzed in the following way:

codayitrī́
P P A U
└─┘
sarvānudātta

Every Vedic word normally is accented and has only one *udātta*. But some words have a double accent (*bṛ́haspáti*, for example), and others have no accent at all. Among the accentless words are those which are naturally enclitic (certain pronouns and particles) and those which lose accent by their position in the sentence (for example, finite verbs, in principal clauses, not at the beginning of the sentence or quarter-verse [*pāda*]).[10]

A phenomenon occasionally met is the so-called independent *svarita*--a *svarita* not dependent on a preceding *udātta*, which has disappeared as a result of euphonic combination (*sandhi*). The method of accentuation is altered only when an *udātta* follows the *svarita*. In this case the figure 1 follows if the *svarita* vowel is short, the figure 3 if it is long. A vertical line and a horizontal stroke are placed above and below the figures, respectively. The following is an example of this type of independent *svarita* from Ṛgveda 1.2.6:

makṣv i1tthā́.

Here the *udātta* ordinarily occurring on the last syllable of the first word (*makṣū́*) has been lost because of the rule that *u* followed by a dissimilar vowel changes to *v*. The vowel (*i*) bearing the *svarita* is short, and the next syllable has the *udātta*; therefore the numeral 1 is placed after the *svarita* vowel.

Forms of Ṛgvedic Recitation

Vedic texts ordinarily observe the laws of coalescence (*sandhi*) between the end of one word and the beginning of another. This type of recitation (*saṃhitāpāṭha*) is thus differentiated from the analytical word-by-word recitation (*padapāṭha*), which presents each individual word in its original, radical form. The following verse, Ṛgveda 1.1.2, reads in this manner when the sandhi laws prevail:

agníḥ pū́rvebhir ṛ́ṣibhir ī́dyo nū́tanair utá /

sá devā́m̐ éhá vákṣati //

But the pada analysis of the same text has this form:

/ agníḥ / pū́rvebhiḥ / ṛ́ṣi 'bhiḥ / ī́dyaḥ / nū́tanaiḥ / utá /

/ sáḥ / devā́n / ā́ / ihá / vakṣati //

The padapāṭha is the basis for other derivative recitations (vikṛtis), which combine the words according to specified schemes. After the padapāṭha itself, the three main vikṛtis learned by the Mahārāṣṭrian Ṛgvedīs are krama ("progression"), jaṭā ("braid"), and ghana ("bell"). If the words of a verse are symbolized by / a / b / c / d / e / . . . , then krama reads / ab / bc / cd / de / . . . , jaṭā / abbaab / bccbbc / cddccd / deedde / . . . , ghana / abbaabccbaabc / bccbbcddcbbcd / cddccdeedccde / . . . . The lines separating the sections designate places where sandhi is absent. A person who has mastered the ghana recitation (ghanapāṭha), and therefore the previous vikṛtis as well, is called ghanapāṭhī. These repetition patterns have been cultivated doubtlessly to insure that not a single element of the text is lost in the process of transmission.

A distinctive feature of the vikṛtis is the use of the word íti ("thus," "in this manner") in certain circumstances. For example, it is the custom to follow a compound, after its final appearance in the vikṛti, by íti and then to break the compound into its two elements. The compound devátātā, on its last statement in a vikṛti, would therefore be recited in this way:

/ devátātéti devá--tāta /.

Vikṛtis on Ṛgveda verses accentuate the members of an analyzed compound as though they were not separated. However, adherents to the Taittirīya school of Kṛṣṇa Yajurveda give to each member its own accentuation.[11] Hence, according to the two practices, the units of accentuation of the word devátātā are bracketed as follows:

Ṛgveda: devátātéti devá--tātā

Black Yajurveda: devátātéti devá--tātā

The term for this use of íti, in compound analyzation, is parigraha ("seizing on both sides").

The particle íti appears also in conjunction with words which are final in the verse or section of the verse. If not a compound, the word is simply stated before and following íti, a procedure called pragraha ("seizing"). Hence the word vắram occurring in final position is treated thusly:

/ vắram íti vắram /.

The pragraha appears immediately after the sandhi segment in which the word first occurs.

Among the other uses of íti should be mentioned its association with pragṛhya-padas, words whose final vowels are not subject to the rules of sandhi. Dual endings in ī, ū, and e, for instance, remain uncombined.

Euphonic Combination (Sandhi)

Since sandhi (junction) between one word and another is one of the most important characteristics of Veda recitation, the rules which pertain to the text examples quoted below and in Part II are now given. In brackets at the end of each rule is a reference to the applicable section of Macdonell's Vedic Grammar, which should be consulted for a complete exposition of the subject.

A. Final a, i, and u are often lengthened when followed by a single consonant. [68]

B. Final a or ā contracts with initial a or ā to form ā; final i or ī contracts with initial i or ī to form ī; final u or ū contracts with initial u or ū to form ū. [69]

C. Final a or ā contracts with initial i or ī to form e, with initial u or ū to form o, with initial e or ai to form ai, and with initial o or au to form au. Final a or ā is not contracted with initial ṛ in the Ṛgveda and the Vājasaneyi-Saṃhitā. [70]

D. Final i or ī is changed to y and final u or ū to v before dissimilar vowels. [71(1)]

E. Final e and o do not change before initial a, but this a is often dropped. [72(1)a]

F. Final e before vowels other than a changes to a through the intermediate stage ay, and the resulting hiatus remains. Final o changes to av, but the v is dropped before u or ū. [72(1)b]

G. Final ai before all vowels except a becomes ā, through the intermediate stage āy, and the resulting hiatus remains. Final au before vowels except a is written āv, but the v is dropped before u or ū. [73]

H. Final voiceless consonants become voiced before voiced sounds; final voiced consonants become voiceless before voiceless sounds. [74]

I. Final voiced stops (or final voiceless stops made voiced by assimilation) may change to nasals of their own class when followed by a nasal. [74a]

J. Final m, when followed by a stop or nasal, becomes a nasal of the same class as the stop or nasal and is written as anusvāra (ṃ). [75(2)]

K. Final m becomes anusvāra (ṃ, m̐ in the Vājasaneyi-Saṃhitā) before r, ś, ṣ, s, and h. [75(3)]

L. Final m and initial y, l, or v become nasalized y̐, l̐, v̐, the m represented in the printed texts by anusvāra. [75(4)]

M. Final t becomes l before l, c before c, ch, and ś, and j before j. A following ś is changed to ch. [76]

N. Final n is doubled when preceded by a short vowel and followed by any vowel. [77(1)a]

O. Final n becomes m̐ if preceded by ā and followed by any vowel. [77(1)b]

P. Final n before s remains, but t may be placed between the two. Final n before c sometimes changes to m̐, and ś is inserted between m̐ and c. Final n before t sometimes changes to m̐, and s is inserted. [77(2)]

Q. Final s preceded by all vowels except a and ā changes to r before voiced sounds, but s is often retained before dental t, regardless of the preceding vowel. [78(1-2)]

R. Final as drops the s before vowels other than a, and the resulting hiatus remains. [78(1)b]

S. Final as becomes o before voiced consonants and a, and this initial a is often dropped. [78(1)b]

T. Final ās drops the s before vowels (where the hiatus remains) and voiced consonants. [78(1)b]

U. Final s becomes the palatal sibilant ś before the palatals c, ch, and ś. [78(2)a]

V. Final s before voiceless gutturals and voiceless labials is written usually as ḥ, but often as or ās remains. [78(2)c]

W. Final s before ś, ṣ, or s is written usually as ḥ. [78(2)e]

X. Final r before vowels and voiced consonants remains, when preceded by a, ā, i, ī, u, or ū. [79(1)a]

Y. Initial h after a final voiced mute may be changed to the aspirate form of that mute. [80b].

These laws of sandhi will henceforth be designated by the appropriate capital letters, placed above the text. Sandhi between the members of compounds will not be so indicated; likewise, the pause form of final s, visarga (ḥ), will not be especially labelled.

Recitations

A study of Vedic recitation must always rely on the actual oral testimony of those Brāhmaṇs who have spent a large portion of their lives mastering the Veda to which they belong by birth. Little knowledge can be gained from a mere perusal of the printed text, for the accentuation presented there gives only a bare outline. The correct interpretation of this outline is left up to the specialist, who today realizes the accents by the use of musical pitches.

The transcriptions below furnish musical renditions of five extracts from the Ṛgveda, as recited by two undisputed masters of the Mahārāṣṭra tradition. The first hymn and the first version of the second hymn are interpreted by Śrī Anant Rām Puṇtāmbekar. He belongs to the Bhāradvāja gotra and studied under Anant Rāmjī Paṭvardhan. The second version of the second hymn and the remaining extracts are recited by Śrī Viśvanāth Vāman Dev, who was quoted extensively in the Introduction. He belongs to the Viṣṇuvṛddha gotra and had his Vedic training at the feet of Bhikojī Paṭvardhan and Bālkṛṣṇa Mahādev Bhaṭṭ Sapre.

Every fifth syllable has the appropriate number placed above. The first note of each transcription is set equal to the actual sung pitch; metronomic readings are given for all extracts. Tape numbers refer to a catalogue of recordings appearing in a previous publication.[12]

Regarding the translations appearing throughout this book, I have derived great benefit from numerous suggestions made by Prof. Jan Gonda and Prof. George Cardona, as well as from Karl Friedrich Geldner's German translation of the Ṛgveda,[13] which should be consulted for clarifications on any questionable points.

(1) Ṛgveda 1.1.1-9: Hymn to Agni

1. ōm agním īḷe puróhitam yajñásya devám ṛtvíjam /
hótāraṃ ratnadhā́tamam //

2. agníḥ pū́rvebhir ṛ́ṣibhir ī́ḍyo nū́tanair utá /
sá devā́m̐ éhá vakṣati //

3. agnínā rayím aśnavat póṣam evá divédive /
yaśásaṃ vīrávattamam //

4. ágne yáṃ yajñám adhvarám viśvátaḥ paribhū́r ási /
sá íd devéṣu gacchati //

5. agnír hótā kavíkratuḥ satyáś citráśravastamaḥ /
devó devébhir ā́ gamat //

6. yád aṅgá dāśúṣe tvám ágne bhadrám kariṣyási /
távét tát satyám aṅgiraḥ //

7. úpa tvāgne divédive dóṣāvastar dhiyā́ vayám /
námo bhárantā émasi //

8. rā́jantam adhvarā́ṇāṃ gopā́m ṛtásya dī́divim /
várdhamānaṃ své dáme //

9. sá naḥ pitéva sūnáve 'gne sūpāyanó bhava /
sácasvā naḥ svastáye //

Translation:

1. I praise (īḷe) Agni (agnim), put at the head (purohitam) of the sacrifice (yajñasya), God (devam), priest (ṛtvijam); Hotṛ (hotāram), distributing great riches (ratnadhātamam).

2. Agni (agniḥ) is fit to be praised (īḍyaḥ) by former (pūrvebhiḥ) and also (uta) by present (nūtanaiḥ) seers (ṛṣibhiḥ); he (saḥ) shall bring (ā vakṣati) the gods (devān) here (iha).

3. Through Agni (agninā) one expects to gain (aśnavat), day by day (divedive), wealth (rayim), indeed (eva) prosperity (poṣam) [which is] honorable (yaśasam), most abundant in heroes (vīravattamam).

4. Agni (agne), the ritualistic (adhvaram) sacrificial worship (yajñam) which (yam) you are pervading (paribhūr asi) everywhere (viśvataḥ) assuredly (it) goes (gacchati) to the gods (deveṣu).

5. Agni (agniḥ), Hotṛ (hotā), wise (kavikratuḥ), truthful (satyaḥ), having most wonderful fame (citraśravastamaḥ); God (devaḥ), may he come (ā gamat) with the gods (devebhiḥ).

6. Indeed (aṃga), O Agni (agne), when (yat) you (tvam) intend to bestow (kariṣyasi) good fortune (bhadram) to the worshipper (dāśuṣe), that (tat), Aṅgiras (aṃgiraḥ), is surely (it) your (tava) truth (satyam).

7. Daily (divedive), O Agni (agne), lighter of darkness (doṣāvastaḥ), we (vayam) come (emasi) to (upa) you (tvā) with prayer (dhiyā), bearing (bharaṃta) obeisance (namaḥ).

8. [We come to you who are] ruler (rājaṃtam) of sacrificial rites (adhvarāṇām), guardian (gopām) of cosmic law

(ṛtasya), bright (dīdivim), growing (vardhamānam) in your (sve) house (dame).

9. Agni (agne), be (bhava) easily accessible (sūpāyanaḥ) to us (naḥ), like father (piteva) to son (sūnave); accompany (sacasva) us (naḥ) for good fortune (svastaye).

(2) Ṛgveda 1.2.1-9: Hymn to Vāyu, Indra, Mitra, and Varuṇa

F 1 T
1. vā́yav ā́ yāhi darśatemé sómā́ áraṃkṛtāḥ /
J A
téṣāṃ pāhi śrudhī́ hávaṃ //

F Q A
2. vā́yā ukthébhir jaraṃte tvā́m ácchā́ jaritā́raḥ /
T
sutásomā aharvídaḥ //

1
3. vā́yo táva prapṛñcatī́ dhénā jigāti dāśúṣe /
urūcī́ sómapītaye //

T Q
4. índravāyū imé sutā́ úpa práyobhir ā́ gataṃ /
S
índavo vām uśánti hí //

F U W L
5. vā́yav índraś ca cetathaḥ sutā́nāṃ vājinīvasū /
G 1
tā́v ā́ yātam úpa dravát //

F U R 1
6. vā́yav índraś ca sunvatá ā́ yātam úpa niṣkṛtám /
D
makṣv itthā́ dhiyā́ narā //

K L J
7. mitráṃ huve pūtádakṣaṃ váruṇaṃ ca riśā́dasam /
J K
dhíyaṃ ghṛtā́cīṃ sā́dhantā //

G G
8. ṛténa mitrāvaruṇāv ṛtāvṛdhāv ṛtaspṛśā /
J
krátuṃ bṛhántam āśāthe //

♩=192
e=f#
Tape IVa(1)
1.
óm a gní mi ḷe pu ró hi taṃ ya jñá sya de
vá mṛ tví jaṃ / hó ta raṃ ra tna dhā́ ta maṃ //
2.
a g níḥ pū́ r ve bhi r ṛ́ ṣi bhi rī́ ḍyo
nū́ ta nai ru tá / sá de vā́ m̐ é há va kṣa ti //
3.
a g ní na ra yí ma śna va tpó ṣa me vá di

65 70
vé di ve / ya śá saṃ vī rá va tta maṃ //
4. 75 80
á g ne yáṃ ya jñá ma dh va ráṃ vi ś vá taḥ pa
85 90 95
ri bhū́ rá si / sá í dde vé ṣu ga ccha ti //
5. 100 105
a g ní r hó ta ka ví k ra tuḥ sa tyá ści t
110 115 120
rá ś ra va sta ma ḥ / de vó de vé bhi rā́ ga ma t //

6.
125
130
yá daṃ gá dā śú ṣe tvá má g ne bha d
135
140
ráṃ ka ri syá si / tá vé ttá tsa tyá maṃ gi ra ḥ //
7.
145
150
155
ú pa t vā g ne di vé di ve dó ṣa va sta
160
165
r dhi yá va yáṃ / ná mo bhá raṃ ta é ma si //
8.
170
175
rá jaṃ ta ma dh va rá ṇa ṃ go pá mṛ tá

180 185
sya̱ dī́ di viṃ / vá r dha mā na̱ ṃ své dá me //
9. 190 195 3 200
sá naḥ pi̱ té va sū̱ ná vé 'g ne sū pā
205 210
ya̱ nó bha va / sá ca s vā naḥ s va̱ stá ye //

9. kavī no mitrāvaruṇā tuvijāta urukṣaya /

dákṣam dadhāte apásam //

Translation:

1. Beautiful (darśata) Vāyu (vāyo), come (ā yāhi): these (ime) Soma drops (somāḥ) have been made ready (araṃkṛtāḥ); drink (pāhi) of them (teṣām), hear (śrudhi) the call (havam).
2. Vāyu (vāyo), the chanters (jaritāraḥ) who have pressed the Soma juice (sutasomāḥ), knowing the days (aharvidaḥ), praise (jaraṃte) you (tvām) with eulogies (ukthebhiḥ).
3. Vāyu (vāyo), your (tava) flowing (prapṛṃcatī) voice (dhenā), far-reaching (urūcī) for the Soma draught (somapītaye), goes (jigāti) to the worshipper (dāśuṣe).
4. Indra and Vāyu (iṃdravāyū), these (ime) [stalks of Soma] are pressed (sutāḥ): with pleasure (upa prayobhiḥ) come (ā gatam); the Soma drops (iṃdavaḥ) have desire (uśanti) indeed (hi) for both of you (vām).
5. Vāyu and Indra (vāyav iṃdraś ca), rich in booty (vājinīvasū), you take notice (cetathaḥ) of the pressed Soma juices (sutānām); come (ā yātam) swiftly (dravat) near (upa).
6. Vāyu and Indra (vāyav iṃdraś ca), come (ā yātam) to (upa) the rendezvous (niṣkṛtam) of him who presses Soma (sunvataḥ), promptly (makṣu), with such (itthā) vision (dhiyā), O Lords (narā).
7. Mitra (mitram) I call (huve), of pure expertness (pūtadakṣam), and Varuṇa (varuṇam ca), the destroyer of enemies (riśādasam); [they render] prayer (dhiyam), abounding in clarified butter (ghṛtācīm), successful

♩=192
g=a
1.
5
Tape IVa(1)
♩=224
e=e
vā́ ya̲ vā́ ya hi da r
Tape Ia(2)
10
15
śa te̲ mé só mā̲ á raṃ kṛ tā ḥ / té
20
ṣa ṃ pā hi ś ru̲ dhī́ há vaṃ //

2.
25
30
vā́ ya u kthé bhi r ja raṃ te t vā́ má ccha
35
40
45
3
ja ri tā́ ra ḥ / su tá so mā a ha r ví da ḥ //
3.
50
55
60
vā́ yo tá va praprṃ ca tī́ dhé na ji gā ti dā

65
70
śú ṣe / u rū cī só ma pī ta ye //
4.
75
80
ín d ra vā yū i mé su tā́ ú pa p rá yo
85
90
bhi rā́ ga taṃ / ín da vo vā mu śán ti hí //

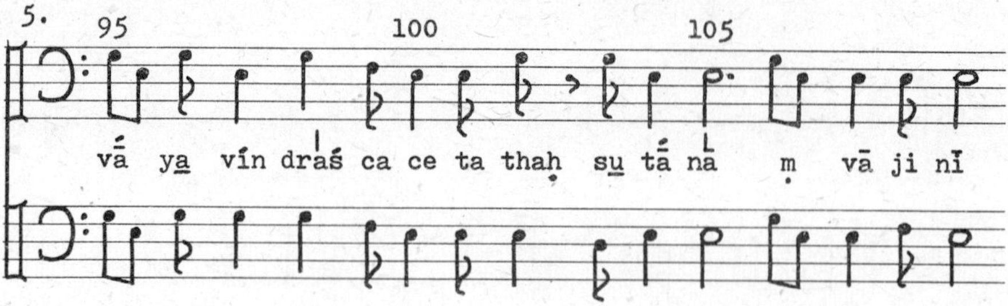
5.
95
100
105
vā́ ya̱ vín draś ca ce ta thaḥ su̱ tā́ na ṃ vā ji nī

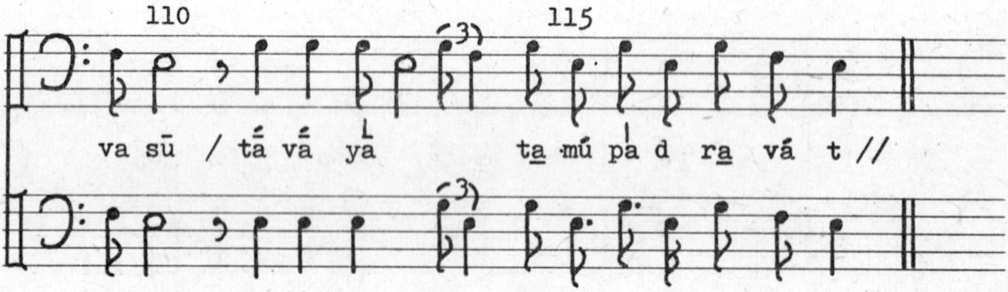
110
115
va sū / tā́ vā́ ya ta̱ mú pa d ra̱ vá t //

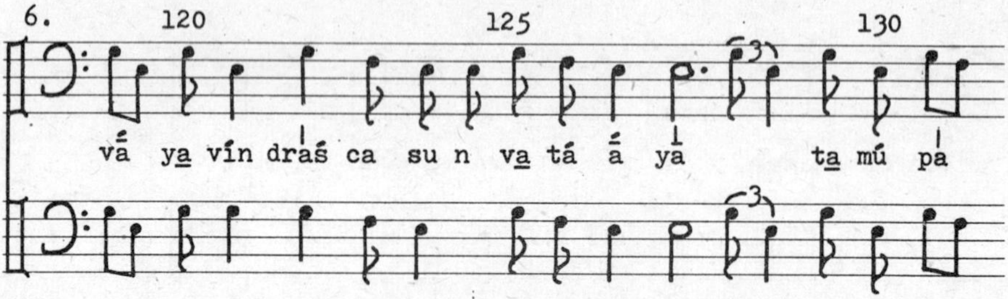
6.
120
125
130
vā́ ya̱ vín draś ca su n va̱ tá ā́ ya ta̱ mú pa

135
140
ni ṣkṛ táṃ / ma kṣvil tthá dhi yā́ na rā //
7.
145
150
mi t rā́ṃ hu ve pū tá da kṣam vá ru ṇaṃ ca ri
155
160
3
165
śā́ da saṃ / dhí yaṃ ghṛ tā́ cī m sā́ dhan tā //

8. 170 175
ṛ té ná mi t rā va ru ṇā vṛ tā vṛ dhā vṛ ta
180 185
spṛ śā / krá tum bṛ hán ta mā śā the //
9. 190 195 200
ka ví no mi t rá vá ru ṇā tu vi jā tā u

205
210
ru̲ kṣá ya / dá kṣaṃ da dhā te a̲ pá saṃ //

8. Through cosmic law (ṛtena), Mitra and Varuṇa (mitrā-varuṇau), who make truth grow (ṛtāvṛdhau), touching truth (ṛtaspṛśā), you have gained (āśāthe) great (bṛhantam) power (kratum).

9. Our (naḥ) sages (kavī) Mitra and Varuṇa (mitrāvaruṇā), of powerful nature (tuvijātau), occupying spacious dwellings (urukṣayā), impart (dadhāte) skillful (apasam) ability (dakṣam).

(3) Ṛgveda 1.3.1-12: Hymn to the Aśvins, Indra, Viśve Devāsa, and Sarasvatī

1. áśvinā yájvarīr íṣo drávatpāṇī śúbhas patī /
púrubhujā canasyátam //

2. áśvinā púrudaṃsasā nárā śávīrayā dhiyá /
dhíṣṇyā vánatam gíraḥ //

3. dásrā yuvákavaḥ sutá násatyā vṛktábarhiṣaḥ /
á yātam rudravartanī //

4. índrā yāhi citrabhāno sutá imé tvāyávaḥ /
ánvībhis tánā pūtásaḥ //

5. índrā yāhi dhiyéṣitó víprajūtaḥ sutávataḥ /
úpa bráhmāṇi vāghátaḥ //

6. índrā yāhi tútujāna úpa bráhmāṇi harivaḥ /
suté dadhiṣva naś cánaḥ //

7. ómāsaś carṣaṇīdhṛto víśve devāsa á gata /
dāśváṃso dāśúṣaḥ sutám //

S W

8. víśve devāso aptúraḥ sutám ā gamta tūrṇayaḥ /

T

usrā iva svásarāṇi //

S R S

9. víśve devāso asrídha éhimāyāso adrúhaḥ /

J

médhaṃ juṣaṃta váhnayaḥ //

W Q

10. pāvakā naḥ sárasvatī vājebhir vājínīvatī /

L

yajñám vaṣṭu dhiyávasuḥ //

J

11. codayitrī sūnŕtānāṃ cétaṃtī sumatīnām /

J

yajñáṃ dadhe sárasvatī //

S W

12. mahó árṇaḥ sárasvatī prá cetayati ketúnā /

S T

dhíyo víśvā ví rājati //

Translation:

1. Aśvins (aśvinā), having swift horses (dravatpāṇī), lords (patī) of splendor (śubhaḥ), enjoying much (purubhujā), enjoy (canasyatam) the sacrificial (yajvarīḥ) refreshment (iṣaḥ).

2. Aśvins (aśvinā), abounding in mighty deeds (purudaṃsasā), heroes (narā), benevolent (dhiṣṇyā), acquire (vanatam) the invocations (giraḥ) with powerful thought (śavīrayā dhiyā).

3. Dasra (dasrā), Nāsatya (nāsatyā), the Soma libations (sutāḥ) of him who has prepared the sacrificial grass (vṛktabarhiṣaḥ) are for you (yuvākavaḥ); come (ā yātam), you who move in mighty paths (rudravartanī).

4. Indra (iṃdra), you of visible splendor (citrabhāno), come (ā yāhi): these (ime) Soma libations (sutāḥ), continually (tanā) purified (pūtāsaḥ) by fine-holed

strainers (*anvībhiḥ*), desire you (*tvāyavaḥ*).

5. Indra (*iṃdra*), moved (*iṣitaḥ*) by prayer (*dhiyā*), urged by the wise (*viprajūtaḥ*), come (*ā yāhi*) to (*upa*) the prayers (*brahmāṇi*) of the one who has pressed Soma juice (*sutāvataḥ*), the institutor of the sacrifice (*vāghataḥ*).

6. Indra (*iṃdra*), hastening (*tūtujānaḥ*) to (*upa*) the prayers (*brahmāṇi*), owner of the bay horses (*harivaḥ*), come (*ā yāhi*); take (*dadhiṣva*) delight (*canaḥ*) in our (*naḥ*) pressed Soma (*sute*).

7. All-the-gods (*viśve devāsaḥ*), helping (*omāsaḥ*), protecting men (*carṣaṇīdhṛtaḥ*), presenting offerings (*dāśvāṃsaḥ*), approach (*ā gata*) the Soma juice (*sutam*) of the worshipper (*dāśuṣaḥ*).

8. All-the-gods (*viśve devāsaḥ*), who cross the waters (*apturaḥ*), come (*ā gaṃta*) quickly (*tūrṇayaḥ*) to the libation (*sutam*) as (*iva*) cows (*usrāḥ*) [who] approach the pastures (*svasarāṇi*).

9. All-the-gods (*viśve devāsaḥ*), never failing (*asridhaḥ*), whom one wants to come and does not want to leave (*ehimāyāsaḥ*), free from malice (*adruhaḥ*): bearers (*vahnayaḥ*), may you enjoy (*juṣaṃta*) the strengthening drink (*medhaṃ*).

10. Sarasvatī (*sarasvatī*), shining (*pavakā*), rich in prizes (*vājinīvatī*) through strength (*vājebhiḥ*), possessing treasure through wisdom (*dhiyāvasuḥ*), desire (*vaṣṭu*) our (*naḥ*) sacrificial worship (*yajñam*).

11. Sarasvatī (*sarasvatī*), promoter (*codayitrī*) of delightful things (*sūnṛtānām*), observer (*cetaṃtī*) of kindnesses (*sumatīnām*), accept (*dadhe*) the sacrificial worship (*yajñam*).

♩=224
e=e
Tape Ia(2)
1.
á śvi nā yá jva rī rí ṣo drá va tpa nī śú
bha spa tī / pú ru bhu jā ca na syá taṃ //
2.
á śvi nā pú ru daṃ sa sā ná rā śá vī ra yā
dhi yā / dhí ṣṇyā vá na taṃ gí ra ḥ //
3.
dá srā yu vā ka vaḥ su tā nā sa tyā vṛ ktá ba

65 70
r hi ṣa ḥ / ā́ ya taṃ ru dra va r ta ṇī //
4. 75 80
íṃ drā́ ya hi ci t ra bhā no su̱ tā́ i̱ mé tvā̱
85 90
yá va ḥ / áṇ vi bhi̱ stá na pū̱ tā́ sa ḥ //
5. 95 100 105
íṃ drā́ ya hi dhi̱ yé ṣi̱ tó ví pra jū taḥ su̱ tā́
110 115 3
va ta ḥ / ú pa̱ brá hma ṇi vā̱ ghá ta ḥ //

6.
120
125
130
íṃ drā́ ya hi̲ tū́ tu jā na̲ ú pa̲ brá hma ṇi
135
140
ha ri va ḥ / su̲ té da dhi ṣva na̲ ścá na ḥ //
7.
145
150
ó ma sa śca r ṣa ṇī dhṛ to̲ ví śve de vā
155
160
165
sa̲ ā́ ga ta / dā̲ śvā́ ṃ so dā̲ śú ṣaḥ su̲ táṃ //
8.
170
175
ví śve de̲ vā́ so a ptú raḥ su̲ tá mā́ gaṃ

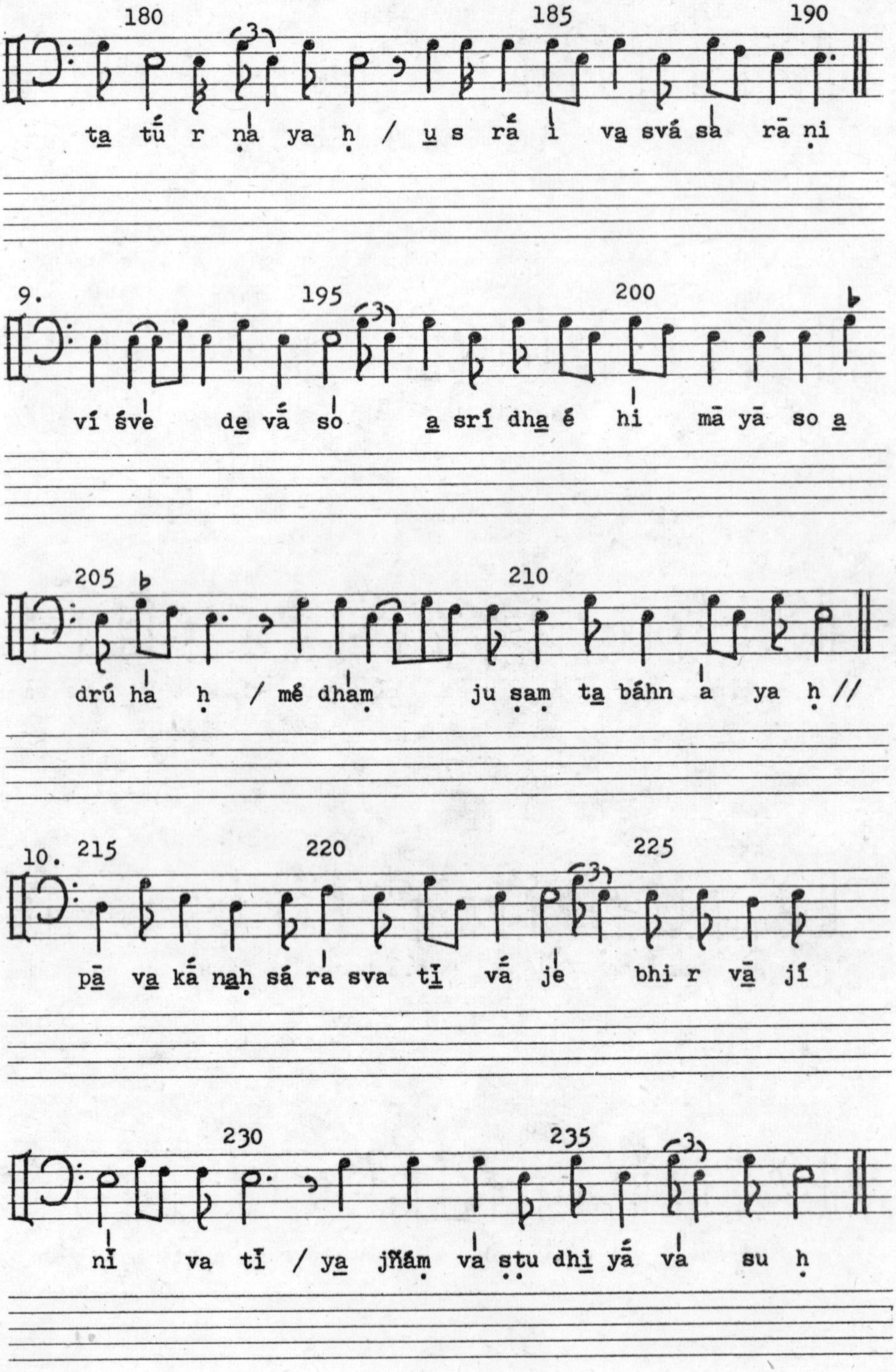
180 185 190
ta̲ tū́ r ṇa ya ḥ / u̲ s rā́ i va̲ svá sa rā ṇi
9. 195 200
ví śve de̲ vā́ so a̲ srí dha̲ é hi mā yā so a̲
205 210
drú ha ḥ / mé dhaṃ ju ṣaṃ ta̲ báhn a ya ḥ //
10. 215 220 225
pā̲ va̲ kā́ naḥ sá ra sva tī̲ vā́ je bhi r vā̲ jí
230 235
nī va tī / ya̲ jñā́ṃ va ṣṭu dhi̲ yā́ va su ḥ

11. 240 245
co da yi trī́ sū nṛ́ ta nā ṃ cé taṃ tī
250 255 260
su ma tī nā́ṃ / ya jñā́ṃ da dhe sá ra sva tī //
12. 265 270
ma hó á r ṇaḥ sá ra sva tī prá ce ta ya ti
275 280 285
ke tú na / dhí yo ví śvā ví ra ja ti//óm//

12. Sarasvatī (sarasvatī), the great (mahaḥ) river (arṇaḥ), makes visible (pra cetayati) through brightness (ketunā); she governs (rājati) all (viśvāḥ) religious thoughts (dhiyaḥ).

(4) Ṛgveda 9.45.1-6: Hymn to Soma Pavamāna

1. sá pavasva̱ mádāya̱ káṃ nṛcákṣā̱ de̱vávītaye /
   íṃda̱v íṃdrāya pī̱táye //

2. sá no arṣā̱bhí dū̱tyaṃ̱ tváṃ íṃdrāya tośase /
   de̱vánt sákhibhya̱ á váraṃ //

3. u̱tá tváṃ aru̱ṇáṃ va̱yáṃ góbhir aṃjmo̱ máda̱ya̱ káṃ /
   ví no rā̱yé dúro vṛdhi //

4. áty ū pa̱vítram akramīd vā̱jī́ dhúra̱ṃ ná yámani /
   íṃdur de̱véṣu patyate //

5. sáṃ ī̱ sákhāyo asvara̱n váne̱ krīḷaṃta̱m átyaviṃ /
   íṃduṃ na̱vā́ anūṣata //

6. táyā pavasva̱ dhárayā̱ yáyā pī̱tó vi̱cákṣase /
   íṃdo sto̱tré su̱vī́ryaṃ //

Translation:

1. Indu (iṃdo), flow (pavasva) you (saḥ) well (kaṃ) for excitement (madāya), beholding men (nṛcakṣāḥ), providing enjoyment for the gods (devavītaye): [you are] for Indra (iṃdrāya) to drink (pītaye).

2. Rush (arṣa) you (saḥ) for us (naḥ) to (abhi) the embassy (dūtyaṃ); you (tvaṃ) drip (tośase) for Indra (iṃdrāya):

you prefer (ā varam) the gods (devān) to [your] friends (sakhibhyaḥ).

3. We (vayaṃ) anoint (aṃjmaḥ) you (tvāṃ) also (uta) with cows' [milk] (gobhiḥ), red-colored one (aruṇaṃ), for excitement (madāya): for us (naḥ) open (vṛdhi) up (vi) the doors (duraḥ) of wealth (rāye).

4. [Soma] has passed through (aty ū akramīt) the filter (pavitraṃ) as (na) a horse (vājī) going (yāmani) to the place of honor (dhuraṃ); Indu (iṃduḥ) belongs (patyate) to the gods (deveṣu).

5. All (sam ī) friends (sakhāyaḥ) have praised (asvaran) [him], sporting (krīḷaṃtaṃ) in the woods (vane) across the fleece (atyaviṃ); the singers (navāḥ) have praised (anuṣata) Indu (iṃduṃ).

6. Flow (pavasva), Indu (iṃdo), with that (tayā) stream (dhārayā), with which (yayā), having drunk (pītaḥ), to proclaim (vicakṣase) heroism (suvīryaṃ) for him who chants praises (stotre).

Krama:

1. sá pavasva / pavasva mádaya / mádaya káṃ / káṃ nṛcákṣaḥ / nṛcákṣa devávītaye / nṛcákṣa íti nṛ--cákṣaḥ / devávītaya íti devá--vītaye / íṃdav íṃdrāya / íṃdo ítīṃdo / íṃdrāya pītáye / pītáya íti pītáye //

2. sá naḥ / no arṣa / arṣābhí / abhí dūtyaṃ / dūtyaṃ tváṃ / tváṃ íṃdrāya / íṃdrāya tośase / tośasa íti tośase / devánt sákhibhyaḥ / sákhibhya á váraṃ / sákhibhya íti sákhi--bhyaḥ / á váraṃ / váram íti váraṃ //

3. utá tvā́m / tvā́m aruṇā́m / aruṇā́m vayā́m / vayā́m gṓbhiḥ /

gṓbhir aṃjmaḥ / aṃjmo mádaya / mádaya kā́m / kā́m íti kā́m /

ví naḥ / no rāyé / rāyé dū́raḥ / dū́ro vṛdhi / vṛdhī́ti

vṛdhi //

4. áty u pavítram / ūm íty ūm / pavítram akramīt / akramīd

vājī́ / vājī́ dhū́ram / dhū́ram ná / ná yā́mani / yā́manī́ti

yā́mani / ímdur devéṣu / devéṣu patyate / patyata íti

patyate //

5. sám ī sákhāyaḥ / īm ítīm / sákhāyo asvaran / asvaran váne /

váne krī́lamtam / krī́lamtam átyavim / átyavim íty

áti--avim / ímduṃ nāvā́ḥ / nāvā́ anūṣata / anūṣatéty

anūṣata //

6. tā́yā pavasva / pavasva dhā́rayā / dhā́rayā yā́yā / yā́yā

pītā́ḥ / pītṓ vicákṣase / vicákṣasa íti vi--cákṣase /

ímdo stotré / ímdo ítīmdo / stotré suvī́ryam / suvī́ryam

íti su--vī́ryam // ṓm //

(5) Ṛgveda 2.12.1: to Indra

yṓ jātá evá prathamṓ mánasvān devṓ devā́n krátunā

paryábhuṣat /

yásya śúṣmād rṓdasī ábhyasetām nṛmṇásya mahnā́ sá

janāsa ímdraḥ //

♩=252
e=e
Tape XXVb(27)
1.
sá pa va sva / pa̱ va̱ sva̱ má da ya / má da ya̱ kám̥ /
kám̥ nṟ cá kṣa ḥ / nṟ cá kṣa de̱ vá vi ta ye /
nṟ cá kṣa̱ í ti nṟ cá kṣa ḥ / de̱ vá vi ta ya̱
í ti de̱ vá vi ta ye / ím̥ da̱ vím̥ dra ya /
ím̥ do̱ í tí m̥ do / ím̥ dra ya pi̱ tá ye /

65
70
pi̱ tá ya̱ í ti pi̱ tá ye //
2.
3
75
80
sá na ḥ / no̱ a̱ r ṣa̱ / a̱ r ṣā̱ bhí / a̱ bhí dū̱
85
tyaṃ / dū̱ tya mi̱ tváṃ / tvá míṃ dra ya /
90
95
100
íṃ dra ya to śa se / to̱ śa̱ sa̱ í ti to śa se /
105
110
de̱ vā́n tsá khi bhya ḥ / sá khi bhya̱ ā́ vá raṃ /

115 120 125
sá khi bhya í ti sá khi bhya ḥ / ā́ vá raṃ /
130
vá ra mí ti vá ram
3.
135 140
u tá tvā́ṃ / tvā́ ma ru ṇā́ṃ / a ru ṇā́ṃ va yáṃ /
145 150
va yáṃ gó bhi ḥ / gó bhi raṃ jma ḥ / aṃ jmo má
155 160 165
da ya / má da ya káṃ / ká mí ti káṃ / ví

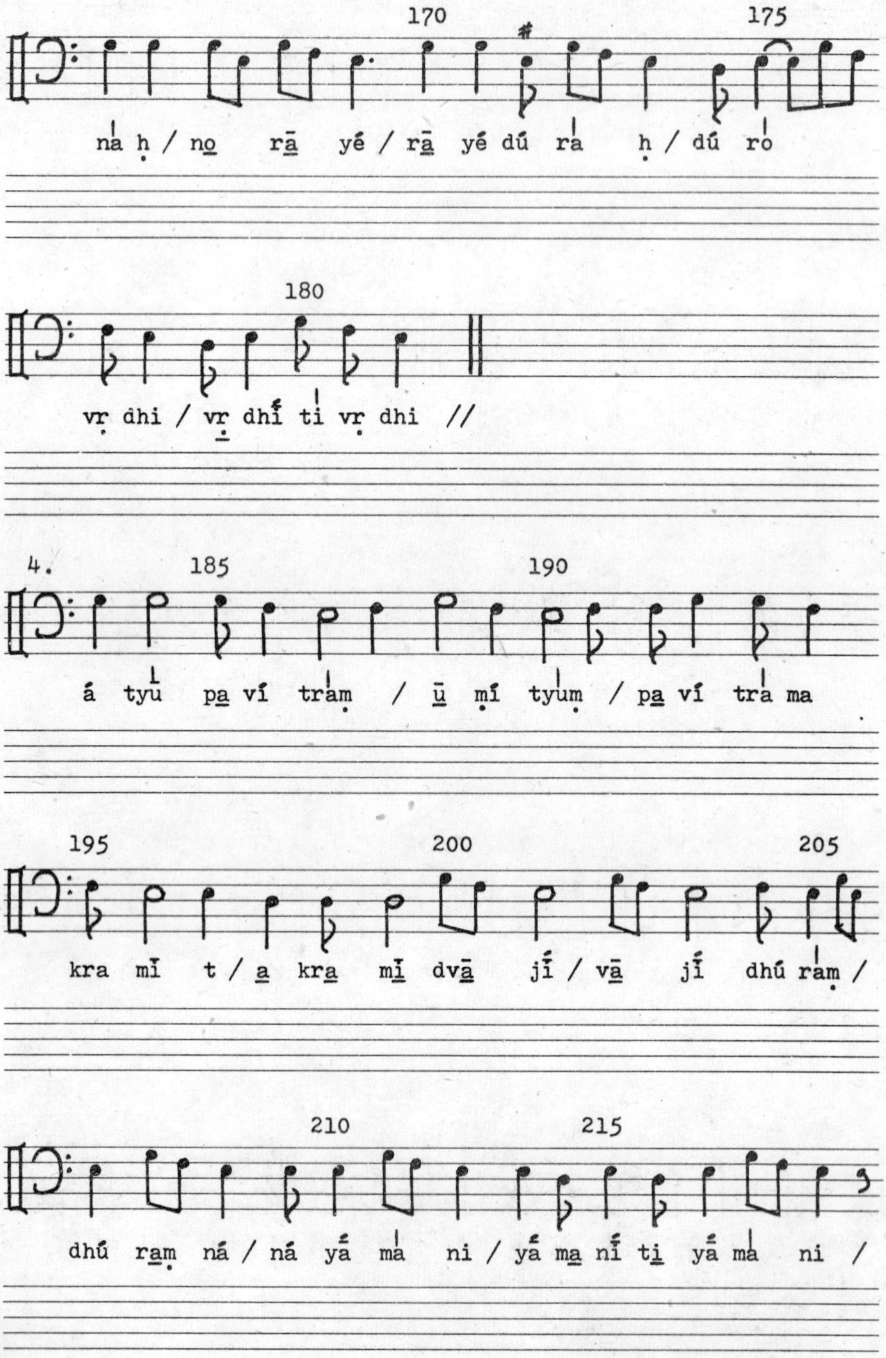
170 175
na ḥ / no rā yé / rā yé dú ra ḥ / dú ro
180
vṛ dhi / vṛ dhī́ ti vṛ dhi //
4. 185 190
á tyu pa ví traṃ / ū ṃí tyuṃ / pa ví tra ma
195 200 205
kra mī t / a kra mī dvā jī́ / vā jī́ dhū́ raṃ /
210 215
dhū́ raṃ ná / ná yā́ ma ni / yā́ ma nī́ ti yā́ ma ni /

220 225 230
íṃ du r de vé ṣu / de vé ṣu pa tya te / pa tya
235
ta í ti pa tya te //
5. 240 245
sá mi sá kha ya ḥ / I mí ti ṃ / sá
250 255
kha yo a sva ran / a sva ran vá ne /
260 265
vá ne krī ḷaṃ taṃ / krī ḷaṃ ta mā tya viṃ/

270 275 280
á tya vi mí tyá ti a viṃ / íṃ duṃ nā vā́
285 290
ḥ / nā vā́ a nū ṣa ta / a nū ṣa té tya nū ṣa ta //
6. 295 300 305
tá ya pa va sva / pa va sva dhā́ ra yā /
310 315
dhā́ ra yā yá ya / yá ya pī tá ḥ / pī tó vi cá
320 325 330
kṣa se / vi cá kṣa sa í ti vi cá kṣa se /

335
340
ím̥ dó sto tré / ím̥ do í tī́m̥ dó / sto
345
350
tré su vī́ r yam̥ / su vī́ r ya mí ti su
vī́ r yá m̥ óm

Translation:

He who (yaḥ), just (eva) born (jātaḥ), first (prathamaḥ) god (devaḥ) in intellect (manasvān), with resolution (kratunā) protected (paryabhūṣat) the gods (devān); from whose (yasya) strength (śuṣmāt), through greatness (mahnā) of courage (nṛmṇasya) heaven and earth (rodasī) shook (abhyasetām): he (saḥ), O men (janāsaḥ), is Indra (iṃdraḥ).

Ghana:

yố jā́tố jā́tố yố yố jā́tá eváivá jā́tố yố yố jā́tá evá / jā́tá
eváivá jā́tố jā́tá evá práthamáḥ práthamá evá jā́tố jā́tá evá
práthamáḥ / evá práthamáḥ práthamá eváivá práthamố mánasvān
mánasvān prathamá eváivá práthamố mánasvān / prathamố mánasvān
mánasvān prathamáḥ práthamố mánasvān devố devố mánasvān
prathamáḥ práthamố mánasvān deváḥ / mánasvān devố devố
mánasvān mánasvān devố devā́n devā́n devố mánasvān mánasvān
devố devā́n / devố devā́n devā́n devố devố devā́n krátunā
krátunā devā́n devố devố devā́n krátunā / devā́n krátunā
krátunā devā́n devā́n krátunā paryábhuṣat paryábhuṣat krátunā
devā́n devā́n krátunā paryábhuṣat / krátunā paryábhuṣat
paryábhuṣat krátunā krátunā paryábhuṣat / paryábhuṣad íti
pari--ábhuṣat / yásya śúṣmāc chúṣmād yásya yásya śúṣmād
ródasī ródasī śúṣmād yásya yásya śúṣmād ródasī / śúṣmād

rṓdasī rṓdasī śū́ṣmāc chū́ṣmād rṓdasī ā́bhyāsetām ā́bhyāsetām

rṓdasī śū́ṣmāc chū́ṣmād rṓdasī ā́bhyāsetām / rṓdasī ā́bhyāsetām

ā́bhyāsetām rṓdasī rṓdasī ā́bhyāsetām nṛmṇā́sya nṛmṇā́syā́bhyāsetām

rṓdasī rṓdasī ā́bhyāsetām nṛmṇā́sya / rṓdasī́tī rṓdasī /

ā́bhyāsetām nṛmṇā́sya nṛmṇā́syā́bhyāsetām ā́bhyāsetām nṛmṇā́sya

mahnā́ mahnā́ nṛmṇā́syā́bhyāsetām ā́bhyāsetām nṛmṇā́sya mahnā́ /

nṛmṇā́sya mahnā́ mahnā́ nṛmṇā́sya nṛmṇā́sya mahnā́ sá sá mahnā́

nṛmṇā́sya nṛmṇā́sya mahnā́ sáḥ / mahnā́ sá sá mahnā́ mahnā́ sá

janāso janāsaḥ sá mahnā́ mahnā́ sá janāsaḥ / sá janāso janāsaḥ

sá sá janāsa ī́mdra ī́mdro janāsaḥ sá sá janāsa ī́mdraḥ / janāsa

ī́mdra ī́mdro janāso janāsa ī́mdraḥ / ī́mdra ítī́mdraḥ //

Tape XXVb(29)

♩=276
e=c#
5 10 15
yṓ jā̲ tṓ jā̲ tṓ yṓ yṓ jā̲ tá e̲ vái vá jā̲ tṓ yṓ
20 25 30
yṓ jā̲ tá e̲ vá / jā̲ tá e̲ vái vá jā̲ tṓ jā̲ tá e̲
35 40
vá pra tha̲ má ḥpra tha̲ má e̲ vá jā̲ tṓ jā̲ tá
45 50 55
e̲ vá pra tha̲ má ḥ / e̲ vá pra tha̲ má ḥpra tha̲ má
60 65
e̲ vái vá pra tha̲ mṓ má na svā̲n má na svā̲n

70 75 80
pra tha má e vái vá pra tha mó má na svān /
85 90
pra tha mó má na svān má na svān pra tha má
95 100 105
ḥpra tha mó má na svān de vó de vó má na svān
110 115
pra tha má ḥpra tha mó má na svān de vá ḥ /
120 125
má na svān de vó de vó má na svān má na svān

130 135 140
de̲ vố de̲ vā́n de̲ vā́n de̲ vố mā́ na svā̲n mā́ na svān
145 150 155
de̲ vố de̲ vā́n / de̲ vố de̲ vā́n de̲ vā́n de̲ vố de̲ vố
160 165 170
de̲ vā́n krā́ tu nā̲ krā́ tu nā de̲ vā́n de̲ vố de̲ vố
175 180
de̲ vā́n krā́ tu nā / de̲ vā́n krā́ tu nā̲ krā́ tu
185 190 195
nā de̲ vā́n de̲ vā́n krā́ tu nā pa̲ r yā́ bhu ṣa

205
tpa̲ r yá bhu ṣa̲ tkrá tu nā de̲ vā́n de̲ vā́n
210
215
krá tu nā pa̲ r yá bhu ṣa t / krá tu nā pa̲
220
225
r yá bhu ṣa tpa̲ r yá bhu ṣa̲ tkrá tu nā̲ krá
230
235
240
tu nā pa̲ r yá bhu ṣa t / pa̲ r yá bhu ṣa̲ dí ti
3
245
250
pa ri̲ á bhu ṣa t / yá sya̲ śú ṣmā̲ cchú

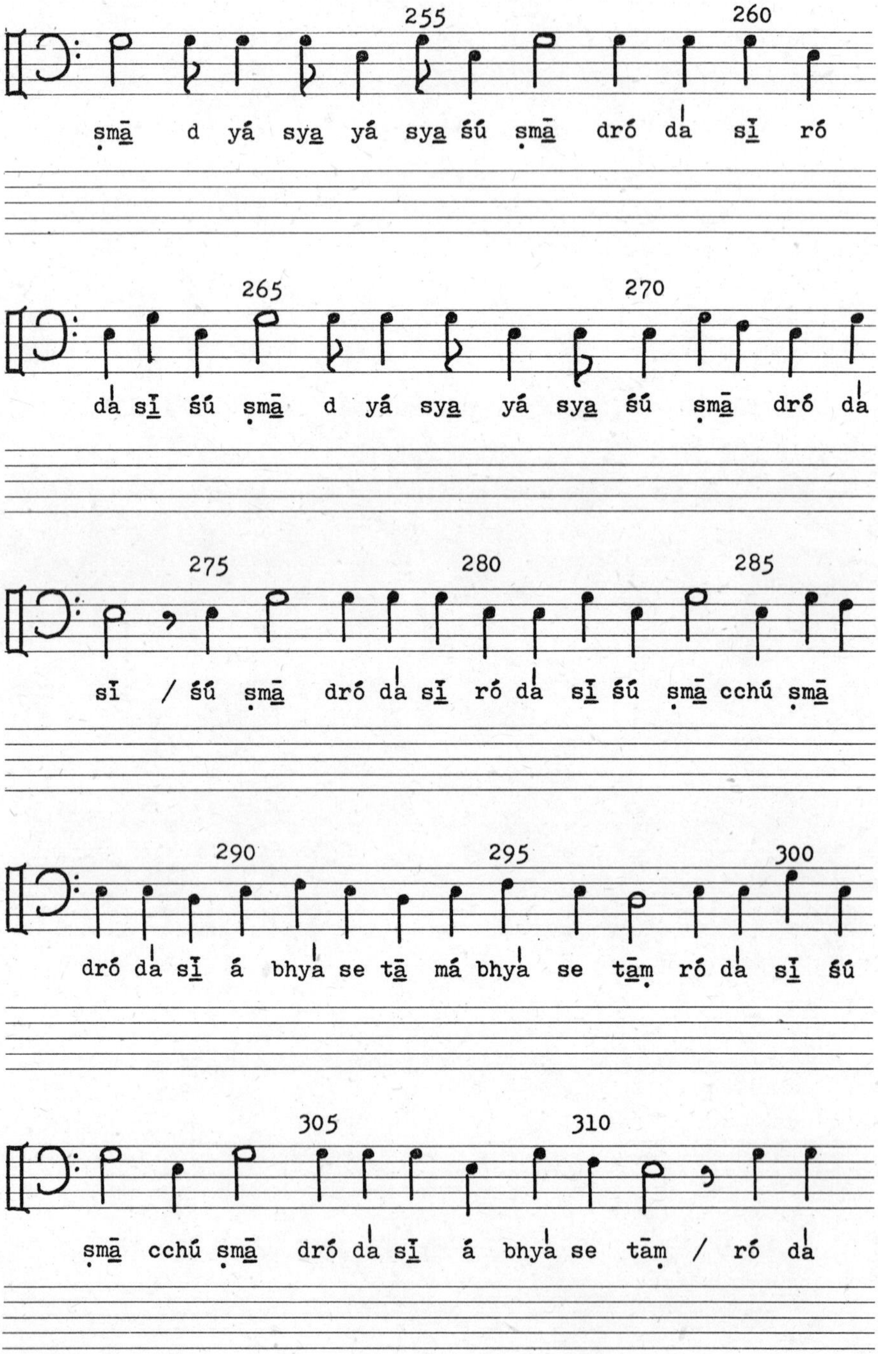
255 260
ṣmā d yá sya yá sya śú ṣmā dró da sī ró
265 270
da sī śú ṣmā d yá sya yá sya śú ṣmā dró da
275 280 285
sī / śú ṣmā dró da sī ró da sī śú ṣmā cchú ṣmā
290 295 300
dró da sī á bhya se tā má bhya se tāṃ ró da sī śú
305 310
ṣmā cchú ṣmā dró da sī á bhya se tāṃ / ró da

315 320 325
sī á bhya se tā má bhya se tāṃ ró da sī ró
330 335
da sī á bhya se tāṃ nṛm ṇá sya nṛm ṇá syá
340 345 350
bhya se tāṃ ró da sī ró da sī á bhya se tāṃ
355 360
nṛm ṇá sya / ró da sī ti ró da sī / á bhya
365 370 375
se tāṃ nṛm ṇá sya nṛm ṇá syá bhya se tā má bhya

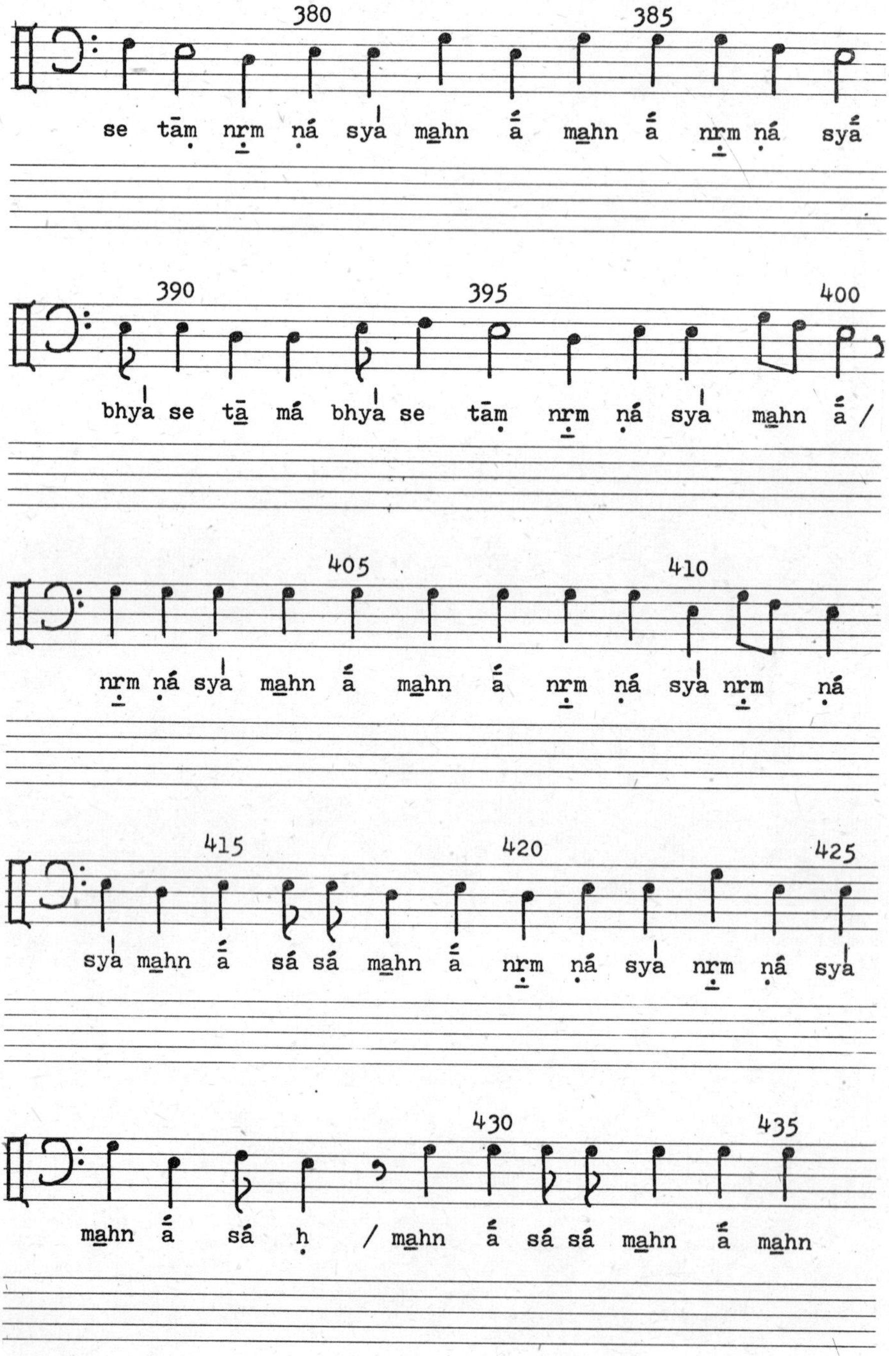
380
385
se tāṃ nṛm ṇá sya mahn ā mahn ā nṛm ṇá syā
390
395
400
bhya se tā má bhya se tāṃ nṛm ṇá sya mahn ā /
405
410
nṛm ṇá sya mahn ā mahn ā nṛm ṇá sya nṛm ṇá
415
420
425
sya mahn ā sá sá mahn ā nṛm ṇá sya nṛm ṇá sya
430
435
mahn ā sá ḥ / mahn ā sá sá mahn ā mahn

440 445
ā sá ja nā so ja nā sa ḥsá mahn ā mahn ā
450 455 460
sá ja nā sa ḥ / sá ja nā so ja nā sa ḥsá sá
465 470
ja nā sa íṃ dra íṃ dro ja nā sa ḥsá sá ja
475 480 485
nā sa íṃ dra ḥ / ja nā sa íṃ dra íṃ dro
490 495
ja nā so ja nā sa íṃ dra ḥ / íṃ dra

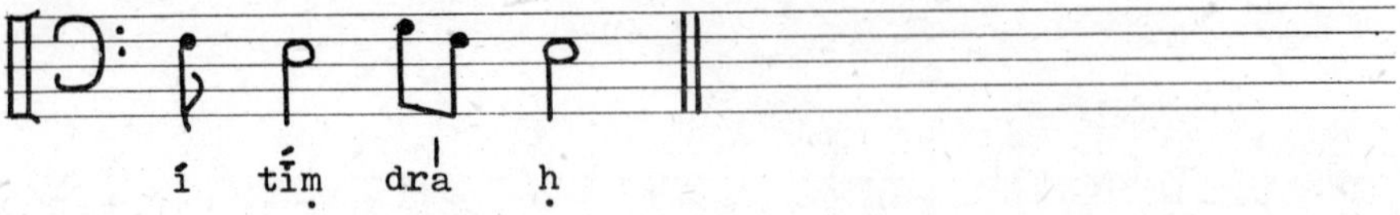
í tī́ṃ dra ḥ

Analysis

Four principal tones are sounded in the above examples: a middle tone (M), a low tone (L) a major second below, a high tone (H) a minor third above, and a tone only a minor second above which can be designated upper middle (UM). Vedic meters count syllables long if they have a long vowel or a short vowel followed by conjunct consonants. In the analyses below superscripts are attached to the pitch symbols to indicate tone length: therefore M^{s} shows short middle tone (an eighth note or less in the transcriptions), M^{l} long middle tone (more than an eighth note), and M^{sl} a middle tone that is sometimes short, sometimes long. Short syllables before a pause are always counted long. Each accent is taken in turn; the tones and tone groups corresponding to that accent are then listed, and reference is made to applicable syllables in each of the five recitations (referred to by numbers, in parentheses--the two versions of the second hymn are listed as 2a and 2b, respectively). The enumeration of syllables associated with each tone or tone group makes use of asterisks to show whether a syllable is long because of vowel length (one asterisk) or long by position (two asterisks): thus *3 shows that the third syllable of a particular recitation has a long vowel, **7 that the seventh syllable of a certain hymn has a short vowel followed by conjuncts.

Udātta

I. M^{sl}

(1) *1,3,*7,**11,14,16,*18,*23,**27,*28,31,*34,*36, *40,41,*43,*44,45,50,53,*57,60,*62,66,69,**75,77, **80,82,*86,87,*92,**98,*99,102,**106,**108,*114, *116,*118,121,123,125,127,**128,**131,134,*137, **138,140,144,*149,*152,*157,*159,160,162,*165, *168,*176,**178,*180,*187,190,*193,196,*197,*202, 205,210.

(2a) *3,*9,*10,12,*21,*27,*32,**33,*37,45,49,*54,*55, 61,*65,*66,79,81,*84,*94,**97,*104,115,**121, *127,130,*134,*137,*139,147,150,*155,*161,*163, **185,*194,195,*201.

(2b) *1,*3,*9,*10,12,*16,*21,22,*27,*32,**33,40,45,*47, 49,*54,*55,**71,*78,79,*84,**87,**92,*94,*104,*111, *112,115,*127,130,*134,*137,*139,147,150,*155,158, *161,*163,**185,*191,*194,195,*201,204.

(3) **1,7,9,13,17,25,28,33,35,*40,43,46,48,*55,*56, 60,*64,*81,*83,85,**87,90,**95,*96,*102,**103, *108,111,117,**119,*120,*123,127,141,*156,*160,163, **166,*170,173,176,*177,*180,187,**191,*194,197, 205,**212,*217,219,*223,227,*236,*242,*247,*253, 258,266,270,276,*286.

(4) 1,8,**14,**15,**17,**47,**49,**52,61,64,66,69,71, 78,80,**85,86,**87,99,109,*112,115,118,120,*123, 126,128,130,**138,**141,**143,**145,*146,*148, 161,162,**164,165,*169,172,*179,*201,*203,206,208, 209,*210,*213,*215,*217,234,239,245,256,258,*260, **269,273,*282,*290,*303,*306,309,*316,**318,**322, 325,**328,**335,*338,*341,348,*351,*353.

(5) *1,*5,*6,*7,9,*11,12,*14,*15,*16,18,20,22,*24,25, *27,29,**31,**34,**37,39,*41,43,**45,**48,**56, *58,**59,*62,63,66,*73,**74,*77,78,*95,96,*100, *102,103,*111,112,**116,117,*123,124,127,*131,*133, *135,*137,138,141,*145,*147,*157,*159,160,163, *167,*171,*173,174,182,*186,*188,189,200,*204, *206,207,214,222,225,228,239,243,**254,**256,*261, **264,**268,**270,*272,**275,*280,**283,**285, *287,**290,**294,*298,**301,**303,**308,*326,**329, **334,**337,*338,*345,**353,**362,**371,**380,

*383,*388,**397,*400,**412,*415,416,417,*419,
421,424,*427,*436,437,444,*446,*448,449,453,
460,461,**465,**467,472,473,**477,**482,**492,**494,
*497.

II. H^{sl}

(1) 89,**90.

(2a) *16,*111,*112,158,182,**206.

(2b) *65,*76,**97,**121,**143,*167,182,**206.

(3) **4,**41,*51,**72,*73,*93,*100,**113,*136,*143,
167,*184,*207,232,244,*263,**280.

(4) **28,36,40,**57,**105,106,**133,*134,*135,*171,
183,192,**220,*223,*226,247,**266,**272,**277,
295,**331,*346.

(5) *3,**50,**53,71,*83,84,87,**92,**108,*121,*149,
*151,*153,*155,*169,*178,179,218,**246,**248,**250,
252,*258,266,*277,*305,*312,**315,**319,*342,
*355,*357,*359,**367,*385,**402,*407,**409,*430,
431,432,*434.

III. UM^{sl}

(1) 136,188.

(2a) 22,40,126,204,212.

(2b) 61,81,126,212.

(3) 23,**129,**151,282.

(4) 23,30,**33,54,113,124,154,**186,**189,204,241,337.

(5) 197,236,*323,**370,**387,**484,496.

IV. H^{sl}-M^{s}

(1) **73,**183.

(2a) *1,*24,*47,**71,*76,**87,**92,*95,*119,**143,*167.

(2b) *24,*37,*66,*95,*119.

(3) *199,**255,**264.

V. L^{sl}

(3) 278.

(4) 11,**20,**90,157,174,*263,311.

(5) 193,211,232,**348,**375,**392.

VI. M^{l}-UM^{sl}

(1) *173.

(2a) *78,*191.

(4) *55,*160,*280,*334,*343.

VII. UM^{sl}-M^{l}

(2a) **118.

(2b) **118.

(4) *314.

(5) *428.

VIII. M^{s}-H^{s}

(4) 43.

Anudātta

I. H^{sl}

(1) 6,**15,33,39,65,79,85,**105,117,**133,**139,156, 158,164,177,179,192.

(2a) 2,*11,20,**26,36,39,53,75,77,83,91,93,96,103,114, 117,120,125,129,133,**135,138,**142,154,160,166, 184,190,**203,211.

(2b) 2,20,**26,36,39,*48,53,*64,75,77,**80,83,93,96, 114,117,120,125,129,133,**142,166,184,190,**193, **203,211.

(3) *3,**22,*27,39,*42,**45,50,82,*84,**89,*92,99,101, **112,122,126,**128,135,*150,*162,*169,**172,175, 179,**183,**186,*193,**196,198,**204,211,216,**231, 235,**241,*243,**254,*257,262,**265,*279.

(4) 13,16,*22,**27,*29,32,*35,39,*42,48,*53,*60,*63, 65,*68,79,98,*104,111,117,119,127,129,132,137,142, 144,*153,159,163,*170,185,*188,*222,*225,*240,265,

271,*308,*313,327,*336,345,350.

(5) *2,*4,*8,*10,*19,*21,*23,*26,*28,*30,36,47,*49, 52,70,*72,82,*86,91,94,110,*120,*122,*132,*136, *146,*148,*150,*152,*154,*156,*158,*162,*168,*170, *172,*177,*181,*187,**196,*205,217,**221,**224, **235,242,247,*249,*251,253,255,*257,*260,*263,*265, 267,*276,*279,*282,*284,*300,*302,*304,*307,*314, *318,*322,**336,*344,*356,358,**366,**369,**382, **384,**386,**401,**404,**406,**408,**423,**426, **429,**433,**435,**459,481,483,491,495.

II. L^{sl}

(1) **10,22,52,**56,*59,61,**76,81,101,148,172,201, **209.

(2a) **193.

(2b) **44,91,103,**135,138,**149,154,160.

(3) *12,*34,54,**59,80,107,*116,**140,155,**218,*226.

(4) 7,19,*83,140,178,214,216,233,**255,*281,289,302, *315,317,321,324,342.

(5) *13,*17,33,*42,*44,61,*65,76,*99,*101,*115,*126, *130,*134,*140,*144,*166,*185,**192,**199,*203, **210,**231,238,*289,*293,*297,*325,*328,**333, *347,**352,*374,**379,*391,**396,**414,**418,**420 **443,**445,**447,464,466,**471,476.

III. H^s-L^s

(1) *13,*35,*68,*113,*115,*122,*124,**130,*175.

(2a) *8,**44,*48,*64,*146,*200.

(2b) *8,*11,*146,*200.

(3) *6,*32,*222.

(5) *38,*40.

IV. M^{sl}-H^s-L^{sl}

(1) *42,*74,*91,*126,*151,*161,**186,*195.

(2a) *31,*60,**149,*162.

(2b) *31,*162.

(3) *8,*159,*246,*269.

(4) *81,*244,*340.

V. $H^{sl}-UM^{sl}$

(3) *252.

(4) *77,*168,*200,*202,*207,*279,*333.

(5) *271,*286,**399,**411.

VI. $H^{sl}-M^{s}$

(1) **26,**49,**97,**107.

(2a) **80.

(5) *57.

VII. $M^{sl}-H^{sl}$

(2b) *60.

(3) *275.

(5) *227,*341.

VIII. UM^{sl}

(1) **2.

(3) 165.

(4) 191.

(5) 55.

IX. M^{s}

(4) 347.

(5) 107,269.

X. $M^{s}-L^{s}$

(1) **30.

XI. $M^{s}-H^{s}-M^{s}$

(3) *281.

XII. $M^{s}-H^{s}-UM^{l}$

(4) *259.

<u>Svarita</u>

I. H^{sl}

(1) 8,**46,**70,**83,93,109,184,**191.

(2a) **50,67,72,88,**98,**122,144,**148,196.

(2b) **50,**98,**122,196.

(3) **10,**14,18,**57,124,**164,**174,**233,**259,
**267.

(4) *37,41,*58,100,**107,**116,**121,*166,180,*184,
193,**221,*224,227,235,*274,**278,283,291,*332.

(5) 51,**79,**85,**88,**118,175,180,215,*219,259,273,
278,306,309,313,330,339,343,349,360,363,372,376,
403,438,450,454,474.

II. M^{sl}

(2b) **148.

(3) 61.

(4) *12,*24,31,*62,67,*82,*110,*114,*158,**264,*310,
*312,323,326,349.

(5) 32,35,46,54,60,**67,75,93,109,**125,**139,161,190,
*194,*198,201,208,*212,*223,226,*233,*237,240,262,
281,288,299,324,327,335,346,368,381,389,393,398,
410,413,422,425,462,*485.

III. H^{s}-UM^{s}

(1) 24,63,150,166,181,203.

(2a) 85,131,140,151,156.

(2b) 67,72,85,88,131,140,144,151,156.

(3) 29,52,104,157,188,200.

(4) 149,211,218,267,304,319,329.

(5) 354.

IV. M^{l}-H^{s}-M^{sl}

(1) **67,**163,**174.

(2a) *82,*105,*128,*213.

(2b) *4,**13,*17,*23,*34,*62,*105,*113,*128,*205,*213.

(3) *24,*49,*88,*91,*121,*171,**178,*192,*195,*224, *271,*277,*283.

(4) *125,*205,*344.

V. H^s-M^s

(1) 12,32,**78,88,103,119,132,135,**145,194,**206.

(2a) 25,**28,**116,202.

(2b) 25,**28,**116,202.

(3) 2,5,26,44,109,181,185,213,237,256.

(4) 2,136,270,307.

VI. M^{sl}-H^s-UM^{sl}

(1) *19.

(2a) **13,*41,*56,**164,168,186,*192.

(2b) *41,*56,*82,**159,**164,168,186.

(3) *36,*65,*97,*130,137,*152,*161,*228,**248.

(4) *88,*155,*175,*242,**261,*339.

(5) *244.

VII. UM^{sl}

(1) 37,**54.

(3) **220.

(5) **64,**97,**104,**113,**128,**142,164,183,229, 291,295,316,320.

VIII. M^l-H^{sl}

(1) *17,*129,*153,*189,*211.

(2a) *23,*34,*62,*205.

(4) *44,*56,*70,*91,*131.

IX. H^s-UM^{sl}-M^l

(2a) *38.

(2b) *38.

(3) *47,*86,*94,*142,*206.

(4) *72,*147,*173.

(5) *478,*493,*498.

X. $H^{sl}-M^{l}-H^{s}-UM^{sl}$

(1) *198.

(2a) *113,**159,**207.

(2b) **183,**207.

(3) *74,*114,*144,**208.

XI. $M^{l}-UM^{sl}$

(1) *4.

(4) *9,*21,*50,*187,*190,*257.

(5) *468.

XII. $M^{l}-H^{s}-M^{sl}-UM^{s}$

(1) *29,*100,**141.

(2a) *4.

(4) *352.

XIII. $M^{sl}-H^{s}-UM^{s}-M^{l}$

(2a) *46.

(2b) *46.

(3) *118.

(4) *34,*246.

XIV. $H^{sl}-M^{l}-H^{s}-M^{sl}$

(2a) **183.

(3) *168,*245.

XV. $M^{s}-H^{s}-M^{l}-H^{s}-L^{l}$

(2a) **136.

(2b) **136.

(4) **84.

XVI. $M^{l}-UM^{s}-M^{s}$

(1) **169.

(4) *18.

XVII. $H^{l}-M^{l}-H^{s}$

(4) *248,*296.

XVIII. H^s-M^s-UM^s

(1) 58.

XIX. M^l-H^s-M^s-H^s

(1) *51.

XX. H^l-M^l-UM^s-H^s-M^s

(2a) *17.

Pracaya

I. M^{sl}

(1) *5,**9,**20,**21,*25,*38,47,*48,55,*64,*72,84,**94,*96,**104,**110,111,142,*146,*147,*167,170,171,*182,*185,*199,*200,*204,*207,**208.

(2a) 5,7,**19,**30,35,*42,43,**52,*58,59,*68,*70,*74,*86,*90,*100,*101,*106,107,*108,*110,**124,**132,*141,*145,153,*157,*165,**169,*170,171,*173,*175,*177,**179,*181,*189,*197,198,199,*210.

(2b) 5,7,14,*18,**19,29,**30,35,*42,43,**52,57,*58,*68,*70,*73,*74,*86,*90,*100,101,**102,*106,*108,*110,**124,**132,*141,*145,153,*157,*165,**169,*170,171,*173,*175,*177,**179,*181,*187,*188,*189,*197,198,199,*209,*210.

(3) 11,*16,21,**30,31,37,*38,**53,*58,62,**66,**67,68,**69,70,*71,75,**76,77,*78,*79,98,*105,**106,115,132,133,**138,139,**145,**146,147,*148,149,*153,*154,*158,*189,*190,*201,*202,*203,**210,221,**225,*230,234,*249,250,251,*261,268,272,273,274,*285.

(4) *4,*10,*26,38,45,*51,*89,*93,94,*95,97,*101,102,*103,**150,*156,*177,*182,*196,*212,*219,**228,229,*230,**236,237,*238,*243,*249,**250,*252,*262,*268,275,*276,*286,*292,*294,297,**298,*299,*320,*330.

(5) *68,69,*80,*89,90,*98,*105,106,*114,*129,*143,*165,*176,*184,*191,**195,*202,*209,*230,*274,*292,*296,

*311,*317,*321,*332,*351,*361,*365,*378,*390,*395,
*439,*440,441,*442,*451,*463,469,*470,*475,479.

II. UM^{sl}

(1) 71,95.

(2a) 14,29,51,57,69,99,109,123,172,176,178,180,208.

(2b) 51,59,69,99,107,109,123,172,174,176,178,180,208.

(3) 15,131,209,229,260,284.

(4) **3,25,92,176,181,**194,195,251,*284,285,293.

(5) *310,*331,*340,*350,*364,*373,*377,*394.

III. H^{sl}

(1) **154.

(2a) **102.

(3) 19,*20.

(4) 59,*96.

(5) 81,*119,*216,**220,*455,*456,457,*458,*480,486,
*487,*488,489,*490.

IV. L^{sl}

(2a) 63.

(2b) 63.

(4) *73,**74,*75,**76,**197,198,*199,**231,232,**253,
254,287,*288,300,**301.

(5) 241.

V. H^{sl}-M^{sl}

(1) *112,*120,*143,**155.

(3) *63,*110,*125,*134,*182,*214,*238.

(4) *108,*167.

(5) *213,*234.

VI. M^{sl}-UM^{s}

(2a) *18,*73,*89,**152,*187,*188,*209.

(2b) *89,**152.

(4) *46,*122,*305.

VII. UM^s-M^l

(4) *151.

(5) *245, *452.

VIII. L^s-UM^s

(2a) **6.

(2b) **6.

IX. M^l-H^s-M^s

(2a) *15.

(2b) *15.

X. L^l-M^s-L^l

(4) **152.

Conclusions

The following interpretation of the data just presented takes each accent in turn. Tabulations of the totals and percentages of tones and tone groups connected with the accents precede each discussion.

Udātta

M^{sl}:	423 =	70.1%
H^{sl}:	98 =	16.3
UM^{sl}:	34 =	5.6
H^{sl}-M^s:	21 =	3.5
L^{sl}:	14 =	2.3
M^l-UM^{sl}:	8 =	1.3
UM^{sl}-M^l:	4 =	.7
M^s-H^s:	1 =	.2

The middle tone is obviously the choice in most cases, where it is used for both long and short syllables: of the 423 M^{sl} udāttas, 266 are long and 157 short. But circumstances exist for which H^{sl} is acceptable:

A. an udātta or series of udāttas initial in the line

(1) 89,**90.

(2a) *16,*111,*112,158,182,**206.

(2b) 182,**206

(3) **41,**72,*73,*143,**167,*207.

(4) **57,*135,**183,**220,**277,295,**331.

(5) **246,*312,*355.

B. one or more *udāttas* following high-tone *anudātta*

(2b) *65,*76,**97,**121,**143,*167.

(3) **4,*51,*93,*100,**113,*136,*184,**232,244,*263, **280.

(4) **28,36,40,**105,106,**133,*134,*171,**192,*223, *226,**272,*346.

(5) *3,**50,**53,71,*83,84,87,**92,*121,*149,*151, *153,*155,*169,*178,179,218,**248,**250,**252, *258,**266,*277,*305,**315,**319,*342,*357,*359, **367,*385,**402,*405,**409,*430,431,432,*434.

Therefore high-tone *udātta* is not at all uncommon in Mahārāṣṭrian Ṛgveda, although it occurs only under special conditions. At the beginning of the line (and less often in medial position) a series of syllables with different accents are sometimes sung to H^{sl}. This is especially true in the *vikṛtis*, as the following examples from *ghana* indicate: 49-53, 81-88, 118-122, 148-156, 177-181, 215-221, 246-253, 276-279, 312-315, 355-360, 401-409, 429-435, 454-459. *Udāttas* on UM occur mainly on short syllables followed by long syllables on M; however, long *udāttas* on UM may appear when the preceding syllable is sung on H^{sl} and the following syllable on M^{sl}. *Udāttas* on L^{sl} may be found in initial position (syllable 278 of the third recitation [3.278], for example) or following an *anudātta* on L^{sl} (5.193, for example). Those sung H^{sl}-M^{s} are found only on long syllables either in initial position (2a.1) or following a syllable sung on H (3.199). The pattern M^{s}-H^{s} appeared only once (4.43), on a syllable prior to the separation between members of a compound in parigraha analysis. The M^{l}-UM^{sl} scheme is but a variant of mid-tone udātta, with UM^{sl} functioning as an auxiliary tone between two middle tones: it occurs only on long syllables. The four examples of UM^{sl}-M^{l} appear on short vowels followed by final consonants or visarga. The above observations are at great variance with the specimens offered by J. E. B. Gray, who specifies only mid- and low-tone udāttas.[14]

Anudātta

H^{sl}:	249 =	59.0%
L^{sl}:	96 =	22.7
H^{s}-L^{s}:	24 =	5.7
M^{sl}-H^{s}-L^{sl}:	21 =	5.0
H^{sl}-UM^{sl}:	12 =	2.8
H^{sl}-M^{s}:	6 =	1.4
M^{sl}-H^{sl}:	4 =	.9
UM^{sl}:	4 =	.9
M^{s}:	3 =	.7
M^{s}-L^{s}:	1 =	.2
M^{s}-H^{s}-M^{s}:	1 =	.2
M^{s}-H^{s}-UM^{l}:	1 =	.2

A sizable majority, nearly 60%, of all anudāttas prefer H^{sl}. This percentage encompasses 118 short syllables, 131 long syllables. Of the latter, 87 appear in the two vikṛti recitations. The next highest number (22.5%) is associated with L^{sl}, which comprises 37 short and 59 long syllables. Here also many long syllables (43) are found in the vikṛtis; therefore these two recitations, with their faster tempi, use mainly single pitches, H or L, for long anudāttas, while the slower saṃhitā recitations make more extensive use of two- and three-tone anudāttas. For example, the pattern H^{s}-L^{s}, used only for long syllables, is found 22 times in the first three recitations, only twice in the fifth, and not at all in the fourth. Similarly, the M^{sl}-H^{s}-L^{sl} group occurs 21 times, with only 3 appearances in the fourth recitation and none in the fifth. A seeming exception is H^{sl}-UM^{sl}, with 11 of its 12 occurrences in the vikṛtis; however, UM^{sl} functions merely as a passing tone to an udātta on M^{sl}. The combination H^{sl}-M^{s} sometimes results when the first of following conjunct consonants is sounded in anticipation of the next syllable. H^{sl}-UM^{sl} and M^{sl}-H^{sl} are variants of H^{l} and occur only on long syllables. UM^{sl} and M^{s} are employed only rarely as substitutes for H^{sl}. The remaining patterns, appearing only one time each, are deviations from the normal long-tone schemes. In summary, H is preferred for short syllables, although L is also used frequently. No rule can be stated as to when H or L is employed. The two possibilities are reflected in the second recitation, where occasionally one reciter sings H, the other L, on the same syllable: see 91, 103, 135, 138, 154, 160, 193. Although the employment of L for anudāttas on short syllables is common in the above recitations, L anudāttas are completely absent in Gray's analysis,[15] where he specifies only H, H-M, or H-L schemes for anudāttas. In the above transcriptions the utilization of single pitches or two- and three-tone patterns appears to be about equally divided in the saṃhitā sections: 58 syllables are sung to single tones, 50 to tone patterns.

Svarita

H^{sl}:	79 = 22.3%
M^{sl}:	59 = 16.7
H^{s}-UM^{s}:	34 = 9.6
M^{l}-H^{s}-M^{sl}:	34 = 9.6
H^{s}-M^{s}:	33 = 9.3
M^{sl}-H^{s}-UM^{sl}:	32 = 9.0
UM^{sl}:	16 = 4.5

M^{l}-H^{sl}:	14 =	4.0
H^{s}-UM^{sl}-M^{l}:	13 =	3.7
H^{sl}-M^{l}-H^{s}-UM^{sl}:	10 =	2.8
M^{l}-UM^{sl}:	8 =	2.3
M^{l}-H^{s}-M^{sl}-UM^{s}:	5 =	1.4
M^{sl}-H^{s}-UM^{s}-M^{l}:	5 =	1.4
H^{sl}-M^{l}-H^{s}-M^{sl}:	3 =	.8
M^{s}-H^{s}-M^{l}-H^{s}-L^{l}:	3 =	.8
M^{l}-UM^{s}-M^{s}:	2 =	.6
H^{l}-M^{l}-H^{s}:	2 =	.6
H^{s}-M^{s}-UM^{s}:	1 =	.3
M^{l}-H^{s}-M^{s}-H^{s}:	1 =	.3
H^{l}-M^{l}-UM^{s}-H^{s}-M^{s}:	1 =	.3

The saṃhitā recitations ordinarily use a falling pattern for short svarita. This usually takes the form H^{s}-UM^{s} (of which M^{s}-H^{s}-UM^{s} is a variant) or H^{s}-M^{s} (of which the scheme H^{s}-$\dot{M}^{s}$-UM^{s} is an extension). The H^{s}-UM^{s} version appears usually when a following anudātta or pracaya begins with, or consists of, middle tone; the UM functions, therefore, as a passing tone between H^{s} and M^{sl}. On the other hand, H^{s}-M^{s} svaritas are followed mostly by syllables which begin with H^{sl}; when this svarita type is followed by conjuncts, the M^{s} may be sung with the first consonant. Both H^{s}-UM^{s} and H^{s}-M^{s} svaritas increase the value of a short syllable by one unit (that is, in the transcriptions each tone has the duration of an eighth note). The vikṛti recitations, taken at a faster speed, are partial to single-tone short svaritas, H, M, or UM. These are sometimes held for twice the expected duration (a quarter note instead of an eighth), which may imply that the single pitch is an abbreviation for H^{s}-M^{s} or H^{s}-UM^{s} and retains the longer temporal value. Long svaritas differ widely in their tonal make-up; both saṃhitā and _vikṛti_ passages have one- and multi-tone realizations of this accent. Among the patterns of several pitches, the rising-falling scheme is the prototype: either M^{l}-H^{s}-M^{sl} or M^{l}-H^{s}-UM^{sl} seem to be the standard tone sequences, and several of the remaining patterns are but modifications of these. For example, to M^{l}-H^{s}-M^{sl} (which in the transcriptions is often followed by nasal + consonant or final ṃ) are related the following:

(1) M^{l}-UM^{s}-M^{s}, where UM^{s} is substituted for H^{s}.

(2) M^{l}-H^{s}-M^{sl}-UM^{s}, an extension by the addition of UM^{s}.

(3) H^{sl}-M^{l}-H^{s}-M^{sl}, an extension at the beginning to obtain a transition from a preceding H^{sl} _udātta_.

(4) M^{l}-H^{s}-M^{s}-H^{s}, an extension at the end.

Likewise, M^{l}-H^{s}-UM^{sl} is modified in these ways:

(1) H^{sl}-M^{l}-H^{s}-UM^{sl}, which follows an H^{sl} _udātta_.

(2) M^{sl}-H^{s}-UM^{s}-M^{l}, which occurs on final long _svarita_s closed by _visarga_.

(3) H^{s}-UM^{sl}-M^{l}, an abbreviation of the preceding scheme, also appearing on final syllables followed by _visarga_.

Among the remaining tone types are:

(1) M^{l}-UM^{sl}, an extension of mid-tone _svarita_.

(2) M^{l}-H^{sl}, which appears usually before a pause (at the end of a _sandhi_ unit or before breath within that unit).

(3) H^{l}-M^{l}-H^{s}, found occasionally when an H^{sl} _udātta_ precedes.

(4) H^{l}-M^{l}-UM^{s}-H^{s}-M^{s}, found only once in the transcriptions and followed by nasal + consonant.

(5) M^{s}-H^{s}-M^{l}-H^{s}-L^{l}, the combination for an independent _svarita_, on a short vowel, not followed by _anudātta_.

Pracaya

M^{sl}:	260 = 67.4%
UM^{sl}:	53 = 13.7
H^{sl}:	20 = 5.2
L^{sl}:	18 = 4.7
H^{sl}-M^{sl}:	15 = 3.9
M^{sl}-UM^{s}:	12 = 3.1
UM^{s}-M^{l}:	3 = .8
L^{s}-UM^{s}:	2 = .5
M^{l}-H^{s}-M^{s}:	2 = .5
L^{l}-M^{s}-L^{l}:	1 = .3

Most pracaya syllables (91%) are sung to a single tone, usually M^{sl}. This pitch is preferred for both long and short syllables; however, UM^{sl} is frequently employed for short pracayas when long M follows. High-tone pracayas were used mainly in the recitation of ghana, where a succession of syllables, regardless of accent, are occasionally sung to this pitch alone. Pracayas on L^{sl} are almost invariably sarvānudāttas, initials in the line preceding anudātta. Of the two-tone pracayas (all long), the most numerous are M^{sl}-UM^{s}, a mere extension of M^{l}, and H^{sl}-M^{sl}, which occurs mainly on final syllables closed by a consonant or visarga. The pattern UM^{s}-M^{l} also has this finality function. The remaining three schemes appear but rarely, in the following contexts:

(1) L^{s}-UM^{s}, on a short vowel followed by conjuncts plus a succeeding pracaya on a short vowel.

(2) M^{l}-H^{s}-M^{s}, on a final long-vowel pracaya followed by visarga (which is sung to the -H^{s}-M^{s} portion).

(3) L^{l}-M^{s}-L^{l}, on an initial pracaya followed by nasal + conjunct.

General remarks

The recitations just described consist of a sufficient number of variables to make one hard pressed to point, without uncertainty, to elements which can be ascertained as "stable." The controversy over the nature of the Vedic accent stems not only from the perplexities of the oral traditions but also from treatises which purport to define that accent. Certainly the most famous of these is the great *Aṣṭādhyāyī* ("Eight Chapters") of the grammarian Pāṇini, whose *sūtras* on accent (particularly 1.2.29-32) have caused a great stir among phonologists. These four aphorisms are now stated; each is followed by two translations, one belonging to the nineteenth century, the other by a scholar living today. The first, by S. C. Vasu,[16] follows rather closely a relatively late commentary known as the *Kāśikā*. The second I owe to personal communications from Dr. Sumitra M. Katre, who recently has completed a translation of the entire *Aṣṭādhyāyī*. Dr. Katre has supplemented his interpretation by referring to *sūtras* throughout Pāṇini's grammar where pertinent technical terms occur. He has advised me on several questions I have raised and has given a clear and logical explanation of the import of Pāṇini's maxims.

29. *uccair udāttaḥ*

(1) The vowel that is perceived as having a high tone is called *Udâtta* or acutely accented.

(2) [The technical term] *udātta* ("high pitched") denotes [a vowel] with rising tone (*uccaiḥ*). (As a technical term it occurs in 1.2.32,37,40; 3.3.96; 3.4.103; 4.1.37,52; 4.4.108; 5.2.44; 6.1.159-223; 6.2.64-126; 6.4.71; 7.1.75,98; 8.2.5,82-108; 8.4.66)

30. *nīcair anudāttaḥ*

(1) The vowel that is perceived as having a low tone is called *Anudâtta* or gravely accented.

(2) [The technical term] anudātta ("low pitched") denotes [a vowel] with falling tone (nīcaiḥ). (As a technical term it occurs in 1.2.38-39; 2.4.32,33; 3.1.4; 4.1.38; 6.1.59,120,161,190; 8.2.6)

31. samāhāraḥ svaritaḥ

(1) The vowel that has the combination of Udâtta and Anudâtta tones is said to be svarita or circumflexly accented.

(2) [The technical term] svarita denotes [a vowel] having a combination (samāhāra) [of rising (uccaiḥ) and falling (nīcaiḥ) tones]. (As a technical term is occurs in 1.2.37,39; 1.3.11; 6.1.185; 8.2.4,6,103; 8.4.66,67)

32. tasyādita udāttam ardhahrasvam

(1) Of it (svarita) the first portion is Udâtta, to the extent of a half measure of prosodical length.

(2) Of that (svarita) the duration of half a short (ardha-hrasvam) [vowel] from the beginning (āditaḥ) is udātta ("high pitched") [= with rising tone].

While Vasu's loose, non-literal readings contrast sharply with Katre's pointedly precise translations, both scholars believe ucca, nīca, and so on to refer to tone levels; hence, if this were true, the udātta would originally have been spoken or recited at a high pitch.

In explaining to me his understanding of these sūtras, Dr. Katre makes the point that they are essentially definitions of technical terms used by Pāṇini in his grammar. The terms have a dual role in the language described by him: (1) metalinguistic within the framework of his corpus, and (2) indicative of the actual situation in the spoken language of his time, when accent was still an important linguistic factor in conveying meaning. Concerning this spoken language, which was similar to that of the brāhmaṇa portion of Vedic literature, it is probable that a tonal system was still in use in Northwest India during Pāṇini's time. The replacement of the tonal system by one of stress appears to have been gradual, but fully realized by the time of his commentators Kātyāyana and Patañjali, residents of regions far removed from Pāṇini's sphere of activity. While it is likely that Pāṇini 1.2.29-40 have primary relevance to Vedic recitation (the examples cited by Patañjali are all from Vedic texts), sūtras 29-31 apply to both Vedic and non-Vedic situations. This fact is emphasized by both commentators, who state that grammarians or linguists must depend solely on popular usage.

Other modern writers also endorse a tonal or musical interpretation, among them Siddheshwar Varma[17] and W. S. Allen.[18] However, Kātyāyana and Patañjali (via Kātyāyana's Mahāvārttika) avoid a literal interpretation of the terms ucca and nīca. J. E. B. Gray, in an unconventional and controversial translation[19] of the Pāṇini passage, reflects this impreciseness and provides a directional point of view: "the important vowel (udātta) is upwards, . . . the unimportant vowel (anudātta) is downwards, . . . the resounded vowel (svarita) is a combination (of the two preceding), . . . half (the length of) a short vowel is 'udātta' (important) at the beginning (of svarita)." Commenting on the first two sūtras, Patañjali, in his Mahābhāṣya ("Great Commentary") on Pāṇini and Kātyāyana, provides a fuller exposition on the terms uccais and nīcais. Gray has translated the passage as follows:

> These terms do not ensure any correct interpretation, however, since "upwards" and "downwards" have no settled meaning. In other words, "upwards" (or "up", "high", "top") and "downwards" (or "down", "low", "bottom") are

> words without any predetermined significance. What is upwards or high for one person may be downwards or low for another . . . . One must resort to definition by saying that tension, hardness, and narrowness of the intrabuccal space are the factors which make a sound "upwards". By tension is meant a general tightening up of the body. Hardness pertains to the vowel, and for hardness one might say roughness (creakiness). Narrowness of the intrabuccal space involves a closing up of the throat. Such are the factors which make a sound "upwards". Relaxation, softness, and wideness of the intrabuccal space are the factors which make a sound "downwards". By relaxation is meant a slackening of the body. Softness pertains to the vowel, and for softness one might say smoothness (rounded quality). Wideness of the intrabuccal space involves amplitude of the throat. Such are the factors which make a sound "downwards".[20]

The phonetic treatise belonging to the Ṛgveda, the Ṛk-Prātiśākhya, seems to be in agreement when it describes udātta, anudātta, and svarita as having tenseness (āyāma), laxness (viśrambha), and withdrawal (ākṣepa), respectively.[21] The treatise refers to the accents as svaras, which Allen translates as "tones."[22] But the ancient use of this term may be in the context of "sound" in general. Certainly this is the case with the Sāmaveda, where the notations of svaras do not correspond to the tones of secular music but signify rather the motives and phrases of the chant.[23]

In formulating his theory on accent realization, Gray places pivotal emphasis on Patañjali's use of the terms alpaprāṇa and mahāprāṇa. When employed to describe non-aspirate and aspirate consonants, they may be translated "little breath" and "big breath," respectively. Gray has taken the same terms and applied them to the tension-release concept. Alpaprāṇa, therefore, is used to denote "(i) the quality of udātta, (ii) the quality of the initial component of svarita, and (iii) the quality of the absence of aspiration." Mahāprāṇa, on the other hand, denotes "(iv) the quality of anudātta, (v) the quality of the final component of svarita, and (vi) the quality of aspiration."[24] If one accepts these correlations as facts, many of the seemingly inexplicable factors in the recitations transcribed above could be assumed to result from the interaction of alpa- and mahāprāṇa. For example, the instances in the second hymn where the two reciters are in conflict should not be taken as errors on the part of one man or the other. Gray, who has compared the Mahārāṣṭrian style to Nambudiri Ṛgveda,[25] has discovered that proponents of the two traditions react to identical conditions in precisely opposite ways. If his theory is accepted, the aforementioned finding can be augmented by stating that two Brāhmaṇs from the same stylistic background can be in disagreement but that both can be judged faithful to the tradition. Indeed, a single paṇḍit might realize a verse differently on subsequent repetitions. This is not to say that Mahārāṣṭrian Ṛgveda should be considered basically improvisatory in nature. A norm does exist, as can be gathered from the analyses above (for example, that udātta is normally mid-tone). In Gray's view, departures from the norm are not to be deemed mistakes or weaknesses of the tradition but rather to be considered results of the inexorable interplay of tension and release.

Gray's theory has not found unanimous acceptance among the scholarly community. The present writer has solicited an opposing viewpoint from Prof. George Cardona, whose reply is summarized in the next paragraph.

Gray's translation of udātta and anudātta as "important vowel" and "unimportant vowel," respectively, cannot be justified. The term udātta is a combination of ud ("up") and ātta (from ā-dā: "uttered"). Anudātta is a negation of this. In addition, Patañjali, in his discussion of Pāṇini 1.2.31 (samāhāraḥ svaritaḥ) makes the statement that the combination (samāhāra) must be of properties (guṇa), not of vowels, since in Pāṇini's system one vowel replaces two vowels and does not result from their fusion. Moreover, the terms uccais and nīcais have both locatival and descriptive meanings. The former may signify either "high up, on high" or "loud(ly)," the latter "low, at a low place" or "soft(ly)." Patañjali's commentary on Kātyāyana's vārttika 1 of Pāṇini 1.2.29-30 (uccair udāttaḥ; nīcair anudāttaḥ) begins by presuming that uccais and nīcais refer to relative loudness:

> Someone says to some (student) doing his lesson, "Why are you bellowing loudly? Let it be softly (done)." Another person says to the same (student) doing his lessons in that manner, "Why are you doing your lessons mumbling behind your teeth? Let is be (done) loudly."[26]

A solution to this problem, involving such factors as tension and glottal aperture, is then offered. But the commentators note that the listener has no way of directly determining whether a person is speaking softly or loudly: what is loud for one person may be soft for another, and vice versa. The person speaking may be a mahāprāṇa ("one who has a great deal of breath"), a person with great lung power, who with minimum exertion obtains the same degree of loudness and carrying power as an alpaprāṇa ("one who has little breath") at his maximum capacity. Undoubtedly this is the meaning Patañjali has in mind when he says that what is as high as possible in respect of an alpaprāṇa (alpaprāṇasya sarvoccaiḥ) is as low as possible in respect of a mahāprāṇa (mahāprāṇasya sarvanīcaiḥ). Therefore, Gray is not justified in rejecting this usual interpretation of alpa- and mahāprāṇa, two terms which are not used in connection with vowels. Hence, Pāṇini has used uccais and nīcais in the locatival sense; it follows that the terms udātta and anudātta referred originally to pitch levels and vowels characterized by these pitch levels. In Gray's view, however, the tonal composition of the accents is a function of the amount of air emitted for different sounds relative to each other, consequent on the glottis being closed or open for alpaprāṇa and mahāpraṇa, respectively. Patañjali's final position, that uccais and nīcais pertain to relative positions of organs, is problematic. To be sure, Kātyāyana states in his first vārttika on 1.2.29-30 that high and low are relative, not absolute. In his second vārttika he suggests that all is in order if one speaks samānaprakrame. If prakrama is taken to refer to a relative pitch position from which one starts (prakramyate 'smin: "that at which one starts"), then this is reconciled with the fact that we are dealing with properties of vowels--namely, relative pitches. There is no absolute pitch, but, once the starting pitch is chosen, the proper intervallic realizations of the accents are maintained from that point on. Ṛk-Prātiśākhya 3.2 supports this interpretation by declaring that the three sounds (svaras) associated with udātta, anudātta, and svarita have vowels as their loci: they are properties of vowels. Also, Śaunakīyā Caturādhyāyikā 1.14 states that the same relative pitch level is what one starts with for the intervals associated with udātta, anudātta, and svarita vowels. Finally, Pāṇini 1.2.40 employs the term sannatara ("more depressed") to describe an anudātta vowel followed by an udātta or a svarita vowel. Of course, there was some variation in the manner in which the pitch levels connected with the accents were realized, as can be surmised from prātiśākhya descriptions. But there can be no doubt that pitch levels and vowels characterized by pitch levels are the qualities to which the earliest texts allude when they speak of accent. Patañjali, on the other hand, in the end uses uccais and nīcais to refer to relative positions at places of production of sounds. This is a later tradition and one quite distinct from that of Pāṇini and (probably also) Kātyāyana. When Pāṇini says that an udātta vowel is pronounced "high," he is speaking not of any specifically Vedic matter but rather of what is practiced in the speech of his time. Likewise, Kātyāyana and Patañjali, in their commentaries on this sūtra, reflect the normal usage of their day and are not expounding on anything particular to Vedic. The discussions of these grammarians imply nothing about any particular mode of Vedic recitation.

These last three sentences may cause trouble for some scholars, for Pāṇini 1.2.34-38, which follow his characterizations of the accents, deal unmistakably with Vedic matter. These aphorisms pertain to ekaśruti (monotone recitation: sūtra 33 defines ekaśruti as the sound obtained when addressing someone from a distance), the manner in which mantras are intoned at the Vedic sacrifices, as it is applied (or disregarded) in the following circumstances: at sacrifices, during murmured prayers (japa),[27] during insertions of o-vowels (nyuṅkha)[28] at certain syllables in sacrificial Ṛgveda recitation, in the chanting of the Sāmaveda, in uttering the sacrificial cry vauṣaṭ ("may [Agni] lead"), in ordinary recitation of the Vedas,[29] and in the subrahmaṇyā invocation, which precedes the soma sacrifice.[30] The sūtras on accent conclude with two aphorisms (1.2.39-40) which describe syllables following the svarita. The first of these pertains to a series of anudāttas (pracayas, for Pāṇini uses anudātta for any syllable not udātta or svarita), which should sound the same. We have seen, in fact, that the Mahārāṣṭrians recite these syllables primarily on the middle pitch. The final sūtra declares that an anudātta prior to udātta or svarita is sannatara ("more depressed"). This, of course, is the true anudātta according to our present-day use of the term. It seems logical, therefore, that sūtras 1.2.29-40 refer specifically to Veda recitation: 29-32 and 39-40 describe conditions under which the Vedas are normally chanted, while 33-38 state exceptions to the rules. One cannot deny that certain of the sūtras may have relevance to the spoken language. But Dr. Katre has called my attention to the fact that Patañjali describes as customary the practice for scholars to acquire competency in the oral tradition of Veda recitation before embarking on a study of grammatical analysis, which was considered uttarā vidyā ("subsequent knowledge"). It is at least possible, therefore, that Pāṇini has defined the terms udātta, anudātta, and svarita in their Vedic sense before using them later on, in a technical capacity, to refer to the spoken language of his day.

In seeming support of Pāṇini's description of the udātta as "high," J. F. Staal has described a type of recitation by Nambudiri Brāhmaṇs in which this accent (short and long) invariably makes use of the highest pitch intoned in the recitation.[31] On July 4, 1971, I visited the Brahmasva Maṭham, a Ṛgveda seminary at Trichur, and recorded several specimens of this recitation, which the paṇḍits refer to as jaṭamātrā (that is, sung with the same mātrā or time values as their jaṭā recitation). The following transcription of the first ṛk of the Ṛgveda, in jaṭamātrā, is realized by Śrī Tiruttumukku Nārāyaṇa Parameśvaran Nambudiri, who hails from the village Muṇṭamuka (Palghat District, Kerala).

Tape IXa(2)

♩=66
G=d
5
a̱ gní mī́ ḷ e (e) pu̱ rő (o)
10
15
hi ta ṃ (ṃ) ya̱ jñá s ya de̱ vám ṛ̱ tv
jaṃ (ṃ) / hő (o) tā́ (ā)
20
ra ṃ (ṃ) ra tna̱ dhā́ (ā) ta ma ṃ
(ṃ) (ṃ)

Although it is a fact that udātta always ascends to the highest pitch (f), this tone is associated with other accents as well. For instance, long udātta and long svarita are recited exactly alike (see syllables 3, 6, 16, 17, 18, 22). Even anudātta on a long vowel employs this highest pitch (syllable 12), and also pracaya (syllable 20) when preceded by another pracaya and followed by anudātta. Therefore, jaṭamātrā appears to be a simplified, albeit elongated, mode of recitation designed to accommodate the special requirements of the Nambudiri jaṭā-vikṛti (which these Brāhmaṇs carry out in a unique way, with two reciters). They now use it, on request, to recite saṃhitā, pada, and other recitations. Their ordinary recitation, however, is taken at a faster tempo and is characterized by mainly mid-tone udāttas.

None of the standard Ṛgvedic recitations of the present day utilize a high udātta to any great extent, a circumstance which leads one to wonder if the principal accent has ever been associated, except under special conditions, with the high tone.[32] It is possible, in fact, that Pāṇini's uccais and nīcais pertain to positions of the right hand during recitation or to bodily postures when recitation is being taught. Gray has described[33] the hand positions (mudrās) employed by a Nepalese Vājasaneyī who probably belongs to the Kāṇva school, members of which recite in almost precisely the same manner as the Mahārāṣṭrian Ṛgvedīs:

udātta: hand to shoulder;
anudātta: hand resting on knee;
svarita: hand to normal position, which is with the forearm bent out to an angle of 45° from the body.

Not coincidentally, perhaps, the Nambudiri teacher impresses the accents on his pupil by keeping the student's head up for udātta, down for anudātta, and sideways for svarita.[34] This scheme is duplicated in the hand positions of the Nambudiris:[35]

udātta: hand up;

anudātta: hand down;

svarita: hand to the right;

pracaya: hand to the left.

Although the above postures differ to a certain extent from descriptions in the *śikṣās* (texts which, to some degree, complement the *prātiśākhyas*), several features are common both to present-day practice and to accounts of these treatises. For example, Pāṇinīya-Śikṣā 43-44 specifies the following positions (my thanks to Dr. Katre for supplying this reference):

udātta: thumb placed on index finger;

anudātta: thumb placed on little finger;

svarita: thumb placed on ring finger;

pracaya: thumb placed on middle finger.

But Yājñavalkya-Śikṣā 51 depicts movements of the entire hand:[36]

udātta: hand to the brow;

anudātta: where the hand lies;

svarita: hand across (the body);

pracaya: hand to the tip of the nose.

All of these descriptions put the *mudrā* for *udātta* in the highest position. Moreover, the *svarita* postures might be considered reflections of Pāṇini 1.2.31 (*samāhāraḥ svaritaḥ*), where *samāhāra* could denote "combination" in the sense of a sum or average of the *mudrās* for *udātta* and *anudātta* (that is, located about halfway between the two). Indeed, Uvaṭa, the commentator on the Ṛk-Prātiśākhya, describes "sideways" as the only possibility for realizing *svarita* as defined by the above *sūtra*.[37] The representations also agree completely with Pāṇini 1.2.40, which portrays *anudātta* as *sannatara*, "lower" than the *pracaya*.

The skeptic may well reply that the prātiśākhyas are essentially phonetic treatises; therefore, their statements must be related to oral and not to visual phenomena. Moreover, if Pāṇini's uccais and nīcais pertain to hand positions, then why was this not made clear by that grammarian? The answer must lie in a traditionally close correlation between accent and mudrā, an association so intimate and inseparable that no distinction was made between the two. W. S. Allen has remarked on the similar terminology of the phoneticians and the authors of works which actually claim to describe manual gestures (the śikṣās, for example)

> We in fact find the terminology of these prescriptions to be related to that of the phonetic accounts. The root kṣip-, "to throw", which was used in the phonetic description of the svarita, appears also in the gestural terms ūrdhva-kṣepa and adhaḥ-kṣepa, "throwing up" and "throwing down", referring to the manual gestures accompanying the udātta and anudātta tones respectively: the gesture for the svarita is said in this case to consist of a combination of the two. The verb praṇihanyate, "is made to fall", likewise used in the phonetic description of the svarita, again appears in the description of the gesture accompanying it. . . . It thus appears probable that some of the tonal terminology is really based on gestural movements, which are of course related in turn to the kinaesthetic and acoustic phenomena.[38]

As will be seen in Part III, the Sāmaveda chants preserve so close a relationship between notation, music, and mudrā that the authors of the Sāmavedic treatises consider them one and the same. Although the musical interpretation of a notated number depends on the context in which that number appears, the mudrā generally remains unchanged. Likewise, the Ṛgvedic recitations show great variety in the manner in which a particular accent is intoned, although the mudrā associated with that accent remains fixed. It should not be alarming, therefore, that 59% of all anudāttas in the transcribed examples prefer the high tone, 22.5% the low pitch. This accent's function is to prepare for a following udātta (which, in the present writer's view, has probably always been mid-tone); therefore, it is immaterial whether the anticipatory anudātta tone is high or low. As seen earlier, in the analyses of the Ṛgveda transcriptions, the musical renditions of udātta, anudātta, and svarita are so complicated as to be practically impossible to describe in a sūtra jargon, such as the one employed by Pāṇini. Therefore, it is at least a possibility that he has not even attempted to do this but has given instead the hand postures associated with these accents. He was able to give a musical description only of pracaya, which could be safely characterized as ekaśruti.

I should state at this point that neither Prof. Cardona nor Dr. Katre would agree with this interpretation. The latter makes the point that mudrās may have been introduced to Veda recitation at a time when the tonal system was entirely foreign to the spoken language. When the tonal structure was lost, it became incumbent on the teacher to indicate the accents in some way while teaching the text. Dr. Katre believes that it was this situation which gave rise to the employment of mudrās, which were then adopted for use in transmitting the Vedas. While his view is certainly a valid one, it is also possible that they were used in a mnemonic capacity from the very advent of Veda recitation. There can be little doubt that the mudrās of the Sāmaveda have played a crucial role in the survival, intact, of complex melodies from ancient times. It is entirely credible that hand gestures have been a significant factor in the transmission process of recited Vedas from a period long before the time of Pāṇini.

As previously noted, an accent's musical disposition depends on several factors, not the least of which is syllable length. The device used by the phoneticians to measure duration is the mātrā ("time unit"), which is equivalent to the length of a short vowel. In Mahārāṣṭrian Ṛgveda, time values are dependent on the following conditions (based on the transcriptions presented above, where an eighth note has the duration of one mātrā):

(1) Udātta, anudātta, and pracaya on short vowels followed by a single consonant + vowel are worth 1 mātrā.

(2) Svarita on a short vowel followed by a consonant + vowel is worth 1 mātrā if the following syllable is pracaya, 2 mātrās if it is anudātta. If the following pracaya occurs before a pause, the preceding svarita is worth 2 mātrās. In the recital of Viśvanāth Vāman Dev, all svaritas in these contexts are worth 2 mātrās in the saṃhitā selections.

(3) Udātta, anudātta, and pracaya on short vowels followed by conjuncts are worth 2 mātrās.

(4) Svarita on a short vowel before conjuncts is worth 2 mātrās, 5-8 mātrās if nasal + consonant follows (as few as 4 mātrās in the vikṛtis).

(5) Udātta, svarita, and pracaya on open short vowels before a pause are ordinarily worth 2 mātrās, occasionally 4 mātrās.

(6) Udātta, anudātta, and pracaya on long vowels followed by a single consonant + vowel are worth 2 mātrās.

(7) Svarita on a long vowel followed by a single consonant + vowel is worth from 4 to 12 mātrās in the standard recitations, as few as 2 or 3 mātrās in the vikṛtis.

(8) Udātta, anudātta, and pracaya on long vowels followed by conjuncts are worth from 4 to 8 mātrās.

(9) Svarita on a long vowel followed by conjuncts is worth from 6 to 8 mātrās.

(10) Udātta (and other accents as well?) on the vowel ā, followed by n changed euphonically to m̐, is worth about 10 mātrās.

(11) An independent svarita on a short vowel preceding udātta is worth 14-16 mātrās.

(12) Udātta and pracaya on long vowels before a pause are worth 3-6 mātrās; however, a 4-mātrā time value is most common. Final long svarita is comprised of 4-8 mātrās.

(13) Udātta and pracaya on a short vowel before a pause contain:

a. 3-5 mātrās if closed by visarga.
b. 3-6 mātrās if closed by a nasal.
c. 3-4 mātrās if closed by a consonant.

(14) Svarita on a short vowel before a pause contains:

a. 4-6 mātrās if closed by visarga.
b. 4-12 mātrās if closed by a nasal.
c. 4-6 mātrās if closed by a consonant? No examples are found in the recited mantras.

(15) Udātta and pracaya on a long vowel before a pause contain:

a. 6-9 mātrās if closed by visarga.
b. 4-6 mātrās if closed by a nasal.
c. about 6 mātrās if closed by a consonant.

(16) Svarita on a long vowel before a pause contains:

a. 5-6 mātrās if closed by visarga.
b. 7 mātrās (or more?) if closed by a nasal.
c. 5-6 mātrās if closed by a consonant? No examples are found in the recited mantras.

(17) The sacred syllable ōm (praṇava), intoned before and after some recitations, comprises 6-8 mātrās.

Although phonologists may frown on the above application of the mātrā concept to the quantity of syllables in their metrical framework, the complex time structure of the recited items made such a correspondence inevitable.

Atharvaveda

Among Vārāṇasī Brāhmaṇs who are currently espousing this Veda are Nārāyaṇ Śāstrī Raṭāṭe, Rāmcandra Āṭhvale, and Gaṅgādhar Dev. Raṭāṭe belongs to a Mahārāṣṭra Ṛgveda family who is specializing in Atharvaveda out of a simple desire to preserve it from extinction. He teaches Atharvaveda at the Nigamāgam Darbhaṅgā Vidyālaya and also is an expert in reciting and discussing the purāṇas (purāṇacarcā pravīṇ). The former head of the family, Āhitāgni Rāmcandra Śāstrī Raṭāṭe, was a product of Dinkar Anna Jośī's vedapāṭhaśālā. He was a true caturvedī, possessing a masterful command of all four Vedas (including Sāmaveda of the Rāṇāyanīya school).[39] For this expertise he is called by the title Vaidik Cakravartī ("Universal Master of the Vedas") and was designated sammānit prādhyāpak ("Revered Reciter of the Veda") by the Vārāṇaseya Saṃskṛta Viśvavidyālaya. He also was a performer of the cāturmāsya sacrifices (more about these in Part III).

During a visit to Naḍiād, Gujarāt, where a vedasammelana was being held, I was successful in recording another Atharvavedī, Lakṣmīśaṅkar Gaurīśaṅkar Rāvaḷ of Bhāvnagar, Gujarāt. This elderly paṇḍit gave Paippalāda as the name of his svaśākhā ("original śākhā"), while maintaining that his recitation was according to the more common Śaunaka school. It is noteworthy that he had his vedādhyayana (Vedic study) at the Sāṅgaveda Vidyālaya in Vārāṇasī, where he was a pupil of Lābhśaṅkar Jhā. Atharvavedic chanters are now extremely rare in North India; there is some doubt that they exist at all in the South.[40] In this regard, J. F. Staal writes that Atharvaveda "seems to be only extant in a few Villages in Gujrat, a fact which was discovered by the Śaṃkarācārya of Dvārakā."[41] Epigraphical references exist across a wide area, however: at Nirmaṇḍa on the Satlaj (probably seventh century); at Nellūr, Āndhra Pradesh (seventh century); near Bijāpur, Karṇāṭaka, not far from the Mahārāṣṭra border (sixth century); and at Bhāvnagar (seventh century).[42]

Not wishing to intrude on the work of another researcher, who is planning a detailed study of Atharvavedic traditions, I shall confine my remarks to a brief comparison of two readings from the well-known "Hymn for Peace." The first version is that of Lakṣmīśaṅkar Gaurīśaṅkar Rāvaḷ, the second that of Nārāyaṇ Śāstrī Raṭāṭe. The transcription is preceded by the source verse and a translation thereof.[43]

Atharvaveda 19.9.1: from the Hymn for Peace

W D | |
śāntā dyáuḥ śāntā pṛthivī́ śāntám idám urv aíntárikṣam /

| Q |W |W D |
śāntā udanvátīr āpaḥ śāntā naḥ santv óṣadhīḥ //

Translation:

Peaceful (śāntā) be (santu) heaven (dyauḥ) for us (naḥ); peaceful (śāntā) be (santu) the earth (pṛthivī) for us (naḥ); peaceful (śāntam) be (santu) this (idam) expansive (uru) atmosphere (antarikṣam) for us (naḥ); peaceful (śāntā) be (santu) the watery (udanvatīḥ) waters (āpaḥ) for us (naḥ); peaceful (śāntā) be (santu) the herbs (oṣadhīḥ) for us (naḥ).

The short analysis which follows is arranged according to accent. The two versions are referred to as (1) and (2), the four tones as L, M, UM, and H.

♩=176
e=c#
e=d
Tape Ia(5)
♩=176
e=c#
Tape IIIa(9)
śā̲ ntā́ dyáu ḥśā̲
5
10
ntā́ pṛ thi̲ vī́ śā̲ ntám i̲ dá mu̲
15
r va1̲ n tá ri kṣam (a) / śā̲

20
25
ntá u da n vá tī rá pa ḥ
30
śā ntá na ḥsan tv ó ṣa dhī ḥ //
3

Udātta

I. M^{sl}

(1) *2,*3,*5,*8,10,12,15,*19,22,*27,*30.

(2) *2,*3,*5,*8,10,12,15,*19,22,*24,*27,*30.

II. L^{l}

(1) *24.

Anudātta

I. M^{s}-H^{s}-L^{l}

(1) *1,*4,*9,*18,*26.

(2) *1,*4,*9,*18,*26.

II. UM^{s}-M^{s}

(1) 7.

III. H^{s}

(1) 11,13.

(2) 7.

IV. L^{s}

(2) 11,13,*23.

V. H^{sl}-L^{sl}

(1) **13,*23,**29.

(2) **21.

VI. H^{sl}-M^{sl}

(1) **21.

(2) **29.

Svarita

I. M^{l}

(1) 6,20,**25.

II. H^{s}-M^{sl}

(1) **28,31.

(2) 6,20.

III. H^{l}-M^{l}-H^{s}-L^{l}

(2) **14.

IV. UM^{l}-M^{l}-H^{s}-L^{l}

(1) **14.

V. H^{sl}

(1) **16.

(2) **16,**25,**28.

VI. M^s-H^s-UM^s

(2) 31.

Pracaya

I. M^l

(1) *17,*32.

(2) *17.

II. M^l-H^s-M^s

(2) *32.

These interpretations are so similar to Mahārāṣṭrian Ṛgvedic recitation that no difference whatsoever may exist in the modus operandi. Attention is drawn immediately to the preponderance of mid-tone udāttas--the low tone appears only once. All but one of the anudātta schemes occurs in the Ṛgveda examples, although the Atharvavedīs have a decided preference for M^s-H^s-L^l on long vowels. The svarita tones and tone patterns employed here are likewise heavily drawn upon by the Ṛgvedīs, notably H^{sl}, M^l, H^s-M^{sl}, and M^s-H^s-UM^s. The patterns for the independent svarita followed by udātta are also identical (minus the first tone of the Ṛgveda examples). Pracaya syllables as a rule utilize M^l, but one instance of final visarga altered the recitation to M^l-H^s-M^s.

II

YAJURVEDA

The preponderant Veda in Vārāṇasī, as indeed throughout northern India, is the White (Śukla) Yajurveda. It has this name undoubtedly for the reason that it is clear of exegetical material which is mixed with the sacrificial formulas of the Black (Kṛṣṇa) Yajurveda.[1] Another name for the White Yajus is the Vājasaneyi-Saṃhitā, an appellation perhaps derived from the patronymic Vājasaneya, "son of Vājasani." This is the surname of Yājñavalkya, who is credited with the authorship of the White Yajus.[2] According to legend, Yājñavalkya learned the original Yajurveda (at this time not divided into Black and White) from his teacher Vaiśampāyana, who became angry with his pupil and forced him to regurgitate all the verses committed to memory. These were picked up by Vaiśampāyana's remaining disciples, who had taken the form of partridges (tittiri). The dirty text came to be known as the Black Yajurveda; its principal school was called Taittirīya, after the partridges. Yājñavalkya, deprived of the yajus, paid homage to the Sun, who in gratitude took the form of a horse (vājin) and brought fresh yajus (ayātayāma yajūṃṣi) not known to Vaiśampāyana.[3]

Geography of the White Yajus, with Relation to Vārāṇasī

The White Yajurveda has been passed down in two recensions, Mādhyandina and Kāṇva. According to Weber,[4] the Mādhyandinas were a people mentioned in a textbook on India by Megasthenes, the ambassador sent by the Greek general Seleukus Nikator to the Mauryan court of Candragupta at Pāṭaliputra (present-day Patna). Megasthenes, quoted by Arrian in his Indika, referred to the Mādhyandinas in connection with the river Andhomatī, mentioned along with other tributaries of the Gaṅgā. In relation to the Indus

> the Ganges is much the larger, and other writers who mention the Ganges agree with him; for, besides being of ample volume even where it issues from its springs, it receives as tributaries the river Kaīnas, and the Erannoboas, and the Kossoanoas, which are all navigable. It receives, besides, the river Sonos and the Sittokatis, and the Solomatis, which are also navigable, and also the Kondochatês, and the Sambos, and the Magôn, and the Agoranis, and the Omalis. Moreover there fall into it the Kommenasês, a great river, and the Kakouthis, and the Andomatis, which flows from the dominions of the Madyandinoi, an Indian tribe. In addition to all these, the Amystis, which flows past the city Katadupa, and the Oxymagis from the dominions of a tribe called the Pazalai, and the Errenysis from the Mathai, an Indian tribe, unite with the Ganges.[5]

McCrindle identifies the Errenysis with Vārāṇasī, "so called from the rivers Vârâna and Asi, which join the Ganges in its neighbourhood."[6] He connects the Andhomatī with the Dammuda (Sanskrit: Dharmadaya), which flows through Bardvān (in present-day Bengāl);[7] but this is disputed by Renou,[8] who describes it as a tributary of the Gaṅgā below the Yamunā, and by Weber,[9] who claims the country of the Mādhyandinas to be located in the center of the Middle Country (Madhyadeśa), around present-day Delhī. This was an area occupied by the Kurus and (farther eastward) the Pañcālas.

> . . . the Middle Region [is] the land between the Himālaya in the north, the Vindhya--which does not seem to have been reached in Vedic times--in the south, the confluence of the Ganges and Jumnā [Yamunā] in the east and the place where the Sarasvatī river disappears in the west. Its main inhabitants were the Kurus and Pañcālas, whose brahmins gained fame and eminence. While the Punjab has receded in importance, the Doāb (between the two great rivers), the land of the Kosalas, has come into prominence and the eastern countries of the Magadhas and the Videhas (the modern S. and N. Bihar), though not completely aryanized and brahminized, successively make their appearance in the texts. The Yajurveda Saṃhitās and most of the brāhmaṇa literature were compiled in this large tract of land, the Middle Region, in which the four Vedas in general must have been forming before they dispersed in "schools". The White Yajurveda may to a certain extent be excepted, because there are--outside the Śāṇḍilya books [of the Śatapatha-Brāhmaṇa] which point to the north-west--some indications of a more easterly origin.[10]

Thus the Kuru-Pañcāla territory appears to have been the original home of all the major Yajurvedic schools: "It is beyond all reasonable doubt that the home of the Taittirīya school was the middle country, just as much as it was the home of the Kāṭhaka, the Maitrāyaṇī, and even the Vājasaneyi and the Śatapatha [-Brāhmaṇa] . . . ."[11] Moreover, this is the area where all four Vedas were cultivated before the dispersion of the schools to the four corners of India.[12] We are not privy to the details of this diffusion; but it is a certainty that the White Yajurveda soon spread eastwards, down the valley of the Gaṅgā. This is known from passages in the Śatapatha-Brāhmaṇa which allude to King Janaka of Videha, a kingdom which was located in present-day Bihār.

> East of the Madhyadeśa, we meet with another confederacy of kindred peoples, of hardly less importance than the Kuru-Pañcālas, at the time of the redaction of the Brahmaṇa, viz. the Kosala-Videhas. . . . They are said to be the descendants of Videgha Māthava, and to be separated from each other by the river Sadānīrā (either the modern Gaṇḍakī or Karatoyā). The country of the Videhas, the eastern branch of this allied people, corresponding to the modern Tirhut or Puraniya, formed in those days the extreme east of the land of the Āryas. In the later books of the Śatapatha, king Janaka of Videha appears as one of the principal promoters of the Brahmanical religion, and especially as the patron of Yājñavalkya. In IX,6,2,1, Janaka is represented as meeting, apparently for the first time, with Śvetaketu Āruṇeya, Somaśuṣma Sātyayajñi, and Yājñavalkya, while they were travelling (dhāvayadbhiḥ). Probably we are to understand by this that these divines had then come from the west to visit the Videha country. A considerable portion of the Bṛhadāraṇyaka deals with learned disputations which Yājñavalkya was supposed to have held at Janaka's court with divers sages and with the king himself. In Bṛh[ad] Ār[aṇyaka] II,1,1 (and Kauṣ[ītaki] Up[aniṣad] IV,1) Janaka's fame as the patron of Brāhmanical sages is said to have aroused the jealousy of his contemporary, Ajātaśatru, king of the Kāśis.[13]

The Kingdom of Kāśi surrounded Vārāṇasī, so the reference to Ajātaśatru's jealousy at least hints that the city may have been associated with the White Yajurveda at an early date. Indeed it can be argued that Mādhyandina is the Vedic school which, historically, has been the most familiar to the Vārāṇasī area. There is little evidence that the school has but rarely existed outside North India, although it is widely scattered across this vast area.[14]

According to one text, the Mahārṇava, the Mādhyandina school extended from Gurjara in the West to Aṅga (situated along the present Bihār-Beṅgāl border) and Vaṅga (occupying the area near the mouth of the Gaṅgā) in the East.[15] From the informatior collected on the geographical distribution of existing Vedic schools by Raghavan, we learn that Mādhyandinas are to be found presently (or were found recently) in the following locales: (1) around Nāsik, in western Mahārāṣṭra; (2) at the Bhonsle Sanskrit Mahāvidyālaya at Nāgpur, in eastern Mahārāṣṭra; (3) at Indore and Ujjain, in Madhya Pradesh; (4) at Vārāṇasī; (5) at Ambāla, in Haryana; (6) at Jullundur, in Pañjāb; (7) at the Sanskrit College in the Raghunāth Temple at Jammu (?--the "Śukla Yajurveda" mentioned by Raghavan as prevalent in this region may well be the Mādhyandina type).[16] Although Raghavan has not said so specifically, Mādhyandinas possibly are found as well in other cities, especially in those which possess _vedapāṭhaśālās_ or Sanskrit colleges (Baroda, for example); but their presence may not imply a local tradition, for several Sanskrit colleges in the North employ teachers who have undergone their Vedic training in Vārāṇasī.[17] It should not be surprising that "wherever Vedic traditions are weakened at home or in the villages, vaidikas learn the recitation of their _śākhā_ from famous centers (e.g. Banaras)."[18]

While the Mādhyandinas have not, as a rule, strayed beyond the upper reaches of the Deccan, the Kāṇvas have migrated "everywhere."[19] The pertinent inscriptions, which refer to them as Vājikāṇva, are found (1) at Vizagapatam (Vishākhapatnam), on the Bay of Beṅgāl in northeastern Āndhra Pradesh; (2) on the Godāvarī River; (3) across an arch extending from Kaṭhiāvāṟ

(Gujarāt) to Kaliṅga (a territory comprising modern Orissā and the coastal strip of northeastern Āndhra Pradesh) to Dacca (Baṅgladesh).[20] Citations of the Kātyāyana-Sūtra in inscriptions from Karṇāṭaka and Tirunelvēli[21] may be indirect references to the Kāṇva śākhā. All of these epigraphical allusions belong to relatively late periods (thirteenth to sixteenth centuries).[22]

Such a wide dispersion is reflected in the present distribution of the school. Again it is Raghavan who has provided much explicit information. He has had contacts with Kāṇvas in the following cities or regions:[23] (1) in Orissā, specifically at the Sanskrit Vidyālaya at Purī, from whence Śukla Yajurvedīs journey to Vārāṇasī to learn the proper manner of reciting; (2) in the Tañjāvūr (Tanjore) District of Tamilnāḍ at Iñjikkollai, Alivalam, Śedinipuram, and Tiruvārūr; (3) in the Tiruccirāppaḷḷi (Trichinopoly) District of Tamilnāḍ, at Śiruhamaṇi, Peruhamaṇi, Tiruccirāppaḷḷi City, Vaihanallūr, and Śrīraṅgam; (4) in the Tirunelvēli (Tinnevelly) District of Tamilnāḍ, near Śermādevi; (5) in the North Arcot District of Tamilnāḍ at the Varadarāja Temple in Kāñcīpuram; (6) in Karṇāṭaka (Mysore);[24] (7) in the Nāsik area of northwestern Mahārāṣṭra; (8) in the Bhonsle Sanskrit Mahāvidyālaya at Nāgpur; (9) at Jaipur, in Rājasthān; (10) in Vārāṇasī. Staal has made tape recordings of Kāṇva recitation from Tiruvidaccheri, near Nannilam in the Tañjāvūr District,[25] from Veṅganellur, near Chelakkara in Kerala (this last recording that of a transplanted Tamil Brāhmaṇ),[26] and from Bangalore.[27] The present writer recorded two Kāṇva paṇḍits. The first was G. Nārāyaṇa Bhaṭṭa, a Professor of Śukla Yajurveda at the Mahārājā's Sanskrit College in Mysore City.[28] He learned Kāṇva recitation at Bangalore from a Chidambara Ghanapāṭhikat, whose name reveals a Tamil provenance. The second was Lakṣmīkānt Śāstrī Khanaṅg, a Professor of Mīmāṃsā at the Saṃskṛta Mahāvidyālaya of Banāras Hindu University. He had his _vedādhyayana_ in Vārāṇasī, although his family hails from Mahārāṣṭra.

Finally, J. E. B. Gray (referring to recordings made by Arnold Bake) has documented the presence of Vājasaneyīs from as far north as Nepal.[29] It may be assumed that they are Kāṇvas; for the recitation here "may represent a southern tradition . . . , since these Vājasaneyīs have traditional connexions with Kannaḍiga Brahmans."[30]

The Mādhyandina School: Recitations

It is essential that a description of Yajurveda recitation in Vārāṇasī focus primarily on the Mādhyandina school, the Yajurvedic _śākhā_ which claims the most representatives in the city and which has the closest ties to North India as a whole. The outstanding feature of the Mādhyandina tradition is its cultivation of numerous _vikṛtis_. While it is not common in South India to find Vaidikas who have mastered formulas beyond the triumvirate _krama_-_jaṭā_-_ghana_, in the North one comes across paṇḍits who are familiar not only with the traditional eight _vikṛtis_ (_aṣṭa_-_vikṛti_) but also with certain esoteric patterns found nowhere else.

The _vikṛti_ expositions presented below are based upon renditions by Śrī Dr. Gajānan Śāstrī Musalgā̃vkar, well-known Mādhyandinīya of Vārāṇasī and a professor in the Department of Mīmāṃsā, Saṃskṛta Mahāvidyālaya, Banāras Hindu University. He had his Vedic training in the former Gwalior State from Gaṅgādhar Śāstrī Musalgā̃vkar. He has recited the eight _vikṛtis_[31] in the traditional order: _jaṭā_ ("braid"), _mālā_ ("garland"), _śikhā_ ("topknot"), _rekhā_ ("row"), _dhvaja_ ("flag"), _daṇḍa_ ("staff"), _ratha_ ("chariot"), and _ghana_ ("bell"). Two types of _mālā_ exist: kramamālā ("ordered garland") and (more commonly) puṣpamālā ("garland of flowers"). Moreover, three species of ratha are practiced--dvipāda, tripāda, catuṣpāda--depending on whether the chariot has two, three, or four wheels (dvicakra, tricakra, catuścakra). Each "wheel" corresponds to a quarter-verse (pāda) of the text. The dvipāda and catuṣpāda varieties are the ratha types most widely cultivated today.

According to Gajānan Śāstrī, the names of the vikṛtis correspond to their qualities. For instance, two strands of hair are made into one by entwining to form a tress. In that very manner, by entwining two words of a mantra the vikṛti named jaṭā comes into being. Similarly, a garland of flowers is formed by an entwining process involving reversal of the stems. A unit of two words is treated in precisely the same way in the type of mālā known as puṣpamālā. To fashion a top-knot, a coiffure adopted especially by sādhus and other ascetics, the hair is bound and encircled around the top of the head, with the end of the strand left over after each encirclement. In śikhā the basic jaṭā scheme is adopted, but one word is added to the end of each unit. In rekhā ("row") the words are deposited in series of straight lines: hence the obvious appellation. The names of the four remaining vikṛtis are likewise reflected in their modus operandi.[32]

The vikṛti presentations below begin with a musical transcription of jaṭā. The tones of the remaining vikṛtis (minus ghana, which has been demonstrated in Part I, but plus pañcasandhi, a vikṛti found only in the North) are indicated by the numbers 1-2-3, in descending order, beneath the syllables of the texts. In relation to the central pitch (2 = f), the other tones are a minor third below (3 = d) and a major second above (1 = g). An italicized number (*1*, *2*, *3*) shows that the tone is long (more than an eighth note). Syllables having more than one tone are realized according to the following rhythmic schemes:

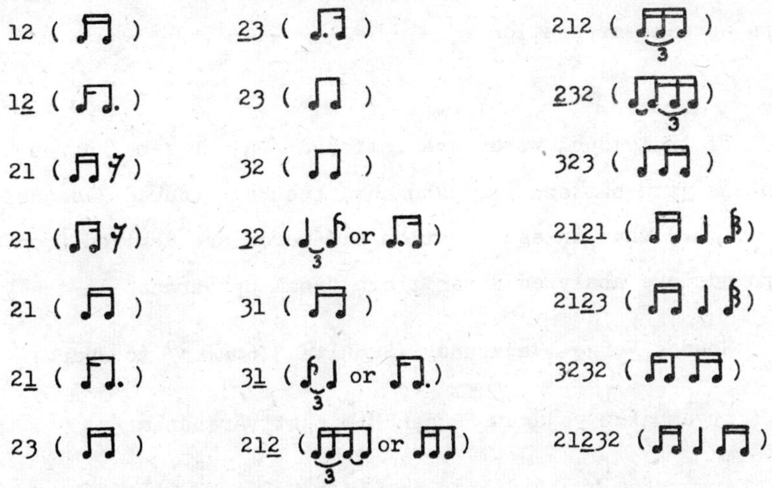

Numbering of syllables is by phonetic unit, with every fifth unit indicated by the appropriate figure (in brackets). Applicable rules of *sandhi* (see Part I) are indicated by capital letters above the text. Asterisks mark spots where breath is taken within sections. The sign ≁ shows that breath is not taken at the end of the phonetic unit.

Mādhyandina Yajurveda is taken at a slower pace than other types of Veda recitation. Short vowels are always short, no matter if conjunct consonants follow; the only exception to this rule is following nasal + consonant, which renders the syllable long. Gray has remarked that "this careful counting of time for long and short vowels gives a rather stately character to the reciter's performance."[33] Another distinguishing feature of this recitation is the pronunciation of *anusvāra* (*ṁ*) before *ś*, *ṣ*, *s*, and *r* as *ghuṃ*: thus the repetition, in *jaṭā*, of the word *sugandhim* is carried out *sugandhighuṃ sugandhim*.[34] A peculiarity associated with the retroflex sibilant *ṣ* is its pronunciation as *kh*, unless combined with a retroflex consonant:

therefore the word *puruṣa* sounds as though uttered *purukha*.[35] Compounds are analyzed according to the method of the Ṛgveda. That is, the two words following *iti* are accented as though there were no separation.

Jaṭā

If individual words are lettered / a / b / c / d / e . . . , then the *jaṭā* pattern is / abbaab / bccbbc / cddccd / deedde /, and so on. Thus in each section six words are derived from two. Compounds are analyzed after their final appearance in the *vikṛti*.

Source Verse (Vājasaneyi-Saṃhitā 3.60a),[36] to Rudra:

L J
tryambakaṃ yajāmahe sugandhíṃ puṣṭivárdhanam /

I Q B
urvārukámiva bándhanān mṛtyór múkṣīya māmṛ́tāt //

Translation:

We worship (*yajāmahe*) he who has three mothers (*tryambakam*), fragrant (*sugandhim*), increasing prosperity (*puṣṭivardhanam*); cucumber-like (*urvārukamiva*), may I escape (*mukṣīya*) from the bond (*bandhanāt*) of death (*mṛtyoḥ*), not (*mā*) from immortality (*amṛtāt*).

Pada:

tryambakam íti trí--ambakam / yajāmahe / sugandhím íti su--gandhím / puṣṭivárdhanam íti puṣṭi--várdhanam /

C D
urvārukámivéty urvārukám--iva / bándhanāt / mṛtyóḥ /

H D
mukṣīya / mā́ / amṛ́tād íty amṛ́tāt //

Kramamālā

This *vikṛti* is similar to *krama*[37] in that two-word units with the characteristic overlapping are the foundation. The

♩=56
d=a
Tape IIa(6)
L
tryam ba kaṃ ya jā ma he ya jā ma he
J L
tryam ba kaṃ tryam ba kaṃ ya jā ma he /
tryam ba ka mí ti trí -- am ba kam (a) /
K
ya jā ma he su gan dhí m̐ su gan dhím
ya jā ma he ya jā ma he su gan

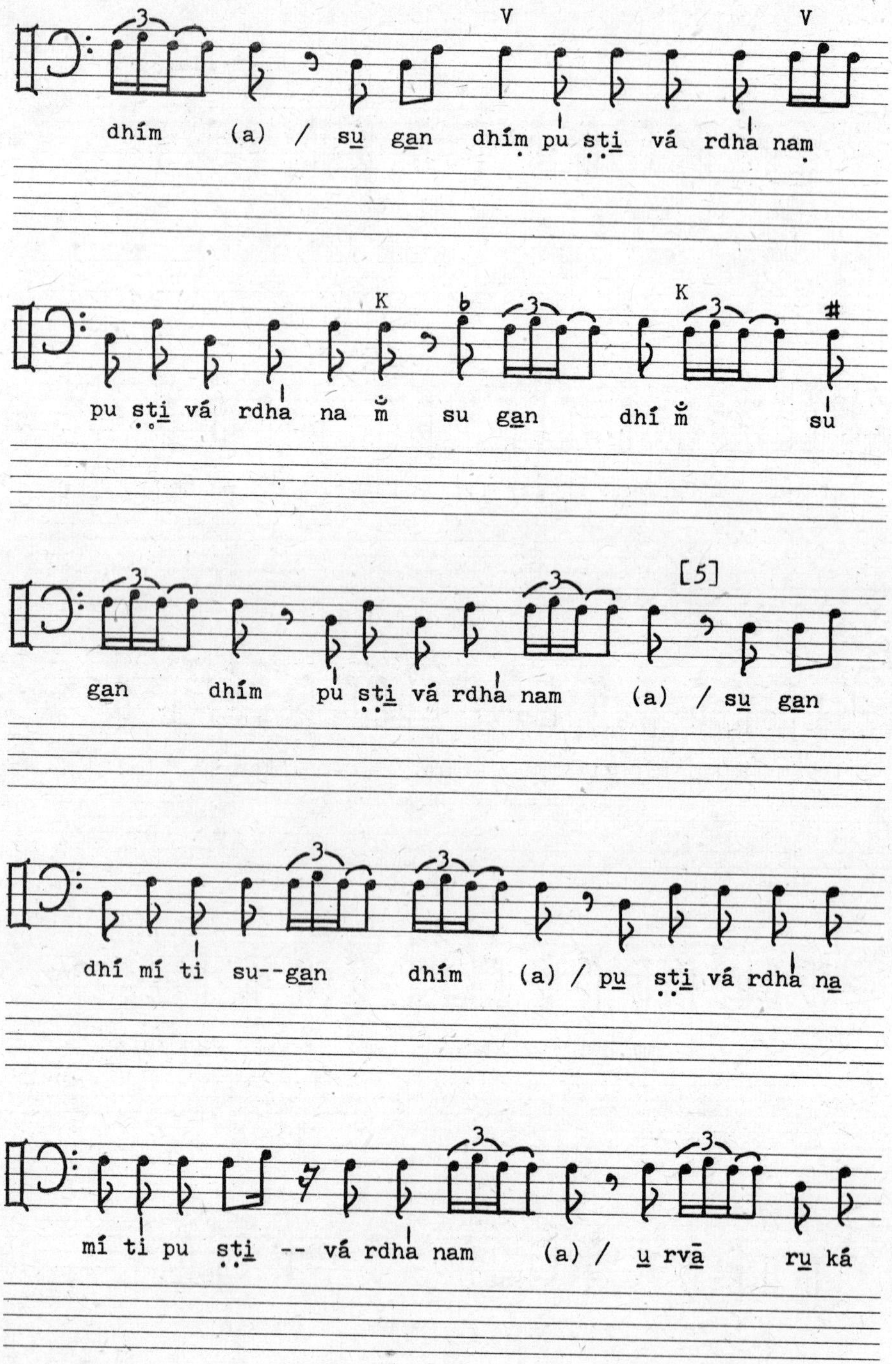
V V
dhím (a) / su gan dhíṃ pu ṣṭi vá rdha naṃ
K K
pu ṣṭi vá rdha na m̐ su gan dhí m̐ su
[5]
gan dhím pu ṣṭi vá rdha nam (a) / su gan
dhí mí ti su--gan dhím (a) / pu ṣṭi vá rdha na
mí ti pu ṣṭi -- vá rdha nam (a) / u rvā ru ká

H H
mi va bán dha nā dbán dha nā du rvā ru ká
C
mi vo rvā ru ká mi va bán dha nā t(a) /
C D
u rvā ru ká mi vé tyu rvā ru kám (a) --
I Q Q
i va / bán dha nān mṛ tyó rmṛ tyó rbán dha
H I [10] Q
nā dbán dha nān mṛ tyó ḥ / mṛ tyó rmu

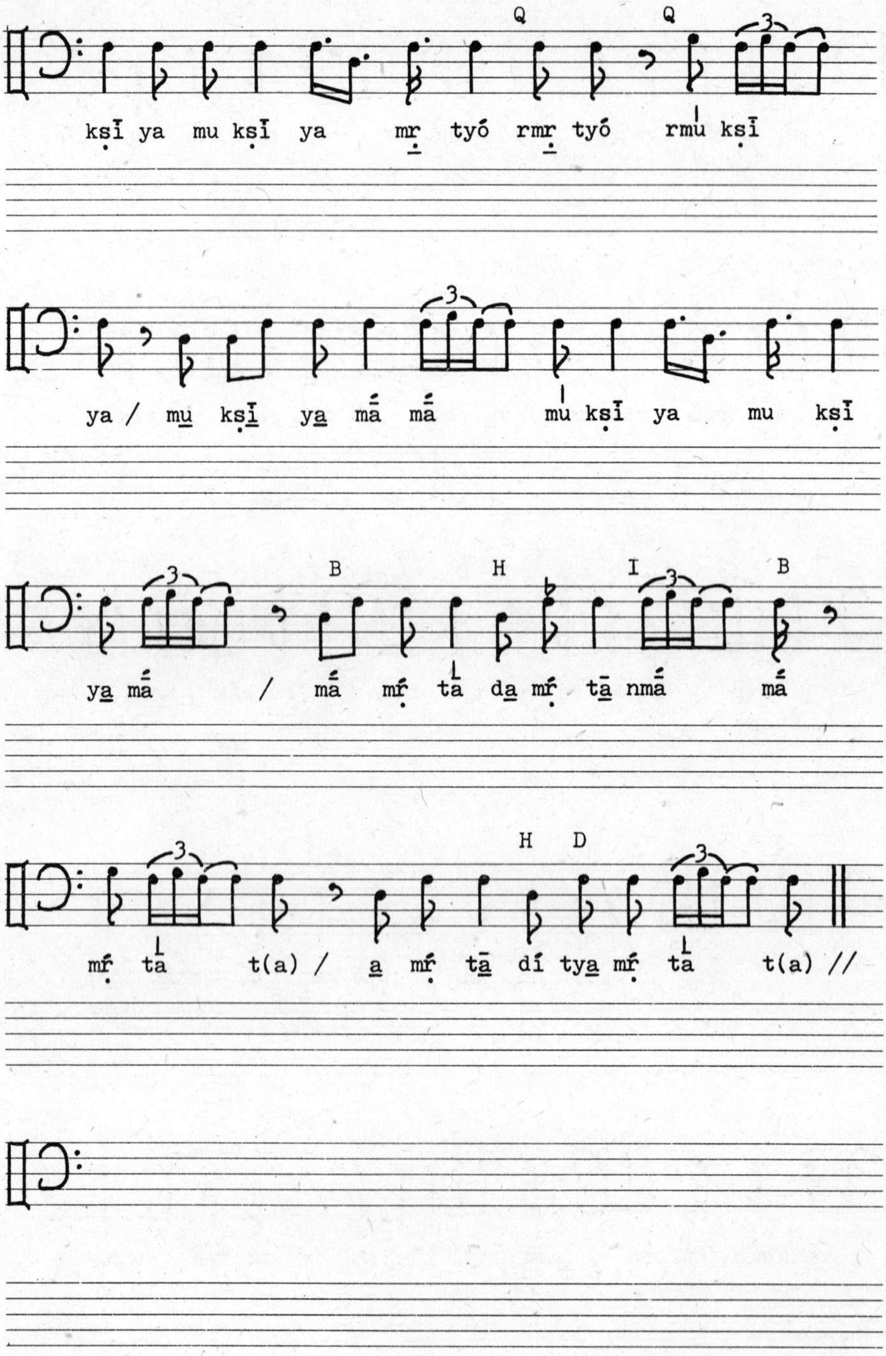
Q Q
kṣī ya mu kṣī ya mṛ tyó rmṛ tyó rmu kṣī
ya / mu kṣī ya mā mā mu kṣī ya mu kṣī
B H I B
ya mā / mā mṛ́ ta da mṛ́ tā nmā mā
H D
mṛ́ ta t(a) / a mṛ́ tā dí tya mṛ́ ta t(a) //

difference is that in *kramamālā* forward motion in groups of two is alternated with movement from the end of the hemistich, in which the two-word sections present the words in reverse order. Thus there is simultaneous action in two directions, from the beginning of the hemistich to the end and from the end to the beginning--with the two paths crossing in the middle. After the completion of one hemistich, the identical operation is performed on the other. Because the final word of a hemistich occurs both near the beginning and near the end of the *vikṛti* (thus reflecting the movement in two directions), the *pragraha* appears twice in each hemistich. The example below is based upon eighteen words. If the first hemistich has words a-h and the second i-r, then the *vikṛti* takes this form:

/ ab / h *iti* h / bc / hg / cd / gf / de / fe / ef / ed /
/ fg / dc / gh / cb / h *iti* h / ba //
/ ij / r *iti* r / jk / rq / kl / qp / lm / po / mn / on /
/ no / nm / op / ml / pq / lk / qr / kj / r *iti* r /
/ ji //

It may be assumed that compounds are likewise analyzed twice, both in forward and backward directions.

Source Verse (Vājasaneyi-Saṃhitā 31.16), from the Puruṣa hymn:

yajñéna yajñám ayajanta devās tāni dhármāṇi prathamāny
āsan /

té ha nākaṃ mahimānaḥ sacanta yátra pūrve sādhyāḥ sánti
devāḥ //

Translation:

Through the sacrifice (*yajñena*) the gods (*devāḥ*) sacrificed (*ayajanta*) the sacrifice (*yajñam*); these (*tāni*) were (āsan) the first (prathamāni) statutes of law (dharmāṇi). Indeed (ha) these (te) great ones (mahimānaḥ) reached (sacanta) the vault of heaven (nākam), where (yatra) the ancient (pūrve) Sādhya (sādhyāḥ) gods (devāḥ) dwell (santi).

Pada:

yajñéna / yajñám / ayajanta / devā́ḥ / tā́ni / dhármāṇi /

N D L
prathamā́ni / āsann íty ā́san / té / ha / nā́kam / mahimā́naḥ /

T
sacanta / yátra / pū́rve / sādhyā́ḥ / sánti / devā́ íti devā́ḥ //

Vikṛti:

N D L
yajñéna yajñám(a) / āsann íty ā- san(a) / yajñám ayajanta /
3 2 2 2 212 2 3 2 2 212 212 2 3 2 3 2 2 2

[5]
ā-san prathamā́- ni / ayajanta de- vā́- ḥ / prathamā́ni
1 212 2 2 212 212 3 2 2 2 212 212 2 3 2 2 2

Q
dhármā- ṇi / devā́s tā́-ni / dhármā- ṇi tā́-ni / tā́-ni
2 212 2 32 2 1 212 1 212 2 2 212 323 2

[10] T
dhármā- ṇi / tā́-ni de- vā́- ḥ / dhármāṇi prathamā́ni / devā́
2 212 2 1 12 212 212 2 32 2 2 2 2 2 2 32 21

D L
a- ya-janta / prathamā́ny ā- san(a) / ayajanta yajñám(a) /
12 12 212 2 3 2 2 212 212 2 3 2 2 23 2 2 2

[15] N D L L
ā-sann íty ā- san(a) / yajñám yajñéna //
32 2 2 212 212 2 2 2123 2 2 212

T [20] W
té ha / de-vā́ íti de- vā́- ḥ / ha nā́- kam(a) / devā́-ḥ sá-nti /
1 212 32 21 2 2 212 212 2 1 212 212 2 32 2 2 21 212

J W
nā́kam mahimā́nā- ḥ / sá-nti sā- dhyā́-ḥ / mahimā́nā- ḥ sacanta /
32 2 2 2 2 2122 1 212 212 212 2 3 2 2212 23 2 2 2

V [25]
sādhyā́-ḥ pū́rve / sacan- ta yátra / pū́rve yátra / yátra
32 2 2 1 212 1 212 23 2 212 1 212 2 2 3 2

[30]
pūrvé / yátrá sa-can-ta / pūrvé sādhyā́-ḥ / sa-can-ta
2 212 1 12 12 212 2 1 212 2 212 2 1 212 2

W S
mahimānā́- ḥ / sādhyā́-ḥ sánti / ma-hi-mā́- no nā́- kám(a) /
2 2 2 212 2 3 2 2 1 212 1 12 212 212 212 212 2

K [35] T
sánti de-vā́- ḥ / nā́ká-m̐ ha ≠ de-vā́ íti de-vā́- ḥ /
3 2 2 212 2 1 1 212 2 2 21 2 2 2 212 2

ha té //
1 123

Puṣpamālā

This vikṛti's formula is similar to that of jaṭā (abbaab/ bccbbc . . .), but puṣpamālā takes two words in each section instead of six: / ab / ba / ab / bc / cb / bc / cd / dc / cd / . . . . The pragraha and parigraha processes occur in the expected places.

Source Verse (Vājasaneyi-Saṃhitā 32.11), on the sacrificer of the sarvamedha (universal sacrifice):

V
parītyá bhūtā́ni parītyá lokā́n parītya sárvāḥ pradíśo

U
díśáś ca /

B B L
upasthā́yá prathamajā́m ṛtásyātmánātmā́nam abhí sám viveśa //

Translation:

Circumambulating (parītya) living things (bhūtāni), circumambulating (parītya) the worlds (lokān), circumambulating (parītya) all (sarvāḥ) directions (pradiśaḥ) and all quarters (diśaḥ ca), placing himself near (upasthāya) the origin (prathamajām) of cosmic order (ṛtasya), with the Self (ātmanā) he entered (viveśa) unto (abhi sam) the Self (ātmānam).

Pada:

C C
parītyéti pari--ítyá / bhūtā́ni / parītyéti pari--ítyá /

lokā̄n / parītyéti pari--ítyá / sárvāḥ / pradíśa íti pra--díśaḥ

díśaḥ / céti ca / upasthāyéty upa--sthāyá / prathamajā́m íti

prathama--jā́m / ṛtásyá / ātmánā / ātmā́nam / abhí / sám /

viveśéti viveśa //

Vikṛti:

parītyá bhū-tā́- ni / bhūtā́-ni parītyá / parī́- tyá bhūtā́- ni /
2 2 2 212 212 2 32 2 23 2 2 2 1 212 2 2 212 2

pa-rītyéti pari--ítyá [5] / bhūtā́-ni parītyá / pa-rī́- tyá
3 32 2 2 2 21 1 212 32 2 23 2 2 2 1 212 2

bhū-tā́- ni / bhūtā́-ni parī́-tyá / parī́-tyá lo- kā́n(a) /
2 212 2 32 2 23 2 2 212 1 1 212 212 212 2

lokā́n parītyá [10] / pa-rī́- tyá lo- kā́n(a) / parītyéti pari--
32 23 2 2 2 1 212 2 212 212 2 3 3 2 2 2 21

í-tyá / lokā́n parī́-tyá / parī́-tyá lo- kā́n(2) / lokā́n parītyá /
1 212 32 23 2 2 212 1 1 212 212 212 2 32 23 2 2 2

[15] pa-rī́- tya sárvā-ḥ / sárvā- ḥ parītyá / parī́-tya sárvāḥ /
1 212 23 2 2 2 1 212 23 2 2 2 1 1 212 2 22

pa-rī́- tyéti pa-ri--ítyá / sárvā- ḥ pradíśa-ḥ [20] / pradíśa-ḥ
1 212 2 23 2 21 1 212 1 212 2 3 2 2 2 3 3 3 3

sárvā-ḥ / sárvā- ḥ pradíśa-ḥ / pradí-śo díśa-ḥ / díśa-ḥ
2 2 2 1 212 2 3 2 2 2 3 2 212 3 2 2 1 1 2

pradí-śa-ḥ / pradí-śo dí-śa- ḥ [25] / pra-dí-śa í-ti pra--
3 2 21 2 3 2 212 2 212 2 1 12 21 12 1 21

dí-śa-ḥ / dí-śaś ca / ca dí-śa-ḥ / dí-śaś ca / cé-ti ca /
12 12 2 3 31 212 212 2 21 2 3 31 212 31 12 212

[30] upasthāyá prathama-jā́m(a) / prathamajā́m upasthāyá /
3 2 2 2 2 2 1 212 2 3 23 2 2 3 2 2 2

C D
upasthāya prathama-jām(a) / upasthāyéty u-pa--sthāya /
3 2 2 2 2 23 2 212 2 3 2 2 2 2 21 212 2

[35]
prathamajām rtá-sya / rtásya pra-tha-ma- jām(a) /
3 23 2 2 2 1 212 3 2 2 2 212 212 212 2

prathamajām rtásya / prathamajām íti prathama--jām(a) /
3 23 2 2 3 2 2 3 23 2 2 3 2 2 2 21 212 2

B C [40] B B
rtá-syātmánā / ātmánā rtá-sya / rtásyātmánā / ātmánātmā-nām(a)
3 2 212 2 2 3 2 2 2 1 212 3 2 2 2 2 3 2 2 21 212 2

B
ātmānam ātmá-nā / ātmá-nā- tmā-nām(a) / ātmānam a-bhí /
3 2 2 2 12 212 1 12 212 212 212 2 32 2 1 12 212

[45]D
abhy ā-tmā-nām(a) / ātmānām a-bhí / abhí sám(a) /
1 212 21 12 2 3 2 1' 12 212 1 12 212 2

[50] L
sám a-bhí / abhí sám(a) / sám vi-ve- śa / vi-ve- śa sám(a)
1 12 212 12 12 212 2 1 12 212 2 3 323 2 212 2

L C
sám vi-ve- śa / vi-ve- śéti vi-ve- śa //
1 12 212 2 32 232 2 2 2 212 2123

Pañcasandhi

The basic pattern of this vikṛti consists of five sandhi units (pañcasandhi = "five sandhis"): / ab / bb / ba / aa / ab / . . . . According to Gajānan Śāstrī, these five divisions have the names anukrama ("succession"), utkrama ("ascent"), vyutkrama ("inversion"), abhikrama ("beginning"), and saṃkrama ("coming together").

Source Verse (Vājasaneyi-Saṃhitā 33.39), to Sūrya and Āditya:

I O H O
báṇ mahām̐2 asi sūrya báḍ āditya mahām̐2 asi /

Q S E O
mahás té sató máhimā panasyate 'ddhā deva mahām̐2 asi //

Translation:

Sūrya (sūrya), you are (asi) truly (baṭ) great (mahān); Āditya (āditya), you are (asi) truly (baṭ) great (mahān). Being (sataḥ) great (mahaḥ), your (te) greatness (mahimā) excites admiration (panasyate); certainly (addhā), god (deva), you are (asi) great (mahān).

Pada:

báṭ / mahā́n / asi / sūrya / báṭ / āditya / mahā́n / asi / maháḥ / te / satáḥ / mahimā́ / panasyate / addhā́ / deva / mahā́n / asi //

Vikṛti:

I H
báṇ ma-hā́n(a) / ma-hā́n ma-hā́n / mahā́n báṭ(a) / báḍ(a) báṭ(a) /
2 2 212 2 2 212 2 23 2 2 1 2 1 1 1 2

[5] I O D
báṇ mahā́n(a) / ma-hā́m2 a- si / asy a-si / a-si mahā́n(a) /
212 2 2 2 1 212 212 212 3 2 212 3 23 2 2 2

[10] O
ma-hā́n ma-hā́n(a) / ma-hā́m2 a- si / asi sū- rya / sū-rya
2 212 2 212 2 1 212 212 212 3 2 212 212 1 212

B D [15]
sū- rya / sūryā-si / asy a-si / asi sū-rya / sūrya
212 2 32 2 212 1 12 212 3 2 2 212 1 12

H
báṭ(a) / báḍ(a) báṭ(a) / báṭ(a) sū- rya / sūrya sū-rya /
1 2 1 2 1 2 1 1 212 212 1 12 1 212

[20] H B
sūrya báṭ(a) / báḍ ā- di-tya / ādityāditya / ādi-tya
1 12 1 2 1 212 2 212 3 2 23 2 2 1 1 212

H [25] H
báṭ(a) / báḍ(a) báṭ(a) / báḍ ā-di-tya / āditya mahā́n(a) /
1 2 1 2 1 2 1 212 2 212 3 2 23 2 2 2

B [30]
ma-hā́n ma-hā́n(a) / mahā́n ā-ditya / ādityādi-tya / āditya
1 212 2 212 2 1 1 212 2 2 3 2 2 2 212 3 2 23

ma̱-hā́n(a) / ma̱-hā́m2 ȧ-si / a̱-sy a̱- si̱ / a̱-si ma̱hā́n(a) /
2 212 2   1 212 212 212 1   212 212   3 23 2 2 2

ma̱-hā́n ma̱-hā́n(a) [35] / ma̱-hā́m2 ȧ- si / a̱-si̱-ty ȧ- si //
1 212 2 212 2   12 212   212 212   1 212   212 212

ma̱hā́s te / te̱ te / te̱ ma̱- hā́- ḥ [40] / ma̱-hṓ mahā́-ḥ / ma̱hā́s
3 2 2   212 2   1 212 212 2   1 2123 2 2 2   1 1

té / te̱ sa̱-tā́- ḥ / sa̱-tā́-ḥ satā́-ḥ / satā́s te [45] / te̱ te /
212   212 2 212 2   1 12 2̱ 2 2 2̇   3 2 212   1 212

te̱ satā́-ḥ / sa̱- tó máhi̱mā́ / ma̱hi̱mā́ ma̱hi̱mā́ / ma̱hi̱-mā́
12 2 2 2̇   212 212 2 2 2   3 2 2̱ 2 2 2   1 1 212

sa̱-tā́- ḥ [50] / satā́-ḥ satā́-ḥ / sa̱tó ma̱-hi̱-mā́ / ma̱hi̱mā́
2 212 2̇   1 1 23 2 2 2̇   1 1̱ 12 12 212   3 2 2̱

pā́-na-sya-te / pa̱- nasya-te panasya̱te / panasya-te
212 1 212 212   212 1 12 2123 2 2 2 2   1 1 1 212

ma̱hi̱mā́ [55] / ma̱-hi̱-mā́ máhi̱mā́ / ma̱hi̱mā́ panasya-te / panasyate̱
2 2 2   1 12 212 2 2 2   1 1 1̱ 12 1 12 212   3 2 2 2̱

'ddhā́ / a̱ddhā́ddhā́ / a̱ddhā́ panasyate [60] / panasya̱te panasya̱te /
212   1 12 212   1 212 2 2 2 2   3 2 2̱ 2 3 2 2 2

panasya-te̱ 'ddhā́ / a̱ddhā́ de̱- va / de̱-va de̱- va̱ / de̱vā́ddhā́ /
1 1 1 212   212   1 12 212 2   1 12 212 2   32 2̱ 212

[65] a̱ddhā́ddhā́ / a̱ddhā́ dé- va / de̱va ma̱-hā́n(a) / ma̱hā́n ma̱-hā́n(a) /
1 12 2   1 12 212 2   32 2 2 212 2   1 1̱ 12 212 2

ma̱-hā́n dé- va [70] / de̱-va de̱- va / de̱-va ma̱hā́n(a) / ma̱-hā́m2
1 212 212 2   1 12 212   2   2 23 2 2̱ 2   1 212

ȧ- si / a̱sy a̱-si̱ / a̱-si ma̱- hā́n(a) [75] / ma̱-hā́n ma̱-hā́n(a) /
212 212   3   2 212   1 12 212 212 2   1 2123 2 212 2

ma̱hā́m2 ȧ- si / a̱si̱ty ȧ- si //
2 2̱   212 212 1 1̱   12 2123

Śikhā

With its forward-reverse-forward movement this *vikṛti* is similar to *jaṭā*. The only difference is that an extra word is picked up at the end of each phonetic section. Thus instead of / abbaab / bccbbc / . . . , *śikhā* reads / abbaabc / bccbbcd / . . . .

Source Verse (Vājasaneyi-Saṃhitā 31.22), to Sūrya:

U U G
śrī́ś ca̱ te la̱kṣmī́ś ca̱ pátnyāv ahorā̱tré pā̱rśvé nákṣatrāṇi

rū̱pám a̱śvína̱u vyā́ttam /

N B F F
i̱ṣṇánn iṣāṇā̱mū́ṃ má iṣāṇa sarvalo̱kā́ṃ má iṣāṇa //

Translation:

Radiance (*śrīḥ*) and (*ca*) good fortune (*lakṣmīḥ*) are your (*te*) wives (*patnyau*); on both sides (*pārśve*) of you are day and night (*ahorātre*); the heavenly bodies (*nakṣatrāṇi*) are your form (*rūpam*); the Aśvins (*aśvinau*) are your open jaws (*vyāttam*). Seeking (*iṣṇan*), seek (*iṣāṇa*); seek (*iṣāṇa*) that (*amum*) for me (*me*); seek (*iṣāṇa*) the whole world (*sarvalokam*) for me (*me*).

Pada:

D
/ śrī́ḥ / ca̱ / te̱ / la̱kṣmī́ḥ / ca̱ / pátnyau / a̱ho̱rā̱tré íty aho--rā̱tré / pā̱rśvé íti pā̱rśvé / nákṣatrāṇi / rū̱pám / a̱śvínau / vyā́tta̱m íti vi̱--ā́ttam / i̱ṣṇán / i̱ṣā̱ṇa̱ / a̱mū́m / me̱ / i̱ṣā̱ṇa̱ / sa̱rva̱lo̱kā́m íti sarva--lo̱kā́m / me̱ /

C B
i̱ṣā̱ṇétīṣāṇa //

Vikṛti:

U W U
śrīś cá ca śrī-ḥ śrīś cá te ⁄ ca te te ca ca te lakṣmī-ḥ /
2 2 2 212 2 2 2 212 2 2 212 2 2 2 2 212 2

Q Q U U
te lakṣmīr lakṣmīs té te * lakṣmīś cá ⁄ lakṣmīś cá ca
23 2 2 2 212 212 2 2 212 23 2 2 2 2

Q U [5]
lakṣmīr lakṣmīś ca pátnyáu ⁄ ca pátnyau * pátnyáu ca ca
2 212 2 212 23 2 2 23 2 2 2 212 2 23

G G
pátnyāv a-ho- rā- tré / pátnyāv aho-rā- tré á- ho- rā- tré
2 2 2 212 232 2 2 212 2 2 232 21 12 212 232 2

G
* pátnyau pátnyāv a-ho- rā- tré * pārśvé / a-ho- rā- tré
1 2123 2 2 2 212 21232 2 1 212 1 212 232 2

pā-rśvé pā-rśvé á-ho- rā- tré * á-ho-rā- tré * pārśvé
212 212 232 21 12 212 232 21 1 12 232 2 32 2

D
nákṣát(a)rā- ṇi / a-horātré ity á-ho--rā- tré / pārśvé
1 2 2 212 2 3 32 2 21 2 2 212 212 2 3 2

nákṣát(a)rā- ṇi nákṣát(a)rā- ṇi pā- rśvé * pārśvé
2 2 2 212 23 2 2 2 212 2 212 2 3 2

[10]
nákṣát(a)rā- ṇi rū- pám(a) / pārśvé í-ti pā- rśvé /
2 2 2 212 2 212 212 2 32 21 1 212 212 2

K J
nákṣát(a)rāṇi rū- pá-m̐ rūpám nákṣát(a)rā-*-ṇi nákṣát(a)rāṇi
3 2 2 2 2 212 1 12 2 2 2 2 2 2 3 3 2 2 2 2

G K
rūpám aśví-náu / rūpám aśví-nāv aśvínáu * rūpá-m̐ rūpám
21 12 1 12 212 32 2 3 2 212 2 2 2 1 1 12 2 2

L G
aśví-nau vyáttám(a) / aśvínau vyáttaṃ vyáttám aśvínā-*-v
2 2 212 212 212 2 3 2 2 212 21232 2 2 2 2 2

aśví-nau vyáttám(a) / vyáttam íti ví--á-ttám(a) //
3 2 212 2 212 2 1 212 2 2 21 12 212 2

N C C N N B
iṣnánn i-ṣā- ne- ṣā- neṣnánn iṣnánn * i-ṣā- nā- múm(a) /
1 12 2 232 212 232 2 2123 2 2 2 212 212 212 2

B C B J E
i-ṣā- nāmúm a-múm i-ṣā- ne- ṣānā-*-múm me / a-múm me me
3 323 2 2 2 212 2 212 21232 2 2 1 212 1 212 212 212

J F F C F
'múm a-múm ma i- ṣā- na / ma i-ṣā- ne- ṣā-na me ma
2 2 212 1 12 212 2 1 1 212 21232 2 23 2 1

K
i- ṣā-*-na sarvalo- kám(a) / i-ṣāna sarvalo- ká-m̐
12 212 3 2 2212 212 2 3 32 2 2 2 212 2 2

C J
sarvalo-*-kám iṣā-ne- ṣāna sarva-lo- kám me /
3 2 2 3 2 2 21232 2 2 2 2 21232 212 2

J K J F
sarvalo-kám me me sarvalo-*-ká-m̐ sarvalo-kám ma i- ṣā- na /
3 2 2 21 12 12 2 2 2 1 12 3 2 2 212 1 12 212 2

F C
sarva-lokám íti sar-va--lo- kám(a) / ma i- ṣā- ne- ṣāna me
3 3 32 2 2 2 2 21 212 212 2 1 12 212 212 2 2 2

F C B
ma i- ṣā- na / i-ṣāné-ti- ṣā- na //
1 12 212 2 3 32 2 212 212 2123

Rekhā

The demonstration of rekhā, one of the more complicated vikṛtis, utilized a verse of sixteen words, symbolized below by the letters a-p. Words e, g, h, and j are compounds, subject to parigraha analysis; words g and p are final in the hemistich.

/ ab / ba / ab / bcd / dcb / bc / cd / defg / gfed /

/ de / ef / e iti e^1e^2 / fg / g iti g^1g^2 / hijkl /

/ lkjih / h iti h^1h^2 / ij / jk / j iti j^1j^2 / kl /

/ lmnop / ponml / lm / mn / no / op / p iti p //

Thus the repetition scheme of this vikṛti is as follows (both diagonal lines and plus signs denote absence of sandhi):

/ ab + ba / ab + bcd + dcb / bc + cd + defg + gfed /

/ de + ef + e iti e^1e^2 + fg + g iti g^1g^2 + hijkl + lkjih /
/ h iti h^1h^2 / ij + jk + j iti j^1j^2 + kl + lmnop + ponml /
/ lm + mn + no + op / p iti p //

At least theoretically, therefore, each section (demarcated above by diagonal lines) is longer than the previous section, although adjustments must be made toward the end of the vikṛti when the supply of words is depleted.

This northern rekhā[38] is different from that of the South, where this scheme predominates:[39]

/ ab / ba / ab / bcd / dcb / bc / cdef / fedc / cd /
/ defgh / hgfed / . . . .

Source Verse (Vājasaneyi-Saṃhitā 17.36), to Bṛhaspati:

bṛ́haspate pári dīyā ráthena rakṣohā́mítrān apabā́dhamānaḥ /
prabhañjánt sénāḥ pramṛṇó yudhā́ jáyann asmā́kam edhy avitā́
rā́thānām //

Translation:

Bṛhaspati (bṛhaspate), killer of demons (rakṣohā), driving away (apabādhamānaḥ) enemies (amitrān), soar (dīya) about (pari) with [your] chariot (rathena). Crushing (prabhañjan) armies (senāḥ), destroying (pramṛṇaḥ) through combat (yudhā), conquering (jayan), be (edhi) protector (avitā) of our (asmākam) chariots (rathānām).

Pada:

/ bṛ́haspate / pári / dīya / ráthena / rakṣohéti rakṣaḥ--
hā́ / amítrān / apabā́dhamāna íty apa--bā́dhamānaḥ /
prabhañjánn íti pra--bhañján / sénāḥ / pramṛṇá íti pra--

mṛṇáḥ / yudhā́ / jáyan / asmā́kam / edhi / avitā́ / ráthānām

íti ráthānām //

Vikṛti:

bṛ́haspate pá- ri / pári bṛ́haspa-te / bṛ́haspate pá- ri /
3 2 2 2 212 212 2 2 2 1 12 212 3 2 2 2 212 212

A [5]
pári dīyā * rá-the-na / ráthena dī- ya pá- ri / pári dīya /
2 2 2 2 1 212 23 2 2 2 212 2 212 212 2 2 2 2

A B O
dī- yā * rá-the-na / ráthena rakṣo-hā́- mítrā́m apabā́-*-
212 2 1 212 23 2 2 2 2 2 212 2 2 2 2 2

S
dha-mā- na- ḥ / apabā́dhamā-no 'mítrān rakṣo-hā́ rá-the-na /
1 212 212 2 3 2 2 2 2 212 2 2 2 21 212 2 212 23

[10] B C
ráthe-*-na ra-kṣo-hā́ / ra-kṣohāmí-trān(a) / rakṣohéti
2 2 2 2 232 212 2 232 2 1 212 2 3 32 2 2

O
rakṣa- ḥ--hā́ / amítrā́m apabā́-*-dha-mā- na-ḥ /
1 212 2 212 3 2 2 2 2 2 2 212 2 2

R D
apabā́-dha- mā- na íty a- pa--bā́- dha-mā- na-ḥ /
3 2 2 212 212 21 1 212 21 212 212 212 2 2

[15] P V S
prabha-ñjánt sé- nā-ḥ pramṛṇó yudhā́ * já-yan(a) / já-yan
1 212 212 212 2 2 3 2 2 2 2 1 212 2 1 212

W V N
yudhā́ pra-mṛ- ṇá- ḥ sé-nā- ḥ pra-bhañján(a) / prabhañjánn
2 2 1 12 212 212 21 212 2 2 212 212 2 3 32 2

V S
íti pra--bhañján(a) / sé-nā- ḥ pramṛ-ṇá- ḥ / pramṛṇó yu- dhā́ /
2 2 2 212 212 2 1 212 2 2 2 212 2 3 2 2 212 212

[20] R N
pramṛ-ṇá í-ti pra--mṛṇá-ḥ / yu-dhā́ já- yan(a) / já-yann
3 2 21 1 12 21 2 2 2 2 212 12 212 2 1 212

D C D
asmā́kam edhy avi-tā́ rá-tha-nām(a) / ráthanām avi-tā́idhy
2 2 2 2 2 2 212 1 212 212 2 3 32 2 2 2 212

J N [25]
asmá-*-kam já-yan(a) / já-yann asmá-kam(a) ≁ asmá-kam
2 2 212 1 212 2 1 212 2 2 212 23 2 2 212

D
e- dhi / edhy a- vi- tá ≁ avitá rá-thā-nām(a) / ráthānām
212 2 1 212 212 212 2 2 2 1 212 212 2 3 32 2

íti rá-thā-nām(a) //
2 2 2 212 21 2123

Dhvaja

Dhvaja is similar to kramamālā in that both vikṛtis alternate forward and reverse movement of two-word segments with the characteristic overlapping; however, two major differences exist. First of all, dhvaja does not take each hemistich separately but proceeds from the beginning and from the very end of the verse (that is, from the end of the second hemistich). Secondly, the word-groups which occur in the backward movement present the words in their original order, without reversing them. Therefore, if the words are lettered a-p, the vikṛti reads:

/ ab / p iti p / bc / op / cd / no / . . . / op / bc /
/ p iti p / ab //

Source Verse: same as for rekhā.

Vikṛti:

bṛhaspate pári ≁ ráthā-nām íti rá-thā-nām(a) / pári dī- ya /
3 2 2 2 2 2 2 2 212 2 2 2 212 212 2 3 2 212 2

[5] D
avitá rá-thā-nām(a) / dī-ya [rá-thena] / e- dhy a-vi-tá /
3 2 2 1 212 212 2 21 12 2 212 2 212 2 12 212

B
rá-the-na rakṣo-há / asmá-kam e- dhi / rakṣohámí-trān(a) /
1 212 23 2 2 212 1 21 212 212 212 3 32 2 1 212 2

[10] N C
já-yann asmá-kam(a) / ra-kṣohéti ra-kṣa-h--há / yudhá
2 2123 2 2 212 2 2 212 2 2 1 212 21 212 2 21

```
                  10                                          S
já-yan(a) / amítram apabādha-mā- na-ḥ / pra-mr- nó  yudhá /
 1 212 2    3 2 21  2 2 2 12 212  2 2      2 212 212  2  2

[15]        P                V                           N
pra-bha-ñjánt sé-na- ḥ / séna-ḥ pramrná-ḥ / prabhañjánn
  2 212 212     2 212 2  32 2 2   2 2 2 2     2 21 212

            V                                           P
íti pra--bhañ-ján(a) / séna-ḥ  pra-mr-ná- ḥ / prabhañ-jánt
2 2  21   212 212 2    32 2 212  1 12 212 2     1  1  212

     [20]       S                            R    D
sé- na- ḥ / pra-mr-nó  yu-dhá / apabādhamā-na íty á- pa--
212 212 2    1 12 212 12 212   3 2 2  2 2 21 1   212 21

              R                                       10
bā-dhamāna-ḥ / pramr-ná í-ti pra--mr-ná- ḥ / amít(a)ram
212  2 2 2 2     3 2 21 1 12  21  12 212 2   1 1  2 2121

                                          [25]       C
apabā-dha-mā- na-ḥ / yu-dhá já- yan(a) / ra-kṣohéti
2 2 2 212 212  2 2   2 212 212 212 2     2 212 2 2

              N                                B
rakṣa-ḥ--há / já-yann as-mā- kam(a) / rakṣohāmítran(a) /
 2  2 21 12    1 212  1  212 212 2    3 32 2 1 212 2

                                     [30]  D
asmá-kam e-  dhi / rá-the-na rakṣo-há / edhy a-  vi- tá /
1  1 212 212 212    1 212 23  2  2 212  1   212 212 212

   A
dī-yā  rá-thena / avitá rá-thā-nām(a) / pá-ri  dī- ya /
21 212  2 212 2   3 2 2  1 212 212 2    1  212 212  2

                             [35]
rá-thā-nām íti rá-thā-nām(a) / bṛhaspate pá-ri   //
 1 212 212 2 2  2 212 212 2     3 2  2 2  1 2123
```

Daṇḍa (Kramadaṇḍa)

Like rekhā, daṇḍa has sections of unequal length, but here the procedure is simpler. The first two words are recited, then repeated in reverse order; then the first and second, followed by the second and third, words are uttered, after which all three are given in backward motion. The same operation is applied until the end of the verse is reached: four words are taken, then five, then six, and so on--a continual interplay of advancement and withdrawal. Forward movement is always from the beginning of the verse in groups of two, with the overlapping reminiscent of krama. Backward movement, however, takes all words covered by the preceding krama operation in one group (one sandhi section). Compounds are analyzed following their final statement in each forward process, but they are never subjected to parigraha in the retraction procedure. The method is illustrated in the ensuing outline (words e and f are compounds):

/ ab / ba / ab / bc / cba / ab / bc / cd / dcba / ab /
/ bc / cd / de / edcba / ab / bc / cd / de / ef / fedcba /
/ ab / bc / cd / de / ef / e iti e^1e^2 / fg / gfedcba /
/ab / bc / cd / de / ef / e iti e^1e^2 / fg / f iti f^1f^2 /
/ gh / hgfedcba / ab / bc / cd / de / ef / e iti e^1e^2 /
/ fg / f iti f^1f^2 / gh / hi / ihgfedcba / . . . .

Source Verse (Vājasaneyi-Saṃhitā 23.20), on the aśvamedha (horse sacrifice):[40]

tā́ ubhā́u catúraḥ padáḥ samprásārayāva svargé loké

prórṇuvāthām vṛ́ṣā vājī́ retodhā́ réto dadhātu //

Translation:

May we (tau) both (ubhau) stretch (samprasārayāva) [our] four feet (caturaḥ padaḥ); let us envelop (prorṇuvāthām) [ourselves] in heaven (svarge loke); the virile (vṛṣā), impregnating (retodhā) horse (vājī) must impregnate (reto dadhātu).

Pada:

táu / ubhā́u / catúraḥ / padáḥ / samprásārayāvéti sam--prásārayāva / svargá íti svaḥ--gé / loké / prá / ūrṇuvāthām / vṛ́ṣā / vājī́ / retodhā́ íti retaḥ--dhā́ḥ / rétaḥ / dadhātv íti dadhātu //

Vikṛti:

```
 G                      G
tá u-bháu ≁ u-bháu táu / tá u-bháu ≁ ubháu catúrà-ḥ /
21 12 212   12 212 212   21 21 212   2  2   3 2 2 212

[5] R              G
catúrà u-bháu táu / tá u-bháu / u-bháu catúrà-ḥ /
 3 2 2 12 212 212   1 12 212   12 212  2 2 2 2

       V               U    R           [10]G
catúrà- ḥ pa-dá- ḥ / padáś catúrà u-bháu táu / tá u-bháu /
 1 1 12 2 12 212 2    3 2   2 2 1 12 212  2    32 12 212

                          V                   W
ubháu ca-tú-rà- ḥ / catú-rà- ḥ pa-dá- ḥ / pa-dá- ḥ
1 1  12 12 212 2    1 1 212 2 12 212 2    1 212 2

                                             U      R
samprá-sā- ra- yā- va / samprásāra-yā- va padáś catú-rà
212  2 212 12  212  2   323  2 2 2 212  2  2 1  12 2 21

        [15]G                                          V
u-bháu táu / tá u-bháu / ubháu ca-tú- rà- ḥ / catú-rà- ḥ
12 212 212   32 2  212   1  1  12 212 212 2   2 1 212  2

          W
pa-dá- ḥ / padá-ḥ samprá-sā- ra-yā- va  / samprásārayāva
12 212 2    2 2 2 212  2 212  2 212 212   32   2 2 2 2 2

    [20]                              U           R
sva-rgé / sva-rgé samprá-sā- rayā-*-va padáś ca-tú- rà u-bháu
 12 212   1 212 212  2 212  2 2   2  1 1  12 212  1 12 212

      G                                    V
táu / tá u-bháu / ubháu catúrà-ḥ / catú-rà- ḥ pa-dá- ḥ /
212   32 12 212   1 212  2 2 2 2   2 2 212  2 12 212 2

       W                     [25]
pa-dá- ḥ samprá-sā- ra-yā- va / samprásāra-yā- va sva-rgé /
 1 212 2 212  2 212  2 212  2   32    2 2 2 212  1  12 212

                 C
samprá-sā- rayā-vé- ti sam(a)--prá-sā- ra-yā- va / sva-rgé
 2    2 212  2 2 212  2 212 2      2 212  2 212  2    1 212

                                                U      R
lo- ké  / loké svargé samprásā-*-ra-yā- va padáś ca-tú-rà
212 212   32 2  2 2 2  2 2   1 212  2 12 1  12 12 21

              G         [30]                       V
u-bháu táu / tá u-bháu / ubháu ca-tú-rà- ḥ / catú-rà- ḥ
12 212 212   32 12 212   1  1  1 12 212 2    1 1 212  2
```

W L L
pa-dá- ḥ / pa-dá- ḥ samprá-sā- ra-yā- va / samprásāra-yā- va
12 212 2 1 212 2 212 2 212 2 212 2 323 2 2 2 212 1

C
svа-rgé / samprá-sā- ra-yā- vé- ti sam(a)--prá-sā-*-ra-yā- va /
12 212 1 1 212 2 212 212 2 212 21 12 21 21 212 2

[35] F
sva-rgé lo-ké / svargá í-ti svaḥ--gé / lo-ké prá / prá
1 212 1 212 2 2 12 2 121 212 1 212 212 1

L U R
lo-ké sva-rgé samprásā-*-rayāva padáś ca-túrā u-bháu táu /
1 212 2 212 212 2 2 2 2 2 2 1 12 12 1 12 212 212

G [40] V W
tá u-bháu / ubháu ca-tú-rā- ḥ / catúrā-ḥ pa-dá- ḥ / pa-dá- ḥ
32 12 212 1 1 12 12 212 2 3 2 2 2 12 212 2 2 212 2

samprá-sā- ra-yā- va / samprásārayāva sva-rgé / samprá-sā-
212 2 212 2 212 2 323 2 2 2 2 1 12 212 2 2 212

C [45]
rayāvé-*-ti sam(a)--prá-sā- ra-yā-va / svargé lo- ké /
2 2 2 2 212 21 12 212 2 212 2 32 2 212 212

F C
svargá í- ti sva-ḥ--gé / lo-ké prá / prórṇu- vā- thām(a) /
212 1 12 12 1 21 212 1 212 212 1 212 212 212 2

J U
ū-rṇuvāthām prá lo- ké * sva-rgé samprásārayā-*-va padáś
32 2 2 212 2 212 2 2 212 212 2 2 2 2 3 2 1

R [50]G
catúrā u-bháu táu / tá u-bháu / ubháu ca-tú-rā- ḥ /
2 2 1 12 212 212 32 12 212 1 1 12 12 212 2

V W L
ca-túrā-ḥ pa- dá- ḥ / pa-dá- ḥ samprá-sā- ra-yā-va /
3 23 2 2 212 212 2 1 212 2 212 2 212 2 212 2

L [55] C
samprá-sā- rayāva sva-rgé / samprá-sā- ra-yā- vé- ti sam(a)--
1 1 212 2 2 2 12 212 1 1 212 2 212 212 2 212 21

F
prá-sā- ra-yā- va / svargé lo-ké / svargá í-ti sva-ḥ--gé /
12 212 2 212 2 32 2 1 212 212 2 1 12 12 21 212

C [60] L
lo-ké prá / prórṇu-vā- thām(a) / ū-rṇuvāthām vṛ-ṣá /
1 212 212 1 12 212 212 2 32 2 2 212 1 212

```
  C     J                           L
vr-sórnu-vā-thām prá lo- ké svargé * samprásara-yā- va
 1  1 12 212 212   2 212  2  2  2   323  2 2 2 212  2

 U         R           G
padáś ca-tú-ra u-bháu táu / tá ubháu / ubháu ca-tú- ra- ḥ /
 2 1  12 12 21 12 212 212   32 2  2     2  1  12 212 212 2

     V        [65]      W          
catúra-h pa-dá-h / pa-dá- h samprá-sā- rayā-va /
 3 2 2 2  1 12 2    2 212 2 212  2 212  2212 2

                           L             C
samprá-sā- rayāva sva-rgé / samprá-sā- ra-yā- vé- ti sam(a)--
 2   2 212  2 2 2  2 212     1   1 212  2 212 212  2 212 21

                                       F
prá-sā-*-ra-yā- va / svargé lo- ké  / svargá íti sva-ḥ--gé /
12 212  2 212  2    32  2 212 212     1  1 1 1   1 21 212

[70]         C                     L
lo-ké  prá / prórnu-vā-thām(a) / ū-rnuvāthām vr-sá  / vrsá
 1 212 212    1 12 212 212 2    32  2 2 212  2 212    1 1

                C         J
vā-jī  / vā-jī  vr-só- rnuvāthām prá loké * svargé
12 212   1 212  2 212   2 2  2    2  2 2    32  2

                      U                [75]G
samprá-sā- rayā-va padáś ca-tú-ra ubháu táu / tá ubháu /
212  2 212  2 2 23  2 1  12 12 21 2 212 212   32 2  2

                           V                     W
ubháu ca-tú-ra- h / ca-túra-h pa-dá- h / padá-h
1  1  12 12 212 2   3 23 2 2  1 212 2   1 1 1

                                             [80]
samprá-sā- ra-yā-va / samprásarayāva sva-rgé / samprá-sā-
212  2 212  2 212 2   323  2 2 2 2 2  12 212    1   1 212

    C
ra-yā- vé- ti sam(a)--prá-sā- ra-yā-va / sva-rgé lo-ké /
 2 212 212  2 212 21   12 212  2 212 2   32 212  21 12

   F                              C
svargá í-ti sva-ḥ--gé / lo-ké  prá / prórnu-vā-thām(a) /
  2  2 12 1  1 21 212    1 212 212    1 12 212 212 2

[85]       L
ū-rnuvāthām vr-sá  / vrsá vā- jī / vā-jī  re- to-dhā-ḥ /
32  2 2 212  1 212    2 2 212 212   1 212 212  2 212 2

  T          C          J
retodhá vā- jī  vr-só- rnuvāthām * prá lo- ké   svargé
32 2   2 212 212 2 212   2 2 2      21 212 2123  2  2
```

U R G
samprá-sā- rayā-*-va padā́s catúrà u-bhā́u tā́u / tā́ u-bhā́u /
212 2 212 2 2 3 2 1 1 1 1 12 212 212 32 12 212

[90]
V W
ubhā́u ca-tū́-ra- ḥ / catū́ra-ḥ padā́-ḥ / padā́-ḥ samprá-sā-
1 1 1 12 212 12 3 2 2 2 112 2 2 1 1 212 2 212

C
ra-yā-va / samprā́sāra-yā-va sva-rgé / samprá-sā- rayā-vé- ti
12 212 2 323 2 2 2 212 2 12 212 2 1 212 2 2 212 2

[95] F
sam(a)--prá-sā-ra-yā-va / svargé lo-ké / svargā́ íti
212 21 12 212 2 212 212 1 1 212 2 32 2 2 2

C L
sva-ḥ--gé / lo-ké prá / prórṇu-vā-thām(a) / ūrṇuvāthām
1 21 212 1 212 212 1 12 212 212 212 2 1 1 212

[100] T
vṛ-sā́ / vṛsā́ vā- jī́ / vā-jī́ re-to- dhā́-ḥ / reto-dhā́
12 212 1 1 212 212 1 212 2 212 212 2 32 2 212

S T C J
ré-ta- ḥ / rétó re-to- dhā́ vā-jī́ * vṛ-só- rṇu-vā- thām
1 212 2 1 1 1 212 212 212 2 2 212 2 212 212

U R
prá lo- ké svargé samprā́sā-*-rayā-va padā́s ca-tú-rà u-bhā́u
2 212 2 2 2 212 2 2 2 2 23 2 1 12 12 21 12 212

G [105] V
tā́u / tā́ u-bhā́u / ubhā́u catū́ra-ḥ / catū́ra-ḥ pa-dā́-ḥ /
212 2 12 212 2 212 2 2 2 2 3 3 3 2 1 12 2

W
padā́-ḥ samprá-sā- ra-yā-va / samprā́sārayāva sva-rgé /
1 1 1 12 2 212 2 212 2 32 2 2 2 2 1 12 212

C [110]
samprā́sāra-yā-vé- ti sam(a)--prá-sā-ra-yā-va / sva-rgé
1 1 1 1 12 212 2 212 21 12 212 2 212 1 1 212

F C
lo- ké / svargā́ íti sva-ḥ--gé / lo-ké prá / prórṇu-vā-
212 2 32 2 1 1 1 2 12 1 212 212 1 12 212

L [115]
thām(a) / ū-rṇuvāthām vṛ-sā́ / vṛsā́ vā- jī́ / vājī́ re-to-
212 2 32 2 2 212 1 12 1 1 212 212 1 1 12 212

T T
dhā́-ḥ / re-to-dhā́ rétā-ḥ / re-to- dhā́ íti re-ta-ḥ--dhā́-ḥ /
212 2 1 12 212 2 2 2 1 212 21 2 2 2 21 2 212 2

$$
\begin{array}{l}
\overset{S}{\text{ré-tó}}\ \text{da-dhātu}\ /\ \overset{[120]}{\text{da-dhātu}}\ \text{ré-tó}\ \overset{T}{\text{retodhā}}\ \text{vājī}\ *\ \overset{C}{\text{vṛ-ṣó-}}\\
\ 2\ 21\underline{2}\ \ 2\ 21\underline{2}\ 2\quad\ 2\ 21\underline{2}\ 2\ \ \underline{2}\ 21\underline{2}\ \ \underline{2}\ \underline{2}\ \ \underline{2}\ 1\ 1\quad\ \overline{\underline{2}}\ 21\underline{2}
\end{array}
$$

rṇu-vā-tha̱m prá lo-ké svargé * samprá-sā- raya-va pa̱dáś[U]
2 21<u>2</u> 21<u>2</u>   1 1<u>2</u> 21<u>2</u>   1 1   <u>1</u> 1 21<u>2</u> 2 <u>2</u> 23 2 1

ca-tú-ra̱[R] u-bháu táu / tá[G] u-bháu / u̱bháu catúra-h / catúra-h[V]
12 12 21 12 21<u>2</u> 21<u>2</u> <u>1</u> 12 21<u>2</u>   2 <u>1</u>   1 2 1 2̇   3 2 2 <u>2</u>

pa̱dá-h / pa̱dá-h[W] sa̱mprá-sā-rayāva / [125] sa̱mprá-sā-rayāva svargé /
2 1 2̇   2 1 <u>2</u> 21<u>2</u> 2 21<u>2</u> 2 <u>2</u> <u>2</u>   <u>2</u> 2 21<u>2</u> 2 <u>2</u> 1 12 12

samprá-sā-rayā-vé-ti[C] sam(a)--prá-sā-ra-yā- va / svargé
<u>2</u>   1 21<u>2</u> 2 <u>2</u> 21<u>2</u> 2 21<u>2</u> 2<u>1</u>   12 21<u>2</u> 2 21<u>2</u> 12   <u>2</u> <u>1</u>

lo-ké / svargá[F] íti sva-h--gé / [130] lo-ké prá / prórṇu-vā-[C]
12 12   <u>1</u> 1 1 1   1 <u>2</u> 12   <u>1</u> 12 21<u>2</u>   <u>1</u> 12 21<u>2</u>

thām(a) / ū̱rṇuvāthā̱m[L] vṛ-sá / vṛsá vā-jī / vā-jī ré- to-
21<u>2</u> 2   <u>1</u> 1 <u>1</u> 21<u>2</u> 1<u>2</u> 12   <u>2</u> <u>1</u> 12 12   <u>1</u> 21<u>2</u> 21<u>2</u> 21<u>2</u>

dhá-h / retodhā[T] réta-h / [135] re-to- dhā[T] íti reta-h--dhá-h /
21<u>2</u> 2̇   32 <u>2</u> 2 <u>1</u> 2 2̇   <u>1</u> 21<u>2</u> 2<u>1</u> 2 2 <u>2</u> 1 <u>2</u> 21<u>2</u> 2̇

rétó[S] dadhā-tu / da̱dhā̱tv[D] íti da-dhā-tu //
<u>1</u> <u>1</u> 1 1<u>2</u> 21<u>2</u>   1 1<u>2</u>   1 1 1 21<u>2</u> 212<u>3</u>

Ratha (Catuṣpāda)

The <u>catuṣpāda</u> ("four quarter-verses" = "four wheels") brand of <u>ratha</u> distributes the <u>daṇḍa</u> apparatus across the four <u>pāda</u>s of the verse, which are analogous to the four wheels of a chariot. Letters may be assigned to the words of the four <u>pāda</u>s in this manner:

> P̄āda 1: abcd
> P̄āda 2: efgh
> P̄āda 3: ijkl
> P̄āda 4: mnop

The recited example of catuṣpāda ratha takes shape according to this plan (words d, h, and l are compounds):

/ ab / ef / ij / mn / ba / fe / ji / nm / ab / ef / ij /
/ mn / bc / fg / jk / no / cba / gfe / kji / onm / ab /
/ ef / ij / mn / bc / fg / jk / no / cd / gh / kl / op /
/ dcba / hgfe / lkji / ponm / ab / ef / ij / mn / bc /
/ fg / jk / no / cd / gh / kl / op / d iti d^1d^2 /
/ h iti h^1h^2 / l iti l^1l^2 / p iti p //

Source Verse (Vājasaneyi-Saṃhitā 25.19), to Indra, Pūṣan, Tārkṣya, and Bṛhaspati:[41]

R S | W |V
svastí na índro vṛddháśravāḥ svastí naḥ pūṣā́ viśvávedāḥ /
Q S | W S |Q
svastí nas tā́rkṣyo áriṣṭanemiḥ svastí no bṛ́haspátir dadhātu //

Translation:

May Indra (indraḥ), of great renown (vṛddhaśravāḥ), grant (dadhātu) us (naḥ) prosperity (svasti); may Pūṣan (pūṣā), omniscient (viśvavedāḥ), grant (dadhātu) us (naḥ) prosperity (svasti); may Tārkṣya (tārkṣyaḥ), the rim of whose wheel is unbroken (ariṣṭanemiḥ), grant (dadhātu) us (naḥ) prosperity (svasti); may Bṛhaspati (bṛhaspatiḥ) grant (dadhātu) us (naḥ) prosperity (svasti).

Pada:

/ svastí / naḥ / índraḥ / vṛddháśravā íti vṛddhá--śravāḥ /
svastí / naḥ / pūṣā́ / viśvávedā íti viśvá--vedāḥ / svastí /
naḥ / tā́rkṣyaḥ / áriṣṭanemir íty áriṣṭa--nemiḥ / svastí /
naḥ / bṛ́haspátiḥ / dadhātv íti dadhātu //

Vikṛti:

svastí na-ḥ ≠ svastí na-ḥ ≠ svastí na-ḥ ≠ svastí na-ḥ ≠
3 2 2 2 3 2 2 2 3 2 2 2 3 2 2 2

[5]W W W W
na-ḥ * sva-stí ≠ na-ḥ svastí ≠ na-ḥ*sva-stí ≠ na-ḥ svastí ≠
2 2 1 212 2 2 1 2 2 2 1 212 1 2 1 2

[10]
svastí na-ḥ ≠ svastí na-ḥ ≠ svastí na-ḥ ≠ svastí na-ḥ ≠
3 2 2 2 3 2 2 2 3 2 2 212 2 2 2 2

R V [15] Q S
na índra-ḥ ≠ na- ḥ pūṣā / nas tā-rkṣya-ḥ ≠ no bṛhaspáti-ḥ /
21 12 21 2 212 2 2 2 1 212 1 2 2 3 2 2 2 2

S W W S W
índro na-ḥ sva-stí ≠ pū- ṣā na-ḥ * sva-stí ≠ tārkṣyo na-ḥ
1 212 2 2 1 212 232 2 2 2 1 212 2 212 1 2

[20] Q W
svastí / bṛhaspátir na-ḥ svastí ≠ svastí na-ḥ / svastí na-ḥ ≠
1 2 3 2 2 2 1 2 1 2 3 2 2 2 2 1 1 2

[25]R V Q
svastí na-ḥ ≠ svastí na-ḥ / na índra-ḥ ≠ na-ḥ pū-ṣā / nas
3 2 2 2 3 2 2 2 2 1 21 2 1 2 232 2 1

S S [30]
tā-rkṣya-ḥ ≠ no bṛhaspáti-ḥ / ín-dro vṛddháśravā-ḥ / pūṣā
212 1 2 2 3 2 2 2 2 1 212 2 3 2 2 2 1 1

S Q
viśvá-ve- dā- ḥ / tārkṣyo áriṣṭa-ne- mi-ḥ / bṛhaspá-tir
1 12 212 212 2 1 21 2 2 2 212 2 2 3 2 2 212

T S W V
da-dhātu / vṛddháśra-vā ín- dro na-ḥ sva-stí / viśvá-ve- dā- ḥ
2 212 2 1 1 1 21 212 212 2 2 1 212 1 1 212 212 2

W [35] Q S W
pū- ṣā na-ḥ sva-stí / áriṣṭanemis tā-rkṣyo na-ḥ sva-stí /
3232 2 2 2 1 212 2 2 1 1 1 212 212 2 2 1 212

Q W
da-dhātu bṛhaspá-tir na-ḥ sva-stí / svastí na-ḥ ≠ svastí na-ḥ ≠
1 212 2 2 2 2 212 2 2 1 212 1 1 1 2 3 2 2 2

[40] R V
svastí na-ḥ / svastí na-ḥ ≠ na ín-dra-ḥ / na-ḥ pū-ṣā /
3 2 2 2 1 1 1 2 1 212 2 2 1 2 1 212

Q S [45] S
nas tārkṣya-ḥ ≠ no bṛhaspáti-ḥ / ín-dro vṛddháśravā-ḥ /
1 1 1 2 32 3 2 2 2 2 1 212 2 2 2 2 2

S Q
pūṣā viśvá-ve- dā- ḥ / tārkṣyo áriṣṭanemi-ḥ / bṛhaspá-tir
1 1 1 12 212 212 2 3 21 2 2 2 2 2 2 1 1 1 212

T [50] T
da-dhātu / vṛddháśra-vā íti vṛddhá--śra-vā- ḥ / viśvávedā
2 212 2 1 1 1 21 2 2 2 21 12 212 2 3 2 2 21

Q D
íti viśvá--ve- dā- ḥ / áriṣṭa-ne- mir íty á-riṣṭa--nemi-ḥ /
2 2 2 21 212 212 2 2 2 12 212 2 1 12 1 12 2 2 2

D
dadhātv íti da-dhā-tu //
3 3 2 2 1 212 212

The Mādhyandina School: Analysis

Outline of tone usage

The following outline makes use of all or portions of the vikṛtis just presented:

- Jaṭā (J): complete
- Kramamālā (K): first hemistich
- Puṣpamālā (Pu): first hemistich
- Pañcasandhi (Pa): first hemistich
- Śikhā (Ś): first hemistich
- Rekhā (Re): complete
- Dhvaja (Dh): complete
- Daṇḍa (D): through sandhi unit 28
- Ratha (Ra): complete

Reference is made first to the name (abbreviated) of the vikṛti, then to the section (phonetic unit), and finally to the syllable of that section. For instance, the designation Re 3.4 refers to the third section, fourth syllable, of the rekhā vikṛti.

I. Syllables Sung to Single Pitches

A. High (1 or 1). Total: 210 (170 short, 40 long)

1. Initial in line, preceding syllable with high tone (excluding those initials before which breath is not

taken). Total: 97 (73 short, 24 long)

a. Preceding 1: J 7.10; Pu 23.1; Pa 4.1,18.1,23.1; Ś 12.9; Dh 23.1; D 8.1,12.1; Ra 33.1,34.1,37.1, 40.1,48.1,49.1. Total: 15 (12 short, 3 long)

b. Preceding 1: Pu 8.1,13.1,17.1; Pa 28.1; Dh 19.1, 28.1; D 11.1,16.1; Ra 30.1,43.1,46.1. Total: 11 (9 short, 2 long)

c. Preceding 12: K 10.1; Pu 25.1; Pa 14.1,16.1, 19.1,20.1; Dh 20.1; D 6.1. Total: 8 (3 short, 5 long)

d. Preceding 12: Ś 7.13. Total: 1 (short)

e. Preceding 21: Dh 8.1. Total: 1 (short)

f. Preceding 21: Ra 31.1. Total: 1 (long)

g. Preceding 212: Pa 12.1,32.1; Ś 14.1; Re 26.1; Dh 30.1,33.1; D 13.1,24.1. Total: 8 (4 short, 4 long)

h. Preceding 212: J 3.20,4.15,8.1,10.13,12.9; K 4.1,8.1; Pu 3.1,6.1,10.1,15.1,16.1,18.1,19.1, 21.1; Pa 6.1,10.1,21.1,25.1,27.1,31.1,34.1,36.1; Ś 6.19,7.1; Re 4.5,7.3,8.12,15.1,15.12,16.1,18.1, 22.1,24.1; Dh 7.1,26.1,29.1,34.1; D 20.1,22.1, 27.1,28.8; Ra 5.3,7.3,15.1,17.1,18.5,27.1,29.1, 36.1,45.1. Total: 51 (42 short, 9 long)

i. Preceding 2123: Ś 6.11. Total: 1 (short)

2. Initial in line, preceding 2: Pa 17.1,24.1; Ra 42.1. Total: 3 (short)

3. Medial in line, preceding a syllable with two or more tones, of which one of the tones is high: J 4.17,7.11,8.7; K 7.3; Pu 4.7,8.2,11.7,13.2,17.2, 18.7,25.5; Pa 19.3,23.2,28.2; Ś 11.7,11.23,12.10; Re 2.4,11.4,12.5,16.5,22.10,23.10,27.4; Dh 4.4,9.4,

11.5,12.3,18.4,19.2,26.3,27.4,28.2,32.4,35.5; D 8.2, 11.2,12.2,14.8,16.2,17.2,20.9,20.10,25.6,28.12; Ra 17.5,25.2,30.3,33.3,33.9,34.2,34.10,35.5,35.10, 36.10,41.1,42.3,46.3,48.3,49.3,51.6,51.8,52.5. Total: 63 (51 short, 12 long)

4. Medial in line, preceding a syllable sung to a single high tone: Ra 22.2,30.2,33.2,35.3,35.4, 37.2,40.2,43.2,46.2,48.2,49.2. Total: 11 (7 short, 4 long)

5. Medial in line, preceding visarga: Pu 23.2; Ra 8.1, 15.3,19.3,20.5,22.3,26.1,27.3,37.3,40.3. Total: 11 (short)

6. Medial in line, preceding hiatus: D 9.5,20.13. Total: 2 (short)

7. Medial in line, following hiatus: Ś 10.3; Re 14.7, 20.4; Dh 21.7,22.4. Total: 5 (short)

8. Medial in line, preceding a final retroflex consonant: Pa 3.3,4.3,16.3,17.3,20.3,23.4,24.3. Total: 7 (short)

9. Medial in line, the first of two conjunct consonants (syllable with high tone precedes and follows): Pa 4.2,18.2. Total: 2 (short)

10. Medial in line, preceding middle tone: Ś 7.19; Dh 23.2; Ra 6.3,8.3,19.5,20.7. Total: 6 (short)

B. Middle (2 or 2). Total: 858 (632 short, 226 long)

1. The most often used method of realizing short and long syllables (excluding special cases, listed below). Total: 607 (436 short, 179 long)

   a. Only 31 of these are initial in the line, excluding beginning of sections before which breath is not taken.

(1) Precede short syllables

1: D 17.1,20.8; Ra 22.1

2: Pa 1.1; Ś 1.1; Re 10.3; D 18.1,23.1, 26.1; Ra 35.1,51.1

(2) Precede long syllables

1: Ra 25.1

2: J 1.10; Pu 1.1

21: Dh 12.1,17.1

212: J 3.1,7.1; K 16.1; Pa 2.1,9.1; Ś 3.8, 5.4,6.1; Re 13.7,21.1; Dh 10.1,11.1,14.1 15.1,24.1

2. Short middle tone, occurring on long syllables or ghuṃ immediately before breath is taken. Normally a long tone would appear here, but the syllables are not held for full duration. J 1.9,3.11,3.19,4.14, 4.21,7.19,9.7,10.12,12.8; Ś 3.7,5.3,6.10,6.18,7.16, 9.14,13.10; Re 4.4,7.2,8.11,10.2,13.6,23.8; Dh 14.5, 9.8,20.7,28.7; Ra 14.4,26.4. Total: 28 (short)

3. The a-sound following final consonants: J 2.10, 3.23,4.27,5.9,6.13,7.27,12.15,13.8; K 1.6,2.6,13.6, 14.7,15.6; Pu 8.6,10.6,13.6; Pa 1.4,3.4,4.4,5.4,8.5, 9.5,16.4,17.4,20.4,23.5,24.4,26.6,27.5,30.6,33.5,34.5; Ś 9.24,12.19,13.16,14.8; Re 11.6,15.14,17.9,21.5,22.13, 23.12,27.7; Dh 2.9,4.7,9.6,10.6,12.5,17.9,24.5,26.6, 27.6,32.7,34.9; D 26.9. Total: 55 (short)

4. Final visarga: J 9.16; K 5.7,10.5; Pu 15.6,17.6,19.7, 20.7,21.7,22.6,23.7,24.6,25.9,27.4; Ś 2.9; Re 8.15, 13.10,14.14,16.15,18.7,20.9; Dh 13.10,15.6,16.7,18.7, 19.6,21.14,22.9,23.11; D 7.6,8.7,11.6,12.7,16.6,17.7, 22.6,23.7; Ra 5.2,7.2,10.4,16.6,18.4,21.4,24.4,28.6, 29.7,30.7,31.8,39.4,41.4,44.6,45.7,46.7,47.8,49.11,

50.11,51.12. Total: 56 (55 short, 1 long)

5. Medial visarga: Pu 19.3,21.3,23.3; Ś 1.5; Re 12.7, 15.6,16.11,18.3; Dh 16.3; D 8.4,12.4,13.3,17.4,18.3, 23.4,24.3; Ra 6.2,8.2,14.2,17.4,19.4,20.6,26.2,33.8, 34.5,34.9,35.9,36.9,42.2. Total: 29 (long)

6. Final visarga after which breath is not taken: Ra 1.4, 2.4,3.4,4.4,9.4,12.4,13.4,15.4,22.4,23.4,25.4,27.4, 37.4,38.4,40.4,43.4. Total 16 (long)

7. Final short syllable after which breath is not taken: Ra 6.4,8.4,20.8. Total: 3 (long)

8. First of two conjunct consonants (when first is voiced?): Pa 17.2,24.2. Total: 2 (long)

9. Syllable preceding r plus consonant: K 6.5,9.3; Ra 20.4. Total: 3 (long)

10. Ghuṃ medial in line: J 3.8. Total: 1 (long)

11. Short syllable preceding hiatus: D 5.3; Ra 25.1. Total: 2 (short)

12. Short syllable following hiatus: Ś 8.5; D 15.2; Ra 49.5,50.5. Total: 4 (short)

13. Short syllable following separation in parigraha: J 6.10; Re 20.7; D 26.10; Ra 49.7. Total: 4 (short)

14. Short syllable preceding visarga: Pu 19.6,21.6,22.5; Re 13.9; Dh 13.9,16.6,23.6,25.6; D 4.5,7.5,18.2,22.5; Ra 1.3,2.3,3.3,4.3,5.1,6.1,7.1,9.3,10.3,11.3,12.3, 16.5,17.3,18.3,21.3,23.3,24.3,28.5,33.7,34.8,35.8, 36.8,38.3,39.3,41.3,44.5,47.7,51.11. Total: 40 (short)

15. The a-sound following the first of two conjuncts: Ś 7.21,9.5,9.10,9.19,11.3,11.13,11.18; Dh 23.3. Total: 8 (short)

C. Low (3 or 3). Total: 111 (100 short, 11 long)

1. Initial in line, followed by a low tone or by two or more tones of which the first is low (excluding those

initials before which breath is not taken).

a. Precede short syllables

3: Pu 20.1; Ś 11.15.

31: Pu 26.1,28.1.

b. Precede long syllables

3: Pu 11.1; Ra 52.1.

32: J 3.12,10.1.

32: J 4.1,5.1,11.1; Pu 4.1; Ś 8.1; Re 12.1, 17.1,23.1,28.1; Dh 9.1,27.1

2. Initial in line, followed by middle tone. Total: 47 (40 short, 7 long)

a. Precede short syllables

2: J 4.22,6.1,7.20,9.1,9.8,13.1; K 3.1,5.1,6.1, 13.1,14.1; Pu 22.1,24.1; Pa 7.1,11.1,15.1, 22.1,26.1,29.1,30.1; Ś 11.1,13.1,13.11; Re 1.1,9.1,14.1,19.1,20.1; Dh 1.1,3.1,4.1, 13.1,21.1,22.1,32.1,35.1; D 5.1,9.1; Ra 1.1, 11.1,20.1,32.1,50.1.

b. Precede long syllables

2: K 1.1,2.1; Ś 9.1,9.15.

3. Initial in line, followed by two or more tones of which the first is middle tone. Total: 3 (2 short, 1 long)

a. Precede short syllables

23: Pa 8.1,33.1

b. Precede long syllable

21: Ra 47.1

4. Medial in line, preceded by middle tone or by two or more tones of which the final tone is middle tone, and followed by a single middle tone: J 2.2,2.4,4.9,4.11, 4.24,5.3,7.3,7.15,7.22,8.3,12.4,13.4; K 3.3; Pu 19.4,

21.4,22.4,23.4; Ś 12.3; Re 3.1,13.1,15.7; D 4.3; Ra 2.1,3.1,4.1,9.1,10.1,16.2,21.1,23.1,24.1,28.2, 29.4,38.1,39.1,44.2. Total: 36 (short)

5. Medial in line, preceded by single low tone initial in line and followed by single middle tone: Pu 11.2; Ś 11.16; Ra 52.2. Total: 3 (1 short, 2 long)
6. Medial in line, preceded by single low tone initial in line and followed by low tone: Pu 20.2. Total: 1 (short)
7. Medial in line, preceded by single low tone not initial in line and followed by low tone: Pu 20.3. Total: 1 (short)
8. Medial in line, preceded by single low tone medial in line and followed by middle tone: Pu 20.4. Total: 1 (long)

II. Syllables Sung to Two or More Pitches

A. High-Middle (12, ♫). Total: 63 (short)

1. Medial in line, following high tone or a syllable with several tones of which one is high (syllables following hiatus excluded): K 10.2,12.4; Pu 25.2, 25.8,29.2; Pa 14.2,16.2,19.2,20.2; Ś 11.22,11.24; Re 2.5,16.6,20.5,21.3; Dh 18.5,20.2,20.4,22.5; D 8.3,11.3,11.4,20.11,25.7,28.13,28.14; Ra 30.4,46.4, 51.7,51.9. Total: 30. All but three (Pu 25.8; D 8.3; Ra 51.9) are followed by a syllable that has a high tone.
2. Following hiatus, the preceding syllable usually ending with high tone and the following syllable having a high tone: K 12.3; Pu 25.4; Ś 6.7,7.9; D 1.2,5.4,6.2,9.6,10.2,14.12,20.14,21.2,28.16; Ra 13.2. Total: 14

3. Following the first analyzed component in *parigraha* (the preceding syllable ending with high tone): *Pu* 25.7; *Dh* 22.7,25.8; *Ra* 49.9. Total: 4

4. Initial in line, followed by syllable with a high tone: *Pa* 35.1; *D* 7.1. Total: 2

5. Following middle tone, and followed by a syllable with a high tone: *Dh* 6.3,13.7; *D* 8.5,12.5,19.7,23.5,28.11; *Ra* 51.3. Total: 8

6. Initial in line, before which breath is not taken (syllable with high tone precedes and follows): *D* 2.1. Total: 1

B. High-Middle (1$\underline{2}$, ♫.). Total: 4 (long)

1. Following syllable with high tone (excluding the first syllable following hiatus): *Ś* 7.14,11.8,12.11. Total: 3

2. Following hiatus (*parigraha* separation also here): *Ś* 14.6. Total: 1

C. Middle-High (21, ♫𝄾). Total: 8 (short)

1. Short syllable preceding hiatus: *Pu* 25.3; *Re* 14.6, 20.3; *Dh* 21.6,22.3; *D* 14.11,28.15; *Ra* 13.1. Total: 8

D. Middle-High (21, ♫𝄾, ♫𝄾, ♩♪𝄾). Total: 32 (15 short, 17 long)

1. Preceding the separation in *parigraha*: *J* 2.6,6.9, 8.11; *Pu* 4.6,11.6,18.6,25.6; *Ś* 14.5; *Re* 14.9,20.6; *Dh* 11.7,17.6,21.9,22.6,25.7; *Ra* 49.8,50.8. Total: 17 (15 short, 2 long). The two long syllables constitute *visarga* (*Dh* 11.7,25.7). The separation in five cases (*J* 2.6; *Pu* 4.6,11.6,18.6; *Ś* 14.5) is that of hiatus between vowels.

2. Preceding hiatus (not *parigraha*): *K* 12.2; *Ś* 6.6,7.8, 7.12,8.4,10.2; *D* 1.1,3.1; *Ra* 31.2,33.4,47.2,49.4, 50.4. Total: 13 (long)

3. Syllable where final n preceded by ā has been changed to ṁ (middle tone held longer than usual): Re 13.3; Dh 13.3. Total: 2 (long)

E. Middle-High (21, ♫). Total: 5 (short)

1. Between two short middle tones: Pu 23.6,27.3; Ra 13.3. Total: 3 (short)
2. Between high tone and middle tone: Ra 25.3. Total: 1 (short)
3. Following hiatus: D 3.2. Total: 1 (short)

F. Middle-High (21, ♫.). Total: 8 (long)

1. Preceded by middle tone (or by several tones of which the last is mid-tone) and followed by a syllable having one tone as high tone: Ś 11.21; Re 9.10,16.9, 28.8; Dh 12.2,17.2. Total: 6 (long)
2. Initial in line, followed by syllable having one tone as high tone: Dh 5.1. Total: 1 (long)
3. Preceded by high tone and followed by a syllable with a high tone: Dh 8.2. Total: 1 (long)

G. Middle-Low (23, ♫). Total: 23 (short)

1. Followed by short middle tone: J 10.8,11.8; K 14.4; Pu 2.3,5.3,7.3,15.3,18.4; Pa 8.2,26.3,30.3,33.2; Ś 3.10,4.9,5.1,5.7,9.7; Re 4.7,7.5,9.14,24.6; Dh 7.3,29.3. Total: 23 (short)

H. Middle-Low (23, ♪.♪). Total: 6 (long)

1. Long syllable followed by short middle tone: Pu 9.2, 12.2,14.2,16.3; Pa 2.4,22.3. Total: 6 (long)

I. Middle-Low (23, ♩♩). Total: 1 (long)

1. Long syllable initial in line: Ś 3.1

J. Low-Middle (32, ♩♩). Total: 36 (long)

1. Long syllable initial in line. Total: 24
   a. Precede short syllables

2: J 1.1,12.1; Ś 12.1; D 15.1,19.1,25.1

3: J 2.1

12: D 10.1,21.1

b. Precede long syllables

2: K 7.1,11.1,15.1; Pu 2.1,5.1,7.1,9.1,12.1,14.1; Pa 13.1; Ś 7.17; Dh 16.1,18.1; D 28.1

21: K 12.1

2. Initial in line, before which breath is not taken: Ra 44.1. Total: 1

3. Following an initial short low tone: J 4.2,5.2,11.2; Pu 4.2; Ś 8.2; Re 12.2,17.2,23.2,28.2; Dh 9.2,27.2. Total: 11

K. Low-Middle (32,  ; ). Total: 3 (long)

1. Long syllable following an initial short low tone: J 3.13,10.2. Total: 2

2. Long syllable initial in line: Ś 10.1. Total: 1

L. Low-High (31, ). Total: 2 (short)

1. Short syllable preceded by initial short low tone and followed by syllable with a high tone: Pu 26.2, 28.2. Total: 2 (short)

M. Low-High (31,  ; ). Total: 1 (long)

1. Initial long syllable followed by syllable with high tone: Pu 29.1. Total: 1

N. Middle-High-Middle (212, ; ). Total: 296 (8 short, 288 long)

1. Long syllables (not visarga or ghuṃ). Total: 284. Of these only 5 are in initial position:

a. Preceding short syllables

1: Re 23.9

2: Pu 27.1; Pa 5.1; Dh 6.1

b. Preceding long syllable

212: *Re* 17.7

2. *Ghuṃ* medial in line: *J* 4.18. Total: 1 (long)
3. *Visarga* medial in line or in final position after which breath is not taken: *Re* 16.8; *Dh* 18.3; *Ra* 11.4. Total: 3 (long)
4. Final short syllable of hemistich, not at end of *vikṛti*: *Pu* 27.1; *Dh* 34.3. Total: 2
5. First syllable following *iti* in *parigraha*: *Re* 14.8; *Dh* 21.8. Total: 2 (both on short vowels)
6. Short syllable in final position not followed by breath: *Ra* 5.4,7.4,18.6. Total: 2
7. Final syllable in *vikṛti*: *Ra* 52.7. Total: 1 (short vowel)

D. Middle-High-Middle (212, ). Total: 108 (93 short, 15 long).

1. Short vowel final in line: *J* 8.13; *K* 4.6,7.4,8.5, 16.5; *Pu* 7.6,11.8,12.5,18.8,26.3,28.3,29.3; *Pa* 6.4, 7.3,10.4,11.4,13.3,14.3,15.4,18.4,19.4,21.4,25.4, 29.5,31.4,32.3,35.4,36.4; *Re* 1.6,3.6,5.7; *Dh* 8.5,28.5; *D* 4.6,18.9; *Ra* 17.6,33.10,34.11,35.11,35.11. Total: 40
2. Short syllable penultimate in line: *J* 8.12; *Pa* 6.3, 10.3,31.3,32.2,35.3,36.3; *Re* 1.5,3.5,5.6,19.4,26.3; *Dh* 24.3,30.3. Total: 14
3. Short vowel before *visarga*: *Pu* 24.5; *Re* 8.14,12.6, 16.7,18.6; *Dh* 11.6,18.6,22.8; *D* 8.6,11.5,12.3,12.6, 13.2,16.5,17.3,17.6,23.3,23.6,24.2; *Ra* 14.1. Total: 20. Half are penultimate in line (*Pu* 24.5; *Re* 8.14, 18.6; *Dh* 18.6,22.8; *D* 8.6,11.5,12.6,16.5,17.6,23.6).
4. Long vowel final in line: *Ś* 11.25; *Dh* 6.4,7.6,11.8, 20.5,29.6,30.4; *D* 2.3,10.3,14.14,15.3,19.8,20.16,27.4; *Ra* 42.4. Total: 15

5. Medial in line, short, preceded and/or followed by a syllable with high tone: Pu 8.3,13.3,17.3; Pa 12.2, 23.3; Ś 10.4,14.2; Re 14.4,14.11,25.3,26.2; Dh 8.3, 14.2,23.8,30.2,33.2; D 16.4,20.12. Total: 19

P. Middle-Low-Middle (232, ). Total: 11 (long)

1. Long syllable followed by middle tone or by several tones of which the first is middle tone: Ś 5.12,6.5, 6.9,7.3,7.7,7.11,7.15; Re 10.5,11.2; Ra 18.1,26.3.

Q. Low-Middle-Low (323, 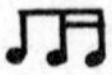). Total: 2 (long)

1. Long syllable initial in line, followed by middle tone: K 9.1; D 14.1.

R. Middle-High-Middle-High (2121, 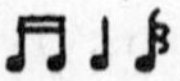). Total: 1 (long)

1. The ā-vowel preceding final n, changed to m̐: Dh 23.4.

S. Middle-High-Middle-Low (2123, 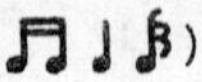). Total: 6 (2 short, 4 long)

1. Vowel followed by final m (changed euphonically to y̐ but written as anusvāra) plus initial y: K 16.2. Total: 1 (long)

2. Long syllable followed by short middle tone: Ś 6.12; Dh 10.2. Total: 2

3. Final syllable in vikṛti: Re 28.9; Dh 35.6. Total: 2 (short)

T. Low-Middle-Low-Middle (3232, ). Total: 1 (long)

1. Long syllable preceded and followed by middle tone: Ra 34.6, a variant of P.

U. Middle-High-Middle-Low-Middle (21232, ). Total: 2 (long)

1. Long syllable followed by middle tone (variant of P): Ś 6.17. Total: 1

2. Vowel plus final m (changed euphonically to v̐ but written as anusvāra) followed by initial v: Ś 13.5. Total: 1

Accent

Recitation of the Mādhyandina recension of the Vājasaneyi-Saṃhitā is in no way connected with the accentuation of the text. By comparing those units which have the same, or nearly the same, sequence of accents, we must conclude that factors other than accentuation are responsible for the tonal composition of the recitation. If A and U denote *anudātta* and *udātta*, respectively, then the series A-U-(-ḥ)-A-U (where *ḥ* is *visarga*) is recited in the following ways.

	A	U	(-ḥ)	A	U . . .
Pu 9:	32	$\underline{23}$		2	$\underline{2}$
Pu 12:	32	$\underline{23}$		2	$\underline{2}$
Pu 14:	32	$\underline{23}$		2	$\underline{2}$
Pu 15:	1	$21\underline{2}$		23	2
Pu 17:	1	$\underline{1}$		212	2
Pu 22:	3	2		$21\underline{2}$	3
Pu 24:	3	2		$21\underline{2}$	2
Pa 2:	2	$21\underline{2}$		2	$\underline{23}$
Pa 9:	2	$21\underline{2}$		2	$21\underline{2}$
Pa 27:	1	$21\underline{2}$		2	$21\underline{2}$
Pa 34:	1	$21\underline{2}$		2	$21\underline{2}$
D 4:	. . . 2	$\underline{2}$		3	2
D 7:	12	$21\underline{2}$		2	2
D 11:	1	$\underline{1}$		12	12
D 16:	1	$\underline{1}$		12	212
D 22:	1	$21\underline{2}$		2	2
D 13:	1	212	$\underline{2}$	$21\underline{2}$	2

	A	U	(-ḥ)	A	U . . .
D 18:	2	2	$\underline{2}$	$21\underline{2}$	2
D 24:	1	212	$\underline{2}$	$21\underline{2}$	2
Ra 16:	. . . $\underline{2}$	3		2	2

Ra 28	. . . 2	3	2	2
Ra 44:	. . . 32	3	2	2
Ra 30:	1	1	1	12
Ra 46:	1	1	1	12

From this list it is apparent that no series of tones can be put forth as standard for the pattern A-U-A-U. Possibly Mādhyandina chanters have cultivated a large number of *vikṛtis* for the very reason that they are not required to pay attention to accent. *Vikṛti* recitation is greatly simplified when the adherence only to correct word order and the rules of *sandhi* is essential. The elimination of accent as an element of recitation removes the need to account tonally for the adjustments in accentuation brought on by the coupling of a word with itself or with a word which precedes or follows. This peculiar characteristic of the Mādhyandina White Yajurveda supports the proposition that this Veda originated after Ṛgveda, Sāmaveda, and Black Yajurveda. It need not be inferred that Kāṇva White Yajurveda and Śaunaka Atharvaveda (both of which are recited with accent) are earlier than the Mādhyandina Yajurveda, for adherents of these two schools seem to model their recitals after Ṛgveda recitation in the Mahārāṣṭrian style.[42] White Yajurvedīs in South India apparently are aware of the esoteric features of Mādhyandina recitation, which they look upon with some trepidation; most claim Kāṇva as their *śākhā*.[43]

Most of the factors which contribute to this unusual mode of recitation have been set forth in the outline previously presented. In drawing conclusions from this data, one can begin with the general statement that syllable length is a major determinant of pitch and that medial short syllables are sung mainly on tone 2, medial long syllables principally on 2 or 212. Other elements which influence the recital relate to line position (initiality, finality, the syllables preceding and following parigraha separation), to phonetics (hiatus, visarga, ghuṃ, conjuncts, final consonants), and to successions of short syllables. These categories will now be dealt with in more detail.

Initiality

In this study an initial is defined as a syllable which occurs either at the beginning of a phonetic unit or after breath is taken within that unit. The first syllables of the units with sandhi in the vikṛtis are, by that definition, initials; but they will not be considered as such if breath is not taken beforehand.

Of the 243 initials in the analyzed portion of Gajānan Śāstrī's program, 41.2% are high-tone; therefore this seems to be the preferred manner of realizing initiality. Fully 100 high tones, 47.6% of their total number, appear in this position. Most are short (76%), 69 of the 100 preceding long syllables; all but three of these are followed by a syllable having a high tone. A smaller number, 31, precede short syllables, all of which have a high tone. Over half (51%) of initial high tones precede the 21<u>2</u> pattern and can be viewed as anticipations of it.

Only 3.6% of all middle tones are initiatory, and a mere 12.8% of initials are mid-tone. Hence this pitch, the most recurrent of all the tones and tone patterns in the recitation, has primarily medial and final functions. Of the 31 middle tones beginning the line, 20 (64.5%) precede long syllables; 15 of these are followed by 21<u>2</u>. All middle tones preceding long syllables are short; only 3 of the 31 are long, and they precede short middle tone.

A substantial majority (61.3%) of all low tones occur as commencing pitches, and the percentage of initials that are low-tone (28.4%) is second only to that for beginning high tones. Most low-tone initials are short (61 of 69, or 88.4%), and 71% are followed by short syllables. Initial low tone is never followed by the 21$\underline{2}$ arrangement. Usually it is succeeded by middle tone (68.1% of all cases); the vast majority of these are short. When a long syllable follows, it is realized, in 75% of the examples, as 32, $\underline{3}$2, or $\underline{3}$--most often as 32.

The tone sequence 32 is found nearly always (97.2% of the time) on either an initial long syllable or else the long syllable following an initial short low tone. When initiatory it ordinarily comes before middle tone (83.3% of the cases), which is mainly long (58.3%). The progression 32 to 12 is the result of hiatus between the syllables; the sole instance of 32 followed by 21 is the consequence of the anticipation of hiatus. The one example of tone 3 following 32 indicates that the former may occur if several short syllables appear together.

Only 1.7% of the 21$\underline{2}$ schemes are found at the beginning of the line, and only 2.1% of all initials are sung in this manner. Most appear before short middle tone.

Other tones and tone sequences occur so rarely as initials that their usage is negligible.

TABLE 1

INCIDENCE OF INITIALITY

	1/$\underline{1}$	2/$\underline{2}$	3/$\underline{3}$	32	21$\underline{2}$
Number of Initials	100	31	69	24	5
Percentage Initial	47.6	3.6	61.3	66.7	1.7
Percentage of Initials	41.2	12.8	28.4	9.9	2.1

Finality

Most final syllables (52%) at the ends of sections,

excluding final consonants and final *visarga*, are sung as 212. When the examples of final 21$\underline{2}$ are added, the percentage rises to 61.2. About one-third of final syllables (33.7%) are confined to short middle tone. The remaining patterns are used so little that they can be discounted entirely: 21$\underline{2}$3 occurs at the conclusion of *dhvaja*, 12 is found only once, and $\underline{2}$ is met thrice. Final syllables within sections are invariably mid-tone. Most (82.8%) are short, regardless of the length of the vowel.

TABLE 2

INCIDENCE OF FINALITY

	2/$\underline{2}$	212	21$\underline{2}$	12	21$\underline{2}$3
Number of Finals	36	51	9	1	1
Percentage Final	4.2	47.2	3.0	1.6	16.7
Percentage of Finals	36.7	51.0	9.2	1.0	1.0

Parigraha Analysis

The syllable prior to separation is usually sung $\underline{2}$1 (73.9% of all cases). Therefore it resembles the syllable just before hiatus (see below), which uses the two pitches 76.5% of the time. Next in order of frequency are 2 and $\underline{2}$ (17.4%), but these and other pitches and patterns are deviations from the norm. Syllables following separation make the most use of 21$\underline{2}$ (39.1%), perhaps because so many of the syllables are long. Also fairly common are the 12 and 1$\underline{2}$ arrangements (21.7%), which characterize many of the syllables immediately after hiatus (see below). Third in order of importance are 2 and $\underline{2}$ (17.4%).

Hiatus

Syllables before hiatus are, in 76.5% of the examples, sung as 21 or $\underline{2}$1, regardless of vowel length. When the anticipatory syllable is initial, it is occasionally sung as 32. The tones 1, 1̲, and 2 appear less often. A significant 85.3% of the syllables make use of high tone either by itself or in conjunction with middle tone. Syllables following hiatus generally reverse the pattern of the preceding syllables, having 12 or 12̲ in 44.1% of the cases. Short and long high tone are next in frequency (29.4%), followed by syllables consisting of, or beginning with, middle tone (26.5%).

Visarga

Whether medial or final, *visarga* is almost always mid-tone (95.3% of all examples). It is long when either medial or final with no breath afterwards. When final before breath, it is normally short--regardless of the length of the preceding vowel. The patterns 2̲1/21 and 212̲ are used but rarely; the former occurs prior to the break in *parigraha*.

Over half (56.3%) of short syllables before *visarga* are mid-tone. Also utilized are 212 (28.2%) and high tone (15.5%). Long syllables preceding *visarga* are largely realized 212̲ (68%), less often as middle tone (32%).

Ghuṃ

Medial *ghuṃ* has the length of a long vowel. It can be sung as 2̲, 212̲, or 12̲. The solitary example of final *ghuṃ* made use of short middle tone, thus echoing the treatment of final long vowels. Where high tone appeared in connection with *ghuṃ*, the anticipatory tone was high. Mid-tone *ghuṃ* is preceded by middle tone.

Conjuncts

The first of two conjuncts is sometimes pronounced with an *a*-vowel. In 83.3% of the examples it is mid-tone, and mainly short (66.7%). The two examples of long middle tone occurred on voiced retroflex consonants. The high-tone conjuncts are short.

Final Consonants

The a-sound following final consonants, including consonants prior to the break in parigraha, is always short mid-tone. All examples except two (Dh 23.3, D 29.9) are found at the end of a sandhi unit. When breath is taken within a section, a preceding nasal is not pronounced with an a-sound; in the same context, stops, semivowels, and fricatives--which would normally be finals--are pronounced after breath is taken.

When a final consonant is a nasal, the preceding vowel, whether long or short, is sung usually as 212 (88.6% of all examples), less often as 2 (11.4%). Final t was always preceded by a long vowel sung 212, and final ṭ by a short vowel realized as short high tone.

Successive short syllables

The most frequently encountered method of singing two or more successive short syllables is the utilization of middle tone and low tone in various permutations. These two pitches are used by a significant 29.7% of the examples, which have them mainly at the beginning of the line, where low tone is the initial pitch. Found mainly within the line are successions of middle tones (21.8%), met only rarely as initials. Also found principally in mid-line is the combination of 23 with 2 (8.7%). The remaining nineteen combinations comprise less than 40% of samples. Of these should be particularly pointed out the series of high tones, which appears always at the beginning of the line.

Protracted syllables

Circumstances arise when syllables are held beyond the normal value of a long vowel. Protraction is predictable on final -ān changed euphonically to -āṁ before an initial vowel. The pattern 212 (final tone extended) is preferred in 50% of the instances. Extensions are occasionally met also in connection with a long syllable followed by short middle tone and with the final syllable in an uninterrupted recitation. The grouping 2123 predominates for both situations.

Other Mādhyandina Recitations

Fragment from a mixed vikṛti

The conclusions reached above are valid only for the recitation of Gajānan Śāstrī Musalgāvkar and not necessarily for Mādhyandina traditions everywhere. By comparing extracts from performances by two additional reciters, we are able to determine the extent of agreement with Gajānan Śāstrī and to isolate characteristics which may apply universally to Mādhyandina recitation.

Transcribed below is a vikṛti fragment sung by Rājārām Bhaṭ Nirmale, another well-known Vārāṇasī Vājasaneyī, who is admired especially for his recitations from the Śatapatha-Brāhmaṇa. He had his vedādhyayana in Vāraṇasī under Babbū Nirmale. The excerpt is from a mixed (saṃyukta) vikṛti which has no independent name. The complete exposition presents jaṭā followed by pañcasandhi, ghana, and puṣpamālā.

Source Verse:

V E S
sá naḥ pitéva sūnávé 'gné sūpāyanó bhava /

A W
sácasvā naḥ svastáye //

Translation:

Agni (agne), be (bhava) easily accessible (sūpāyanaḥ) to us (naḥ), like father (piteva) to son (sūnave); accompany (sacasva) us (naḥ) for good fortune (svastaye).

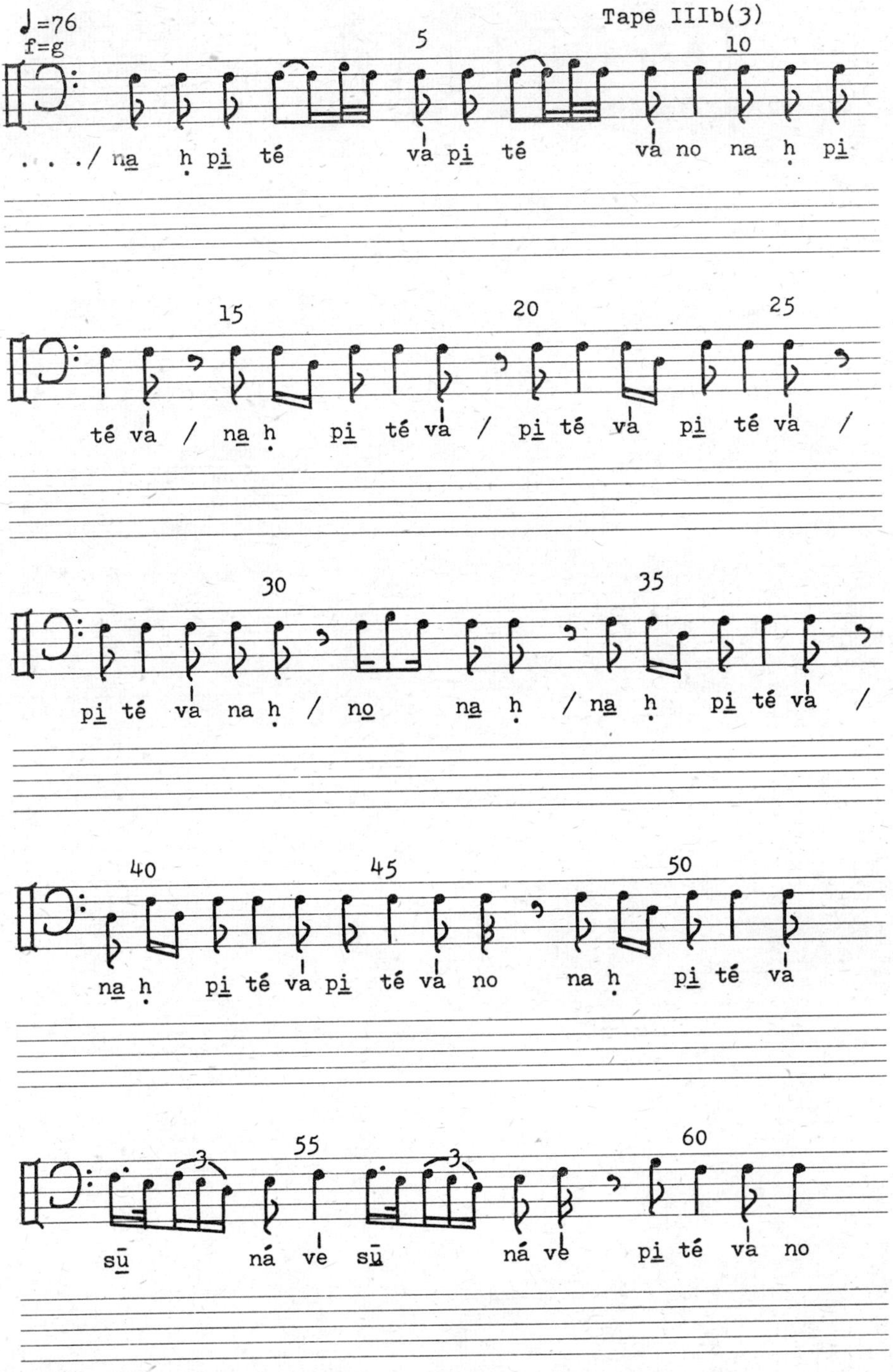

♩=76
f=g
Tape IIIb(3)
. . . / na ḥ pi té va pi té va no na ḥ pi
té va / na ḥ pi té va / pi té va pi té va /
pi té va na ḥ / no na ḥ / na ḥ pi té va /
na ḥ pi té va pi té va no na ḥ pi té va
sū ná ve sū ná ve pi té va no

65
70
na ḥ pi té va sū ná ve . . .

The three tones employed by Gajānan Śāstrī are found here as well, intervallically related in the same way. But one finds also the appearance of a fourth tone, between middle tone and low tone at the interval of a minor second below middle tone. It occurs on long syllables as a passing tone between middle tone and low tone (see syllables 53, 56, 68--this last a variant) and on short syllables between preceding low tone and following middle tone (54, 57, 69). As expected, long vowels have twice the value of short vowels, regardless of the presence of conjuncts (not found in the extract). But medial visarga is short in this performance and is sung either to middle tone (2, 11) or to middle tone followed by low tone (16, 22, 35, 40, 49, 64). Only a quick perusal of the fragment reveals the preponderance of long and short middle tone: 54 of the 70 syllables are sung to this pitch. It follows that this reciter likewise pays no attention to the accentuation of the text. Reference need be made only to syllables 41-48, which have the accents A-U-S-A-U-S-P-P, all sung to middle tone. This pitch predominates even among the initials (all short), which use high tone and low tone only once each (59, 39). The 21<u>2</u> grouping, which appears so often on long syllables in Gajānan Śāstrī's recital, is found here too but with altered rhythm: <u>2</u>12 (see syllables 4, 7). However, Rājārām Bhaṭ also uses patterns not even hinted at by Gajānan Śāstrī (see 53, 56, 68).

The puruṣa hymn

A more tonally varied rendition is that of the famous pûrûṣa-sūkta (Hymn of the Cosmic Man), as performed by Kapildev Prasād Miśr, a pupil of Maṅgal Datt Tripāṭhī (Retired Lecturer, Saṃskṛta Mahāvidyālaya, Banāras Hindu University).

Source Verses (Vājasaneyi-Saṃhitā 31.1-22):

V W
1. sahásraśīrṣā pū́ruṣaḥ sahasrākṣáḥ sahásrapāt /

K B D H
sá bhū́mim̐ sarváta spṛtváty atiṣṭhad daśāṅgulám //

R C K L H L M
2. pū́ruṣa evédám̐ sárvam yád bhūtám yác ca bhāvyam /

B C S H B
utāmṛtatvásyéśāno yád ánnenātiróhati //

B S P
3. etā́van asya mahimā́to jyā́yām̐ś ca pū́ruṣaḥ /

S L H B J
pā́do 'sya víśvā bhūtā́ni tripā́d asyāmṛ́tam diví //

H R H V S C B
4. tripā́d ūrdhvá úd ait pū́ruṣaḥ pā́do 'syehā́bhavat púnaḥ /

S D
táto víṣvaṅ vy akrāmat sāśanānaśané abhí //

S H S
5. táto virā́ḍ ajāyata virā́jo ádhi pū́ruṣaḥ /

S D H
sá jātó áty aricyata paścā́d bhū́mim átho puráḥ //

H W J
6. tásmād yajñā́t sarvahū́taḥ sámbhṛtam pṛṣadājyám /

P P L T U
paśū́m̐s tā́m̐ś cakre vāyavyān āraṇyā́ grāmyā́ś ca yé //

H R W
7. tásmād yajñā́t sarvahū́ta ṛ́caḥ sā́māni jajñire /

H Q H
chándām̐si jajñire tásmād yájus tásmād ajāyata //

H T C
8. tásmād áśvā ajāyanta yé ké cobhayā́dataḥ /

M T
gā́vo ha jajñire tásmāt tásmāj jātā́ ajāváyaḥ //

L J C J
9. tám yajñám barhíṣi práukṣan pū́ruṣam jātám agratáḥ /

T T U
téna devā́ ayajanta sādhyā́ ṛ́ṣayaś ca yé //

L D V D
10. yát pū́ruṣam vy ádadhuḥ katidhā́ vy akalpayan /

J B J G
múkham kím asyāsīt kím bāhū́ kím ūrū́ pā́dā ucyete //

S H V
11. brāhmaṇó 'sya múkham āsīd bāhū́ rājanyàḥ kṛtáḥ /

H H V K S
ūrū tád asya yád vāiśyaḥ padbhyām̐ śūdrō ajāyata //

T S U W S
12. candrámā mánaso jātáś cákṣoḥ sūryo ajāyata /

H U U H Q
śrótrād vāyúś ca prāṇáś ca múkhād agnír ajāyata //

T H K S W
13. nābhyā āsīd antárikṣam̐ śīrṣṇó dyáuḥ sám avartata /

J Q W L O
padbhyām bhūmir díśaḥ śrótrāt táthā lokām̐2 akalpayan //

T
14. yát púruṣeṇa havíṣā devā yajñám átanvata /

S B H J R W Y
vasanto 'syāsīd ājyam grīṣmá idhmáḥ śarád dhavíḥ //

B B Q W V
15. saptāsyāsan paridháyas tríḥ saptá samídhaḥ kṛtāḥ /

T H J T J
devā yád yajñám tanvānā ábadhnan púruṣam paśúm //

Q D
16. yajñéna yajñám ayajanta devās tāni dhármāṇi prathamāny

L
āsan /

J W W
té ha nākam mahimānaḥ sacanta yátra pūrve sādhyāḥ

sánti devāḥ //

Translation:

1. Puruṣa (puruṣaḥ) has a thousand heads (saharaśīrṣā), a thousand eyes (sahasrākṣaḥ), a thousand feet (sahasrapāt). Releasing (spṛtvā) earth (bhūmim) on all sides (sarvata), he (saḥ) is protruding (atiṣṭhat) the length of ten fingers (daśāṅgulam) beyond (ati).

2. Puruṣa (puruṣaḥ) is truly (eva) this (idam) all (sarvam): what (yat) has been (bhūtam) and (ca) what (yat) will be (bhāvyam). He is master (īśānaḥ) also (uta) of immortality (amṛtatvasya)

and whatever (yat) thrives (atirohati) by [consuming] food (annena).

3. So great (etāvān) is his (asya) majesty (mahimā), and yet (ca) Puruṣa (puruṣaḥ) is greater (jyāyān) than this (ataḥ). All (viśvā) beings (bhūtāni) are one-fourth (pādaḥ) of him (asya); three-fourths (tripāt) of him (asya) are the immortal (amṛtam) in heaven (divi).

4. Puruṣa (puruṣaḥ), rising (ūrdhvaḥ), rose (ait) up (ut) by three quarters (tripāt); a quarter (pādaḥ) of him (asya) assumed (abhavat) here (iha) a new state (punaḥ) [of existence]. From there (tataḥ), all-pervading (viṣvaṅ), he advanced (akrāmat) here and there (vi) towards (abhi) that which eats and does not eat (sāśanānaśane).

5. From him (tataḥ) Virāj (virāṭ) was born (ajāyata) and from Virāj (virājaḥ) Puruṣa (puruṣaḥ) besides (adhi). Once born (jātaḥ) he (saḥ) removed himself (aricyata) beyond (ati) the earth (bhūmim), behind (paścāt) and also (athaḥ) before (puraḥ).

6. From that (tasmāt) sacrifice (yajñāt), offered completely (sarvahutaḥ), clarified butter (pṛṣad-ājyam) was collected (sambhṛtam). He made (cakre) those (tān) animals (paśūn) which (ye) are in the air (vāyavyān), in the forest (āraṇyaḥ), and (ca) in the village (grāmyaḥ).

7. From that (tasmāt) sacrifice (yajñāt), offered completely (sarvahutaḥ), the verses (ṛcaḥ) and chants (sāmāni) were born (jajñire). The meters (chandāṃsi) were born (jajñire) from it (tasmāt); the yajus (yajuḥ) was born (ajāyata) from it (tasmāt).

8. From it (*tasmāt*) horses (*aśvāḥ*) were born (*ajāyanta*) and (*ca*) any creatures whatsoever (*ye ke*) with teeth in both jaws (*ubhayādataḥ*). Indeed (*ha*) cows (*gāvaḥ*) were born (*jajñire*) from it (*tasmāt*), and goats and sheep (*ajāvayaḥ*) were born (*jātāḥ*) from it (*tasmāt*).

9. They sprinkled (*pra aukṣan*) that (*tam*) sacrifice (*yajñam*), Puruṣa (*puruṣam*), born (*jātam*) in the beginning (*agrataḥ*) on the sacred grass (*barhiṣi*). With him (*tena*) gods (*devāḥ*), Sādhyas (*sādhyāḥ*), and (*ca*) seers (*ṛṣayaḥ*) sacrificed (*ayajanta*).

10. When (*yat*) they divided (*vy adadhuḥ*) Puruṣa (*puruṣam*), he was disposed (*vy akalpayan*) in how many parts (*katidhā*)? What (*kim*) was (*āsīt*) his (*asya*) mouth (*mukham*), what (*kim*) [were his] arms (*bāhū*)? What (*kim*) were [his] thighs (*ūrū*) and feet (*pādau*) called (*ucyete*)?

11. The Brāhmaṇ (*brāhmaṇaḥ*) was (*āsīt*) his (*asya*) mouth (*mukham*), his arms (*bāhū*) form (*kṛtaḥ*) the Rājanya (*rājanyaḥ*). Consequently (*tat . . . yat*) his (*asya*) two thighs (*ūrū*) were the Vaiśya (*vaiśyaḥ*), and from his feet (*padbhyām*) the Śūdra (*śūdraḥ*) was born (*ajāyata*).

12. The moon (*candramāḥ*) was born (*jātaḥ*) from his mind (*manasaḥ*), from his eye (*cakṣoḥ*) the sun (*sūryaḥ*) was born (*ajāyata*). From his ear (*śrotrāt*) Vāyu (*vāyuḥ*) and (*ca*) Prāṇa (*prāṇaḥ*) [were born], and (*ca*) from his mouth (*mukhāt*) Agni (*agniḥ*) was born (*ajāyata*).

13. From [his] navel (*nābhyāḥ*) the atmosphere (*antarikṣam*) came into existence (*āsīt*); from [his] head

(*śīrṣṇaḥ*) heaven (*dyauḥ*) came into being (*sam avartata*). From [his] feet (*padbhyām*) earth (*bhūmiḥ*) [appeared]; from [his] ear (*śrotrāt*) the quarters (*diśaḥ*) [appeared]; thus (*tathā*) they created (*akalpayan*) the worlds (*lokān*).

14. When (*yat*) the gods (*devāḥ*) performed (*atanvata*) the sacrifice (*yajñam*) with Puruṣa (*puruṣeṇa*) as offering (*haviṣā*), spring (*vasantaḥ*) was (*āsīt*) its (*asya*) clarified butter (*ājyam*), summer (*grīṣmaḥ*) [its] fuel (*idhmaḥ*), autumn (*śarat*) [its] oblation (*haviḥ*).

15. Seven (*sapta*) enclosing sticks (*paridhayaḥ*) were (*āsan*) for him (*asya*), and three times seven (*triḥ sapta*) pieces of firewood (*samidhaḥ*) were fashioned (*kṛtāḥ*) when (*yat*) the gods (*devāḥ*), performing (*tanvānāḥ*) the sacrifice (*yajñam*), bound (*abadhnan*) Puruṣa (*puruṣam*) as victim (*paśum*).

16. Through the sacrifice (*yajñena*) the gods (*devāḥ*) sacrificed (*ayajanta*) the sacrifice (*yajñam*); these (*tāni*) were (*āsan*) the first (*prathāmani*) statutes of law (*dharmaṇi*). Indeed (*ha*) these (*te*) great ones (*mahimānaḥ*) reached (*sacanta*) the vault of heaven (*nākam*), where (*yatra*) the ancient (*pūrve*) Sādhya (*sādhyāḥ*) gods (*devāḥ*) dwell (*santi*).

Three tones are employed, the lowest a minor second below mid-tone, the highest a major second above. Solitary low tone is always short in this performance; it occurs either initially in the line prior to a syllable with middle tone (syllables 11,21,442,495) or else medially, following and/or preceding middle tones (47,49-50,71,81,88,94,99,101,111,114,135, 137,140,142,148,156,171,175,182,191,194,201-2,205-6,213,231,236,

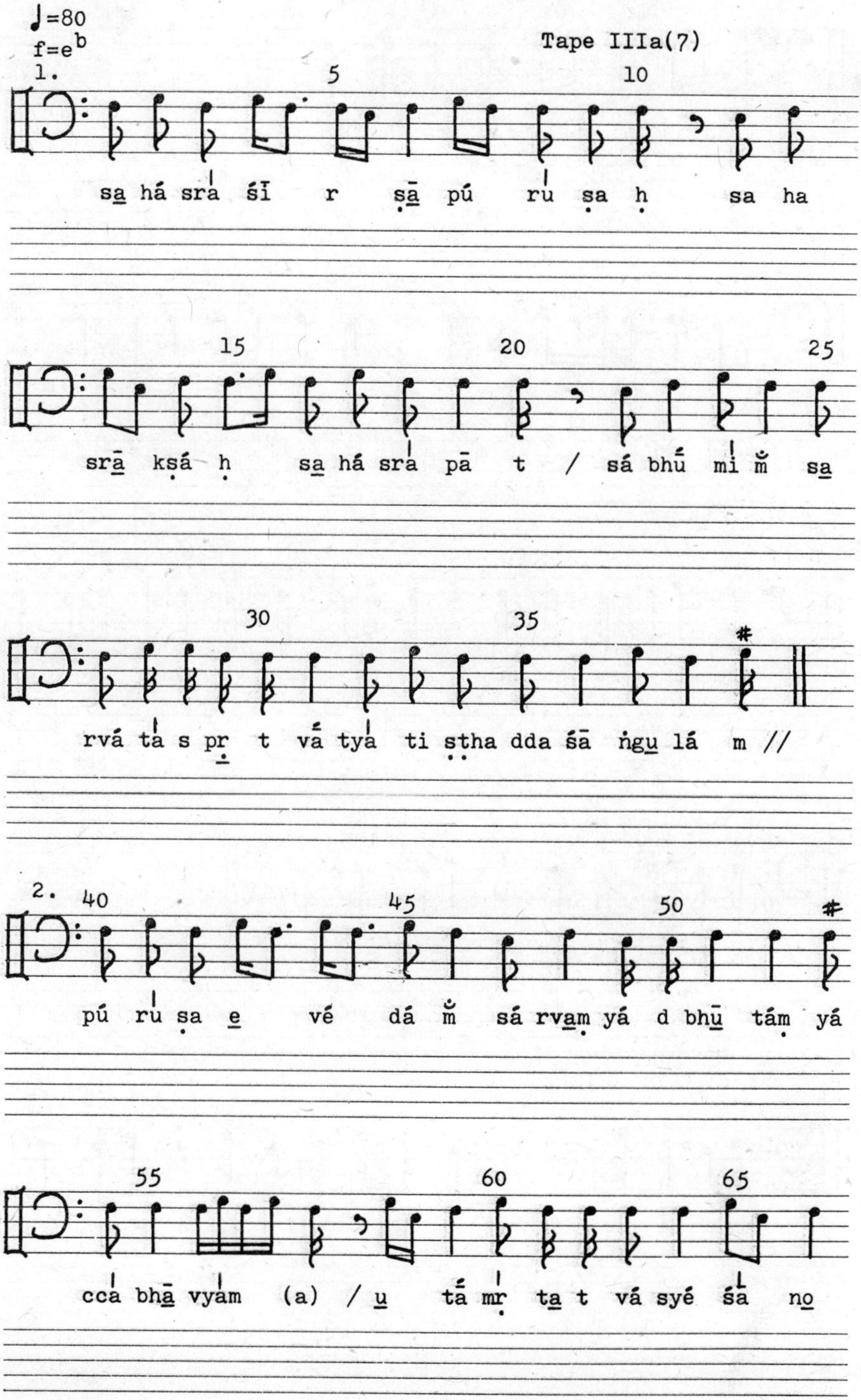

♩=80
f=e♭
Tape IIIa(7)
1.
sa̲ há sra śī r ṣa̲ pú ru ṣa ḥ sa ha
srā kṣá ḥ sa̲ há sra pā t / sá bhū mi m̐ sa̲
rvá ta s pṛ t vá tya ti ṣṭha dda śā ṅgu̲ lá m //
2.
pú ru ṣa e̲ vé dá m̐ sá rvam̱ yá d bhū̲ tám̱ yá
cca bhā̲ vyam (a) / u̲ tā mṛ ta̲ t vá syé śā no̲

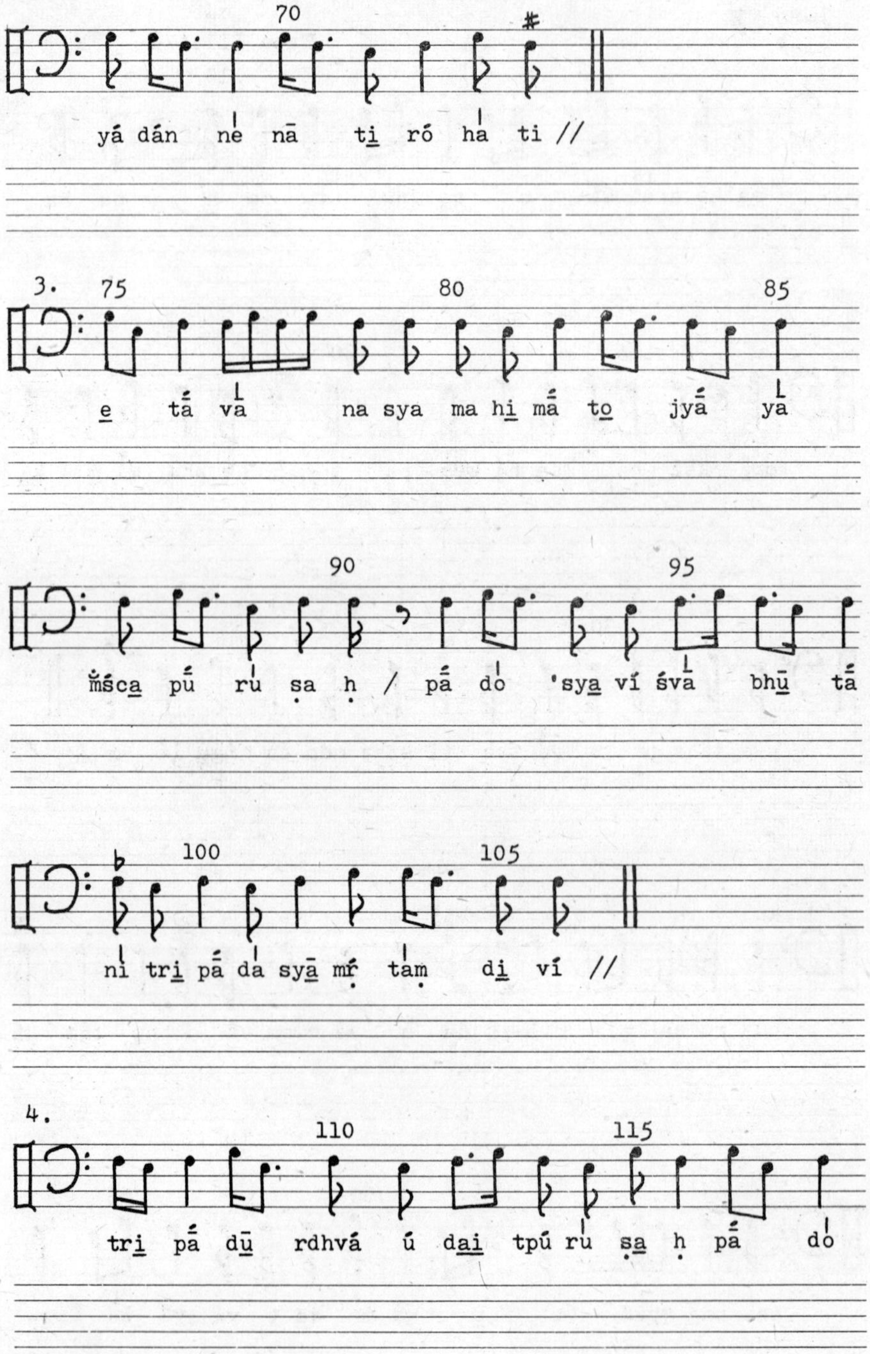
70
yá dán ne nā ti ró ha ti //
3.
75 80 85
e tā́ va na sya ma hi mā́ to jyā́ ya
90 95
m̐śca pū́ ru ṣa ḥ / pā́ do 'sya ví śva bhū tā́
100 105
ni tri pā́ da syā mṛ taṃ di ví //
4.
110 115
tri pā́ dū rdhvá ú dai tpú ru ṣa ḥ pā́ do

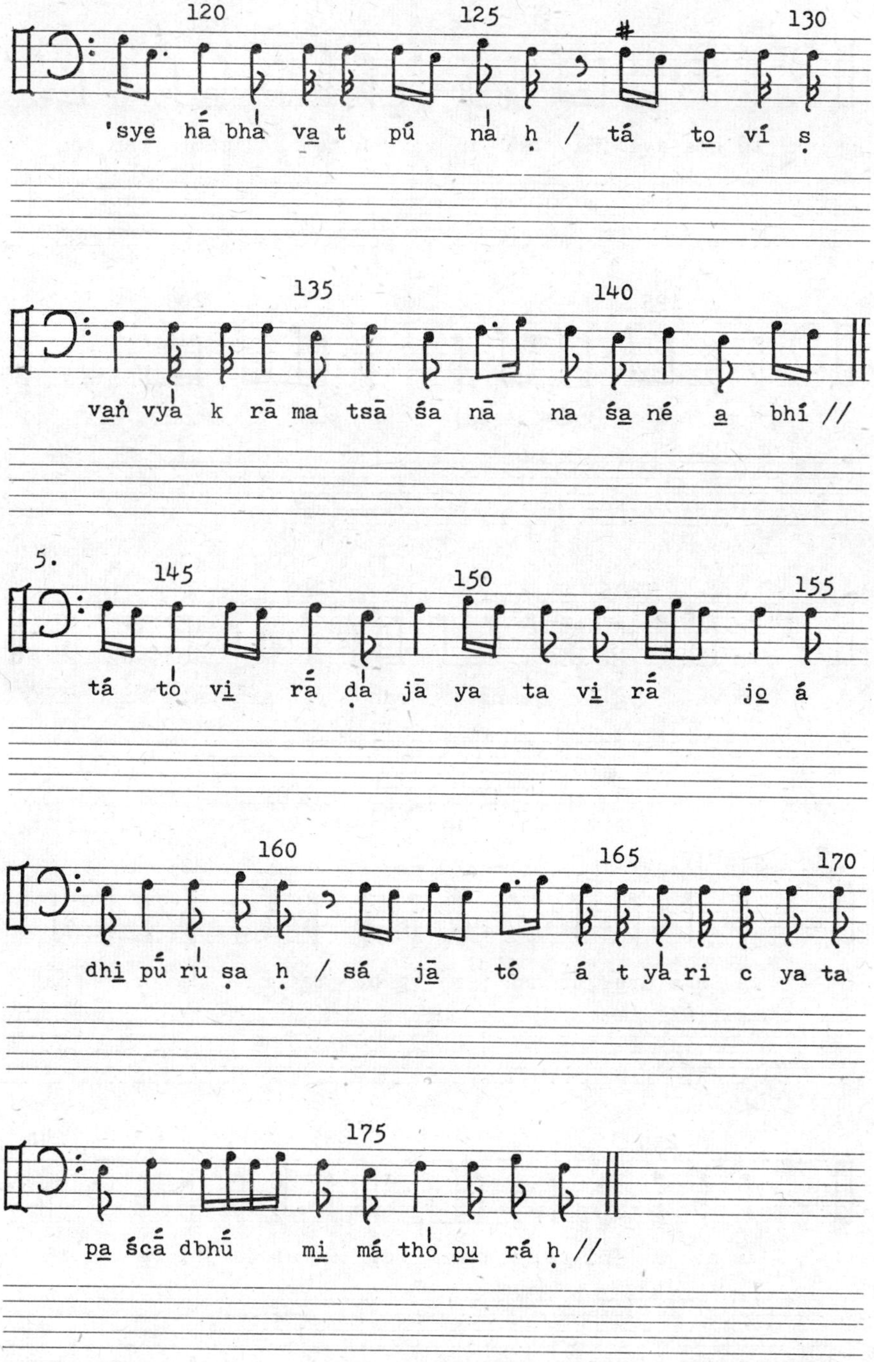
120 125 130
'sye hā bha va t pú na ḥ / tá to ví ṣ
135 140
vaṅ vya k rā ma tsā śa nā na śa né a bhí //
5.
145 150 155
tá to vi rā ḍa jā ya ta vi rā jo á
160 165 170
dhi pū ru ṣa ḥ / sá jā tó á t ya ri c ya ta
175
pa ścā dbhū mi má tho pu rá ḥ //

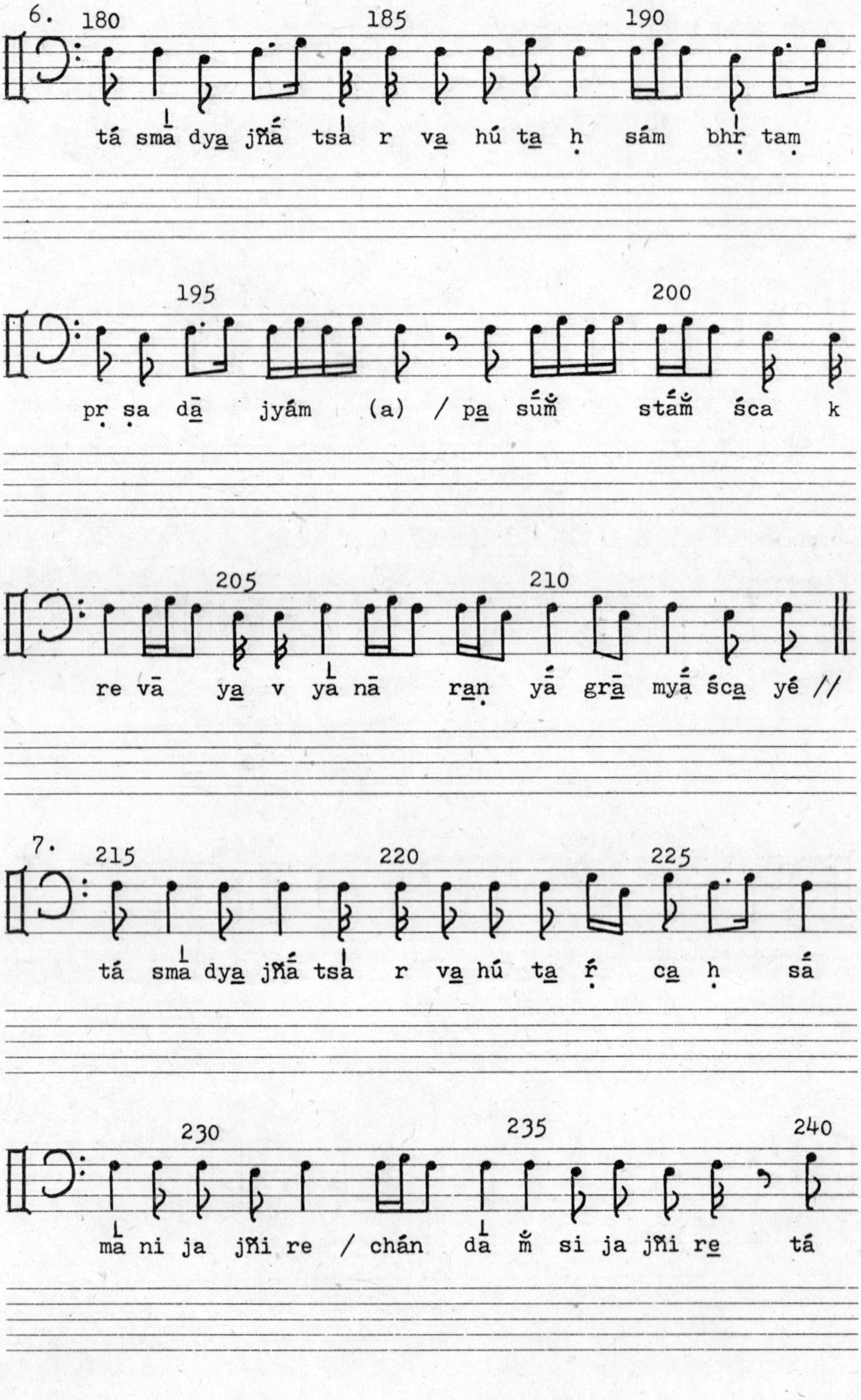
6. 180 185 190
tá smā dya jñā tsa r va hú ta ḥ sám bhṛ taṃ
195 200
pṛ ṣa dā jyám (a) / pa sūṁ stāṁ śca k
205 210
re vā ya v ya nā raṇ yā grā myā śca yé //
7. 215 220 225
tá smā dya jñā tsa r va hú ta ṛ́ ca ḥ sā
230 235 240
mā ni ja jñi re / chán da ṁ si ja jñi re tá

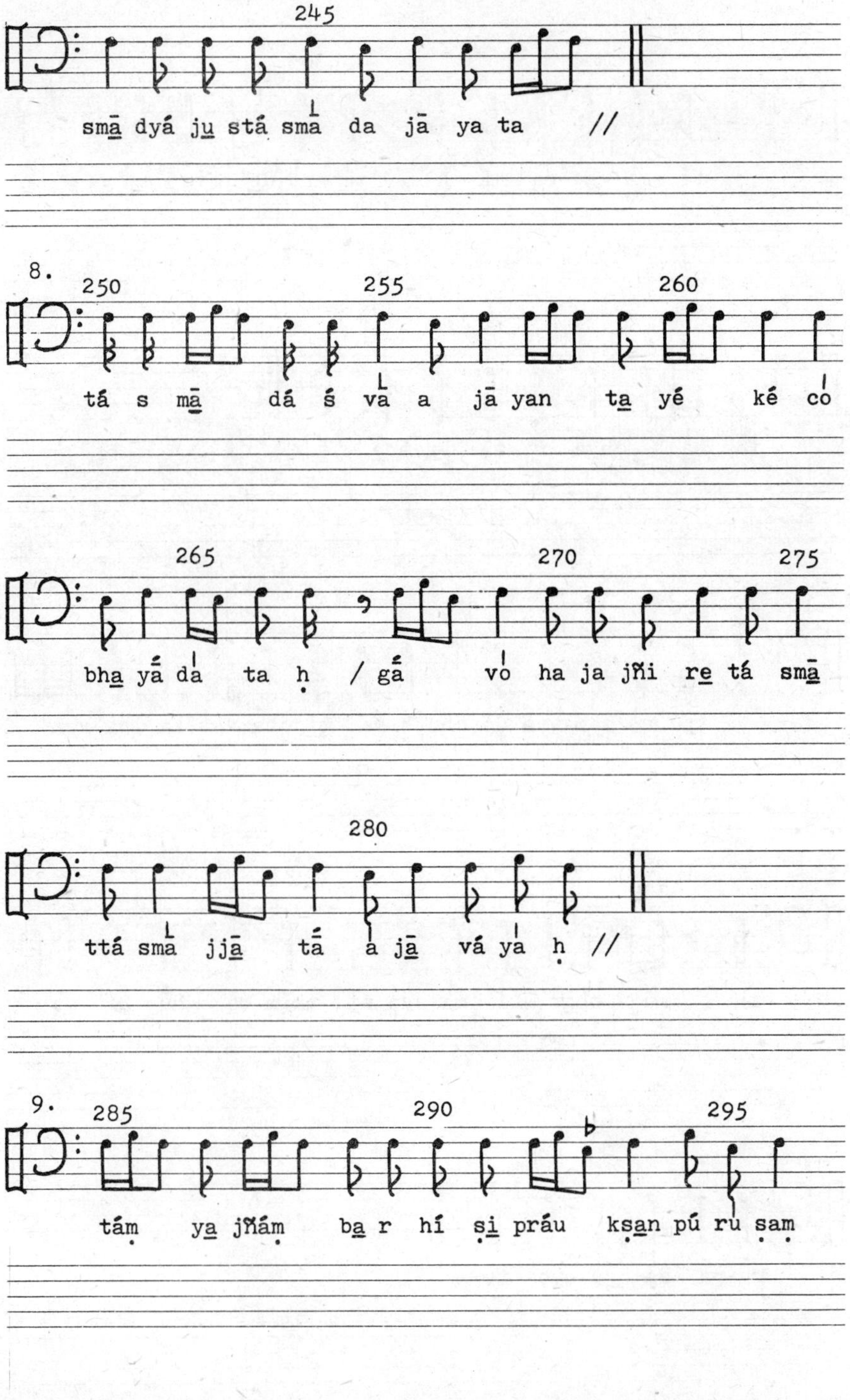
245
smā̲ dyá ju̲ stā́ sma da jā ya ta //
8. 250 255 260
tá s mā̲ dá ś va a jā yan ta̲ yé ké co
265 270 275
bha̲ yā́ da ta ḥ / gā́ vo ha ja jñi re̲ tá smā̲
280
ttá sma jjā̲ tā́ a jā̲ vá ya ḥ //
9. 285 290 295
táṃ ya̲ jñáṃ ba̲ r hí ṣi̲ práu kṣa̲n pú ru ṣaṃ

300 305 310
ja̲ tá ma g ra̲ tá ḥ / té na de̲ vá a ya jan
315
ta sa̲ dhyá ṛ́ ṣa ya śca̲ yé //
10. 320 325 330
yá tpú ru ṣa̲ṃ vyá da dhu ḥ ka ti̲ dhá vya ka lpa yan
335 340 345
(a) / mú kha̲ṃ kí ma syā sī̲ tkím bā̲ hú kí mū̲
350
rū́ pá da u cye te //

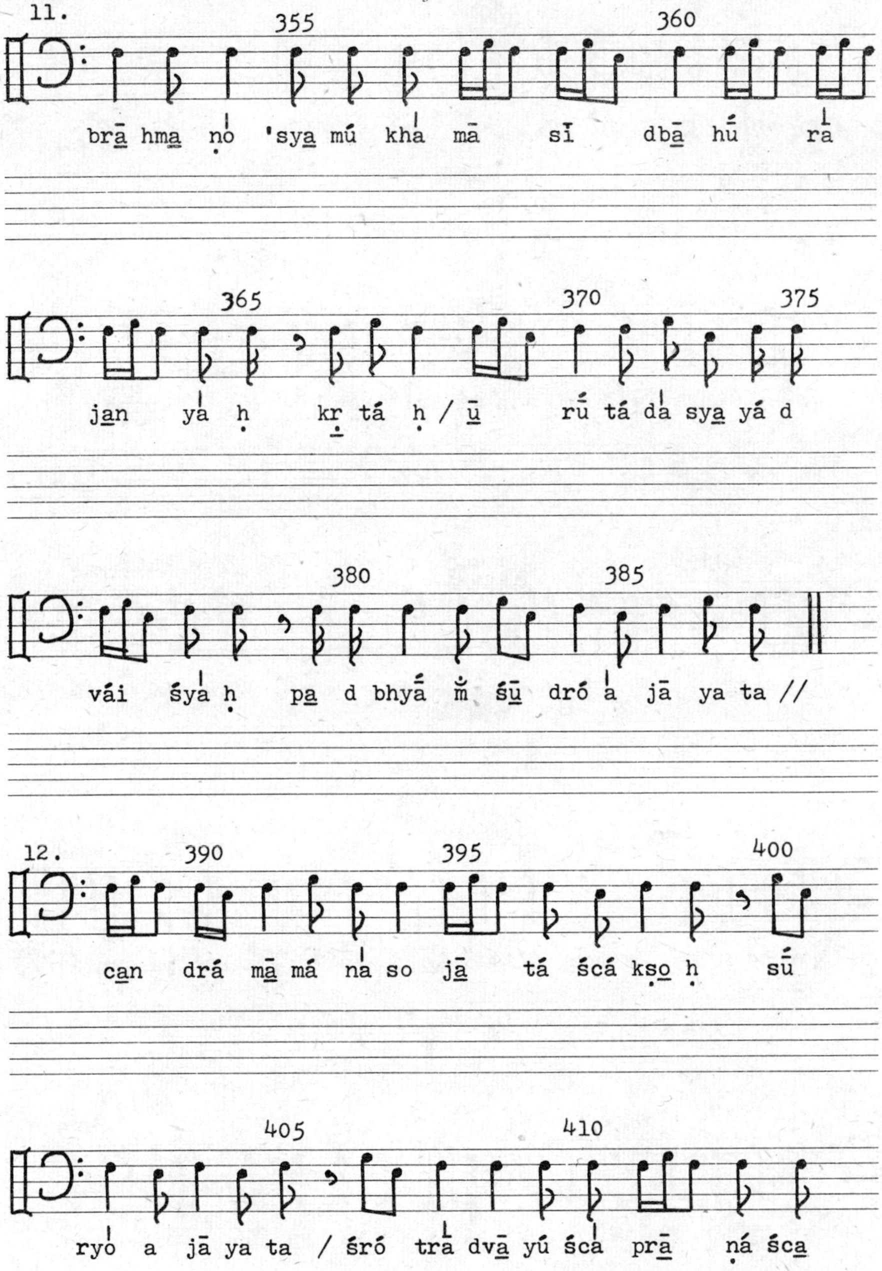
11.
355 360
brā hma ṇo 'sya mú kha mā sī dbā hū ra
365 370 375
jan ya ḥ kṛ tá ḥ / ū rū tá da sya yá d
380 385
vái śya ḥ pa d bhyā m̐ śū dró a jā ya ta //
12.
390 395 400
can drá mā má na so jā tá ścá kṣo ḥ sū
405 410
ryo a jā ya ta / śró tra dvā yú śca prā ṇá śca

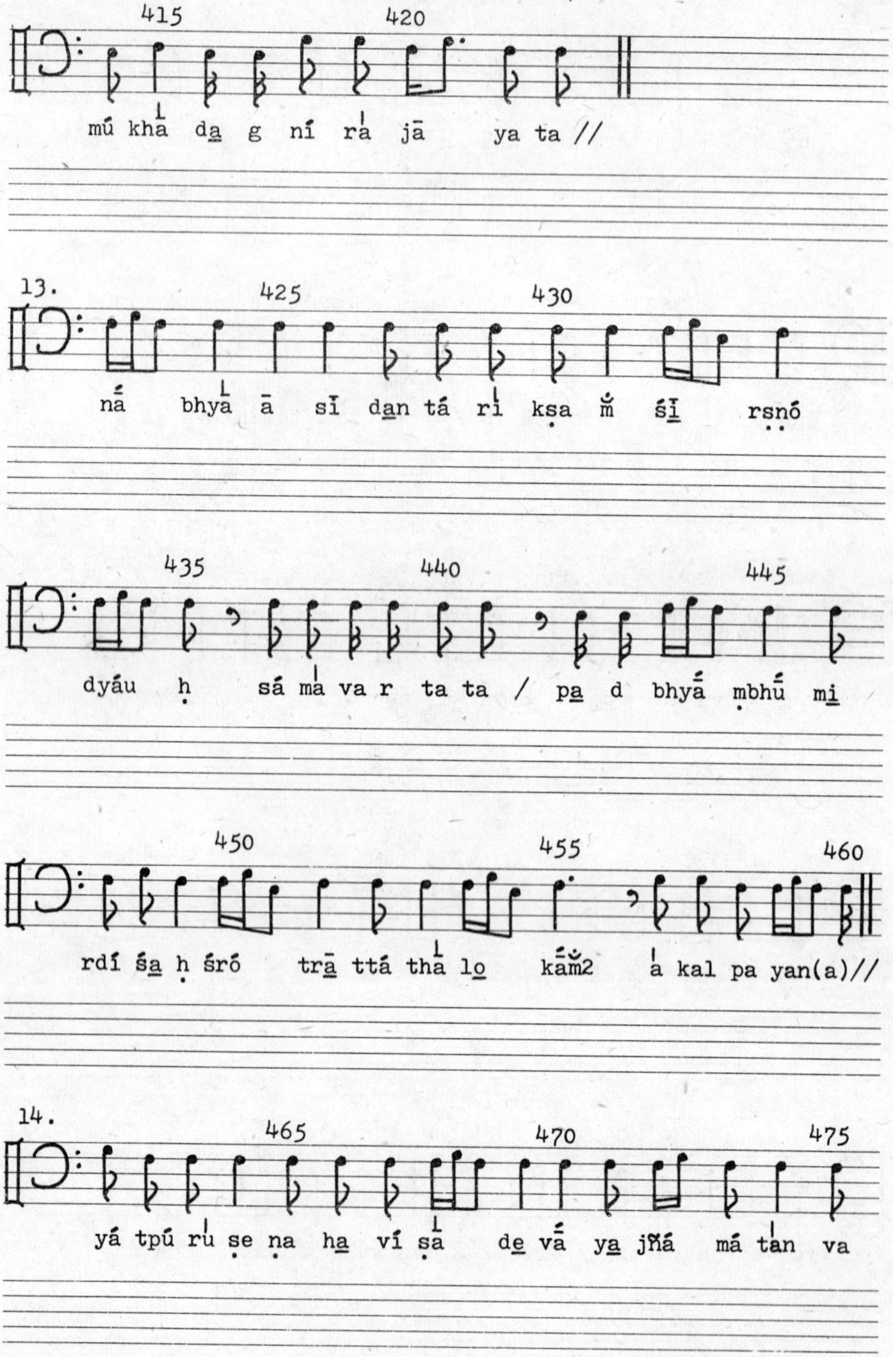
415
420
mú kha da g ní ra jā ya ta //
13.
425
430
nā bhya ā sī dan tá ri kṣa m̐ śī rṣṇó
435
440
445
dyáu ḥ sá ma va r ta ta / pa d bhyā ṃbhū mi
450
455
460
rdí śa ḥ śró trā ttá tha lo kām̐2 a kal pa yan(a)//
14.
465
470
475
yá tpú ru ṣe ṇa ha ví ṣa de vā ya jñá má tan va

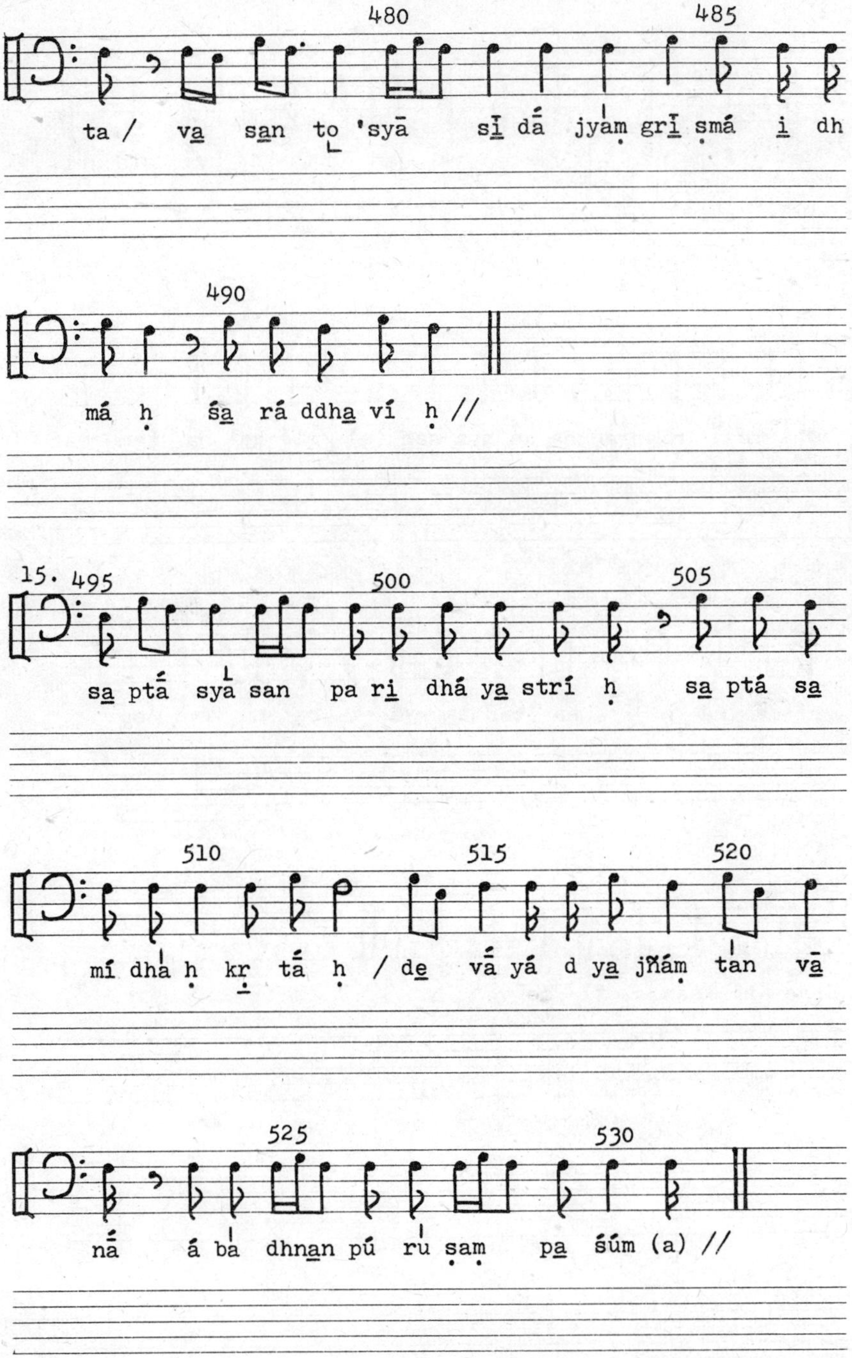
480 485
ta / va san to 'syā sī dá jyaṃ grī ṣmá i dh
490
má ḥ śa rá ddha ví ḥ //
15. 495 500 505
sa ptá sya san pa ri dhá ya strí ḥ sa ptá sa
510 515 520
mí dha ḥ kṛ tá ḥ / de vá yá d ya jñáṃ tan vā
525 530
ná á ba dhnan pú ru ṣaṃ pa śúm (a) //

16.

ya jñé na ya jñá ma ya jan ta de vá stā́ ni
dhá rma ṇi pra tha mā́ nya san (a) / té ha nā́ kaṃ ma
hi mā́ na ḥ sa can ta yá t ra pū́ rve sā
dhyā́ ḥ sán ti de vā́ ḥ //

238,246,248,253-54,256,263,272,280,295,373,385,397,402,404,414, 416-17,544,549). Isolated high tone is here primarily a short medial pitch positioned between mid-tones (2,17,23,27-28,33,37, 41,60,67,73,103,115,125,159,178,188,225,283,294,325,331,367,372, 387,392,448,488,493,512,518,536), thus relieving the monotony of successive middle tones (see, for example, 22-39). Occasionally it has initial (240,319,456,461,490,505) and final (39,318) functions; a few instances of two successive high tones arise (418-19,456-57,484-85,490-91,505-6). Long syllables are sung mainly on single middle tone (6,19,22,31,36,38,48,51,52,55,59, 64,66,69,72,82,85,91,97,100,102,108,118,120,128,131,134,136,141, 145,147,149,154,157,172,176,181,203,207,210,212,216,218,227,228, 232,234,241,245,247,255,257,261,262,264,269,273,275,277,279,281, 293,296,297,304,307,313,322,329,339,340,341,343,344,346,347,348, 350,352,354,360,370,381,384,386,391,398,401,403,407,408,415,424, 425,426,433,445,449,451,453,455,464,469,470,474,479,481,482,483, 497,515,519,521,530,541,542,543,546,550,551,552,554,556,557,560, 564,570,572,576,577). Sometimes, however, other schemes are employed: middle-high-middle or middle-high-middle-high (56,77, 153,173,190,196,199,200,204,208,233,252,258,260,285,287,312,333, 358,361,362,363,389,395,411,423,434,444,459,468,480,498,525,528, 533,539,574), high-middle (4,43,44,68,70,83,87,92,104,478,496, 545), high-low or middle-high-low (13,65,75,109,117,119,209,211, 268,278,292,306,310,342,345,359,369,376,383,400,406,432,450,454, 514,520,569,571), middle-low (84,96,162). Ghuṃ is sung to middle tone (24,46,235,382,431), as is medial visarga, which is always long regardless of the length of the preceding vowel (116,189, 326,368,449,510,573); some instances of visarga add a high tone (15,226). Short syllables are overwhelmingly middle tone--deviations of more than one pitch occurring in initial position (58,107,127,144,161,335,477), after hiatus (274) and in final position (143). Other examples of two-tone short syllables are less numerous (124,150,390,472). A notable characteristic of this recital is the notice taken of the first of two conjuncts, which often is recited with a vowel sound subtracted by half from the duration of the preceding short syllable (5,28,30,50, 62,123,130,133,165,168,185,202,206,220,251,254,289,300,375,380, 417,439,443,487,517,567). Final consonants are likewise given particular attention (20,57,197,334,460,531,553).

General Characteristics of Mādhyandina Yajurveda

The Mādhyandinas are so numerous that a complete list is not possible at this time. In addition to the paṇḍits already mentioned may be added the names of Lakṣmīkānt Dīkṣit Jāvjī Bhaṭṭ (*ghanapāṭhī*) and Śrīnāthjī Sārasvata (*ghanapāṭhī*, *vedācārya*). It may be assumed that the testimony of these and other reciters would merely echo most of the observations made above. Enough information is at our disposal that we are able to list traits which appear to be universally applicable to Mādhyandina recitation.

1. The accentuation of the text is completely ignored.

2. Three tones are employed by most reciters, although a relatively unimportant fourth tone is placed by some paṇḍits between middle and low tones. The middle tone is by far the predominant pitch, and there is no question that it has pivotal or tonic function.

3. Most short and most long syllables are sung to the middle pitch.

4. The circumflex tonal pattern middle-high-middle is a noteworthy characteristic of all recitations. It is found most often on long syllables but is not connected with any particular accent or feature of the recitation.

5. Initial syllables are often rendered in special ways, but no particular tone or tone pattern can be said to be preferred by all reciters. Even less consistency is found in the methods of distinguishing final syllables.

6. Visarga is sung usually to middle tone, although some paṇḍits realize it with middle-low (quickly). Some reciters sound medial visarga the length of a long vowel, regardless of whether the preceding vowel is long or short. Others sing it the duration of a short syllable, if a short vowel precedes.

7. Medial ghuṃ has the duration of a long vowel; mid-tone seems to be preferred.

8. The first of two or more conjunct consonants sounded as a separate syllable is sung usually to middle tone, as are final consonants.

9. Hiatus and the compound separation in parigraha analysis are often rendered in special ways.

10. A succession of short syllables may break the monotony of middle-tone domination by occasionally proceeding to a higher or lower pitch.

11. The ā-vowel preceding final n, which is changed to m̐ before an initial vowel, is protracted beyond the length of a long vowel (the figure 2 follows m̐ in the Vājasaneyi-Saṃhitā).

Other Yajurvedic Recitations

The Taittirīyas

The remaining Yajurvedic śākhās of the city are Taittirīya and Kāṇva, belonging to the Black and White Yajurveda, respectively. About the former little need be written, for the musical realization is simple and straightforward: anudātta, udātta/pracaya, and svarita are recited constantly at low-, mid-, and high-tone, respectively (in relation to the middle pitch the anudātta is a major second below, the svarita a minor second above). Variations in this strict design are achieved only in relation to sarvānudātta syllables, recited below anudātta level, and svaritas made long by ensuing conjunct consonants, recited middle-high.[44] This style, incidentally, is applicable to both Taittirīya Yajurveda and Ṛgveda traditions in Tamilnāḍ and hence has been imported to Vārāṇasī from the Dravidian region. Vārāṇasī paṇḍits belonging to the Black Yajurveda are Gaṇeś Bhaṭṭ Bāpaṭ, Rāmcandra (Bāpaṭ?), and S. Śrīnivās Dīkṣit. All are ghanapāṭhīs; all, presumably, hail from South India. Paṇḍit Śrīnivās Dīkṣit was recorded by the present writer,[45] who found him to be not only an excellent reciter but also an extremely learned individual who is able to deliver extemporaneous lectures, in Sanskrit, on a variety of subjects.

The Kāṇvas

The Kāṇva tradition requires more extensive documentation. The school has not nearly the representation in Vārāṇasī as has the Mādhyandina, but Kāṇva advocates include Lakṣmīkānt Śāstrī Khanaṅg, Lakṣmīkāntācārya Purāṇik (ghanapāṭhī), and Bālājī Peṭhkar (ghanapāṭhī). From the first-named paṇḍit the following verses were taped:

Source Verses: Vājasaneyi-Saṃhitā (Kāṇva) 3.3.1-3, to Agni and Indra.

1. upaprayánto adhvarám mántram vocemāgnáye /
   āré asmé ca śṛṇvaté //

2. agnír mūrdhā́ diváḥ kakút pátiḥ pṛthivyā́ ayám /
   apā́ṃ rétāṃsi jinvati //

3. ubhā́ vām indrāgni āhuvádhya ubhā́ rā́dhasaḥ sahá mādayádhyai /
   ubhā́ dātā́rāv iṣā́ṃ rayīṇā́m ubhā́ vā́jasya sātáye huve vām //

Translation:

1. Approaching (*upaprayantaḥ*) the sacrifice (*adhvaram*), may we utter (*vocema*) a mantra (*mantram*) to Agni (*agnaye*), [who] hears (*śṛṇvate*) even though (*ca*) far from (*āre*) us (*asme*).
2. Agni (*agniḥ*) is the head (*mūrdhā*) of heaven (*divaḥ*), the summit (*kakut*); lord (*patiḥ*) of the earth (*pṛthivyāḥ*) is he (*ayam*). He urges on (*jinvati*) the currents (*retāṁsi*) of water (*apām*).
3. To invoke (*āhuvadhyai*) both (*ubhā*) of you (*vām*), Indra and Agni (*indrāgnī*), is to be powerfully (*saha*) exhilarated (*mādayadhyai*) from the kindness (*rādhasaḥ*) of you both (*ubhā*). I call (*huve*) both (*ubhā*) of you (*vām*), givers (*dātārau*) of refreshing drinks (*iṣām*) and riches (*rayīṇām*), both (*ubhā*) for the gift (*sātaye*) of strength (*vājasya*).

A mere glance at the preceding transcription reveals its similarity to those of Part I; therefore the analytical symbols employed there will be resurrected in order to show the compositions of each accent.

a. *Udātta*

I. M^{l}-UM^{s}: **4,**8,**9,*40,*41,*48,*71,**74.

II. M^{sl}: 14,*23,*27,32,**55,*77,84.

III. H^{sl}-M^{s}: *19,**25,*59,*69,*80.

IV. H^{l}: **29,**31,*58,*79.

V. M^{l}-H^{s}: *17,*36.

VI. UM^{sl}: 63,**66.

VII. M^{l}-UM^{s}-M^{s}: *38.

b. *Anudātta*

I. H^{sl}: 3,7,**18,22,**24,28,37,39,47,54,57,62,65,68,73,78.

II. H^{s}-L^{l}: *16,**35,*70,*76,*83.

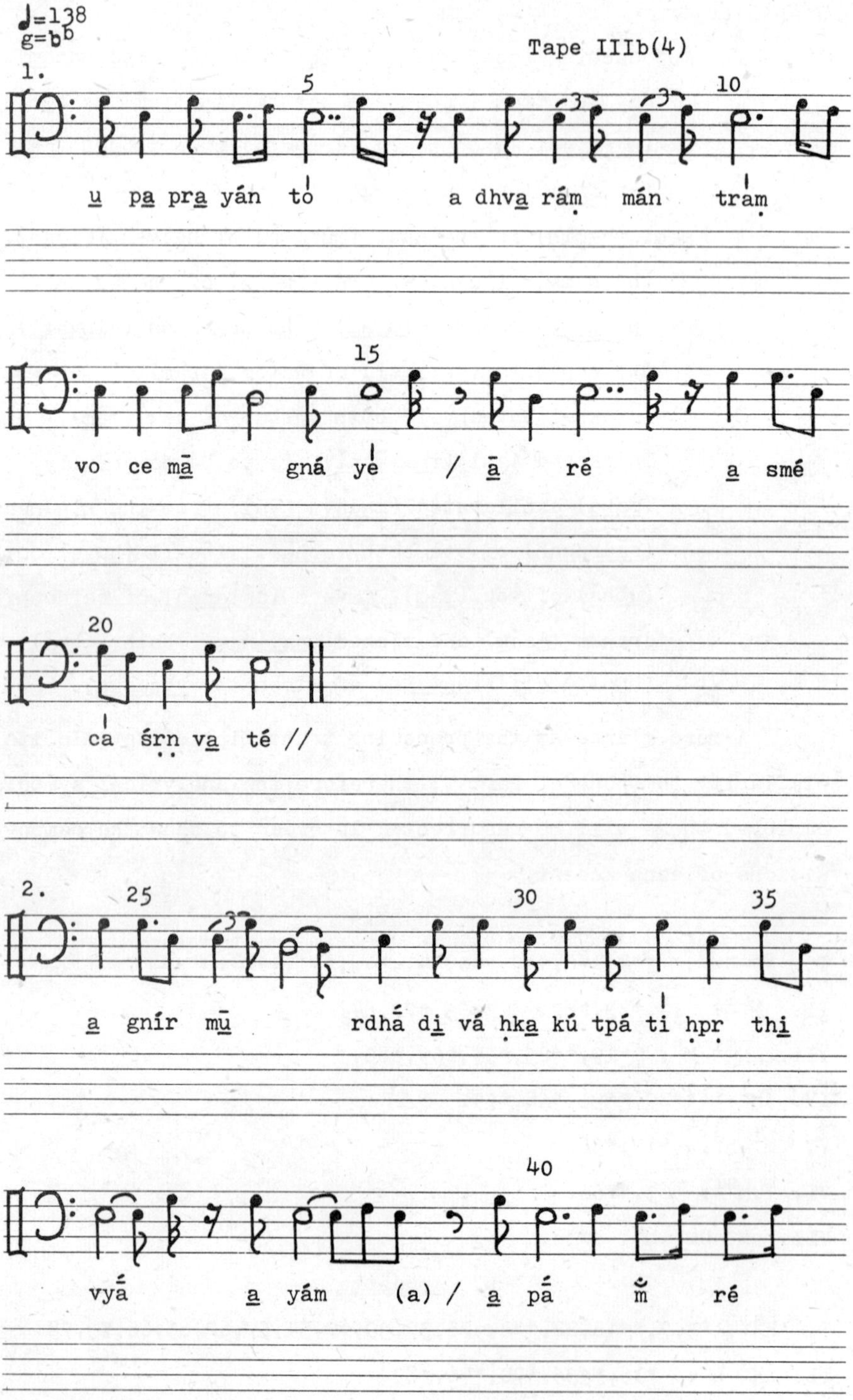
♩=138
g=b♭
Tape IIIb(4)
1.
u pa pra yán tó a dhva rám mán tram
vo ce mā gná yé / ā ré a smé
ca śṛṇ va té //
2.
a gnír mū rdhā́ di vá ḥka kú tpá ti ḥpṛ thi
vyā́ a yám (a) / a pā́ ṁ ré

45
ta m̐ si jin va ti //
3.
50
55
u bhā va min drā gnī ā hu vá
60
65
dhyā u bhā rā dha sa ḥsa há mā da
70
yá dhyai / u bhā dā tā rāv i ṣā m̐
75
80
85
ra yī ṇā mu bhā vā ja sya sā tá ye

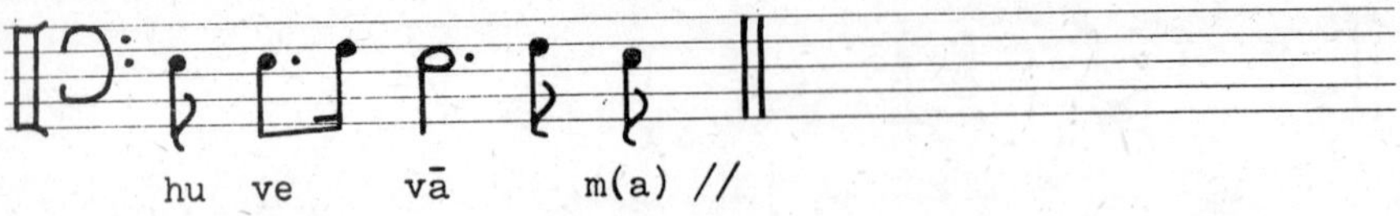
hu ve vā m(a) //

III. M^{sl}-H^{s}-L^{l}: *13,*26.

IV. M^{s}: 30.

c. Svarita

I. M^{l}-H^{s}-UM^{sl}: **10,*64,*72,*85.

II. M^{l}-H^{s}: *15,*56,*67.

III. H^{s}-UM^{s}: **20,60.

IV. H^{l}: **33,**81.

V. M^{l}-H^{s}-UM^{sl}-H^{s}: *42,*49.

VI. H^{s}-M^{s}: 75.

VII. M^{l}-H^{s}-M^{s}: *5.

d. Pracaya

I. M^{sl}: **2,**6,*11,*12,**21,34,**44,46,*53,**61,82,86.

II. M^{l}-UM^{s}: **50,*51,*87,*88.

III. UM^{s}: 43,45.

IV. H^{s}: 1.

V. M^{l}-H^{s}: *52.

With the exception of M^{l}-UM^{s}-M^{s} (closed by a final consonant), all udātta tones and tone combinations found in the transcribed extract occur also in the Ṛgveda specimens of Part I. Kāṇva Yajurveda too prefers udātta on M^{sl}, with the UM^{s} of its variant M^{l}-UM^{s} serving as an auxilliary tone between two middle tones. Also echoing the Ṛgveda practices are the appearances of H^{l} and H^{sl}-M^{s}, both occurring normally after a high-tone anudātta. The succession M^{l}-H^{s} is found prior to hiatus, and UM^{sl} functions as a passing pitch between high-tone anudātta and mid-tone svarita. The predilection for high-tone anudāttas is characteristic also of Kāṇva recitation. The common Ṛgveda schemes for long syllables, H^{s}-L^{l} and M^{sl}-H^{s}-L^{l}, are used here as well. Not a single instance of low-tone anudātta appears in the extract. Anudātta on M^{s} is found once, on a short syllable between *udāttas* on H. The typical falling pattern for Ṛgveda short *svarita* (H^{s}-UM^{s}, H^{s}-M^{s}) is reflected in Kāṇva practice. In addition to H^{l}, the circumflex patterns M^{l}-H^{s}-UM^{sl} (extended twice as M^{l}-H^{s}-UM^{sl}-H^{s}) and M^{l}-H^{s}-M^{s} are usual for long *svarita*. The sequence M^{l}-H^{s} occurs before a pause, as it did in the Ṛgveda pieces. As would be expected, most *pracaya* syllables are mid-tone, with the occasional extension M^{l}-UM^{s} on long syllables. *Pracayas* on UM are short and occur between middle tones. The single example of *pracaya* on H^{s} is a *sarvānudātta* tone initial in the recitation, while the M^{l}-H^{s} *pracaya* anticipates hiatus. The *ghuṃ* of the Mādhyandinas and Tamil Taittirīyas is also a feature of Kāṇva recitation, where it is sung to M^{l} or its extension M^{l}-UM^{s}.

Therefore Kāṇva Yajurveda is closely allied with Mahārāṣṭrian Ṛgveda and hence also with Atharvaveda from the same general region. From the facts before us we are prone to assume that an independent Kāṇva style does not exist and that, at least as far as music is concerned, propagators of the *śākhā* are little more than Ṛgvedīs in disguise. The texts of the White Yajurveda support the contention that the Kāṇvas are under greater Ṛgveda influence. Renou[46] has noticed that where the two *śākhās*, Mādhyandina and Kāṇva, disagree, the disagreement is not always an innovation on the part of one school or the other but rather an attempt to approximate a reading of another Saṃhitā. The Kāṇva recension ordinarily imitates the Ṛgveda or the Taittirīya branch of the Black Yajurveda, whereas the Mādhyandina *śākhā* approaches the Maitrāyaṇī- and Kāṭhaka-Saṃhitās of the Black Yajus.

III

SĀMAVEDA

Saṁhitā of the Kauthuma School

The vast majority of Vārāṇasī's Sāmavedīs are members of the Kauthuma śākhā. Their principal texts comprise the Saṃhitā, which includes not only accented verses (most appearing also in the Ṛk-Saṃhitā) but also four songbooks (gānas) containing chants (sāmans) which utilize these texts in modified form. The source verses are arranged in two ārcikas (collections of ṛc). The Pūrvārcika (First Ārcika) contains verses addressed to Agni, Indra, and Soma Pavamāna; these verses form the basis of the Grāmageyagāna (Village Songbook). This gāna presents one or more musical settings of each verse of the Pūrvārcika, taken in the order in which the verses originally appear. Posterior to the Pūrvārcika is the Āraṇyaka-Saṃhitā, on which the chants of the Āraṇyageyagāna or Āraṇyakagāna (Forest Songbook) are partially composed. The forest chants are, as a rule, longer and more spellbinding. They make great use of repetitive formulas and stobhas (non-textual insertions having magical or perhaps even dangerous properties), and, because of these esoteric qualities, were originally kept secret and sung in solitude in the forest. The Āraṇyakagāna is divided into four sections (arka, dvandva, vrata, śukriya) and draws upon verses of the Āraṇyaka-Saṃhitā, taken in order but not necessarily consecutively. Interspersed among these chants are those based on verses taken here and there from the Pūrvārcika. A pariśiṣṭa ("supplement") is attached at the end.

The second verse collection is the Uttarārcika (Final Ārcika), where the verses are arranged usually in groups of three or two--the first verse of the group ordinarily occurring also in the Pūrvārcika. This type of organization fits the requirements of the complicated Vedic soma rituals, where each group functions as a textual source for a chant complex (stotra). These sacrificial sāmans are found in the two songbooks associated with the Uttarārcika: the Ūhagāna and the Ūhyagāna. The Ūhagāna is made up largely of melodies from the Grāmageyagāna which have undergone modification (ūha) for ritual purposes. The Ūhyagāna, on the contrary, is closely allied with the Āraṇyakagāna. In fact the name of this last songbook is an abbreviation of Ūharahasya, which is evocative of the secret (rahasya) milieu of the Āraṇyakagāna. Both songbooks are divided into seven sections (parvans): daśarātra, saṃvatsara, ekāha, ahīna, sattra, prāyaścitta, and kṣudra. The daśarātra-parvan presents sāmans to be sung during the ten-day period central to the dvādaśāha or twelve-day soma sacrifice. The saṃvatsara-parvan contains chants for the sacrifice lasting a full year. The ekāha-, ahīna-, and sattra-parvans present chants for sacrifices lasting one day, two to twelve days, and twelve days or more, respectively.[1] Featured in the prāyaścitta-parvan are sāmans to be sung for atonement, while the kṣudra-parvan gives chants to be performed at soma rituals carried out to fulfill some wish or desire.[2] The first two songbooks are referred to as the Pūrvagāna (First Gāna) or Prakṛtigāna (Primary Gāna); the last two are sometimes called the Uttaragāna (Last Gāna) or Vikṛtigāna (Derived Gāna). The disposition of the various texts is shown in table 3.

Eight brāhmaṇas and fifteen śrautasūtras belong to the Kauthumas.[3] However, they are like the other Vedic schools in having one main brāhmaṇa, Pañcaviṃśa ([The Brāhmaṇa of] Twenty Five [Chapters]), to which the Ṣaḍviṃśa ([Chapter] Twenty-Six)

TABLE 3

KAUTHUMA SAṂHITĀ

Prakṛti		Vikṛti	
Pūrvārcika + Āraṇyaka-Saṃhitā		Uttarārcika	
Pūrvagāna		Uttaragāna	
Grāmageyagāna	Āraṇyakagāna	Ūhagāna	Ūhyagāna
1. Āgneya-Parvan	1. Arka-Parvan	1. Daśarātra-Parvan	1. Daśarātra-Parvan
2. Aindra-Parvan	2. Dvandva-Parvan	2. Saṃvatsara-Parvan	2. Saṃvatsara-Parvan
3. Pāvamāna-Parvan	3. Vrata-Parvan	3. Ekāha-Parvan	3. Ekāha-Parvan
	4. Śukriya-Parvan	4. Ahīna-Parvan	4. Ahīna-Parvan
	5. Pariśiṣṭa	5. Prāyaścitta-Parvan	5. Prāyaścitta-Parvan
		6. Kṣudra-Parvan	6. Kṣudra-Parvan

is an appendix, and one principal śrautasūtra (that of Lāṭyāyana).

Vārāṇasī As the Center of Kauthuma Tradition

A preliminary analysis of the principal style of Sāmavedic chanting in North India was offered by the present writer in 1977.[4] It was pointed out that the Sāmavedīs of Vārāṇasī who follow this tradition are members of the Kauthuma śākhā and that the unique mode of singing Sāmaveda has been transplanted from Gujarāt: the main authorities are either immigrants from that state or those who have undergone vedādhyayana from a Gujarāti teacher.[5] That the Kauthuma school has been associated with this area for at least four hundred years can be surmised from the statements of Mahidāsa in his commentary on the Caraṇavyūha. Accordingly, the three schools of Sāmaveda are said to be distributed as follows: the Kauthumas in the country of the Gūrjara, the Jaiminīyas in Karṇāṭaka, the Rāṇāyanīyas in Mahārāṣṭra.[6] A more recent survey[7] places Kauthumas among the Śrīmālī Brāhmaṇs of Rājpūtānā, the Vyāsa (Gauḍādya) Brāhmaṇs of Bengāl, and the Tivārīs at Kānyakubja.

Epigraphical references to the Kauthuma school are likewise confined largely to the North, although the inscriptions are spread over a wide area:[8] Baghelkhaṇḍ (Madhya Pradesh, sixth century), Bādāmi (northern Karṇāṭaka, eighth century), Kaṭak (Orissā, eighth century), Dinajpur (Bengāl, eleventh and twelfth centuries), Orissā (tenth century and thirteenth [?] century), Mālva (Madhya Pradesh), Bardvān (Bengāl, eleventh century), and Gañjām (Orissā, seventh [?] century).

The absence of any mention of Kauthumas in the extreme south would ordinarily lead one to suspect that the school exists mainly in North and Central India. However, it is well known that the Tañjāvūr and neighboring districts in Tamilnāḍ have large numbers of Sāmavedīs who call themselves Kauthumas. Nevertheless, reasons have been given[9] to believe that the designation "Kauthuma" is rather new to the Dravidian area and that the true śākhā of these paṇḍits may be Rāṇāyanīya. For one thing, the northern habit of notating the chants with numbers has apparently been introduced to the South only recently. Originally a syllable notation was in use which caused some confusion due to its characteristic of mixing the notational syllables with the words of the text. This particular syllable notation,[10] quite different from the syllable notation of the Jaiminīyas, is associated with the Rāṇāyanīya school; it was replaced in the southern districts of Tamilnāḍ but was kept in North Arcot. The North Arcot Sāmavedīs are now said to belong to the old (prācīna) school because of their adherence to the syllable notation, while the Tañjāvūr chanters are called "new school" Sāmavedīs. Evidently the only "new" feature of their chant is the use of the numeral notation, for stylistically their singing can definitely be connected to that of the North Arcot Sāmagas: in a tape-recording of Śrī Muḷḷanṭiram Rāmanātha Dīkṣitar (Muḷḷanṭiram village, North Arcot) by Mr. T. K. Rājagopāla Aiyar, the chants of the Ūhagāna and Ūhyagāna are rendered in the Tañjāvūr style, while the Grāmageyagāna and Āraṇyakagāna are sung in a manner reminiscent of Rāṇāyanīya chanting in the North Kannaḍa District of Karṇāṭaka.[11] Therefore the prācīna type of Kauthuma chant might be called the "missing link" between two types of Rāṇāyanīya Sāmaveda in widely separated regions of South India. The hybrid nature of the prācīna style was reported by V. Raghavan in 1957; he listed villages in northern Tamilnāḍ where this old style is cultivated:

> Besides Muḷḷandram, other villages in the northern Tamil Dists. having Sāmaveda-families were Aḍayappalam,

Anakkāvūr, Perumāḷ koil (Vaiṣṇavas), Panayūr and Paranūr; the Panayūr-style is a mixed one; the style of Paranūr near Villupuram might be taken as the source of the new style of singing, according to some Sāmagas.[12]

The cause of the schism which produced the separation into two stylistically unified traditions is not known. For the moment it is sufficient to say that the "new school" style of Tañjāvūr appears to be associated with the sacrificial (svarūpa) form of Sāmaveda, while the North Kannaḍa branch may represent a less sacrosanct type of singing employed outside the sacrificial arena (the rūpāntara form).[13] The split may have occurred along lines of caste.

Supporting the contention that southern Kauthumas are perhaps Rāṇāyanīyas is the uncertainty among some singers of their true śākhā.[14] Moreover, a number of chanters who call themselves Gautamas or Chāndosāmas interpret the chants in exactly the same way as the so-called Kauthuma singers of Tañjāvūr. According to the Caraṇavyūha (which may not always be reliable), Gautama is a Rāṇāyanīya sub-school (as is also Kauthuma),[15] and Chāndosāma is a general appellation which tells us little.[16]

One further reason to suspect Rāṇāyanīya as the predominant school of Tamilnāḍ is the total absence of Kauthuma sūtras in that region. Here the Sāmavedīs calling themselves Kauthumas universally follow the Drāhyāyaṇa-Śrauta-Sūtra, a Rāṇāyanīya text, in their sacrificial observances. On the other hand, the northern (primarily Gujarāti) Kauthumas strictly follow sūtras of their own school, namely the Lāṭyāyana-Śrauta-Sūtra and Gobhila-Gṛhya-Sūtra. This fact advances the argument for a purer Kauthuma tradition in the North or West, especially in view of the fact that the name Lāṭyāyana comes from Lāṭa, a name for Gujarāt.[17] According to Asko Parpola,[18] the geographical references in Lāṭyāyana's Sūtra corroborate the proposition of a western or northwestern provenance. Moreover, he states outright that of the two Kauthuma is the principal school.

> They [the two schools] have most texts in common; greater differences appear only from the Śrautasūtras onwards. According to the Caraṇavyūha, a most unreliable source, the Kauthumas (as well as the Śāṭyāyanins = Jaiminīyas!) are a sub-school of the Rāṇāyanīyas . . . ; but since the separation has apparently taken place only at the Sūtra level . . . , and as Drahy[āyaṇa] is later than Lāṭy[āyana] . . . , Kauthuma must be the main school . . . .[19]

Parpola maintains the long-established subsistence of Kauthumas in the South and deduces that a new school, Rāṇāyanīya, was formed as a result of contacts between southern Kauthumas and Jaiminīyas:

> If we now examine the actual ritualistic differences [of the Drāhyāyaṇa-Śrauta-Sūtra] from the LŚS [Lāṭyāyana-Śrauta-Sūtra], differences which are not due only to the individual revisor's desire to improve the work, it is immediately striking that, at least in the part examined by me so far, they are almost invariably based on the Jaiminīyas, and that in general the main reliance is on these . . . . This gives a simple answer to the question of the nature of the Rāṇāyanīya school which is corroborated by the evidence supplied by the other Rāṇ[āyanīya] texts, beginning with the Saṃhitā . . . : the Kauthumas resident in South India were influenced by the neighbouring Jaiminīyas who, in the course of time, became almost totally absorbed into the new sub-school [Rāṇāyanīya] which thus had come into being.[20]

While the assertion of Jaiminīya influence in Rāṇāyanīya texts cannot be faulted, one's attention is irrevocably drawn to the paucity of historical evidence for Kauthumas in the South. As Parpola has pointed out,[21] not a single manuscript of Lāṭyāyana' Sūtra has been found south of Poona, yet the Drāhyāyaṇa-Śrauta-Sūtra is found in profusion in South India. The Jaiminīya influence on Rāṇāyanīya texts extends to the divisions which those texts employ, and thus Parpola has developed a criterion for determining the true school of a Kauthuma-Rāṇāyanīya manuscript:

> The Mss. often attest divisions not recorded in the editions etc., so that, as a rule, the Southern Mss. (grantha, palm leaves) almost invariably have what appears to be the Rāṇāyanīya division and the Northern Mss. (devanāgarī, paper) the Kauthuma division.[22]

If Kauthumas ever existed in the South, it is strange indeed that not a single manuscript of their Śrautasūtra is to be found in the area and that the overwhelming majority of texts shared with the Rāṇāyanīyas preserve distinctive Rāṇāyanīya readings attributable in large part to southern, Jaiminīya influence.

It may be pointed out that no solid conclusion of śākhā provenance can be reached by pointing to the presence or absence of hiatus (the gap between consecutive vowels) in the gānas (songbooks). Hiatus occurs most often when the vowels ā and o are lengthened by the addition of the simple vowels i or u, a prolongation (gati) which is one of the most prominent features of the Sāmaveda chants. Renou[23] has stated that the avoidance of hiatus (for example, the singing of ognā-i as ognā-yi) is a characteristic of the Rāṇāyanīya school, a declaration which is confirmed by the oral tradition of the Hāvik Brāhmaṇs of North Kannaḍa, who definitely belong to this school.[24] However, this contradicts the evidence of the manuscripts, where Kauthuma texts regularly avoid the hiatus and Rāṇāyanīya texts maintain it.[25] Either practice can be said to stem from contacts with the Jaiminīyas: the Tamil exponents of this śākhā often retain the consecutive vowels, but the Nambudiri Jaiminīyas of Kerala interpolate the semivowel.[26]

When the above information on geographical distribution, epigraphy, and textual differences of the schools is compared with the musical facts, which must be considered just as important, one must conclude that an indisputable Kauthuma tradition exists only in North India. In this area it is Vārāṇasī which has emerged as the major Sāmavedic center, attracting with its religious aura the Kauthumas from their original home in Gujarāt. It is mandatory, therefore, that serious study of the Kauthuma mode of chanting be undertaken in the city where its leading proponents reside.

The Sāmaveda Community in Vārāṇasī

Because of the shroud of secrecy surrounding Sāmaveda in Vārāṇasī, the presentation of information concerning the chanters of this city in which northern Sāmavedīs appear in greatest concentration is an appropriate introduction to the chant itself. It should be mentioned at the outset that in Sāmavedic matters Vārāṇasī is a citadel of the most restrictive brand of conservatism. The most orthodox chanters of South India (where Sāmavedic chanting is more widespread) were found to be infinitely more cooperative than those in Vārāṇasī, where the chant is thought (probably incorrectly) to be less pure. Some singers who were inclined to be helpful were scared away by their superiors or suddenly had second thoughts about collaborating with an outsider. Those Sāmagas who did agree to chant before a tape-recorder either were disposed to brevity or else insisted on being recorded outside the center city. These observations are in no way to be construed as criticisms, for several paṇḍits who adamantly refuse to sing for the outsider welcome him in their homes and invariably demonstrate the greatest courtesy and hospitality. More than once the view was expressed that a tape might eventually find its way to a radio station, for instance, and be heard by millions of listeners, including Śūdras. Although many Vaidikas in India would not object to this use of their art, in Vārāṇasī more than the usual apprehension seemed attached to the sudden appearance of a foreigner with his recording apparatus. Eventually, however, this obstacle was overcome, and excellent recordings were made of several able Sāmagas.

Foremost among the city's Vaidikas are those who are _āhitāgni_s or _agnihotrī_s, Brāhmaṇs who maintain perpetual sacred fires in their households. In recent memory several of these high-ranking paṇḍits have been Sāmavedīs. The best-known of the group is Ṛṣiśaṅkar Tripāṭhī Agnihotrī, a Gujarāti Śrīmālī Brāhmaṇ who is a professor (_adhyāpak_) at the J. M. Goenkā Saṃskṛta Mahāvidyālaya. He was the sacrificer (_yajamāna_) at the final _śrauta_ ritual held in the city, a _somayāga_ solemnized April 25-30, 1966. He is the editor of the Kauthuma sacrificial chants appearing in the _agniṣṭoma_ volume of the _Śrautakośa_, an encyclopedia of Vedic ritual,[27] where the following is written:

> Āhitāgni Rishishankar Tripathi of Varanasi extended very valuable help in editing the Kauthuma Sāmans given in this Part. He himself belongs to the Kauthuma recension of the Sāmaveda and hails from a family of Sāmaveda Pandits. He has studied the Sāmaveda together with its ancillary texts, has acquired a detailed practical knowledge of Sāman-chanting, and has officiated

as Udgātṛ in several Soma-sacrifices.[28]
He also is a practitioner of White Yajurveda in the Mādhyandina recension and has performed in the caturmāsya sacrifices. These comprise three rituals performed at the beginning of the three seasons of four months: vaiśvadeva (spring), varuṇapraghāsa (rainy season), sākamedha (autumn). The last of these "includes a funerary ceremony with offerings to Rudra Tryambaka."[29]
Vārāṇasī is the city of Rudra (Śiva); therefore much of the worship (pūjā) is connected with this deity, who has terrible and horrific aspects. The association of Sāmaveda with Rudra-pūjā was vividly documented early in this century by Havell:

> Below the Observatory the lamps get fewer and fewer, and near Manikarnika the whole scene fades away, as the lurid glare of the funeral pyres flashes across the water, amidst the inky blackness of the burning ghât. Dark figures are crouching on the great smoke-begrimed piers which flank the ghât, and demoniacal forms appear moving to and fro between the flaming heaps. A horrid crackling noise arises from the burning wood. From the darkness up above comes the raucous note of a temple conch, and the booming of drums.
>
> Presently a strangely familiar sound comes floating on the still night air, like a Gregorian chant with its slow and solemn cadence. In a distant monastery high above us the Brahmins are chanting the old sacrificial hymns, the Sâm-Ved, which the Aryan priests may have chanted here thirty centuries ago--still held so holy that it is sacrilege for our impure ears to listen. They are singing the praises of Rudra, the Mighty, the Terrible, lord of sacrifices, who has a thousand eyes, and carries a thousand quivers full of arrows of destruction.[30]

This destructive characteristic of Rudra lends a fearful and terrifying aura to those priests who are closely connected with his worship. One Brāhmaṇ who acted as an intermediary between the present writer and the Vārāṇasī Vaidikas was always reluctant to approach Ṛṣiśaṅkar Tripāṭhī. When a meeting was finally arranged, through the offices of Svāmī Maheśānand Giri and Dr. Prem Latā Śarmā, Tripāṭhī merely referred to a book which he had edited giving information on Sāmaveda and containing Sāmavedic hymns to be used during Rudra-pūjā.

This book, Sāmavedīyarudrajapavidhiḥ[31] ("Canon of Sāmavedic Prayers to Rudra"), not only contains valuable information on Sāmaveda as understood by the northern Kauthumas; it presents also a biographical sketch of Yamunā Prasād Tripāṭhī,[32] the compiler, an āhitāgni who has had connections with Vārāṇasī. He was born in 1906 in Markā Village, Bā̃dā District, Uttar Pradesh. His father, Śiv Śaṅkar Lāl Tripāṭhī, was a police officer (thānedār) in Markā. Yamunā Prasād had instruction in foreign languages (Urdū, Fārsī, English) and in 1927 passed the B. A. examination at Prayāg (Allāhābād) University. In 1930 he became a police sub-inspector and worked in Faizābād, Dehrādūn, Āzamgaṛh, Murādābād, Vārāṇasī, and Lakhnaū (Lucknow). For his service in the Police Department, which included the capture of two bandits, he was awarded a medal for heroism by the government. From 1947 to 1951 he was Senior Police Superintendent. On the occasion of the invasion of India by China, the government of Uttar Pradesh appointed him to a position in the security branch of the police espionage department. He retired in 1962. He is a Sāmavedī of the Kauthuma śākhā and a Saryūpārīṇ Brāhmaṇ. He carried on Veda svādhyāya (private recitation) with his police work. Many of his ancestors and relatives have been noteworthy in various fields. His paternal great-grandfather was taken from Saryā Village, Gorakhpur District, Uttar Pradesh, to Pratāpgarh, in order that he could participate in a Vedic sacrifice. After the conclusion of the ritual he took residence in Ajhārā Village of Pratāpgarh District. His paternal grandfather, Kauśilyānand Tivārī, and paternal uncle, Sītārām Tripāṭhī Śāstrī, were famous Sanskrit scholars. His father-in-law, Śyām Sundar Brahmcārī, was a peerless scholar of vyākaraṇa (grammar) and knew by memory Patañjali's Mahābhāṣya. His elder brother was a prominent scholar of Sāmaveda and jyotiṣa śāstra (astronomy).

In 1952 Yamunā Prasād Tripāṭhī made the acquaintance of Satyadev Brahmcārī, an Iṭār Pāṇḍe Brāhmaṇ belonging to the Sāvarṇa gotra and to the Kauthuma school of Sāmaveda. From an early age Brahmcārī developed a love of yogic practices and attended on sādhus and mahātmās. In 1939 he abandoned family and home and took refuge in the āśram of Svāmī Sāligrām Dās. From that time on he led a life of penance. In 1959 Brahmcārī influenced Kṛṣṇa Kumār Goyal, the collector of revenues in Bharthanā (Iṭāvā District, Uttar Pradesh) and later Deputy Collector at Allāhābād, to prepare for the Viṣṇu Mahāyajña at Bharthanā. The yajamāna of this sacrifice was Yamunā Prasād Tripāṭhī (together with his wife); the ācārya (teacher in the law of sacrifice) was Ṛṣiśaṅkar Tripāṭhī Agnihotrī.[33]

Next in the list of āhitāgnis is Agniṣvātt Śāstrī Agnihotrī, a Kauthuma Sāmavedī of the Vatsa gotra. A Bengālī by birth, he came to Vārāṇasī and had instruction in Sāmaveda from Vināyak Rām Dīkṣit. He has never performed in a soma ritual but has attended several as an observer. His non-participation in the sacrifices is clearly not based on his qualifications, for he was able and willing to sing a number of agniṣṭoma chants, including the subrahmaṇyā invocation[34] and the bhakāra-rathantara (a sacrificial form of the rathantara-melody in which certain consonants are replaced by bh). Concerning this last sāman, he is the only Sāmavedī recorded by the present writer who follows the admonition that "the chanting [of the rathantara] should be performed swiftly, for the attainment of the world of heaven."[35] He has resided at the Agnihotrī Āśram in Vārāṇasī, where, according to one of his admiring pupils, he lived as a true paṇḍit in the deepest sense of that word. His authoritative interpretations of the Sāmavedic hymns offer ample confirmation of that statement.

Last but not least is Hari Śaṅkar Agnihotrī, a Sāmavedī who has taught at the Sāṅgaveda Vidyālaya and who learned sāman-singing at that same institution from Dev Śaṅkar.

Despite the title "Agnihotrī" attached to the above names, I am told that Ṛṣiśaṅkar Tripāṭhī is the only practicing āhitāgni left in the city.

Many of the remaining Sāmavedīs in Vārāṇasī are relatives of Ṛṣiśaṅkar Tripāṭhī. Among these are Nārāyaṇ Śaṅkar Tripāṭhī (his brother) and Gopāl Rām Tripāṭhī (his nephew). The former was taught Sāmaveda at the Sāṅgaveda Vidyālaya by Hari Śaṅkar Agnihotrī. The latter, who consented to demonstrate the Kauthuma mudrās (hand positions used while chanting),[36] could not support himself as a practicing paṇḍit and, on last information, was working in the College of Indology at Banāras Hindu University.

To be added to the list of chanters are those who have functioned as udgātṛ (chief Sāmaveda chanter) in the soma rituals: Śiv Rām Tripāṭhī, Dev Kṛṣṇa Tripāṭhī, Nand Kṛṣṇa Tripāṭhī, Śiv Datt Tripāṭhī, Gaṇeś Bhaṭ Bāpaṭ, Kāśīnāth Bāpaṭ, Cintāmaṇi Pāḷande, and Nārāyaṇ Dātār. Dev Kṛṣṇa, a Gujarāti Nāgar Brāhmaṇ, has taught Sāmaveda to the son of the Mahārājā of Banāras, Dr. Vibhūti Nārāyaṇ Siṅgh. Although teaching the

Vedas outside the Brāhmaṇ caste is not too common today, it has been permitted since ancient times for the dvija ("twice-born") castes--Brāhmaṇ, Kṣatriya, Vaiśya.

Among the South Indian Sāmavedīs in the city, two must be singled out for special attention. One of the foremost Tamil paṇḍits here is Prof. A. M. Rāmnath Dīkṣit, Head of the Vedic Department at the Saṃskṛta Mahāvidyālaya of Banāras Hindu University and editor of a recent edition of the Kauthuma Ūha- and Ūhya-gānas--the Sāmavedic songbooks which contain hymns arranged for sacrificial performance. He is now quite old and prefers not to be recorded because of difficulties in hearing. His principal consultant in the gāna edition was P. Kṛṣṇamūrti Śrautigal, an erudite Kauthumin from the village Maraiturai (Vedaprī) in the Tañjāvūr District of Tamilnāḍ who gave me some of my most interesting recordings. Kṛṣṇamūrti had his Vedic training at Tiruvidaimarudūr (Madhyārjunam), near Kumbakoṇam in the Tañjāvūr District. Later he was trained in Madras as a śrautin (sacrificial functionary). In 1955 he came to Vārāṇasī on a pilgrimage and has remained ever since, becoming one of the most highly respected Vaidikas in the city. He has accomplished the incredible feat of committing to memory not only the source verses and hymns contained in the large songbooks, but also the eight brāhmaṇas (Pañcaviṃśa, Ṣaḍviṃśa, Sāmavidhāna, Ārṣeya, Devatādhyāya, Mantra, Saṃhitā-Upaniṣad, and Vaṃśa) and single upaniṣad (Chāndogya) of the Kauthuma (Rāṇāyanīya?) school. All of these texts were recited in the presence of the Mahārājā of Banāras, on which occasion the śrautin was borne on one of the royal elephants to the palace in Rāmnagar, on the east bank of the Gaṅgā. He was subsequently awarded a pension and given inscriptions proclaiming the achievement. His accomplishment is all the more impressive by the fact that the brāhmaṇas and the upaniṣad were not transmitted as accented texts; therefore the chanter had to draw upon his own extensive knowledge of Sanskrit grammar in placing the accents udātta, svarita, and so forth on the correct syllables.

Several Vaidikas who belong to other Vedas have some familiarity with Sāmaveda. For example, Gopāl Candra Śāstrī, head of the Vedic Department at the Vārāṇaseya Saṃskṛta Viśva-vidyālaya, is a Mādhyandina Śukla Yajurvedī who knows the northern Kauthuma style of Sāmaveda. He has passed on the tradition to his sons Yugal Kiśor and Kiśor, who were able to chant any Sāmavedic hymn placed in front of them. Undoubtedly there are other deserving singers whose paths are yet to be crossed.

The Numeral Notation

The Kauthumas notate the four songbooks with numbers, whereas the Rāṇāyanīyas and Jaiminīyas use different types of syllable notations. The notations have been passed down, probably for thousands of years, in the form of hand movements (mudrās). The songbook manuscripts, all of relatively recent origin, therefore do nothing more than preserve, in written form, the sāman texts with the mudrās. Put another way, the notations *are* the hand positions, which have sustained the complicated musical structure of the Sāmavedic hymns and kept it secret from those not among the qualified elite.

Even with manuscripts and printed editions now at his disposal, the scholar seeking to unravel the mysteries of the oldest musical tradition on earth has been hard pressed to find any correlation between the mudrās and the oral interpretations of the Sāmagas who employ them as they sing. A major barrier to research is the distrust and suspicion which the appearance of an outsider elicits among some Vaidikas. The intricacies of their art have been mastered only through long and tedious labor, so the reluctance to share their traditional means of livelihood with a foreigner who suddenly appears on the scene is understandable. Even a Sāmavedī willing to sing before a tape recorder would shy away from explaining the modus operandi of his chant. This would scarcely be possible in any case, for the hymns have been learned not by sitting in a classroom and subjecting the songs to analytical scrutiny but by monotonously repeating over and over again after a teacher (guru). The singers are naturally not familiar with the Western musical notation, so they would not be able to relate the elements of their chant to that medium. The jealousy with which the hymns are protected excludes close and extended study by the non-Brāhmaṇ researcher; hence the only practical method of analysis is through transcription of a sizable body of tape recordings, whereby the transcriber is not required to rely on mere momentary impression but is able to examine the recorded sāmans in minute detail.

Initial steps toward a true understanding of the numeral notation, as it bears upon the hymns as actually sung, were taken in a previous publication[37] by the present writer. It was shown that prior notions as to the symbolic role of the numbers are well off the mark and that the cursory statements, in certain treatises, connecting the mudrās to the tones of secular music are not confirmed in actual practice. Although transcribed examples were offered[38] to illustrate renditions of certain passages, guidelines for the correct interpretation of entire chants could not be given at that time. Now, however, an examination of a larger body of recorded sāmans taken from Vārāṇasī chanters has made it possible to present rules for the correct contextual realization of the mudrās. Before a thorough documentation of the musical facts, a review of the basic features of the numeral notation is necessary.[39]

Numbers 1 through 5 provide the foundation of the system. Five basic numerals are utilized for the simple reason that the human hand has five fingers; the mudrās, all indicated on the right hand, correspond to the figures as follows:[40]

Number 1: the first (prathama) finger, the thumb, is held high and somewhat apart from the other fingers.

Number 2: the thumb touches the middle section of the second (dvitīya) or index finger.

Number 3: the thumb touches the middle section of the third (tṛtīya) or middle finger.

Number 4: the thumb touches the middle section of the fourth (caturtha) or ring finger.

Number 5: the thumb touches the middle section of the fifth (pañcama) or little finger.

In addition to the five fundamental numbers, three additional figures appear in the songbooks: 11, 6, and 7. The first (actually number 1 stated twice), which occurs in only a few chants, is realized in a manner described as kruṣṭa ("clamorous, loud").[41] The second (atisvārya, anusvāra) is used in only a secondary capacity and may have originally signified nazalization, as its name indicates.[42] The third is designated abhigīta ("praised in song")[43] and in the North denotes quick articulation of a textual syllable. Mudrās associated with these numbers are the following:

Numbers 11: same as the mudrā for number 1.[44]

Number 6: the thumb touches the base of the little finger.[45]

Number 7: the thumb is flicked upwards from beneath the index finger.[46]

The special character of these three figures clearly places them subordinate to the first five. It is entirely possible that *kruṣṭa*, for example, is a later addition to the notation.

In the songbooks the numbers appear above and within the line of text. The purpose of following a syllable with one or several figures is the procurement of a combination of tones not obtainable otherwise. The syllable thus affected may or may not be temporally extended as a result. A notated number (and thus the corresponding *mudrā*) is held until the appearance of a different number. Ordinarily the numbers occurring in the line of text (the *vikṛti* or secondary position) are indicated on the fingers in precisely the same way as the figures notated above the syllables (the *prakṛti* or primary position). However, some combinations of a *prakṛti*-number with one or more *vikṛti*-numbers elicit special movements of the fingers:[47]

Preṅkha or *Vinata* ($1_{\bar{2}}$): the thumb glides over the middle sections of the fingers, from forefinger to little finger.[48]

Praṇata (2_3 or $2^{\hat{}}_3$): the thumb glides from base to tip of the forefinger.

Svāra or *Utsvarita* (1^{1111}_{2345}, 2^{111}_{345}, or 3^{1111}_{2345}): the thumb glides over the tips of the fingers, from forefinger to little finger.[49]

Karṣaṇa ($1^{\hat{}}_2$ or $2^{\hat{}}$): the thumb rubs the side of the forefinger as the hand forms a fist.[50]

Much discrepancy exists between the account of time values contained in a relatively recent treatise, the Mātrālakṣaṇa ("Description of Mātrā"),[51] and the actual practices of the Sāmavedic masters. The basic time unit is said to be the *mātrā*, which is equivalent to the length of a short (*hrasva*) vowel. Syllables can also be long (*dīrgha*) or augmented (*vṛddha*). Long syllables invariably have a long vowel, with the letter *r* (*repha*) placed above. Augmented syllables are those with long vowels which lack the superscribed *repha*. Long syllables are said to be worth two *mātrās*, augmented syllables three *mātrās*. The Kauthumas are not at all consistent in following these rules. Were it not a fact that the *mātrā* concept occurs, for instance, in treatises such as the Ṛk-Prātiśākhya, one would be tempted to speculate that the anonymous author of the Mātrālakṣaṇa had taken the term *mātrā* from the classical music, where it denotes a single unit of the *tāla* rhythmic cycle, and then attempted to apply it--with only limited success--to current Sāmavedic practice. At any rate, the Kauthumas have special left-hand *mudrās* to be used in conjunction with the letter *r*, which may appear along with any of the five basic numbers:

1r: the little finger touches the palm.

2r: the ring finger touches the palm.

3r: the middle finger touches the palm.

4r: the forefinger touches the palm.

5r: the thumb touches the forefinger as the fingers retract to form a fist; the hand is opened, then closed again.

The combination of a primary number with one or several secondary numbers, henceforth referred to as a sequence (the author's own term), presents yet another problem in determination of duration. The Mātrālakṣaṇa gives specific values for some sequences but is silent or vague regarding others. Generally, however, the primary number is held for a longer duration (probably two *mātrās*) than the secondary numbers, although this rule does not necessarily apply where special finger movements are involved.

Each Sāmavedic chant is divided into sections (*parvans*) of unequal length. The sections, each to be chanted in a single breath, are separated in the manuscripts by vertical lines (*daṇḍas*). Actually the several thousand Kauthuma chants are constructed from a repository of only about three hundred *parvans*, each with its distinctive sequence of *mudrās*.[52] For example, a *parvan* from the second chant of the Grāmageyagāna is notated as follows:

1 ^ 3 5r r
/barhā2iṣā234 au ho vā/.

This *parvan* presents the notational numbers in the order 1-2-3-2-3-4-5, which gives a musical combination not duplicated by any other *parvan* in the repertoire of three hundred.[53] The Rāṇāyanīyas use the same *mudrās* as the Kauthumas, but some Rāṇāyanīya manuscripts represent the series of *mudrās* in a *parvan* by a particular syllable, which occurs after the first textual syllable of the *parvan*.[54] Therefore the Rāṇāyanīya version of the *parvan* quoted above reads as follows (the zero or *bindu* is used instead of the *repha* in South Indian manuscripts):[55]

o o
/ba*ve*rhāiṣā au ho vā/.

This type of notation obviously makes infinitely greater demands on the chanter, especially if he is inexperienced and relies to some degree on written texts. Not only must he have memorized the series of *mudrās* implied by the syllable *ve*, he must have had sufficient training to know to which textual syllables the *mudrās* are attached. For instance, he might incorrectly sing the *parvan* as

1 2 3 5r r
/barhāiṣā234 au ho vā/

or

1 2 5r r
/barhā3iṣā234 au ho vā/

or

1 5r r
/barhā23iṣā234 au ho vā/.

Because of the impreciseness of the syllable notation (which may indicate that it is older than the numeral notation), variants may have crept into Rāṇāyanīya chanting in some areas. The reverse possibility may also come into play: that some Kauthuma passages may be based on erroneous interpretations of the older syllable notation, the inexact nature of which predetermines usage only by those who have already mastered the chant. This vagueness insured that the secrets of the Sāmaveda would be kept from outsiders, but it lead to confusion among the Sāmavedīs themselves.[56] Therefore the more exact numeral notation is now preferred in both North and South and by both Kauthumas and Rāṇāyanīyas, though some of the latter are still acquainted with the old system.

The Rāṇāyanīya notation (and thus also the Kauthuma, which merely elucidates it by giving the precise spots where the mudrās occur) provides direct evidence of the method by which the Sāmavedic chants are constructed. Because every parvan has a notational syllable that signals a particular mudrā sequence (and hence a particular musical phrase), and since the number of syllables is limited to about three hundred, therefore the chants are formed by piecing together selected parvans from this standard repertoire of three hundred phrases.[57] This technique, which Western musicologists call "centonization," is utilized to a great extent in ancient liturgical music of various countries; it is also the organizational principle behind the classical secular music of a large portion of the earth.[58] There is absolutely no question of this technique's operation in the Sāmavedic chant: the songbooks themselves offer evidence enough, but the existence of a number of treatises[59] which actually list the components of the standard repertoire should be proof even to the most skeptical critic. The procedure can be demonstrated by showing the content of the first ten chants (indicated by Roman numerals) of the Grāmageyagāna. The notational syllables, resulting from a collation of Manuscripts B.89 and B.60a of the India Office Library, represent *mudrās*, and corresponding music, of individual *parvans*. In parentheses following each syllable is the number sequence which it symbolizes (based upon Nārāyaṇasvāmī's edition[60] as collated with Manuscript B.188a of the India Office). Variants are given following each *sāman*.

I. / *ta* (4) / *cho* ($2_3 1_{\bar{2}}$) / *kā* ($1_{\bar{2}}$) / *kā* (12) /
/ *co* ($21_{\bar{2}}$) / *kā* ($1_{\bar{2}}$) / *ghī* (121_{23}) / *ve* ($\hat{1}_2 3_{234} 5$) /
/ *ṭū* ($3_{234} 5$) //

Parvan 5: *chu* (B.60a)

II. / *te* (45454) / *ka* (1) / *kaḥ* ($1_{23} 2$) / *ghai* ($121_{23} 2$) /
/ *ve* ($\hat{1}_2 3_{234} 5$) / *ja* ($2_3 1^{1111}_{2345}$) //

Parvan 1: *tu* (B.89); *Parvan* 2: 41 (N); *Parvan* 6: $2_3 3^{1111}_{2345}$ (N).

III. / *tu* (4545) / *tī* ($4_5 54$) / *ghai* ($12_1 2_3 2$) / *śe* ($23_{234} 5$) /
/ *vi* ($1_{23} 2_3$) / *kū* ($1_{234} 5_6 5$) //

Parvan 1: 45454 (B.188a); *Parvan* 2: *ti* (B.89);
Parvan 3: $12_{31} 2_3 2$ (B.188a); *Parvan* 5: $1_{234} 2_3$ (N).

IV. / *tu* (4545) / *tī* (454) / *ra* (21) / *kaḥ* ($1_{23} 2$) /
/ *jā* ($21_{23} 2$) / *yā* (321) / *cī* ($2_3 45$) / *tā* (4_5) / *pa* (5) //

Parvan 2: *ti* (B.89); *Parvan* 3: *ku* (B.89); *Parvan* 4: *kā* (B.89); *Parvan* 5: *kā* (B.89).

V. / pa (5) / ra (21) / kaḥ ($1_{23}2$) / ra (21) / kaḥ ($1_{23}2$) /
/ ka (1) / ce ($2_{3}32$) / kā (12) / vu ($1_{23}2_{343}$) /
/ ku (1_{2345}) / pa (5) //

Parvan 7: $2_{3}3$ (B.188a); Parvan 8: 1 (B.188a).

VI. / pa (5) / ve ($1^{\wedge}_{2}3_{234}5$) / ṭū ($3_{234}5$) / chu (2121_{2}) /
/ kaḥ ($1_{23}2$) / kā (12) / vu ($1_{23}2_{343}$) / ku (1_{2345}) /
/ pa (5) //

Parvan 2: $1_{2}1_{234}5$ (B.188a); Parvan 4: 21212_{2} (N), cu (B.89); Parvan 5: ka (B.89), 1_{23} (B.188a); Parvan 8: 3_{2345} (B.188a).

VII. / ṭū (32345) / pai (545) / kaḥ ($12^{\wedge}_{3}2$) / vi ($12^{\wedge}_{3}2^{\wedge}_{3}$) /
/ ga ($13_{234}5$) / ghi ($121_{\bar{2}}$) / ki ($12^{\wedge}_{3}$) / ve ($1^{\wedge}_{2}3_{234}5$) /
/ śi (213^{1111}_{2345}) //

Parvan 3: $1_{3}2$ (B.188a); Parvan 4: vi absent (B.89); Parvan 6: gha (B.89), $11_{\bar{2}}$ (N, B.188a); Parvan 8: $1_{2}2_{234}5$ (B.188a).

VIII. / tā (45) / ra (21) / ṭhau ($323_{234}5$) / ro (2121) /
/ ṭhau ($323_{234}5$) / kai (121) / ṭhau ($323_{234}5$) /
/ ti ($4_{5}5_{6}5$) //

Parvan 4: ga (B.89); Parvan 5: ṭhau absent (B.60a); Parvan 7: ṭhau absent (B.60a); Parvan 8: tī (B.60a).

IX. / tī (454) / kaḥ ($1_{23}2$) / kā (12) / jā ($21_{23}2$) /
/ vi ($12_{3}2_{3}$) / vu ($1_{23}2_{343}$) / kū ($1_{234}5_{6}5$) //

Parvan 1: ti (B.89); Parvan 2: kā (B.89); Parvan 4: $31_{23}2$ (N); Parvan 6: 1_{2343} (B.188a); Parvan 7: ku (B.89).

X. / tā (45) / ta (4) / kaḥ ($1_{23}2$) / cā (2_{3}) /

/ *vū* ($1_{\hat{2}}3_{234}5$) / *ra* (2_1) / *ghī* (121_{23}) / *kha* ($1_{23}4_3$) /

/ *cu* ($2_{345}5_65$) //

Parvan 2: *tā* (B.60a); *Parvan* 3: 12_32 (B.188a),

kā (B.60a); *Parvan* 6: *rā* (B.89); *Parvan* 7:

ghi (B.89,B.60a).

Therefore eighty-three phrases (counting the repetitions), all from the pool of three hundred, are used to fashion only ten *sāmans*. However, the musical structure is not nearly as rigid as the outline seems to indicate, for more than one textual syllable and more than one tone are often associated with a single *mudrā*. Further variation is achieved according to whether the number is above or within the text. For example, the fourth *parvan* of chant II (that is, II/4) arranges the *mudrās* $121_{23}2$, whereas III/3 has the identical series but orders them 12_12_32. Similarly, I/3,6 (*kā*) have the arrangement $1_{\bar{2}}$, but I/4, V/8, VI/6, and IX/3 give 12. Likewise,

(1) *tā* = 4_5 (IV/8)

= 45 (VIII/1, X/1)

(2) *kaḥ* = $1_{23}2$ (II/3, IV/4, V/3,5, VI/5, IX/2, X/3)

= 12_32 (VII/3)

(3) *ra* = 21 (IV/3, V/2,4, VIII/2)

= 2_1 (X/6)

(4) *tī* = 4_54 (III/2)

= 454 (IV/2, IX/1)

(5) *vi* = $1_{23}2_3$ (III/5)

= 12_32_3 (VII/4, IX/5).

A *mudrā*'s disposition as *prakṛti* or *vikṛti* affects its musical realization, and even more complication arises when the special *mudrās* for *praṇata*, *svāra*, and so on are indicated in the notation. Since the Kauthuma and Rāṇāyanīya notations are probably in some yet undetermined way connected with the Jaiminīya notation,[61] it too must be based on the centonization principle.

The technique of piecing together melodic fragments to create a musical work undergirds the *rāga* concept of Indian classical music. The operation of this procedure in northern *rāgas* has been demonstrated by Paṇḍit Viṣṇu Nārāyaṇ Bhātkhaṇḍe in his monumental work *Hindustānī Saṅgīt-Paddhati: Kramik Pustak-Mālikā*.[62] Bhātkhaṇḍe concentrates mainly on the presentation, in the North Indian *rāga* notation, of short compositions (*cīz*) which are used in performances of *khyāl* and *ṭhumrī*, the two principal forms of the North. But also, at the end of each volume (except the first), he lists *svaravistāras* (Hindī: *svarvistār*), means of elaborating on the fixed tones (*svaras*) of a *rāga*. These tone patterns are to be mastered by continuous repetition in front of a teacher.[63] The teacher's presence in fact is essential, for Bhātkhaṇḍe gives the bare tones without any indication of duration; therefore the teacher must demonstrate the proper rendition of the important tones (*vādī*, *saṃvādī*, and so on) as well as intonations which cannot be indicated by the notation. Phrases like these, learned through long and arduous practice, are the backbone of a *rāga* performance. Not only is the introductory *ālāp* (performed in a free rhythm, without drums) based upon them, but also much of the material following the *cīz*, including *rūpakālāp* (a "floating" *ālāp* with drum accompaniment) and *tāns* (virtuosic patterns towards the end of the *rāga*). Admittedly, the types of patterns stressed by one teacher or performer may vary somewhat from those emphasized by another artist, but it must be remembered that the *principle* is the same: the building of a musical structure by drawing on phrases and phrase successions learned in study and practice.

Three sections of Bhātkhaṇḍe's *svarvistār* for Rāg Vasant, performed late at night in the spring, may be quoted to demonstrate the above explanation. The names of the seven tones of the scale are abbreviated in the notation as follows: *sā* (*ṣaḍja*), *re* (*ṛṣabha*), *ga* (*gāndhāra*), *ma* (*madhyama*), *pa* (*pañcama*), *dha* (*dhaivata*), *ni* (*niṣāda*). This *rāga* has high *sā* as the *vādī*, *pa* as the *saṃvādī*. The pitches *re* and *dha* are flat (*komal*), and *ma* is sometimes natural (*śuddh*), sometimes sharp (*tīvr*).[64] The transcription below[65] assumes *sā* as equivalent to tone c.

10.

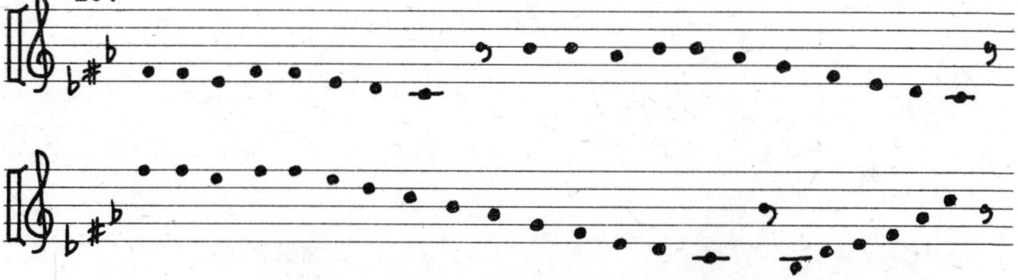

One may presume that a performer, once having memorized and committed these phrases to his repertoire, will use some or all of these fragments in subsequent renditions of Rāg Vasant. Thus he patches together a performance (albeit not haphazardly) in much the same way as the composers (more precisely, arrangers) of the Sāmavedic hymns put together their creations from a preexistent standard repository. In fact it is this very characteristic, more than any other, which ties the ancient Sāmaveda to the contemporary Indian classical music.

Transcriptions of Selected Sāmans

The unschooled researcher is not able to decipher the Kauthuma notation by simple consultation of manuscripts or printed texts. The key to a true understanding of the notation is obtainable only through its comparison with the hymns as actually sung. This conclusion seems to be at variance with certain statements in some Sāmavedic treatises, which relate

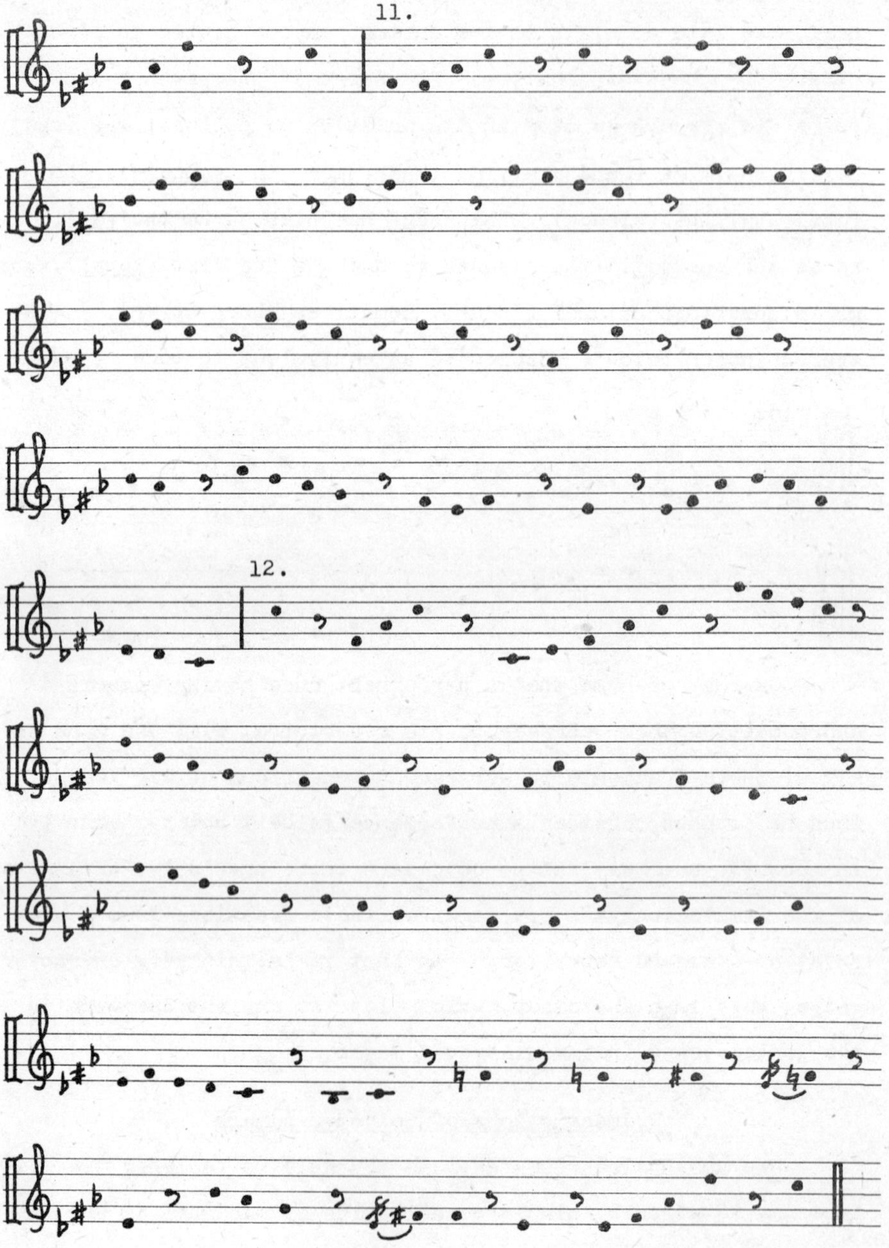
11.
12.

prathama, dvitīya, and so on to the tones of secular music. For example, the Nāradīyā-Śikṣā[66] connects the prathama-mudrā of Sāmavedic chant to the madhyama of the flute, dvitīya to gāndhāra, tṛtīya to ṛṣabha, caturtha to ṣaḍja, pañcama to dhaivata, ṣaṣṭha to niṣāda, and saptama (= kruṣṭa?) to pañcama. But almost in the very same breath Nārada equates the seven tones (listed now in ascending order from ṣaḍja to niṣāda) to the cries of animals: the peacock, cow, she-goat, curlew, cuckoo, horse, and elephant, respectively. Anyone who has heard the peacocks roaming wild near the Music College at Banāras Hindu University knows that their vocal abilities are in direct aesthetic contrast to their physical appearance; it is impossible that the noises made by this and the other animals could serve as the basis of the sophisticated art and liturgical music.

One must conclude that Nārada and other authors of Sāmavedic tracts have made extensive use of symbolism, and that great care must be exercised in not attaching literal meanings to all of their pronouncements. The oral traditions, which are just as important as the texts which claim to explain them, show that the notational numerals (and hence the mudrās) do not signify isolated tones and that the musical realization of a mudrā varies according to context. In the past the Vedic reciters and chanters exercised great power over the populace at large. Only they were privy to the hidden rationale behind the potent and hypnotic verses, formulae, and chants. This power was jealously guarded and protected, so that the true, secret meaning of the mudrās remained their property alone. For example, if each numeral of the Kauthuma notation signified a single tone, a literate Śūdra might be able to pick up enough information to master at least a few Sāmavedic hymns. With a written version in front of him, he would be able to sing everything and thus to usurp the considerable authority and control of the Brāhmaṇs. But the rules for singing the Sāmaveda are not nearly that simplistic, and the intricacies of the chant were preserved in such a way that they could be learned only from a qualified Brāhmaṇ teacher. The complexity of the chants dramatically contradicts the naive assumption that in the course of time certain tones have been "lost" or that corruptive influences have crept in. The very fact that the Sāmavedic chanters do not sing one tone per numeral and have kept the involved structure of their sāmans is indisputable proof of the vitality of the traditions. They have maintained the complicated melodic fabric and have not been influenced by a literal interpretation of the notation.

In order to formulate rules for correct sāman-singing in the northern Kauthuma style, transcriptions of sixteen chants from all four songbooks are now presented.[67] Chants 1-10 and 12 are sung by Hari Śaṅkar Trivedī and Nārāyaṇ Śaṅkar Tripāṭhī, chant 11 is rendered by Jugal Kiśor Śāstrī and his brother Kiśor, and chants 13-16 are interpreted by Agniṣvātt Śāstrī Agnihotrī. The tone material and range are rather small. The principal pitches are a low tone plus the major second and minor third above. A fourth tone, a perfect fourth above the low tone, is not used as frequently. In the transcriptions the lowest pitch is set equal to tone d. Each transcription is preceded by the sāman name, the source verse, a translation of the verse, and the chant as notated. Furthermore, the notation has been reproduced in the musical examples beneath the syllables of the text. Every fifth syllable has the appropriate number placed above.

The source verses of the Kauthuma Saṃhitā use the numbers 1-2-3 to show the accents. Numbers 1 and 3 always represent udātta and anudātta, respectively. Number 2 indicates svarita, but it denotes also an udātta syllable followed by anudātta.

When two or more udātta syllables appear in succession, only the first is marked with 1, but the sign 2r is placed above the following svarita. If, however, an anudātta follows, 2u is placed above the first udātta syllable and the rest are left undesignated. In a series of anudātta syllables at the beginning of the line, only the first is marked with 3. An independent svarita has the sign 2r, and the preceding anudātta is marked 3k. Pracaya syllables have no markings.[68]

(1) Śyena, or Prajāpati, or Dīrghāyuṣya (Grāmageyagāna 73.1, ascribed to Prajāpati)

Source Verse (Sāmaveda-Saṃhitā 1.73):

1 2 3 2 3 2 3 1 2 3 1 2 3 1 2 3 2 3 1 2
abodhy agniḥ samidhā janānaṃ prati dhenum ivāyatīm uṣāsam /

3 1 2 3 2 3 2 3 1 2 3 2 3 1 2 3 2 3
yahvā iva pra vayām ujjihānāḥ pra bhānavaḥ sasrate nākam

1 2
accha //

Translation:

Agni (agniḥ) has wakened (abodhi) by means of the people's (janānām) firewood (samidhā), expecting (prati) the dawn (uṣāsam), [who] has appeared (āyatīm) like (iva) a cow (dhenum). Like (iva) the youngest [birds] (yahvāḥ) flying (ujjihānāḥ) up (pra) to a branch (vayām), [his] rays (bhānavaḥ) spring (sasrate) forth (pra) towards (accha) the vault of heaven (nākam).

Chant:

45r 4 1 2 1 2r 1Sr r 1 2 2
abodhi yā / gnāiḥ samidhā janā2nām / pratāi dhe3nūm /

r 1r r 2 1 2 2 1 Sr 1r 2 12r r
ivāyatīm uṣāsam / yahvā ī3vā / pra vā2yām ujjihānāḥ /

1r 2 r 1r 2 1 2 1 2
pra bhānā23vāḥ / sasrate nākam accha / iḍā23 bhā343 /

1
o2345i / ḍā //

[a] The *parvan* is sung as though notated $123_{234}5$.
[b] Sung as though notated 11r1 or 21r1.

[a]Sung as though notated 2^.

45
ka ma ccha / i dā
2 1 2 1 ·123
bhā
2343
/ o
12345
i / dā

(2) <u>Pāṣṭhauha</u> I (Grāmageyagāna 192.1, ascribed to Paṣṭhavāṭ)

Source Verse (Sāmaveda-Saṃhitā 1.192):

1 2 3 1 2r 3 2 3 1 2 3 2
mahi trīṇām avar astu dyukṣam mitrasyāryamṇaḥ /

3 2 3 1 2
durādharṣaṃ varuṇasya //

Translation:

Great (<u>mahi</u>) be (<u>astu</u>) the protection (<u>avaḥ</u>) of the three (<u>trīṇām</u>): the heavenly (<u>dyukṣam</u>) [protection] of Mitra (<u>mitrasya</u>) and Aryaman (<u>aryamṇaḥ</u>), the invincible (<u>durādharṣam</u>) [protection] of Varuṇa (<u>varuṇasya</u>).

Chant:

3 2^ 3 5 1 1 3 2 3 5
mahāi trā234iṇam / avā2r astū / dyukṣaṃ ma234itra /

1 1 3 2^ 3 5S 2 1r 5
syā2ryamṇāḥ / durādhā234rṣam / var au ho234 / vā /

4 5
nā5syo6 hāi //

(3) <u>Pāṣṭhauha</u> II (Grāmageyagāna 192.2, ascribed to Paṣṭhavāṭ)

Source Verse: same as for (2).

Chant:

5 r r 5 2 1 r
mahi trīṇām avar astū6 e / dyukṣaṃ mitrasyāryamṇaḥ /

21r 2 1 1 1^
durādhā23rṣām / var au ho2 / hiṃ mā2 / ṇa / syo2 /

3 5r r 2r 1 2 1 31111
yā234 au ho vā / hā o vā / o vā2345 //

(4) <u>Dhurāsākamaśva</u> (Grāmageyagāna 193.1, ascribed to Sākamaśva)

Source Verse (Sāmaveda-Saṃhitā 1.193):

1 2 3 1 2
tvāvataḥ purūvaso vayam indra praṇetaḥ /

1 2
smasi sthātar harīṇām //

Translation:

Indra (<u>indra</u>), [our] guide (<u>praṇetaḥ</u>), abounding in

[a]Sung as though notated 1. [b]Sung as though notated 2^.
[c]Unclear on tape: approximate transcription.

[a]Unclear on tape: approximate transcription.

riches (purūvaso), we (vayam) belong to (smasi) [a god] like you (tvāvataḥ), driver (sthātaḥ) of the horses Hari (harīṇām).

Chant:

```
 1r   2      s     2        1 r 2       s     2
tvāvato3 / hāu3 ho3li / purūvaso3 / hāu3 ho3li /

 2 1       2     s     2        1 r 2       s     2
vayam indrā3 / hāu3 ho3li / praṇetā3ḥ / hāu3 ho3li /

 1      2r         s     2       1 r 2       s      2
smasi sthātā3ḥ / hāu3 ho3li / harīṇā3m / hāu3 ho312345i /

ḍā //
```

(5) Gaurīvita (Grāmageyagāna 318.1, ascribed to Gaurīvita)

Source Verse (Sāmaveda-Saṃhitā 1.318):

```
2      3    1 2   3 1  2             3  1       2r    3 1 2 3    2 3    2
indraṃ naro nemadhitā havante yat pāryā yunajate dhiyas tāḥ /

 2 3   1 2 3     1 2      3  2 3 1     2r      3 1   2 3   1    2
śūro nṛṣātā śravasaś ca kāma ā gomati vraje bhajā tvaṃ naḥ //
```

Translation:

In competition (nemadhitā) men (naraḥ) invoke (havante) Indra (indram), that (yat) he may put to use (yunajate) those (tāḥ) effective (pāryāḥ) prayers (dhiyaḥ). You (tvam), hero (śūraḥ) in war (nṛṣātā) and (ca) in (ā) love (kāmaḥ) of glory (śravasaḥ), distribute (bhaja) to us (naḥ) in [our] shed (vraje) full of cows (gomati).

Chant:

```
2      ^  3   5      2 ^ 3      5       2 1             2   ^ 3   5
indran nā234ro / nemādhā234itā / havantā23i / yat pārā234yāḥ /

 2 ^ 3     5S         2 1             2 ^   3     5S    2
yūnājā234tāi / dhiyās tā23ḥ / śūro nā234rṣā / tā

 ^ 3     5S        2  1          2  ^ 3    5        2 ^       3    5
śrāvā234saḥ / ca kāmā23i / ā gomā234tī / vrajāi bhā234jā /

 1   S     2      2     1r 31111
tvan nā3 u vā3 / e3 /  āyū2345ḥ //
```

(6) Tārkṣyasāman I (Grāmageyagāna 332.1, ascribed to Tārkṣya)

Source Verse (Sāmaveda-Saṃhitā 1.332):

♪=120
Tape IVb(2)
d=e♭
ma hi t rī nā ma va ra stū
5 r r 56
e / dyu kṣa
5 2 1
mi t ra s yā r ya m ṇā
r
ḥ / du rā dhā
2 lr 123
r sā m / va rau
2 1

25
ho / hum mā /
na / syo / yā
30
au ho vā / hā o
5r r 2r 1
35
vā / o vā
2 1 111

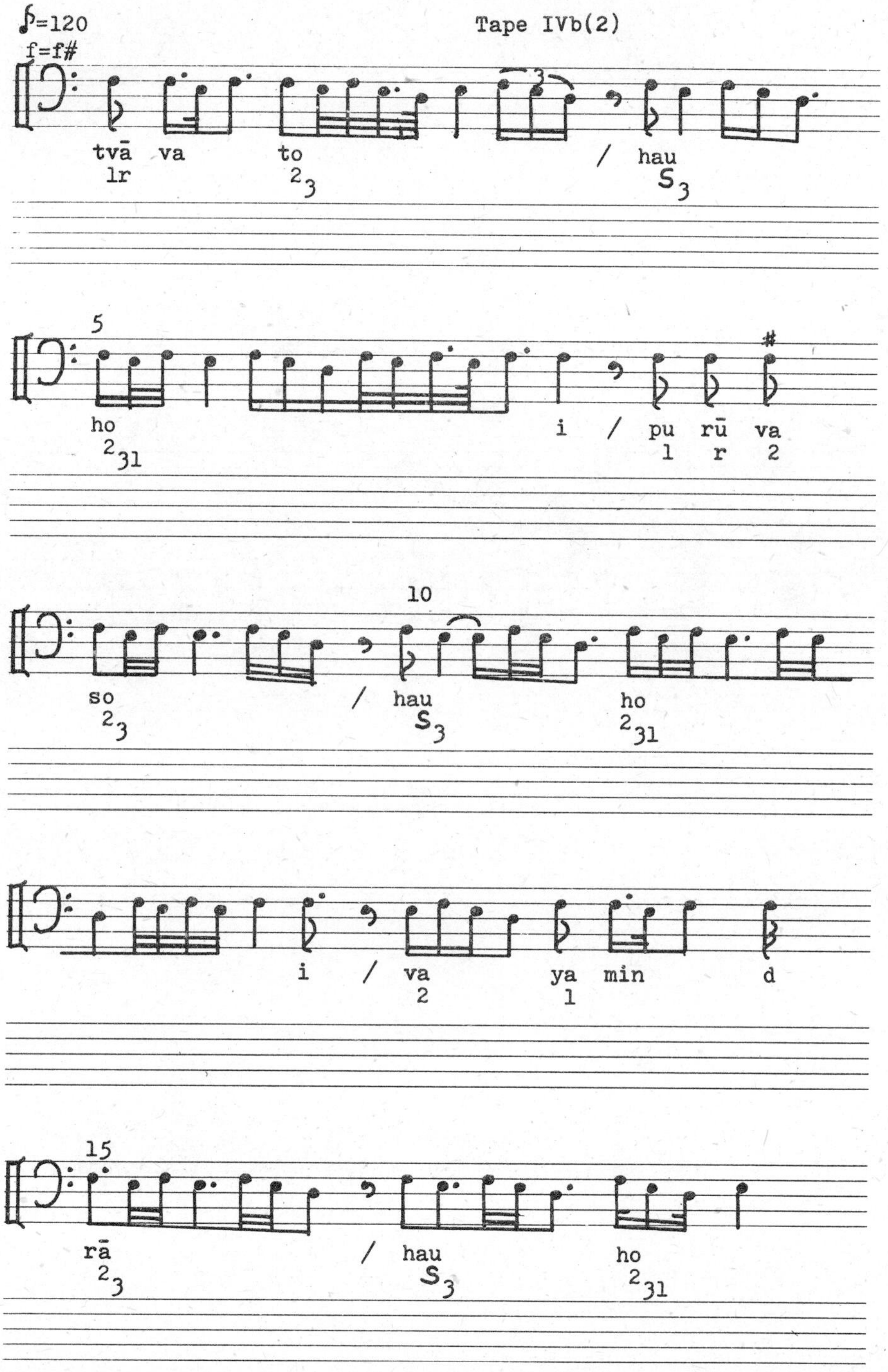
=120
f=f#
Tape IVb(2)
tvā va to / hau
1r 23 S3
5
ho i / pu rū va
231 1 r 2
10
so / hau ho
23 S3 231
i / va ya min d
2 1
15
rā / hau ho
23 S3 231

20
i / pra ne ta
1 r 2 3
h / hau ho i /
S 3 2 31
25
sma si sthā ta h / hau
1 2r 2 3 S 3
30
ho i / ha rī nā
2 31 1 r 2 3
m / hau ho
S 3 2 312345

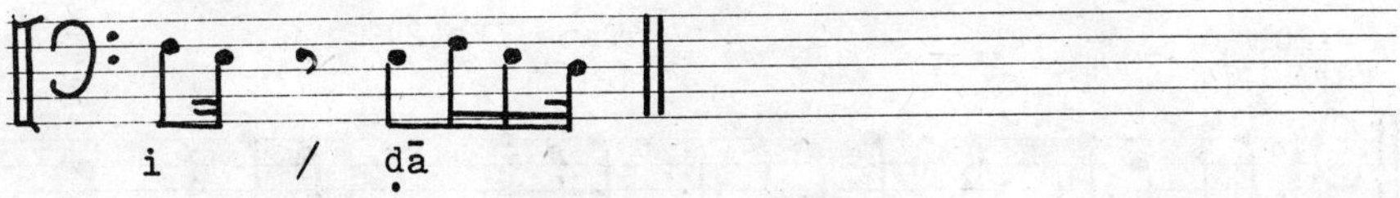
i / ḍā

=120
f=f#
Tape IVb(2)
in d ran nā
2 3234
ro /
5
5
ne mā
2
dhā i tā /
3234 5
10
ha van tā i / ya t
2 1 123 2

[a]At this point the chanters repeat the portion from "havantāi."

25
nā r
3234
sā / tā ś rā
5 2
30
vā sā
3234 5
h / ca kā mā
2 1 123
35
i / ā go
2

mā
3234
tī
5
/
40
vra
2
jā
i
bhā
3234
jā
5
/
tvan
1
nā
S3
45
u
vā
23
/
e
23
/
ā
lr
yū
111
32345
h.

=120
e=f
Tape IVb(2)
5
tya mū ṣū / vā ji / nā
5 r 2r 3 2345
111
10
m / de va jū tā
2r r 3 234
m / sa ho vā nam
5 r 3r 2
15
tā / ru tā /
1 2 2 3
20
ra m̐ ra thā
2 3 4

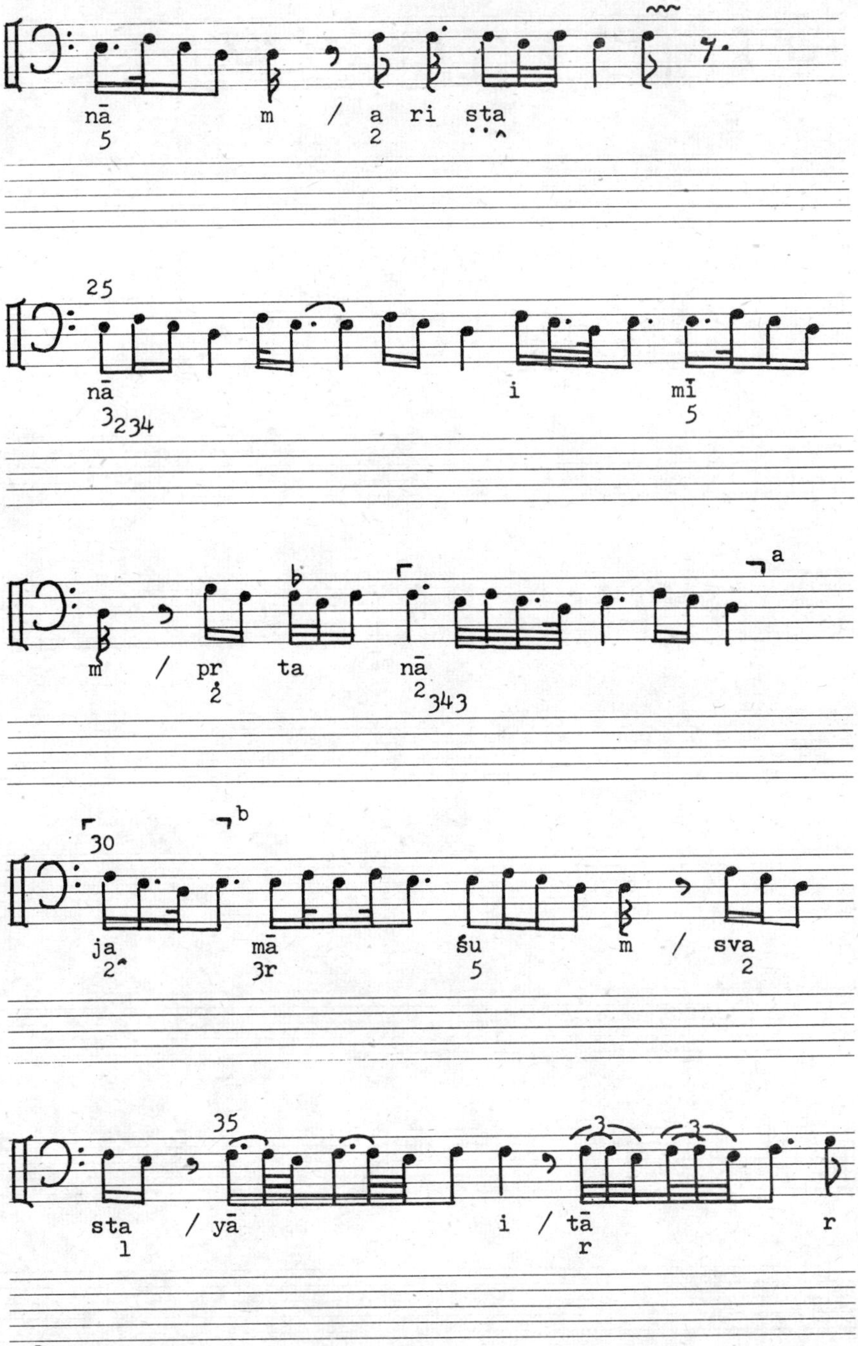

[a]Unclear on tape: approximate transcription.

[b]Sung as though ^ were absent.

ksya
"2"
mi
3
hā
2343
40
hū
23
vā
45
i
mā
5656

2 3 2 3 1 2 3 1 2 3 1 2 3 2 3 1 2
tyam ū ṣu vājinaṃ devajūtaṁ sahovānaṃ tarutāraṁ rathānām /

1 2 3 1 2 3 2 3 2 3 1 2 3 1 2
ariṣṭanemiṃ pṛtanājam āśuṁ svastaye tārkṣyam ihā huvema //

Translation:

For [our] good fortune (svastaye) may we call (huvema) forward (iha), forthwith (ū ṣu), Tārkṣya (tārkṣyam), that (tyam) warrior (vājinam) incited by the gods (devajūtam), mighty (sahovānam), impeller (tarutāraṃ) of chariots (rathānām), he whose rims are unbroken (ariṣṭanemim), hero (pṛtanājam), swift (āśum).

Chant:

5 r 2r 31111 2r r^3 5 r3r 2 1
tyam ū ṣū / vāji / nā2345m / devajūtā234m / sahovānaṃ tā /

2 ^ 2^ 3 4 5S 2 ^3 5 2 2^
rutā3 / raṁ rathānām / ariṣṭanā234imīm / pṛtanā343jam

3r 5 2 1 r 2^ 3 2 2 4
āśum / svasta / yāi / tārkṣyam ihā343 / hū3vā5imā656 //

(7) Tārkṣyasāman II (Grāmageyagāna 332.2, ascribed to Tārkṣya)

Source Verse: same as for (6).

Chant:

2r 2 r r 4 23r 5 3 5
ī ya i yā3 hāi / tyam ū ṣu vājinā3ṃ de3vajūtam / ī4 ya

4 5r 3 5 r3r 2 1 2 2^ 3 4 5S
i yā / hā234i / sahovānaṃ tā / rutā3 / raṁ rathānam /

2r 2 1S 2 1 2^ 3 4 5S
ī ya i yā3 hāi / ariṣṭā3 / nāi / mī3ṃ pṛta / nājam āśum /

3 5 4 5r 31111 2 1 r 2^ 3 2
ī4 ya i yā / hā2345i / svasta / yāi / tārkṣyam ihā343 /

2 4
hū3vā5imā656 //

(8) Indrasya Tāta (Grāmageyagāna 333.1, ascribed to Indra)

Source Verse (Sāmaveda-Saṃhitā 1.333):

3 2 3 1 2 3 2 3 2 3 1 2 3 2 3 2 3
trātāram indram avitāram indraṁ have have suhavaṁ śuram

1 2
indram /

[a]The chanters are singing something other than the notated sequence.

ru tā / ra m̆
2 2 3 2
30
ra thā nā m / ī ya i
3 4 5 2r
35
yā hā i / a ri
2 3 2
40
sta / nā i /
2 3 1
45
mī mpr ta / nā ja
2 3 1 2 3

mā 4 śū 5 m / ī 34 ya 5
50
i 4 yā 5r / hā 32345 111 i /
55
sva 2 sta 1 / yā i /
tā r r kṣya 2 mi 3
60
hā 2343 / hū 23

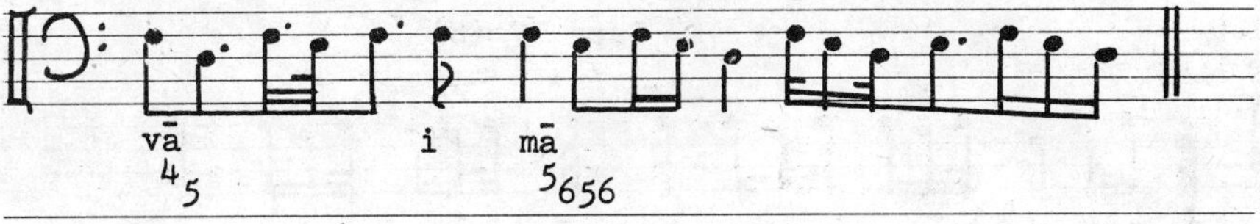
vā
4 5
i
mā
5656

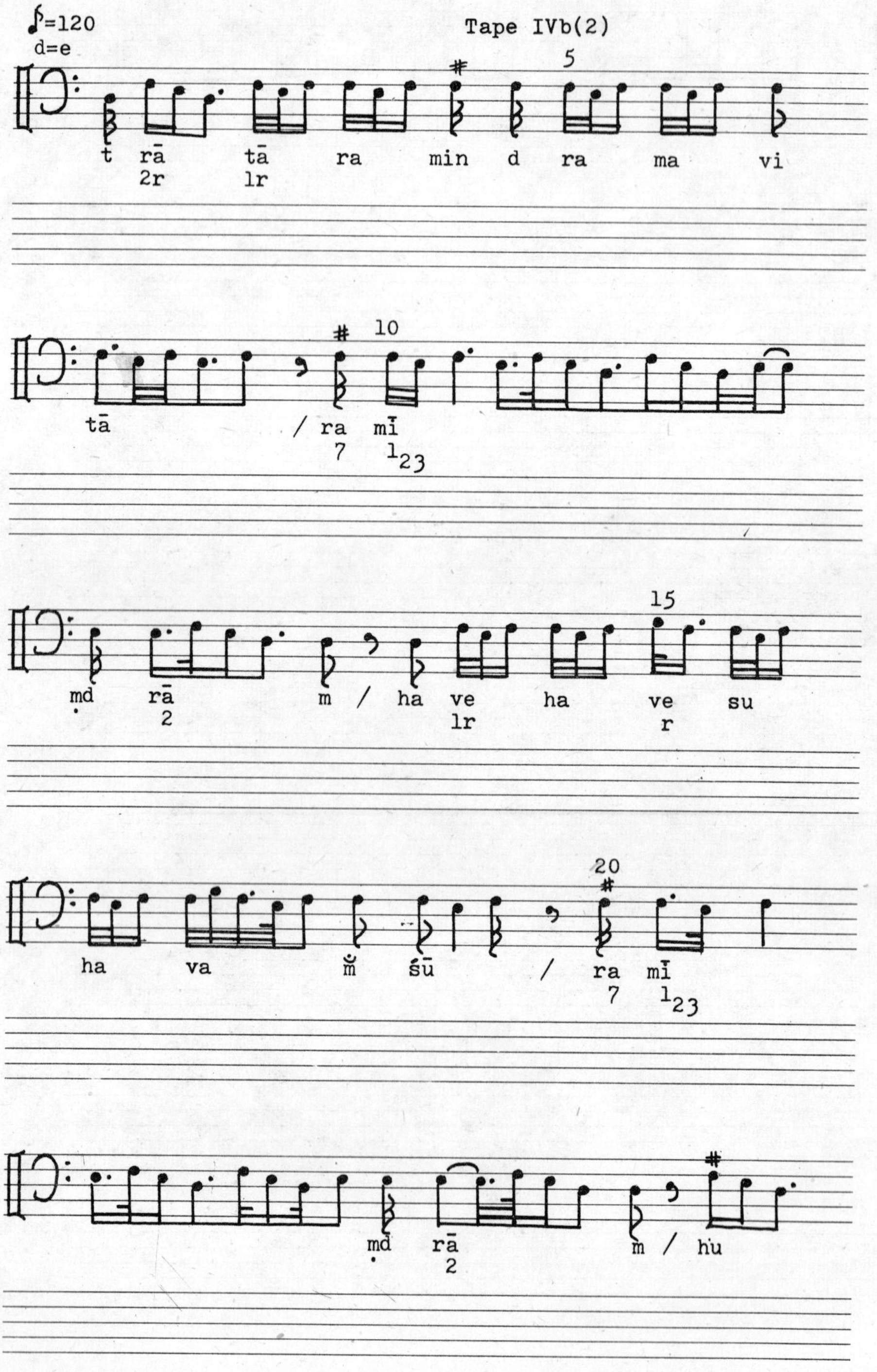
♪=120
d=e
Tape IVb(2)
t rā tā ra min d ra ma vi
2r lr
tā / ra mī
7 123
md rā m / ha ve ha ve su
2 lr r
ha va m̐ śū / ra mī
7 123
md rā m / hu
2

[a]Sung as though notated 2^.

[b]Unclear on tape: approximate transcription.

45
i / tū vā in d
23 45
rā ḥ
5656

32u 3 1 2 3 1 2r 3 2. 3 2 3 1 2 3
huve nu śakraṃ puruhūtam indram idaṁ havir maghavā vetv

1 2
indraḥ //

Translation:

Indra (indram) the defender (trātāram), Indra (indram) the protector (avitāram), Indra (indram), hero (śūram) listening willingly (suhavam) at each invocation (have have): I now (nu) call (huve) the powerful one (śakram), Indra (indram), invoked by many (puruhūtam). May Indra (indraḥ), the munificent one (maghavā), enjoy (vetu) this (idam) oblation (haviḥ).

Chant:

2r1r 7 2S 1r r
trātāram indram avitā / ram ī23ṃdrām / have have suhavaṁ śū /

7 2S 1 7 2S
ram ī23ṃdrām / huvāi nu śakraṃ puruhū / tam ī23ṃdrām /

1. 2 1 r 2 1 r 2 2 4
idaṁ svasti no maghavā / vā343i / tū3 vā5 indrā656ḥ //

NOTE: The parvan / 2 1. 2 1 r 2 1 r idaṁ svasti no maghavā /, after the reading of Ṛgveda 6.47.11, is replaced by / 2 1. 2 idaṁ ha / 1 vāiḥ / 2 1 r maghavā / in the edition of Nārāyaṇasvāmī.

(9) Atīṣādīya (Grāmageyagāna 572.6, ascribed to Prajāpati)

Source Verse (Sāmaveda-Saṃhitā 1.572):

1 2 3 2 3 2u 3 2 3 1 2
somaḥ punāna ūrmiṇāvyaṃ vāraṃ vidhāvati /

1 2 3 1 2r 3 1 2
agre vācaḥ pavamānaḥ kanidradat //

Translation:

Soma (somaḥ), purified (punānaḥ), flows (vidhāvati) with [his] wave (ūrmiṇā) through the woolen Soma strainer (avyaṃ vāram): roaring (kanikradat), flowing clearly (pavamānaḥ), before (agre) [invocatory] Speech (vācaḥ).

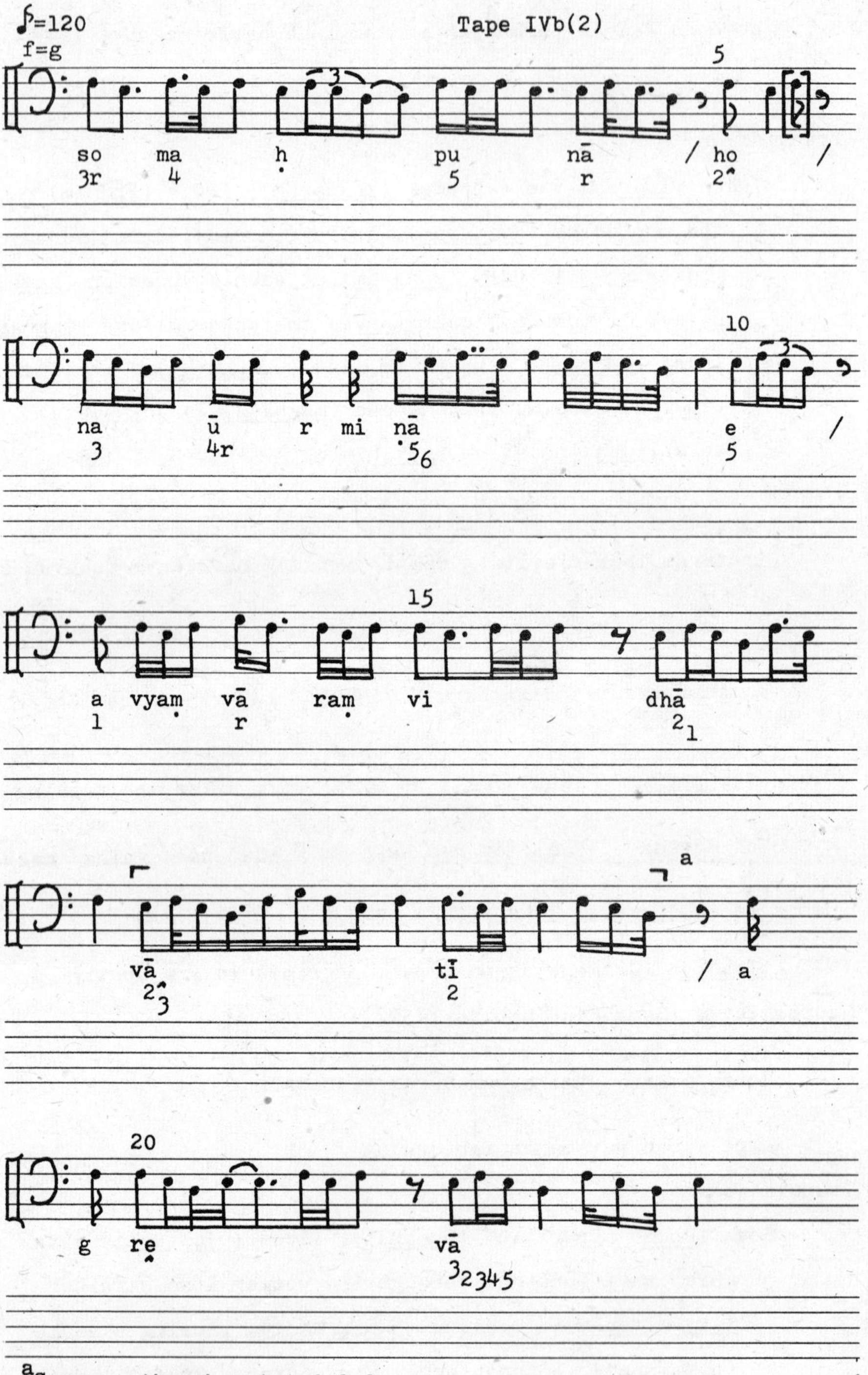

[a]Sung as though notated $2_1 2_3$.

/ cā h /
3 2 111 345
25
pa va mā nā
2 1 1 23 2̂ 3
h / kā nā
1 2̂ 3 234
30
au ho vā /
5r r
kra da de
2 3 2 111 345

Chant:

```
3r 4   5 r    2^     3 4r   5  5   1       r          2  2^ 2
somaḥ punā / ho / na ūrmiṇā6 e / avyaṃ vāraṃ vidhālvā3tī /

  ^ 3          31111       2 1       2^       1^ 3     5r  r
agre vā2345 / cā2345ḥ / pavamā23nā3ḥ / kā2nā234 au ho vā /

  2    31111
kradad e2345 //
```

(10) Loman, Dīrgha (Grāmageyagāna 582.1, ascribed to Bharadvāja)

Source Verse (Sāmaveda-Saṃhitā 1.582):

```
1  2   3  1   2r 3    2  3 1  2 3 1        2r
sa sunve yo vasūnāṃ yo rāyām ānetā ya iḍānām /

2 3  1    2     3 2
somo yaḥ sukṣitīnām //
```

Translation:

Extracted (sunve) is he (saḥ) who (yaḥ) is the bringer (ānetā) of riches (vasūnām), possessions (rāyām), refreshments (iḍānām). Soma (somaḥ) [it is] who (yaḥ) [is the bringer] of places of refuge (sukṣitīnām).

Chant:

```
4   5      1r  r          2          1     1          r r     1      2
sā sū / nve yo vasū23nām / yo rā2yām ā2 / netā ya iḍā23nām /

  1   2      1      2 1      5   5
so23māḥ / yaḥ sukṣitā234ino6 hāi //
```

(11) Rathantara (Āraṇyakagāna 49.1, ascribed to Vasiṣṭha)

Source Verse (Sāmaveda-Saṃhitā 1.233):

```
3  1   2          3 1   2             3 1 2
abhi tvā śūra nonumo 'dugdhā iva dhenavaḥ /

1 2     3   1    2r        3  2 3  1 2             3   1 2
īśānam asya jagataḥ svardṛśam īśānam indra tasthuṣaḥ //
```

Translation:

Like (iva) unmilked (adugdhāḥ) cows (dhenavaḥ), we cry out (nonumaḥ), hero (śūra), to (abhi) you (tvā), ruler (īśānam) of that (asya) which moves (jagataḥ), ruler (īśānam) of that which is immovable (tasthuṣaḥ), whose eye is the sun (svardṛśam), O Indra (indra).

[a]Sung as though notated 2r.

[b]Sung as though notated 2rlrl.

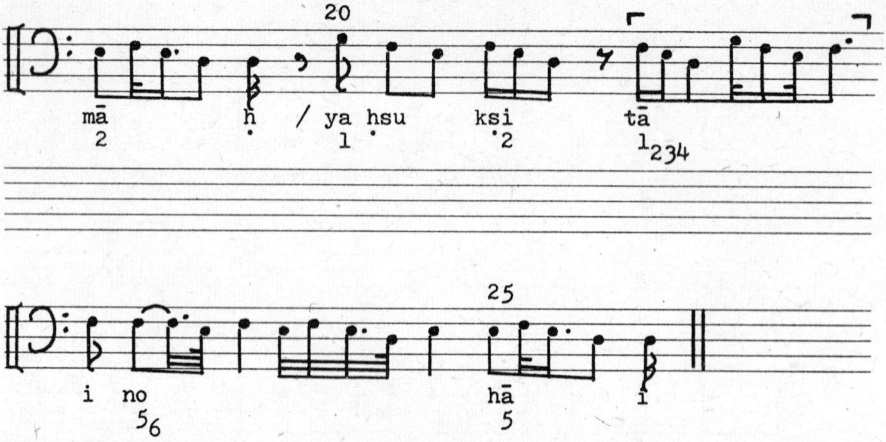

[a]Sung as though notated 2_1.

Chant:

2 r r r 1 2r r r r
ābhi tvā śūra nonumo vā / ādugdhā iva dhenava īśānam

1 2 1 r 2 1 4
asya jagataḥ / suvā23rdṛśām / aiśānam ā23indrā3 /

1 r r 5 5 1
tāsthū234ṣā / o vā6 / hāu vā / as //

(12) Setuṣāman (Āraṇyakagāna 57.1, ascribed to Prajāpati)

Source Verse (Āraṇyaka-Saṃhitā 1.9):

3 1 2 3 2 3 2 3 1 2 3 1 2 3 1 2 3 1 2
aham asmi prathamajā ṛtasya pūrvaṃ devebhyo amṛtasya nāma /

2 3 1 2 3 2u 3 1 2 32u 3 1 2 3 1 2
yo mā dadāti sa id evam āvad aham annam annam adantam admi //

Translation:

I (aham) am (asmi) the primal issue (prathamajāḥ) of cosmic order (ṛtasya), the name (nāma) of immortality (amṛtasya), [existing] prior (pūrvam) to the gods (devebhyaḥ). He (saḥ) who (yaḥ) offers (dadāti) me (mā) assuredly (id evam) is favored (āvat); I (aham) am food (annam), [and] consuming (adantam) I consume (admi) food (annam).

Chant:

2r r r 1r r 2 2 1
hāu hāu hāu / setuṃs tara / (triḥ) / dusta / rān / (dve

r2r1r r 2 r r r
triḥ) / dānenādānam / (triḥ) / hāu hāu hāu / aham asmi

r 1 2111 2r r r 1r r 2
prathamajā ṛtā23syā345 / hāu hāu hāu / setuṃs tara /

1 r 2r 1r 2
(triḥ) / dusta / rān / (dve triḥ) / akrodhena krodham /

1 r 2r 1r 2r r r r
(dviḥ) / akrodhena krodham / hāu hāu hāu / pūrvaṃ

r r r 1 2111 2r r r 1r r 2
devebhyo amṛtasya nā23mā345 / hāu hāu hāu / setuṃs tara /

1 2 1 r 2r
(triḥ) / dusta / rān / (dve triḥ) / śraddhayāśraddhām /

r r r r r r r 1 2111
(triḥ) / hāu hāu hāu / yo mā dadāti sa id evam ā23vā345t /

=138
f=f#
Tape IIIa(1)
ā bhi t vā śū ra no nu mo vā / ā
2 r r r 1
du g dhā i va dhe na va ī śā
2r r r r
na ma sya ja ga ta ḥ / su vā
1 1 23
rdṛ śā m / ā i śā na
2 1 r 2
mā in drā / tā
1 23 4 3 1

[a] Sung as though notated 3_{234}.

[b] Sung as though notated 5.

=120
f=g
Tape IVb(2)
hā u hā u hā u / se
2r r r lr
5 10
tū̃m̐ sta ra / se tū̃m̐ sta
r 2 lr r 2
15
ra / se tū̃m̐ sta ra / du
lr r 2 2
20
sta / rā n / du sta /
1 2 1
rā n / du sta / rā
2 1

25
n / dā ne nā
r 2r lr
30
dā na m / dā ne
r 2 lr 2r
35
nā dā na m / dā
lr r 2 lr
40
ne nā dā na m / hā u
2r lr r 2 r
45
hā u hā u / a ha ma s mi p ra tha
r r

50
ma jā r r tā
r i 1 23
s yā 2111 345 / hā u 2r
55
hā u hā u / se tūṁ
r r lr r
60 65
sta ra / se tūṁ sta ra / se
2 lr r 2 lr
70
tūṁ sta ra / du sta / rā
r 2 1

n / du sta / rā n /
2 1
75
du sta / rā n /
2 1
80
a k ro dhe na k ro dha m /
r 2r 1r 2
85
a k ro dhe na k ro dha m /
1 r 2r 1r 2
90 95
a k ro dhe na k ro dha m / hā
1 r 2r 1r 2r

u hā u hā u / pū r vaṃ
r r r
de ve bhyo am ṛ ta sya nā
r r r 1 1 23
mā 2 111 345
/ hā u
2r
hā u hā u / se tūm̐ sta
r r lr r 2
ra / se tūm̐ sta ra / se
lr r 2 lr

125
tūm̐ sta ra / du sta / rā
r 2 1
130
n / du sta / rā n /
2 1
du sta / rā n / śra
2 1 2
135
ddha yā śra ddhā m / śra
1 r 2r 2
140
ddha yā śra ddhā m / śra
1 r 2r 2

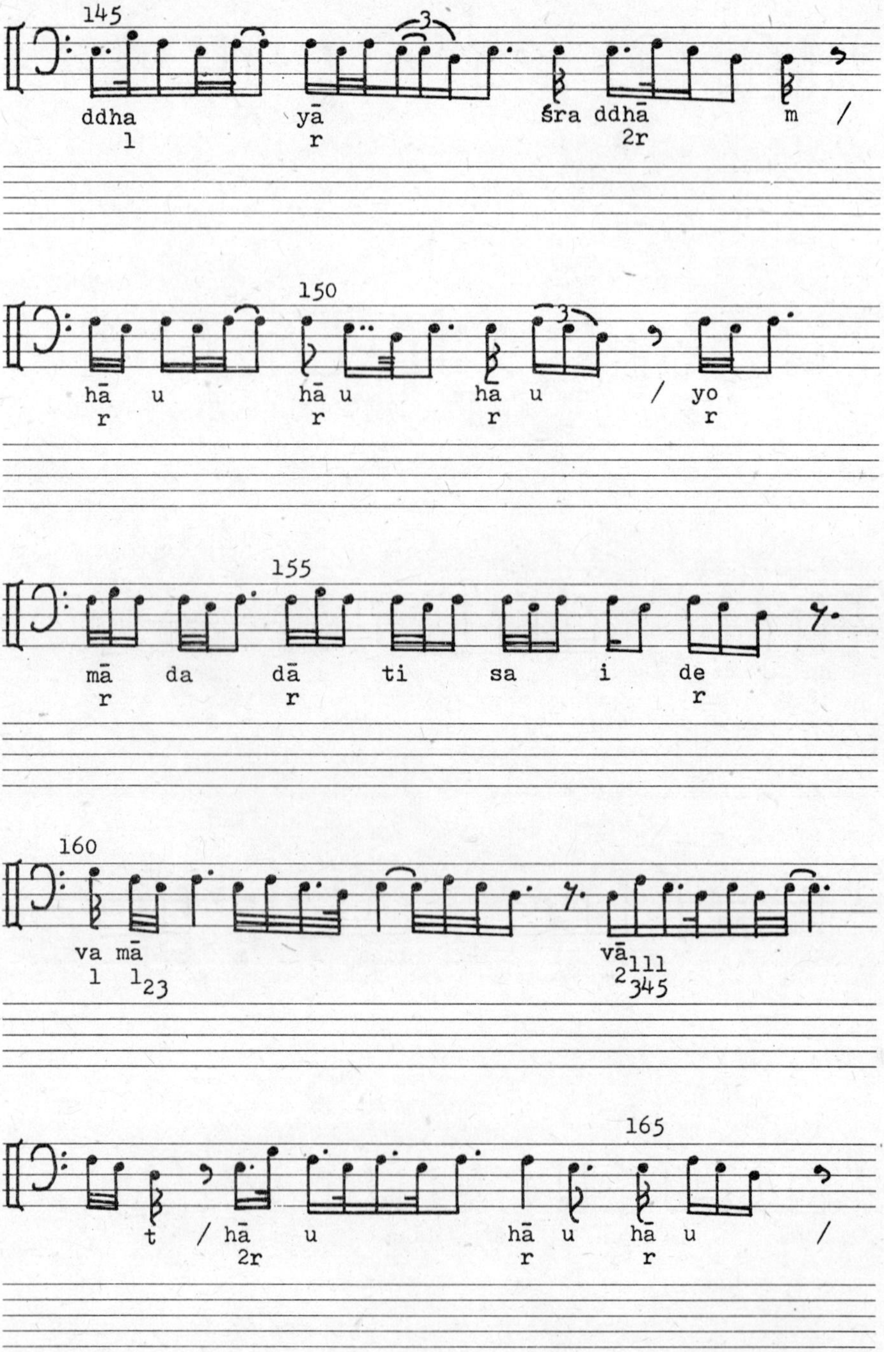
145
ddha yā śra ddhā m /
1 r 2r
150
hā u hā u ha u / yo
r r r r
155
mā da dā ti sa i de
r r r
160
va mā vā111
1 123 2345
165
t / hā u hā u ha u /
2r r r

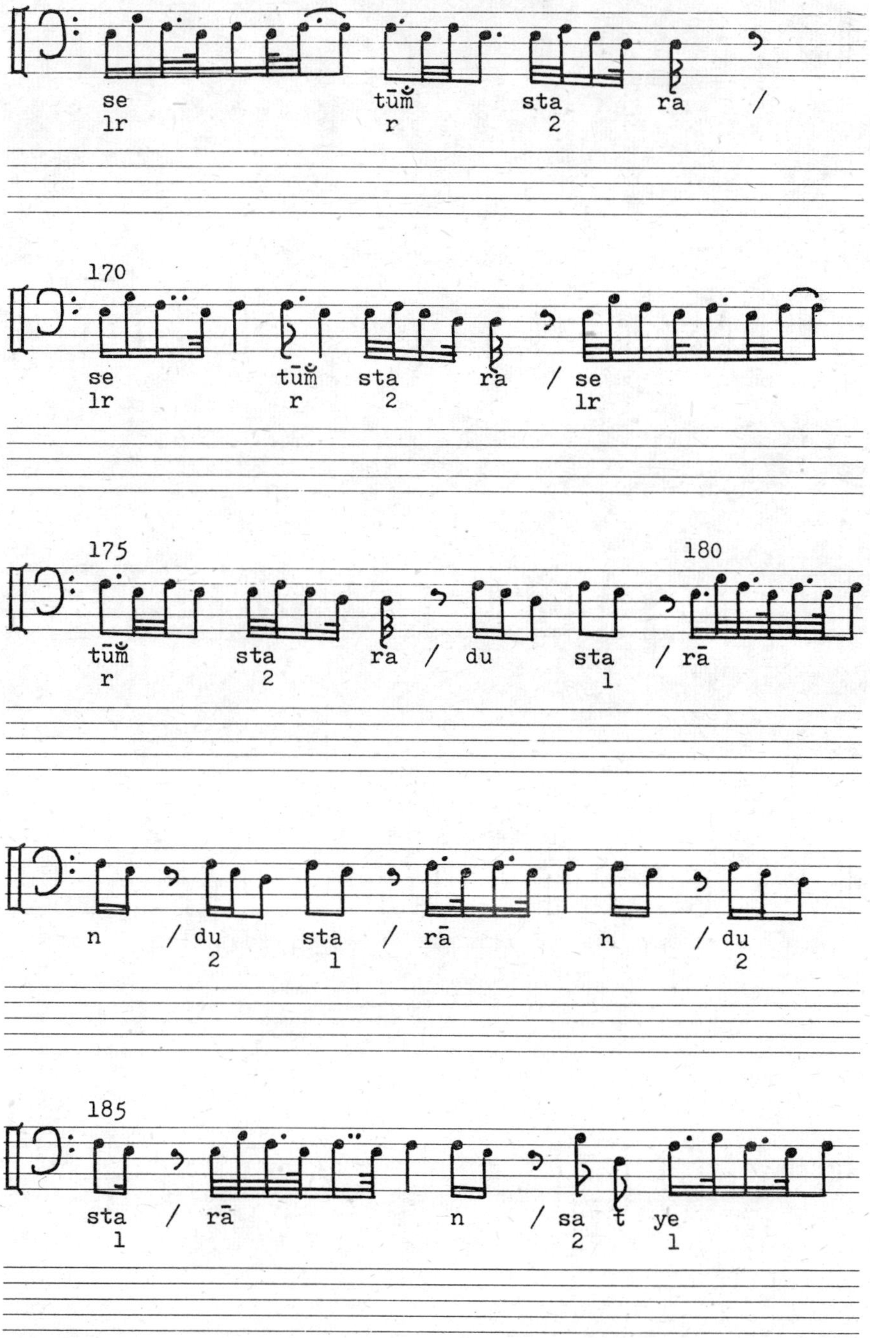
se tūm̐ sta ra /
1r r 2
170
se tūm̐ sta ra / se
1r r 2 1r
175 180
tūm̐ sta ra / du sta / rā
r 2 1
n / du sta / rā n / du
2 1 2
185
sta / rā n / sa t ye
1 2 1

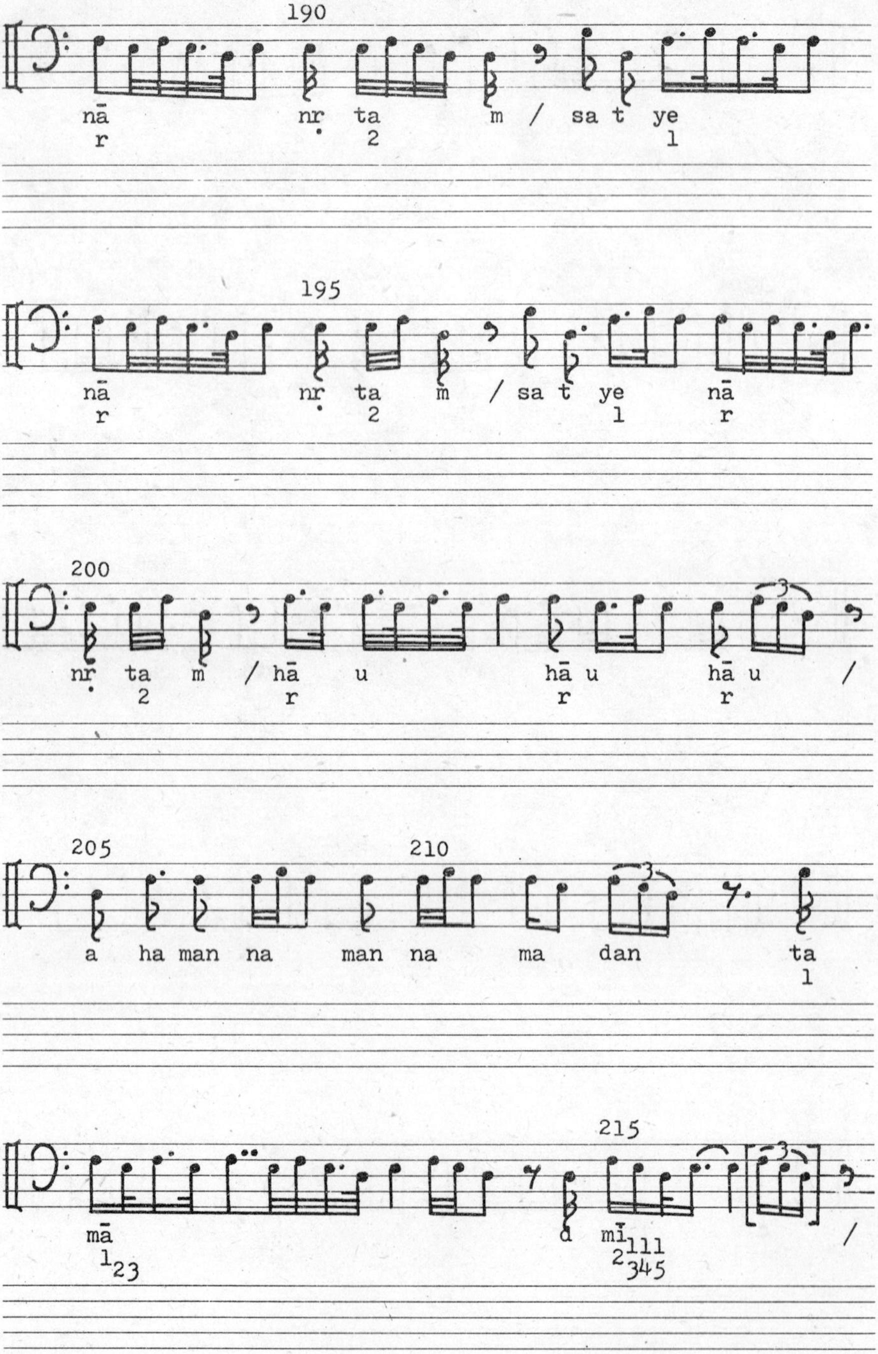
190
nā nṛ ta m / sa t ye
r 2 1
195
nā nṛ ta m / sa t ye nā
r 2 1 r
200
nṛ ta m / hā u hā u hā u /
2 r r r
205 210
a ha man na man na ma dan ta
1
215
mā d mī /
123 2111345

hā u hā u hā u
2S S S
220
vā / e sā ga ti ḥ /
r ir
225
e ṣā ga ti ḥ / e sā
2r ir 2r ir
230 235
ga ti ḥ / e ta da mṛ
2r 1 2 i
240
tam / e ta da mṛ tam / e
2r 1 2 i 2r

[a]Sung as though notated 2r.

2r r r lr r 2 1
hāu hāu hāu / setūṃs tara / (trih) / dusta / rān /

2 1r 2 r r r
(dve triḥ) / satyenānṛtam / (triḥ) / hāu hāu hāu /

1 2111 2S S S
aham annam annam adantam ā23dmī345 / hāu hāu hāu vā /

r1r 2r 1 2 1 1
eṣā gatiḥ / (triḥ) / etad amṛtam / (triḥ) / svar

2 1r 2 1r r
gaccha / (triḥ) / jyotir gaccha / (triḥ) / setūṃs

2r 1r 2 1 1111
tīrtvā caturā2345ḥ //

(13) Āmahīyava (Ūhagāna 1.1.1, ascribed to Amahīyu)

Source Verses (Sāmaveda-Saṃhitā 2.22-24):

3 1 2 3 1 2r 3 1 2r
1. uccā te jātam andhaso divi sad bhūmy ā dade /

3 2u 3 2 3 1 2
ugraṃ śarma mahi śravaḥ //

2 3 1 2 3 1 2 3 1 2 3 1 2
2. sa na indrāya yajyave varuṇāya marudbhyaḥ /

3 1 2r
varivovit pari srava //

3 1 2r 3 2u 3 2 3 1 2
3. enā viśvāny arya ā dyumnāni mānuṣāṇām /

1 2
siṣāsanto vanāmahe //

Translation:

1. High (uccā) is the birth (jātam) of your (te) juice (andhasaḥ). I receive (dade) [the drink], existing (sat) in heaven (divi), on (ā) the earth (bhūmi). Powerful (ugram) is [your] protection (śarma), great (mahi) [your] glory (śravaḥ).
2. Finding an outlet (varivovit), circle you (saḥ) round (pari srava) [the strainer] for us (naḥ), for the sacrifice-worthy (yajyave) Indra (indrāya), for Varuṇa (varuṇāya), for the Maruts (marudbhyaḥ).
3. Wishing to acquire (siṣāsantaḥ) here (enā) all (viśvāni) powers (dyumnāni) of men (mānuṣāṇām), through (ā) the master (aryaḥ) we are victorious (vanāmahe).

=120
e=g
Tape VIIIb(34)
u ccā tā i jā
5 r 2 3 4r
5 10
ta maṅ dha sā ḥ / di vā i sā d
5 2 1 2 1
15
bhū / mi yā da
1 2 1 1 23
20
dā i / u gra m̐ śa rmā / ma hā
2 1 2 1 1 23
25
i ś ra vā u / vā
2 2 3

30
sa na ā in drā ya ya jya
5 2 3 4r 5
35
vā i / va rū nā yā /
2 1 2 1 1 2
40
ma rū d bhi yā h / va ri
1 1 23 2 1
45
vo vā i t / pa rā i
2r 1 1 23
50
ś ra vā u / vā
2 2 3

[a]Displaced tonal center here.

Chant:

5 r 2 4r 5 2 1 2 1
1. uccā tā3i jātam andhasāḥ / divāi sāld bhū2 / mi yā23
2 1 2 1 2
dadāi / ugraṁ śarmā / mahā23i śravāu / vā3 /

5 2 4r 5 2 1 2 1 2
2. sa na ā3indrāya yajyavāi / varūṇālyā2 / marū23dbhiyāḥ /
1 2r 1 2
varivovāit / parā23i sravāu / vā3 /

5r r 2 4r 5 2 1 2 1 2
3. enā vā3iśvāni arya ā / dyumnānāli mā2 / nuṣā23ṇām /
1r 2 1 2 2r 111
siṣāsantāḥ / vanā23mahāu / vā3 / stauṣe345 //

(14) Vāmadevya (Ūhagāna 1.1.5, ascribed to Vāmadeva)

Source Verses (Sāmaveda-Saṃhitā 2.32-34):

1 2 3 1 2r 3 2 3 1 2 3 1 2
1. kayā naś citra ā bhuvad ūtī sadāvṛdhaḥ sakhā /
2 3 1 2 3 2
kayā śaciṣṭhayā vṛtā //

1 2 3 1 2r 3 1 2 3 1 2
2. kas tvā satyo madānāṃ maṁhiṣṭho matsad andhasaḥ /
3 1 2 3 2 3 1 2
dṛḍhā cid āruje vasu //

3 2u 3 1 2 3 1 2 3 2
3. abhī ṣu ṇaḥ sakhīnām avitā jaritṝṇām /
3 1 2 3 1 2
śataṃ bhavāsy ūtaye //

Translation:

1. With what (kayā) help (ūtī) will the wonderful (citraḥ) friend (sakhā), always giving prosperity (sadāvṛdhaḥ), assist (bhuvat) us (naḥ)? With what (kayā) most powerful (śaciṣṭhayā) retinue (vṛtā)?

2. What (kaḥ) true (satyaḥ), most generous (maṁhiṣṭhaḥ) of exhilarating drinks (madānām) of the Soma juice (andhasaḥ) will intoxicate (matsat) you (tvā) [so that you] break open (āruje) even (cit) fortified (dṛḍhā) treasure (vasu)?

3. [You who are] the excellent (su) protector (avitā) of us (naḥ), [your] friends (sakhīnām), [your] invokers (jaritṝṇām), do approach (abhi bhavasi) [us] a hundred times (śatam) for [our] protection (ūtaye).

Chant:

1. 3 r 4 2 4r 5 1 r 21r 2 1
ka5yā / naś ca3itrā3 ā bhuvāt / ū / tī sadāvṛdhas sa /
2 r 2 1 2^ 3 r 2
khā / au3 ho hāi / kayā23 śacāi / ṣṭhayau ho3 /
1 1↑ 2
hum mā2 / vā2rto35 hāi //

2. 3 r 4 2 4 5 1 2r 1 2 1
ka5s tvā / satyo3 mā3dānām / mā / hiṣṭho mātsād andha /
2 r 2 1 2^ 3 r 2 1
sā / au3 ho hāi / dṛḍhā23 cid ā / rujau ho3 / hum
1↑ 2
mā2 / vā2so35 hāi //

3. 3 r 4 2 4 5 1 2r 1 2r 1
ā5bhī / ṣu ṇā3s sā3khīnām / ā / vitā jarāitṝ / ṇām /
r 2 1 2^ 3 r 2 1
au23 ho hāi / śatā23m bhavā / si yau ho3 / hum mā2 /
1↑ 2
tā2yo35 hāi //

(15) Rathantara (Ūhyagāna 1.1.1, ascribed to Vasiṣṭha)

Source Verses (Sāmaveda-Saṃhitā 2.30-31):

1. 3 1 2 3 1 2 3 1 2
abhi tvā śūra nonumo 'dugdhā iva dhenavaḥ /
1 2 3 1 2r 3 2 3 1 2 3 1 2
īśānam asya jagataḥ svardṛśam īśānam indra tasthuṣaḥ //

2. 1 2r 3 2 3 1 2r 3 2 3 1 2r
na tvāvām̐ anyo divyo na pārthivo na jāto na janiṣyate /
3 1 2 3 1 2 3 1 2
aśvāyanto maghavann indra vājino gavyantas tvā
havāmahe //

Translation:

1. Like (iva) unmilked (adugdhāḥ) cows (dhenavaḥ), we cry

Tape VIIIb(31)
=120
f=g
kā yā / na ścā i
t rā yā bhu vā t / ū / tī sa dā
vṛ dha ssa / khā / au ho hā i / ka
yā śa cā i / stha yau ho
/ hum mā / vā rto hā i

[a]Displaced tonal center. [b]Not the usual interpretation.
[c]Sung as though notated 2_3.

[a]Not the usual interpretation of this sequence.

[b]Sung as though notated 2_3.

[a] Not the usual interpretation of this sequence.

[b] Sung as though notated 2_3.

out (nonumaḥ), hero (śūra), to (abhi) you (tvā), ruler (īśānam) of that (asya) which moves (jagataḥ), ruler (īśānam) of that which is immovable (tasthuṣaḥ), whose eye is the sun (svardṛśam), O Indra (indra).

2. None (na) other (anyaḥ) is like you (tvāvān), divine (divyaḥ) nor (na) earthly (pārthivaḥ), born (jātaḥ) nor (na) yet to be born (janiṣyate). Munificent (maghavan) Indra (indra), wishing for horses (aśvāyantaḥ) and cows (gavyantaḥ), we warriors (vājinaḥ) invoke (havāmahe) you (tvā).

Chant:

2 r r r 1 2r r r r
1. ābhi tvā śūra nonumo vā / ādugdhā iva dhenava īśānam

1 2 1 r 2 1 4
asya jagataḥ / suvā23rdṛśām / āiśānam ā23indrā3 /

1 r r 5 5 1
sūsthū234ṣā / o vā6 / hau vā / as //

2r 1 2 r r r r
2. īśo vā / nām indra susthuṣo na tvāvām anyo diviyaḥ /

1 2 1 r2r 1 4 1 r
na pā23rthivāḥ / na jāto nā23 jā3 / nāiṣyā234tā /

r 5 5 1
o vā6 / hau vā / as //

2 1 2 r r r
3. na jo vā / to na janiṣyate aśvāyanto maghavann i /

1 2 1 2 1 4 1 r
dra vā23jināḥ / gavyantas tvā23 hā3 / vāmā234hā /

r 5 5 1
o vā6 / hau vā / as //

(16) Bhakāra-Rathantara

Source Verses: same as for (15).

Chant:

2 r r r 1 1 2r
1. ābhi tvā śūra nonumo vā / om vāk bhā bhu bhā bhi bha

r r r
bhe bha bha bhī bhā bha bha bha bha bha bha

=120
Tape VIIIb(29)
f=e
ā bhi tvā śū ra no nu mo vā /
2 r r r 1
ā du gdhā i va dhe na va ī śā na ma
2r r r r
sya ja ga ta ḥ / su vā rdṛ
1 1 23
śā m / ā i śā na mā in drā
2 1 r 2 1 23 4 3
/ ta sthū sā / o vā /
1 1 234 r r 5 6

hā u vā
5
45 50
ī śo vā / nā min dra su sthu so na
2r 1 2 r
55 60
t vā vām̐ an yo di vi ya ḥ / na pā
r r r 1 1 23
65
r thi vā ḥ / na jā to nā
2 1 r 2r 1 23
70
jā / nā i syā
4 3 1 1 234

75
tā / o vā / hā u vā
r r 56 5
80
na jo vā / to na ja ni ṣya
2 1 2
85 90
te a ś vā yan to ma gha van nin /
r r r
95
dra vā ji nā ḥ / ga
1 123 2 1
100
v yan ta st vā hā /
2 123 43

vā mā hā /
1 1234 r
105
o vā / hā u vā / as
r 56 5 1

=120
f=g
Tape VIIIb(30)
5
ā bhi tvā śū ra no nu mo vā /
2 r r r 1
10 15 20
om vāk bhā bhu bhā bhi bha bhebha bha bhī bhā bha bha
1 2r r r r
25 30
bha bha bha bha bha / su vā
1 123
35
rdṛ śā m / ā i śā na mā
2 1 r 2 123
40
in drā / sū sthū
43 1 1234

45
sā / o vā / hā u vā / as
r r 56 5 1
50
ī śo vā / om vāk bhā bhi bha
2r 1 2
55 60 65
3
bhu bhu bho bha bha bhā bhā bha bho bhi bhi
r r r r
70
bho ḥ / na pā r thi vā ḥ /
r l 123 2
75
na jā to nā jā / nā i
1 r 2r 123 43 1

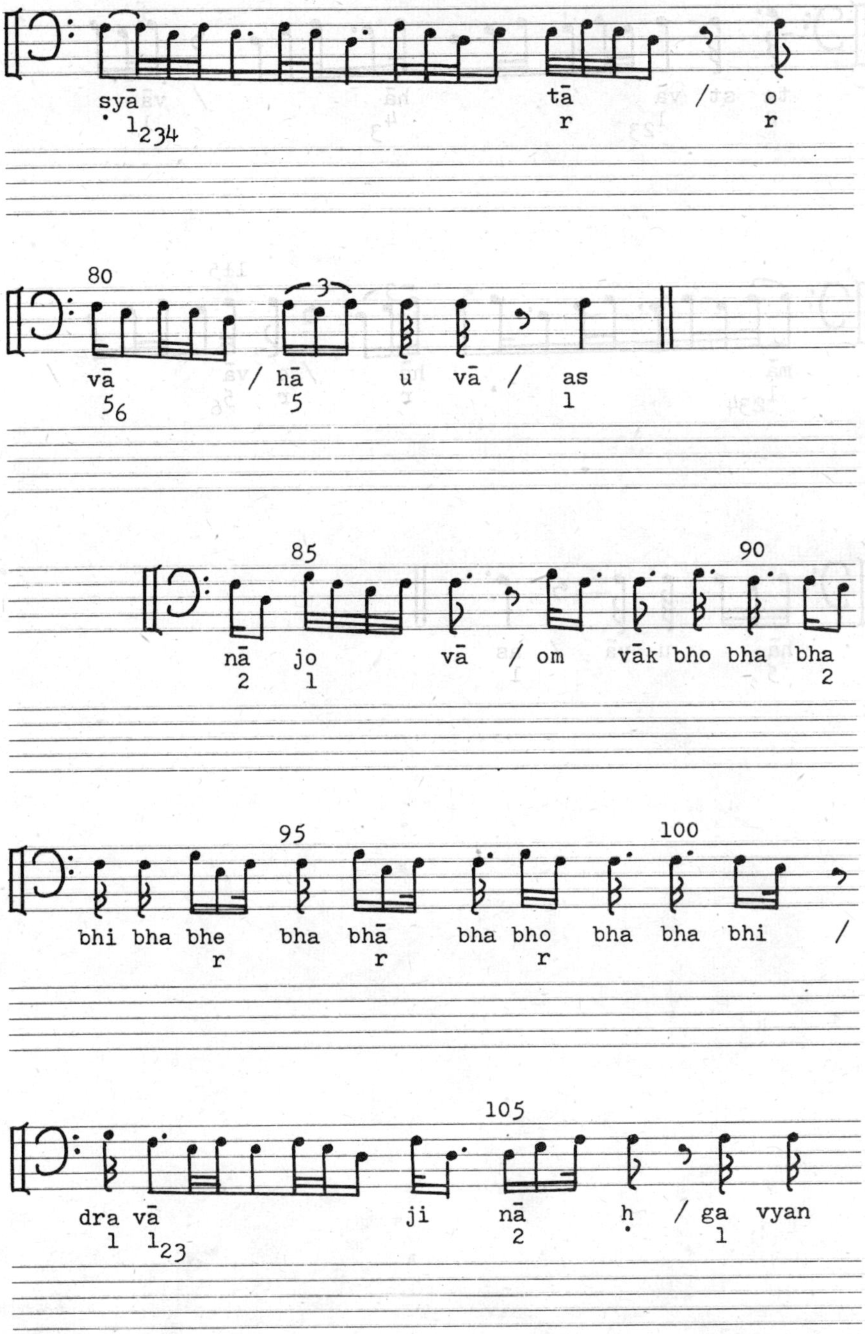
syā tā / o
1234 r r
80
vā / hā u vā / as
56 5 1
85 90
nā jo vā / om vāk bho bha bha
2 1 2
95 100
bhi bha bhe bha bhā bha bho bha bha bhi /
r r r
105
dra vā ji nā ḥ / ga vyan
1 123 2 1

110
ta st vā hā / vā
2 123 43 1
115
mā hā / o vā /
1234 r r 56
hā u vā / as
5 1

1 2 1 r 2 1 4 1 r
suvā23rdṛśām / āiśānam ā23indrā3 / sūsthū234ṣā /

r 5 5 1
o vā6 / hāu vā / as //

2r 1 1 2 r r r
2. īśo vā / om vāk bhā bhi bha bhu bhu bho bha bhā bhā bha

r r 1 2 1 r2r 1 4
bho bhi bhi bhoḥ na pā23rthivāḥ / na jāto nā23 jā3 /

1 r r 5 5 1
nāiṣyā234tā / o vā6 / hāu vā / as //

2 1 1 2 r r
3. na jo vā / om vāk bho bha bha bhi bha bhe bha bhā bha

r 1 2 1 2 1
bho bha bha bha bhi dra vā23jināḥ / gavyantas tvā23

4 1 r r 5 5 1
hā3 / vāmā234hā / o vā6 / hāu vā / as //

Analysis

Comments on motive distribution

If the three principal tones are designated (high to low) by the Roman numerals I, II, and III, then the motives (short pitch patterns) associated with these tones can be symbolized by number-letter combinations. For example, Ia and Ib can represent two motives associated with tone I, the high pitch; likewise, IIIa, IIIb, IIIc, and IIId can denote four different patterns connected with tone III, the low pitch. Careful scrutiny of the transcribed sāmans just presented shows that approximately sixteen different motives are used:

Ia

Ib

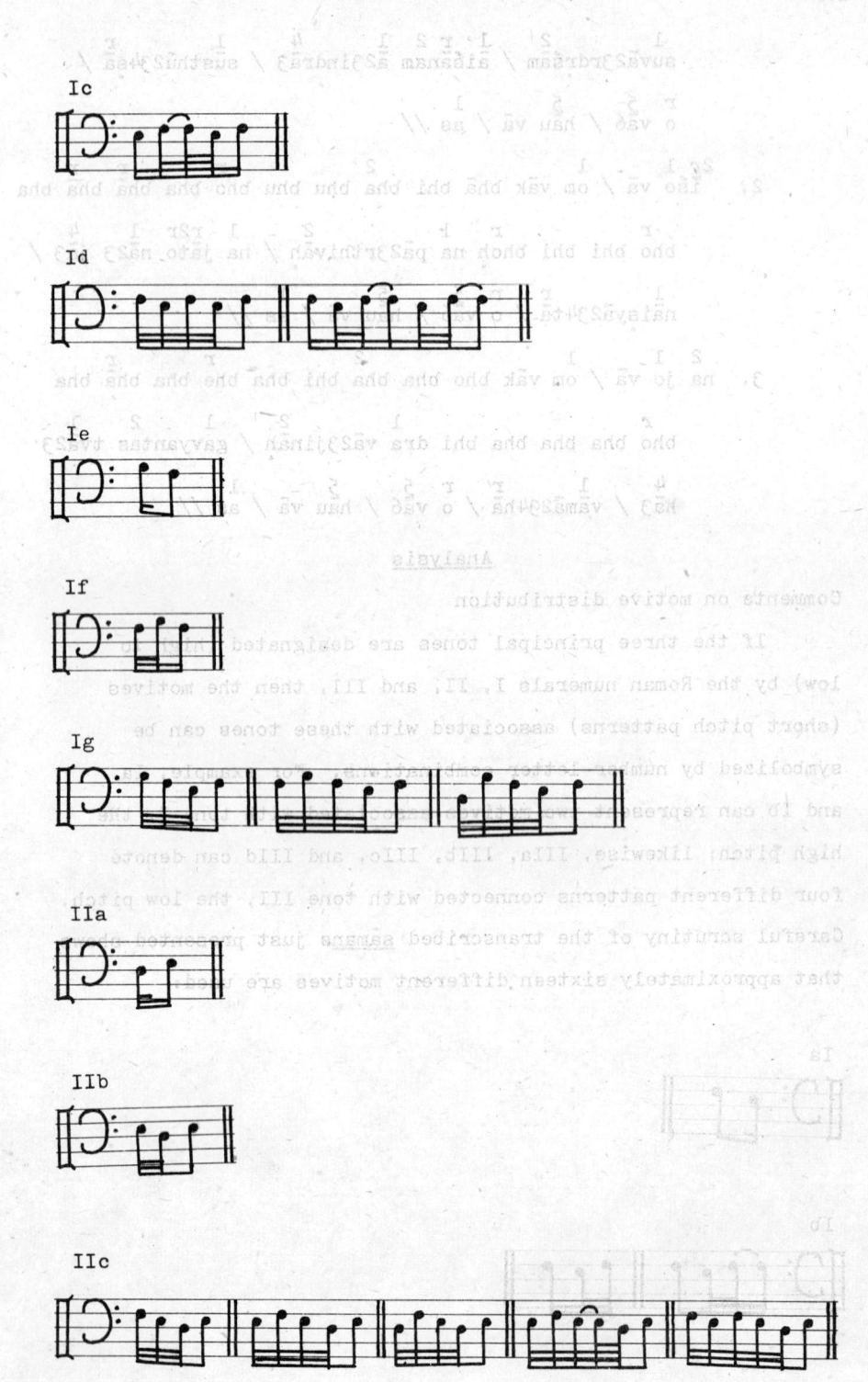

Ic

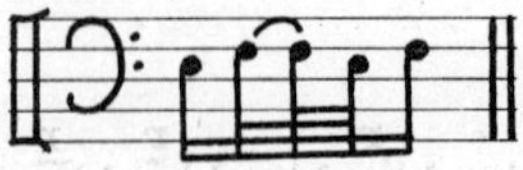

Id

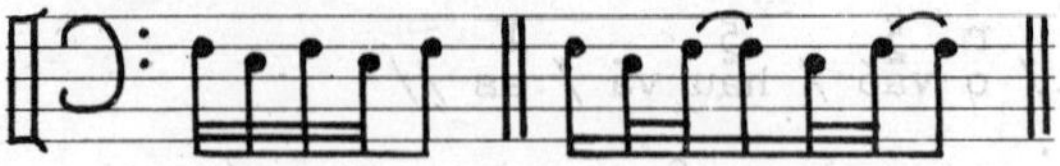

Ie

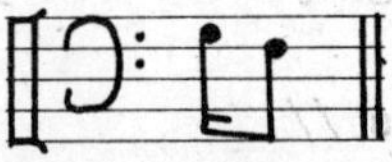

If

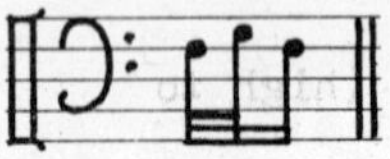

Ig

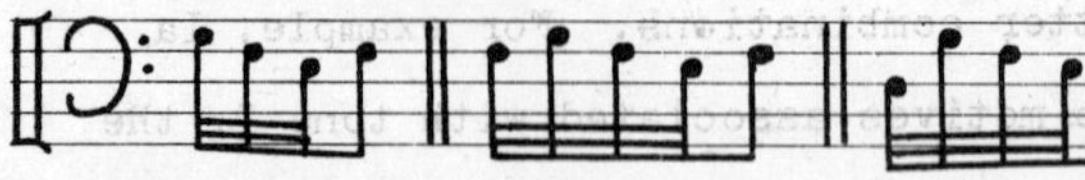

IIa

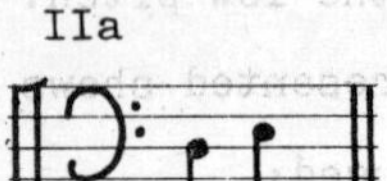

IIb

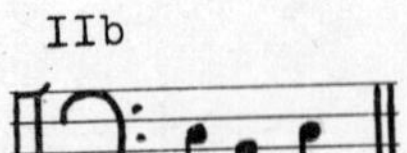

IIc

IId

IIe

IIIa

IIIb

IIIc

IIId

These figurations appear 941 times in the sixteen chants: 245 center around tone I, 324 around tone II, 372 around tone III. This distribution may not give a totally accurate picture of the tonal make-up, for isolated tones (single pitches not connected with a motive) were not taken into account in the analysis. The present writer has already shown[69] that in three versions (A, B, C) of the first chant of the Grāmageyagāna the high pitch was the most conspicuous, the low pitch the least pronounced, of the three tones. This did not necessarily hold true when cognizance was taken of durational value:

> . . . the lowest [tone] is the least prominent in each interpretation, while the highest is the most important pitch in the recitals of A and C. In B's reading, the middle tone (II) is slightly more prominent than its upper neighbor. None of these tones, however, can be said to serve as a tonic or principal pitch.[70]

The pervasive motivic organization of North Indian Kauthuma chanting is shown in table 4. The motives occur mainly on syllables held for some duration and particularly on syllables which are followed by one or more numerals in the line of text. Syllables of relative unimportance are ordinarily sung rapidly to a single pitch. The motives are used to introduce tones, to effect a transition from one tone to another, and to demarcate repeated tones.

By far the most common pattern is IIIb, which constitutes a rapid descent I-II-III. In the recital of Agniṣvātt Śāstrī Agnihotrī this motive is sometimes reversed, giving the scheme III-II-I (motive IIId). In either case, it is clear that tone III is the pivotal pitch of the motive (and also of its variant IIIc); the pattern is often preceded by a motive centered around II (IIc, for example), from which IIIb or IIId provides a bridge to the lowest pitch.

Prakṛti 1

As previously noted in the discussion of the Kauthuma numeral notation, the numbers representing the mudrās appear either above or within the textual line--the basic or prakṛti position and the secondary or vikṛti position, respectively. Since combinations of a prakṛti-number with one or more vikṛti-

TABLE 4

MOTIVE DISTRIBUTION IN SIXTEEN SĀMANS

Sāmans → / Motives ↓	1	2	3	4	5	6	7	8	9	10	11	12	13	14	15	16	Totals
Ia	1	1	1	0	3	0	0	0	0	0	0	2	9	5	1	0	23
Ib	1	1	2	4	4	3	1	14	8	5	1	17	4	1	5	4	75
Ic	0	0	1	0	0	1	0	0	0	0	0	0	0	2	0	0	4
Id	2	0	1	5	1	3	3	1	4	2	0	13	0	0	1	0	36
Ie	0	0	0	1	0	2	1	1	1	0	0	4	0	4	11	5	30
If	0	0	0	0	0	0	0	2	0	0	4	6	0	0	0	0	12
Ig	0	1	1	1	3	1	2	4	1	3	0	37	0	5	1	5	65
IIa	0	0	0	0	0	0	1	0	0	0	0	1	0	0	0	0	2
IIb	2	2	0	2	0	0	2	0	2	1	0	8	0	0	1	0	20
IIc	11	12	4	2	18	10	6	7	8	5	3	16	11	0	14	6	133
IId	1	0	0	0	5	6	10	0	1	1	2	26	4	13	5	15	89
IIe	2	0	3	4	10	6	4	2	3	2	1	18	1	12	5	7	80
IIIa	0	0	0	0	0	0	0	0	0	0	0	0	5	5	4	3	17
IIIb	15	15	10	20	29	13	19	11	15	13	8	39	15	18	16	16	272
IIIc	8	3	4	1	3	5	7	6	1	0	3	25	2	1	2	1	72
IIId	0	0	0	0	0	0	0	0	0	0	0	0	3	3	2	3	11

TOTAL 941

numbers (called sequences in this study) are often sung in distinctive ways, it is desirable to separate the analysis of pure prakṛti-numbers, those not followed by secondary numerals, from that of the numerous sequences. Roman numerals will continue to represent the three basic tones, in descending order. A designation such as Ibcg indicates that tone I is sometimes combined into motives Ib, Ic, and Ig. Textual syllables are shown by Hindu-Arabic numbers. For example, the symbol 7.10 shows that reference is made to the tenth syllable of the seventh chant. Final consonants, visarga, and gati elongation of a vowel are not considered syllables. Occasionally some pitch above tone I is intoned, in which case an asterisk precedes the syllable designation in question.

A. Tone I

(1) Augmented: 1.5,1.13,2.21,3.22,5.21,11.8,11.10, 11.30,11.36,13.36,13.61,13.70,14.9,14.16,14.39, 14.42,14.46,14.69,14.73,14.75,15.9,15.10,15.30, 15.44,15.45,15.46,15.69,15.78,15.79,16.9,16.10, 16.11,16.12,16.33,16.49,16.50,16.51,16.52,16.76, 16.86,16.88,*16.89.

(2) Long: 1.19,1.35,3.18,4.1,4.7,4.30,14.10,*14.12, 15.65,16.72.

(3) Short: 1.9,1.20,1.23,1.31,1.45,2.5,2.7,2.14,3.11, 3.12,3.13,3.15,3.24,4.6,4.13,4.18,4.23,4.24,4.29, 5.10,7.42,8.4,8.7,8.26,*9.11,9.24,10.15,*10.20, 11.11,11.26,*12.51,*12.107,*12.160,*12.213,12.235, 12.240,12.245,12.257,12.261,12.265,12.273,13.13, 13.21,13.39,13.43,14.50,14.57,14.70,14.79,14.86, 15.11,15.47,15.80,15.93,15.97,15.98,16.13,*16.29, 16.46,16.53,16.83,16.90,*16.102,16.106,16.107,16.118.

B. Motive Ia

(1) Augmented: 13.10,13.20.

(2) Long: 13.68.

C. Motive Ib

(1) Augmented: 13.46,15.102,16.39,16.111.

(2) Long: 8.2,8.13,10.4.

(3) Short: 4.2,4.14,8.3,8.5,8.6,8.14,8.16,8.17,8.25, 8.28,8.29,9.12,9.14,10.5,12.222,12.223,12.226, 12.227,12.230,12.231.

D. Motive Id

(1) Augmented: 3.35,6.35,7.40,7.55,8.24,15.77.

(2) Long: 5.47,6.36,7.56.

E. Motive Ie

(1) Augmented: 16.87.

(2) Long: 4.19,8.15,9.13,12.221,12.225,12.229,15.31.

(3) Short: 14.72.

F. Motive If

(1) Augmented: 12.198.

(2) Long: 12.94.

(3) Short: 8.27.

G. Motive Ig

(1) Augmented: 5.32,10.8,10.10,12.188,12.193,16.8, 16.48,16.85.

(2) Long: 3.14,12.4,12.8,12.12,12.27,12.32,12.37, 12.57,12.61,12.65,12.113,12.117,12.121,12.166, 12.170,12.174,12.256,12.260,12.264,16.34.

(3) Short: 5.42,8.18,8.37,8.40,12.135,12.140,12.145.

H. I-Ic

(1) Short: 1.27.

I. IIcde-Ib

(1) Augmented: 6.15,7.25,15.8.

(2) Long: 1.29,1.41,12.79,12.85,12.91,12.269.

(3) Short: 8.35,14.45.

J. I-IIe-Ibd

(1) Augmented: 8.8,8.19,8.30,8.38.

(2) Long: 8.41,12.25,12.30,12.35,12.271.

(3) Short: 9.15,12.233,12.238,12.243.

K. Tone II

(1) Short: 1.7,12.137,12.142,12.147,12.190,12.195, 12.200,15.26,15.60.

L. Motive IIc

(1) Long: 12.88,12.146.

(2) Short: 1.43,12.247,12.250,12.253.

M. Motive IId

(1) Short: 6.34,7.43,7.54.

N. Motive IIe

(1) Augmented: 3.33.

O. Ibdg-IIbcde

(1) Augmented: 2.8,2.15,3.16,11.9,12.18,12.21,12.24, 12.71,12.74,12.77,12.127,12.130,12.133,12.180, 12.183,12.186.

(2) Long: 1.21,11.31,12.5,12.9,12.13,12.28,12.33, 12.38,12.58,12.62,12.66,12.82,12.114,12.118, 12.122,12.136,12.141,12.167,12.171,12.175,12.189, 12.194,12.199.

(3) Short: 10.21,12.17,12.20,12.23,12.70,12.73,12.76, 12.95,12.126,12.129,12.132,12.179,12.182,12.185, 12.236,12.241,12.246.

P. Tone III

(1) Short: 1.12,12.78,12.84,12.90,15.64,16.71.

Q. Motive IIIb

(1) Long: 10.3,12.268.

R. Motive IIIc

(1) Short: 11.43.

S. Motive IIId

(1) Short: 13.18,15.36.

Of the syllables ending with tone II, 35 sound this pitch only briefly before breath is taken by the chanters. Hence tone I is the principal tone of these syllables (see under M and O in the above analysis). When this characteristic is taken into account, 319 syllables notated with 1 (86%) have tone I as the main pitch, 40 (11%) have tone II, and 11 (3%) have tone III.

Rules for singing prakṛti 1

(1) With certain exceptions, all 1-notated syllables are to be sung to tone I or to motives connected with tone I. This includes initials and series of syllables which have this number as the only notational numeral. Example (from 3.11-16):

See also the following: 1.5,1.9,1.13,1.19-20,1.23,1.27,1.29, 1.31,1.35,1.41,1.45,2.5,2.7,2.14,2.21,3.18,3.22,3.24,4.1-2, 4.6-7,4.13-14,4.18-19,4.23-24,4.29-30,5.10,5.21,5.32,5.42,5.47, 6.35,6.36,7.40,7.42,7.55,7.56,8.2-7,8.13-18,8.24-29,8.37,8.40, 9.11-14,9.24,10.4-5,10.8,10.10,10.15,*10.20,11.10-11,11.26,11.30, 11.36,12.4,12.8,12.12,12.25,12.27,12.30,12.32,12.35,12.37,*12.51, 12.57,12.61,12.65,12.79,12.85,12.91,12.94,*12.107,12.113,12.117, 12.121,12.135,12.140,12.145,*12.160,12.166,12.170,12.174,12.188, 12.193,12.198,*12.213,12.221-223,12.225-226,12.229-230,12.235, 12.240,12.245,12.256,12.260,12.264,12.273,13.10,13.13,13.18, 13.20,13.21,13.36,13.39,13.43-44,13.46,13.47,13.61,13.64,13.68, 13.70,13.71,14.9,14.10,*14.12,14.13,14.15,14.16,14.20,14.27, 14.39,14.40,14.42-43,14.45,14.46,14.50,14.57,14.69,14.70,

14.72-73,14.75,14.79,14.86,15.9,15.10-11,15.30-31,15.36,15.44-45, 15.46-47,15.65,15.69,15.77-78,15.79-80,15.93,15.97-98,15.102, 15.109,16.8-9,16.10-13,*16.29,16.33-34,16.39,16.46,16.48-49, 16.50-53,16.67,16.72,16.85-86,16.87-90,*16.102,16.106-107, 16.111,16.118.

(2) Occasionally initial short 1-notated syllables are sung to tones II or III. Example (from 15.60):

See also the following: 1.12,12.78,12.84,12.90,15.26,15.64,16.71.

(3) A 1-notated syllable before final 2 or 2 before a pause is sung to tone II, to II motives, or to I-II. This holds true even if 1 is initial. Example (from 1.7):

See also the following: 1.43,3.33,10.21,11.31,12.5,12.9,12.13, 12.28,12.33,12.38,12.58,12.62,12.66,12.82,12.88,12.114,12.118, 12.122,12.136-137,12.141-142,12.146-147,12.167,12.171,12.175, 12.189-90,12.194-195,12.199-200,12.247,12.250,12.253,12.257, 12.261,12.265. An exception is 1.31 (the following 2 descends to tone II, which is not final).

(4) A final 1-notated syllable may dip to tone II. This may occur on a final consonant (including visarga). Example (from 7.43):

See also the following: 2.8,2.15,3.16,6.34,7.54,12.17,12.18, 12.20,12.23,12.24,12.70,12.71,12.73,12.74,12.76,12.77,12.95, 12.126,12.127,12.129,12.130,12.132,12.133,12.179,12.180,12.182, 12.183,12.185,12.186,12.227,12.231,12.236,12.241,12.246.

(5) Syllables notated with 1 may occasionally be sung II-I or I-II-I. Final augmented 1 syllables are sung this way, as well as 1-notated syllables before a pause (rest) within the parvan. Example (from 9.15):

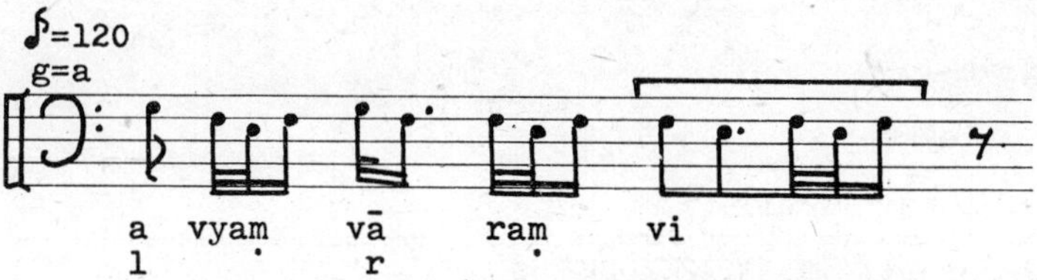

See also the following: 6.15,7.25,8.35 (before anusvāra/anunāsika), 8.38,8.41,12.233,12.238,12.243,12.269,12.271,15.8.

Prakṛti 2

A. Tone 1

(1) Augmented: 1.24,2.17,11.1,13.42,14.19,14.31,15.1, 15.63,15.96,16.1.

(2) Long: 1.17,6.7,7.7,7.9,7.32,11.3,11.4,15.3,15.4, 16.3,16.4,16.14,*16.17,16.20,*16.21.

(3) Short: 1.18,4.8,5.12,5.38,6.8,6.16,6.22,6.23, 7.2,7.3,7.6,7.8,7.10,7.26,7.33,7.34,7.37,7.38, 9.19,9.32,11.2,11.13,11.14,11.16,11.17,11.20, 11.21,11.22,11.23,12.44,12.45,12.46,12.48,12.206, 12.207,12.209,12.248,12.251,12.254,12.258,12.262,

12.266,13.17,15.2,15.5,15.13,15.14,14.16,15.17,
15.20,15.21,15.22,15.23,15.24,15.49,15.50,15.52,
15.55,15.82,15.83,15.85,15.87,15.89.15.90,15.91,
16.2,16.5,16.15,16.16,16.18,16.19,16.22,16.23,16.24,
16.25,16.26,16.27,16.55,16.56,16.58,16.59,16.62,
16.67,16.92,16.93,16.95,16.97,16.99,16.100.

B. Motive Ia

(1) Augmented: 13.16,13.74,14.53,14.61,14.78.

C. Motive Ib

(1) Augmented: 14.49.

(2) Long: 10.13,12.1,12.99,12.152,15.33.

(3) Short: 6.28,10.14,12.47,12.154,12.156,12.157.

D. Motive Ic

(1) Augmented: 13.50.

E. Motive Id

(1) Augmented: 5.5,5.34.

(2) Long: 12.149.

(3) Short: 9.33,12.100.

F. Motive Ie

(1) Long: 6.4,7.1,14.74,15.12,15.15,15.19,15.51,15.54,
15.84,15.86,15.88,16.57,16.61,16.63,16.98.

(2) Short: 6.27,15.48,15.81,16.108.

G. Motive If

(1) Long: 11.12,11.15,11.18,11.19,12.153,12.155.

(2) Short: 12.208,12.210.

H. Motive Ig

(1) Augmented: 5.16,5.23,12.216,12.217.

(2) Long: 4.25,6.9,12.40,12.54,12.96,12.110,12.163,
15.18,16.60,16.94,16.96.

(3) Short: 7.13.

I. I-Ia

(1) Augmented: 5.27.

(2) Long: 12.101.

J. IIbcde-Ib

(1) Augmented: 2.2,7.44.

(2) Short: 1.39,5.2,6.18,6.24,7.28.

K. IIIb-I

(1) Short: 5.1.

L. I-IIe-Ib

(1) Augmented: 5.6,5.13,5.17,5.24,5.28,5.35,5.39, 7.57,9.20.

(2) Short: 2.10,6.37.

M. Tone II

(1) Long: 12.80,12.86,12.92.

(2) Short: 11.5,11.24,13.35,15.57,15.58,15.59,15.92, 16.28,16.64,16.65.

N. Motive IIc

(1) Short: 6.30,15.25.

O. Motive IId

(1) Augmented: *13.45.

(2) Long: *14.41,*14.71,*15.56,*15.66,*16.73.

(3) Short: 6.5,12.49,12.158,12.202,12.211,*14.11, *14.14,*14.44,*15.32,*15.99,*16.35,*16.54,16.91, 16.101.

P. Motive IIe

(1) Short: 12.115.

Q. Id-IIbe

(1) Augmented: 9.5,12.218.

(2) Long: 1.11,1.32,12.2,12.41,12.55,12.97,12.102, 12.111,12.150,12.164,12.203.

(3) Short: 3.26.

R. Tone III

(1) Short: 1.16,1.34,5.20,8.12,11.7,12.43,12.81,12.87, 12.93,12.105,12.106,12.116,12.169,12.173,12.177,

12.205,12.249,12.252,12.255,12.259,12.263,12.267, 13.9,13.19,13.67,13.69.

S. Motive IIIa

(1) Augmented: 16.84.

(2) Short: 9.23.

T. Motive IIIb

(1) Augmented: 11.29.

(2) Long: 3.32,8.1,10.12,11.6,12.159,12.242,15.6-7, 15.43,16.6-7,16.47,16.66.

(3) Short: 1.6,1.30,2.20,3.10,6.33,7.53,8.23,8.34, 10.22,11.25,12.14-15,12.16,12.19,12.22,12.29,12.34, 12.39,12.59-60,12.67-68,12.69,12.72,12.75,12.83, 12.89,12.103-104,12.119-120,12.123-124,12.125, 12.128,12.131,12.134,12.178,12.181,12.184,12.212, 13.60.

U. Motive IIIc

(1) Augmented: 1.26,3.34,8.11,12.3.

(2) Long: 1.8,12.31,12.36,12.50,12.56,12.98,12.165, 12.220,12.224,12.228,12.232,12.237,12.270,12.272, 13.76

(3) Short: 1.22,3.17,3.21,4.12,5.31,6.14,7.24,8.36, 8.39,11.32,12.6-7,12.10-11,12.63-64,12.112,12.139, 12.144,12.148,12.151,12.168,12.172,12.176,12.191, 12.196,12.201,12.219,12.239,12.244.

V. Motive IIId

(1) Augmented: 13.24,13.66,14.23,14.82,14.90,15.29, 16.32,16.70,16.105.

W. I-III

(1) Short: 5.9,*12.187,*12.192,*12.197,15.76.

X. IIe-IIIb

(1) Augmented: 1.15,1.37,3.20,7.5,7.36,8.22,8.33,10.7, 10.17,10.19.

(2) Long: 1.33,1.40,12.26,12.42,12.138,12.143,12.204.

(3) Short: 1.42,1.44,12.234.

Y. I-IIe-IIIb

(1) Augmented: 9.18.

Of the approximately 408 syllables having 2 as the notational numeral, 201 (50%) are associated primarily with tone I, 50 (12%) with tone II, and 157 (38%) with tone III.

Rules for singing prakṛti 2

(1) Initial 2 prior to a 1-notated syllable is sung to tone III or to a motive descending to tone III--usually motive IIIb. Example (from 6.33):

See also the following: 1.34,2.20,3.10,3.17,3.21,3.32,4.12,5.9, 5.20,5.31,7.53,8.1,1.12,8.23,8.34,9.23,12.16,12.19,12.22,12.69, 12.72,12.75,12.125,12.128,12.131,12.134,12.139,12.144,12.178, 12.181,12.184,12.187,12.192,12.197,12.220,12.224,12.228,12.232, 12.237,12.242,13.9,13.60,13.67.

(2) One or a series of initial 2-notated syllables are sung to tone I. If a 1-notated syllable follows or if only 2-notated syllables appear in the parvan, the final 2-notated syllable will descend to tone III. The descent may be spread over several syllables. Example (from 11.1-7):

See also the following: 1.38-40,5.1-2,5.5-6,5.12-13,5.16-17, 5.23-24,5.27-28,5.34-35,5.38-39,6.4-5,6-7-9,6.16,6.22-24,6.27-28, 7.1-3,7.6-10,7.26,7.28,7.32-34,7.37-38,7.44,9.19-20,2.32-33, 12.1-3,12.40-42,12.43-50,12.54-56,12.96-98,12.99-106,12.110-112,12.149-151,12.152-159,12.163-165,12.202-204,12.205-212, 12.216-219,15.1-7,16.1-7.

(3) The first in a series of initial 2-notated syllables may occasionally be sung to tones II or III. Example (from 12.43):

(4) A series of 2-notated syllables final in the line is sung to tone I or to motives connected with tone I. A descent to tone III is made on the final syllable(s). Example (from 11.12-25):

Note: In the recital of A. Ś. Agnihotrī the descent is often to tone II. See also the following: 15.12-25,15.48-59,15.81-92, 16.14-28,16.54-66,16.91-101.

(5) A 2-notated syllable at the end of a <u>parvan</u> descends to tone III. The descent may be spread over several 2-notated syllables. Example (from 12.6-7):

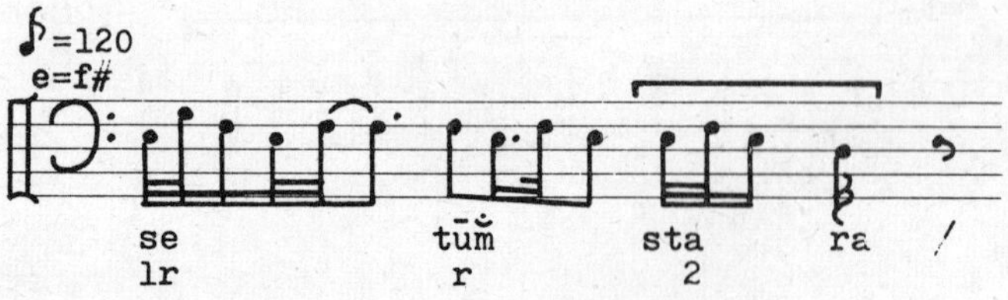

Note: In the recital of A. Ś. Agnihotrī, ascent <u>from</u> III occurs (motive IIId or a portion thereof).

See also the following: 1.22,1.26,1.32-33,1.37,1.44,3.20,3.34, 7.5,7.36,8.11,8.22,8.33,9.18,10.7,10.17,10.19,11.29,11.32, 12.10-11,12.14-15,12.29,12.34,12.39,12.59-60,12.63-64,12.67-68, 12.83,12.89,12.115-116,12.119-120,12.123-124,12.138,12.143, 12.148,12.168-169,12.172-173,12.176-177,12.191,12.196,12.201, 12.248-249,12.251-252,12.254-255,12.258-259,12.262-263,12.266-267, 13.16,13.24,13.42,13.50,13.66,13.74,13.19,13.31,14.49,14.61, 14.74,14.78,14.90,15.29,15.63,15.96,16.32,16.70,16.105.

(6) A 2-notated syllable occurring between 1-notated syllables descends to tone III. The descent may be spread over several 2-notated syllables. Example (from 12.80-81):

Note: In the recital of A. Ś. Agnihotrī the descent is often to II instead of III.

See also the following: 1.6,1.8,1.30,1.42,6.14,7.24,10.22,12.26, 12.31,12.36,12.86-87,12.92-93,12.234,12.239,12.244,12.270,12.272, 13.19,13.45,13.69,14.11,14.14,14.41,14.44,14.71,15.32,15.66,15.99, 16.35,16.73. Exceptions to the rule are 7.13 and 16.108.

(7) The notation 2^ signals the tones I-II-I or motives associated with these tones. This scheme holds regardless of the numerical context. Example (from 5.13):

See also the following: 5.17,5.24,5.28,5.35,5.39,6.9,6.18,6.24,

6.37,7.28,7.44,7.57,9.5,9.20. Exceptions to the rule are 2.2, 6.30,14.23,14.53, and 14.82.

(8) A 2-notated syllable appearing before a sequence having 2 or 3 as the prakṛti numeral is sung to tone I. Example (from 4.25):

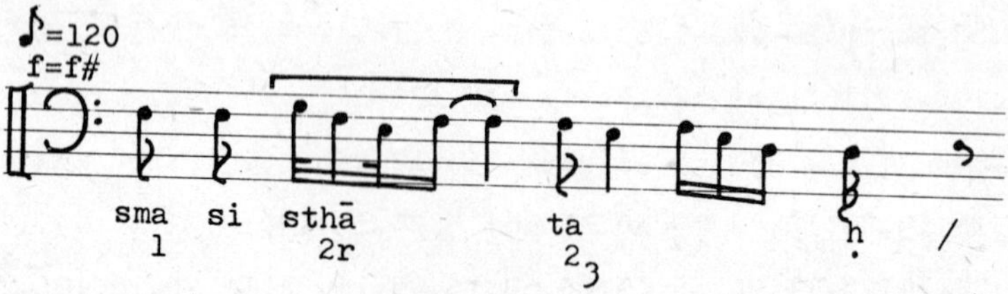

See also the following: 1.24,2.17,4.8,9.33.

Prakṛti 3

A. Motive Ib

(1) Short: 2.9.

B. Motive Ic

(1) Long: 14.25.

C. Motive Ig

(1) Long: 14.55.

D. I-IIe-I

(1) Long: 6.13,7.23.

E. Motive IIc

(1) Short: 11.28.

F. Motive IIe

(1) Long: 6.31.

G. I-IIb

(1) Long: 7.14,9.1

(2) Short: 9.6.

H. Tone III

(1) Short: 11.34,13.23,13.29,13.73,14.24,14.52,14.54, 14.83,15.34,16.31,16.37.

I. Motive IIIa

(1) Long: 14.18,14.77.

(2) Short: 13.15,13.41,13.49,14.22,14.81,15.28,15.62, 15.95,16.69,16.104.

J. Motive IIIb

(1) Long: 14.48.

K. Motive IIIc

(1) Short: 2.1,6.38,7.29,7.58.

L. II-IIIb

(1) Short: 2.16,6.19,7.45.

Hence 5 syllables (12% of the total of 41) are sung to tone I, 5 (12%) to tone II, and 31 (76%) to tone III.

Rules for singing <u>prakṛti</u> 3

(1) An initial 3-notated syllable before following 2- or 3-notated syllables is sung to III or to a motive falling to III. Example (from 14.54):

See also the following: 2.1,2.16,14.24,14.83. An exception to the rule is 2.9, occurring before 2^ and sung to Ib.

(2) An initial 3-notated syllable before a following 4-notated syllable is sung to the tones I-II or motives thereof. Example (from 9.1):

See also the following: 9.6.

(3) A 3-notated syllable following an initial 3-notated syllable is sung to tone I or to motives connected with tone I. Example (from 14.84):

See also the following: 14.25,14.55.

(4) A 3-notated syllable following 2^ and preceding a 4-notated syllable is sung to a motive falling to III. Example (from 7.45):

See also the following: 6.19,6.38,7.29,7.58.

(5) A 3-notated syllable following the sequence 1_{23} and preceding a 4-notated syllable is sung to tone III or to motives thereof. Example (from 11.34):

(6) A 3-notated syllable preceding a 5-notated syllable (a disjunct skip of the fourth finger called atikrama) concludes on tone II or on motives thereof. Example (from 6.31):

See also the following: 7.14.

(7) A 3-notated syllable following a 5-notated syllable (atikrama) is sung I-II-I. Example (from 7.23):

See also the following: 6.13.

(8) A 3-notated syllable before a final 2-notated syllable is sung to tone II or motives thereof. Example (from 11.28):

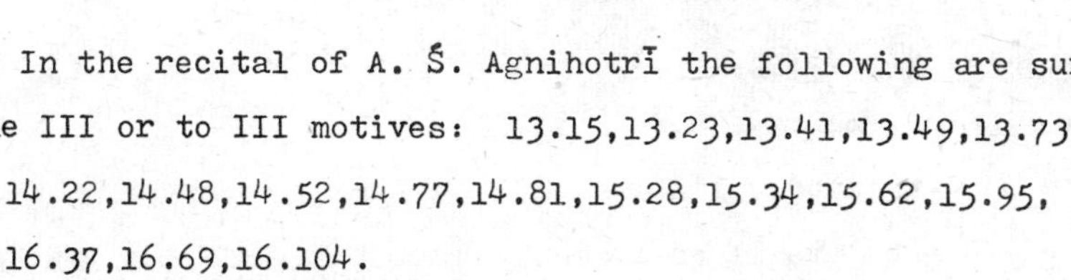

Note: In the recital of A. Ś. Agnihotrī the following are sung to tone III or to III motives: 13.15,13.23,13.41,13.49,13.73, 14.18,14.22,14.48,14.52,14.77,14.81,15.28,15.34,15.62,15.95, 16.31,16.37,16.69,16.104.

Prakṛti 4

A. Tone I

(1) Long: 13.4,13.30,13.55,14.6,15.39,15.72,15.105, 16.42,16.79,16.114.

(2) Short: 9.8.

B. Motive Ib

(1) Long: 9.7.

C. Motive IIc

(1) Augmented: 6.20.

D. Motive IId

(1) Augmented: 14.67.

(2) Short: 7.50.

E. Motive IIe

(1) Augmented: 7.30,7.46,14.37.

F. I-II

(1) Augmented: 10.1.

(2) Long: 11.39.

(3) Short: 7.18.

G. Tone III

(1) Short: 13.5,13.31,13.56,14.7.

H. Motive IIIb

(1) Long: 15.38,15.104,16.41,16.113.

I. Motive IIIc

(1) Long: 11.38,15.71,16.78.

(2) Short: 1.1.

J. II-IIIb

(1) Augmented: 1.4.

K. I-II-IIIb

(1) Short: 9.2.

Of the 35 4-notated syllables, 12 (34%) are sung to I or I motives, 9 (26%) to II or II motives, and 14 (40%) to III or III motives.

Rules for singing <u>prakṛti</u> 4

(1) Initial 4 before a single 5-notated syllable or before 5_6 falls to tone II. Example (from 10.1):

Note: Exceptions, all in the recital of A. Ś. Agnihotrī, are: 15.39,15.72,15.105,16.42,16.79,16.114.

See also the following: 11.39.

(2) Initial 4 before two or more following 5-notated syllables falls to tone III. Example (from 1.1):

(3) A 4-notated syllable following initial 3 is sung to tone I or to motives thereof. Example (from 9.7-8):

See also the following: 9.2. Note that the following visarga descends to tone III.

(4) A 4-notated syllable occurring between preceding non-initial 3 and following 5 is sung to tone II or to motives thereof. Example (from 7.30):

See also the following: 6.20,7.46,14.37,14.67. Exceptions in the recital of A. Ś. Agnihotrī are: 13.4-5,13.30-31,13.55-56, 14.6-7.

(5) A 4-notated syllable occurring between two 5-notated syllables is sung to tone II or to motives thereof. Example (from 7.50):

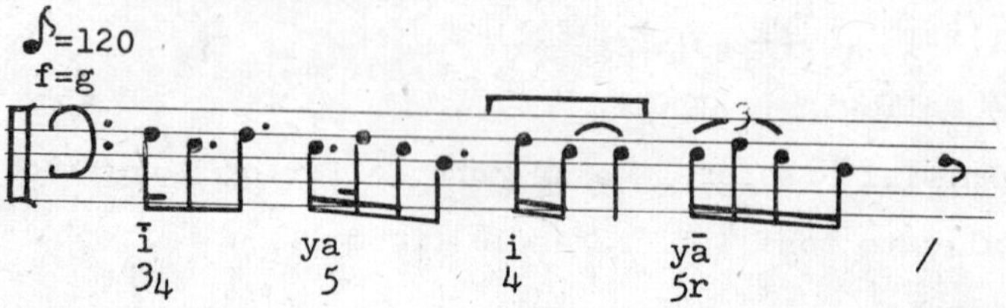

See also the following: 7.18.

(6) A final 4-notated syllable falls to tone III. Example (from 16.113):

See also the following: 1.4,11.38,15.38,15.71,15.104,16.41,16.78.

Prakṛti 5

A. Tone I

(1) Augmented: 3.31,13.34,13.59,15.42,15.75,15.108, 16.45,16.82,16.117.

(2) Long: 1.2,3.4.

(3) Short: 3.5,3.6,3.7,8.45,*13.6,13.26,13.32,*13.57.

B. Motive Ia

(1) Augmented: 13.8,15.41,16.44.

(2) Short: 13.7,13.33.

C. Motive Ib

(1) Augmented: 11.41,15.74,15.107,16.81,16.116.

(2) Long: 13.52.

D. Motive Ig

(1) Long: 7.22.

E. II-Ibd

(1) Long: 3.3,6.12.

F. Tone II

(1) Short: 6.1,13.1,13.58.

G. Motive IId

(1) Augmented: 6.3.

(2) Long: 6.2,13.53.

H. Motive IIe

(1) Short: 9.3.

I. I-II

(1) Augmented: 3.29,9.29,11.42.

(2) Short: 1.3.

J. Tone III

(1) Augmented: 9.31.

(2) Short: 3.1,3.2,6.11,7.21,13.27.

K. Motive IIIa

(1) Short: 14.34,14.64.

L. Motive IIIb

(1) Long: 3.30,9.30,14.33,14.63.

M. Motive IIIc

(1) Augmented: 2.23,3.9,5.8,5.19,6.21,6.26,7.31,
7.47,14.68.

(2) Long: 7.51,13.2.

(3) Short: 7.15,7.49.

N. Motive IIId

(1) Augmented: 14.8.

O. II-IIIb

(1) Augmented: 1.49,2.4,2.12,2.19,2.26,4.34,5.4,5.15,

5.26,5.30,5.37,5.41,6.32,9.10,10.2,10.25.

(2) Long: 7.19,9.4.

(3) Short: 7.17.

Of the 89 5-notated syllables, 33 (37%) are centered around tone I, 11 (12%) around II, and 45 (51%) around III.

Rules for singing prakṛti 5

(1) A series of initial 5-notated syllables in a parvan having additional notational numerals are sung to tone I, with lower tones perhaps occurring over the first syllables. Example (from 7.21-22):

See also the following: 3.1-7,6.11-12. In the recital of A. Ś. Agnihotrī there is instead a descent to tone III: see 13.1-2,13.26-27.

(2) Initial 5 before 4 falls to tone III. Example (from 14.64):

See also the following: 14.34. An exception is 14.3, which is sung to tone I.

(3) Two consecutive 5-notated syllables following initial 4 and prior to final 4 are sung to tones I and I-II, respectively. Example (from 1.2-3):

(4) In a *parvan* having 5 as the only notational numeral, all syllables are sung to tone II or to motives connected with it (exceptions: the *parvans* /$\overset{5}{\text{ḍā}}$/ and /$\overset{5}{\text{hāu}}$ vā/). Example (from 6.1-3):

(5) A 5-notated syllable following the sequences 1_{234}, 3_{234}, 3_4 and 5_6 is sung to a motive falling to tone III. Example (from 9.10):

See also the following: 2.4,2.12,2.19,2.23,2.26,3.9,5.4,5.8, 5.15,5.19,5.26,5.30,5.37,5.41,6.26,7.17,7.49,10.25.

(6) A 5-notated syllable following the sequence 4_5 is sung to tone I. Example (from 8.45):

(7) The first syllable of the *stobha* *au*^{5r} *ho*^{r} *vā* is sung I-II, the second as a motive falling to III, the third to tone III. Example (from 3.29-31):

See also the following: 9.29-31.

(8) The *parvan* consisting of the *stobha* /hā^{5}u vā/ is sung to tone I, sometimes with a descent to II at the end. Example (from 11.41-42):

See also the following: 15.41-42, 15.74-75, 15.107-108, 16.44-45, 16.81-82, 16.116-117.

(9) The *parvan* /ḍā^{5}/, found as the final *parvan* of many chants, is sung as a motive falling to tone III. Example (from 4.34):

See also the following: 1.49.

(10) Two 5-notated syllables final in the *parvan* are centered around tones II and III, respectively. Exceptions to

5r r 5

this rule are the stobhas au ho vā and hau vā. Example (from 9.3-4):

See also the following: 6.21,6.32,7.15,7.19,7.31,7.47,7.51,10.2, 14.33,14.38,14.63,14.68. Occasionally, in the recital of A. Ś. Agnihotrī, a series of 5-notated syllables final in the parvan are sung to tone I: 13.6-8,13.32-34,13.57-59. The final 5-syllable may rise from III: 14.8.

Sequences

The various sequential patterns, combinations of a prakṛti number with one or more vikṛti numbers, demand by definition the utilization of either several basic mudrās or distinctive movements of the fingers. The twenty-six sequences which occur in the sixteen chants are illustrated below by musical examples. The numbers of the sequences are placed underneath the transcription where the respective mudrās are most likely to be realized. Sequences which call for special continuous finger action (vinata, karṣaṇa, abhigīta, praṇata, svāra) cannot be labelled in this manner; in these cases all of the numbers are placed together beneath the textual syllable.[71]

(1) 1_2 (vinata or preṅkha)

a. I-IIce-IIIb: 2.6,3.23,3.25,10.9,10.11.

b. IIcd-IIIb: 2.13,13.12,13.38,13.63,14.28,14.58,14.87.

Five of the above examples start with tone I as a principal pitch. The ones which do not at least have the tone as part of motives IIc and IId. Consequently the typical 1_2 pattern is I-IIcde-IIIb. Example (from 2.6):

(2) $l_{\hat{2}}$ (*karṣaṇa*)

a. Icd-IIc-Ib: 3.27,9.27.

The circumflex signals the basic I-II-I pattern. Example (from 3.27):

(3) lSr_2 (*vinata*)

a. I-IIb-IIIb: 1.10,1.28.

These examples of *vinata* are realized in exactly the same way as $l_{\bar{2}}$, which itself is called *vinata* by the North Indians. Example (from 1.28):

(4) $l_{\hat{2}}$

a. IIIb-Iae: 14.29,14.59,14.88.

Example (from 14.29):

(5) 1_{23}

a. Iabd-IIce-IIIb: 1.46,5.11,5.22,5.33,9.25,10.6, 11.27,12.52,12.108,12.161,12.214,13.14,13.22,13.48,13.65,13.72, 14.21,14.51,14.80,15.27,15.61,15.67,15.94,15.100,16.30,16.68, 16.74,16.103,16.109.

b. Ib-IIbc-IIIb-IIc: 1.36,10.18.

c. Ib-IIIc-IIc: 8.10,8.21,8.32.

d. IId-IIIb: 11.33.

e. II-I-IIc-IIIb: 13.40.

f. Id-IIbcde: 10.16,15.33,16.36.

When 1_{23} is followed by a single primary 2 (concluding the parvan), the patterns I-III-II or I-II-III-II appear to be preferred. When 1_{23} itself concludes the parvan, or when it is followed by two syllables or by one syllable with two or more notated numerals, the scheme I-II-III is predominant. The remaining patterns (d-f above) are deviations from the norm. It is entirely possible that I-II-III should be sung at all times, since the two Brāhmaṇs who chant together appear to be in some disagreement in b and c above. Examples (from 1.46 and 8.32):

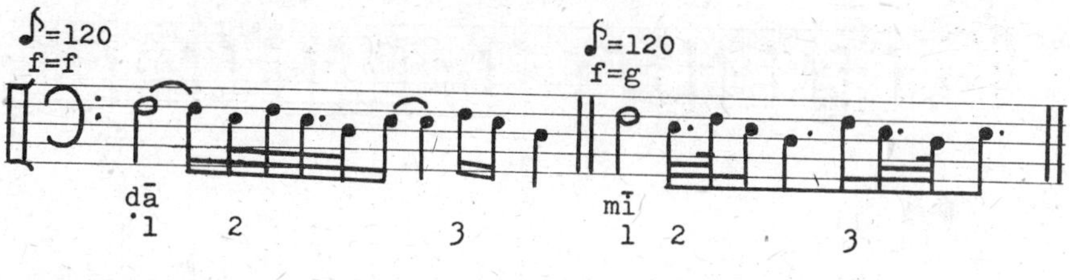

(6) 1_{234}

a. I-IIce-IIIb-IIcd: 2.22,15.37,15.103,16.40,16.77, 16.112.

b. IIIb-IIc-IIIb-IIc: 11.37.

c. IIIb-Ig: 10.23.

d. IIe-I-IIIc-IIc: 15.70.

The scheme I-II-III-II is standard for this sequence. Item b is a reading of the sequence 3_{234}; c and d are obviously mistakes. Example (from 2.22):

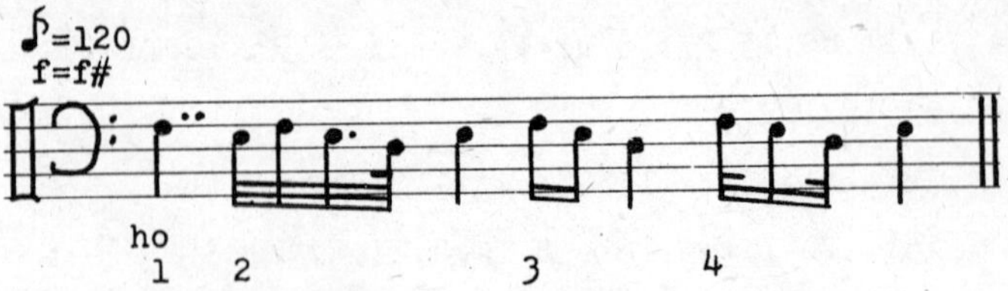

(7) 1_{2345}

a. Ib-IIe-IIIb-IIe: 1.48.

The final two *parvans* of this chant are notated $\overset{1}{\text{o}}$2345i / ḍā //. The first syllable is sung as though 1_{234} were notated; the sound associated with the numeral 5 (II-IIIb) is saved for the syllable ḍā. This peculiarity may imply that originally these two *parvans* were joined as one: /$\overset{1}{\text{o}}$2345 iḍā //. The unseparated type is characteristic of the Jaiminīya school of Sāmaveda,[72] a fact which further establishes that this *śākhā* preserves an older reading than that of the Kauthuma-Rāṇāyanīya schools. Example (from 1.48):

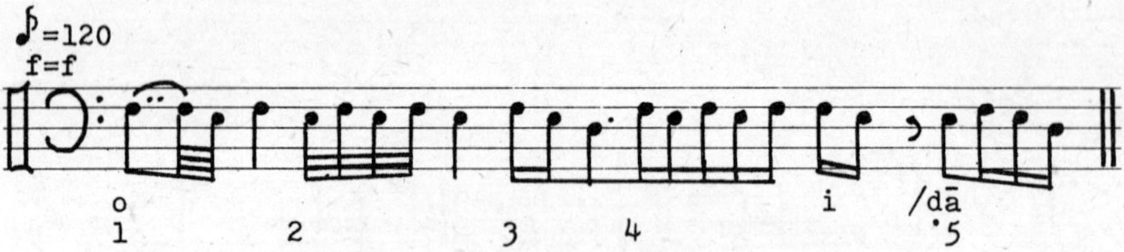

(8) S_3

a. I-II-IIIb: 4.4,4.10,4.16,4.21,4.27,4.32,5.43.

Namana is performed in the same manner as *vinata* (*preṅkha*) and other sequences. Example (from 4.4):

(9) 2_1

a. IIIa-Iab: 13.11,13.37,13.62.

b. II-IIIb-Ib (or IIIc-Ib): 9.16.

The two readings are very nearly identical. This is an example of *pratyutkrama* (ascent). Example (from 13.62):

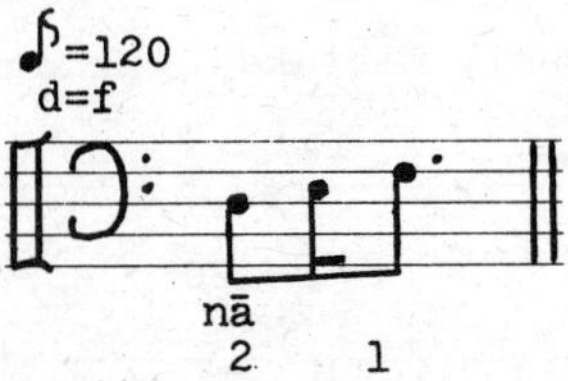

(10) 7 (*abhigīta*)

a. Tone I (sung quickly): 8.9,8.20,8.31.

The shortness of this pitch reflects the special *mudrā* connected with number 7: the thumb is flicked upwards from beneath the forefinger. Example (from 8.9):

(11) 2_3 or $2_{\hat{3}}$ (*praṇata*)

a. I-IIbce-IIIb (or IIcd-IIIb): 4.3,4.9,4.15,4.20, 4.26,4.31,5.45,5.46,6.17,7.11,7.27,7.39,7.41,7.60,8.43,9.26,13.3, 13.25,13.28,13.51,13.75,14.26,14.56,14.85.

b. I-IIb-IId-IIIb: 7.35.

c. II-IIIb-IIc (or IIIc-IIc): 1.25.

d. II-IIIb-Ig: 9.17.

e. Ia-IIcde: 7.4,13.54,14.5,14.17,14.47.

f. I-Ig: 14.36,14.66.

g. IIIc-IIc-IIIb-IIc: 1.14.

Pattern *a* is the typical scheme for this sequence. It occurs when 2_3 appears on the final syllable of a *parvan* or when the following numeral is not higher than 3 (when there is no *pratyutkrama*). Pattern *b* is very similar to *a*, and *d* is but a variant of *c*. Schemes *b*, *c*, and *d* have 2_3 followed by 2 (*pratyutkrama*). Scheme *g* cannot be related at all to the sequence; it is probable that the chanters are singing a completely different sequence here. Type *e* is a shortened version of *a*; the *f* examples are obviously mistakes. Examples (from 4.9 and 1.25):

(12) 2_{31}

a. IIce-IIIb-Id: 4.5,4.11,4.17.

b. I-II-IIIb-Ibd: 4.22,4.28.

Pattern *b* is an elongated variant of *a*. Example (from 4.28):

(13) 2_{343}

a. IIcd-IIIb-IIc-IIIb: 1.47,6.39,7.59,8.42.

b. I-IIc-IIIb: 6.29.

Scheme *b* is probably incorrect, for the two chanters are in disagreement on the initial portion. Example (from 1.47):

(14) $^{2}{}_{312345}$

a. I-II-IIIb-Ib-II-IIIb-Ib / II-IIIb: 4.33-34.

The text reads ho^{2}312345i / dā //. The music associated with the fifth finger is not sung until the syllable dā. See (7) above. Example (from 4.33-34):

(15) $^{2}{}_{35}$

a. I-IIe-IIIb: 14.30,14.60,14.89.

The sequence is interpreted as though only 2_3 were notated. Example (from 14.30):

(16) 3_{234}

a. II-IIIb-IIcd-IIIb-IIc: 2.3,2.11,5.3,5.7,5.14, 5.18,5.25,5.29,5.36,5.40,6.25.

b. I-II-IIIb-IIc-IIIb-IIc: 2.18.

c. II-IIIb-IIc-IIIb-Ib: 3.28,9.28.

d. II-IIIb-IIc-IIIb: 6.10.

All of the a examples are followed by a single 5-notated syllable: thus $3_{234}5$. Wherever the syllable bearing the sequence has been subjected to gati elongation, the music associated with the numeral 4 is sung on the final element of the diphthong. The two c examples occur before the common stobha

5r r
au ho vā. Here only the final tone is different: the tonal level ascends to I instead of II. The d pattern appears when the sequence is attached to the last syllable in a parvan. The tonal composition of the b example is uncertain because of unclearness on the tape; it probably was intended to be sung like a, since the sequence is followed by a single 5 in prakṛti position. Example (from 2.3):

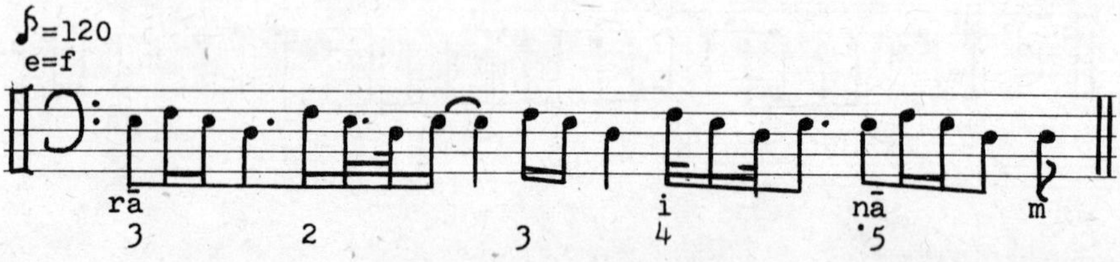

(17) $^{3}2345$

a. II-IIIb-IIc-IIIb-IIc-IIIb: 9.21. Example (from 9.21):

(18) $^{3}4$

a. I-II-I: 7.16.

b. IId-I: 7.48.

Scheme b is a variant of a. Example (from 7.16):

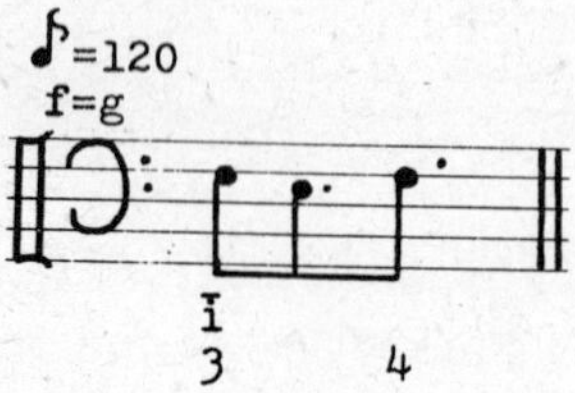

(19) $^{3}5$

a. I-IIe: 14.32,14.62.

The pattern appears when 5r follows to conclude the <u>parvan</u>. Example (from 14.32-33):

(20) 4_3

a. I-II-IIIb: 7.12.

b. IIcd-IIIb: 11.35,15.35,15.68,15.101,16.38,16.75, 16.110.

c. Ia-IId: 14.3.

d. II-Ieg: 14.35,14.65.

Schemes <u>a</u> and <u>b</u> give the accurate tonal movement; <u>c</u> and <u>d</u> are unexplainable deviations from the norm. Example (from 11.35):

(21) 4_5 (<u>utsvarita</u>)

a. IIIbc-Idg: 2.24,6.41,8.44.

b. I-III-Ib: 7.61.

Type <u>b</u> is an <u>a</u> variant. Example (from 2.24):

(22) 5_6

a. Ib-Ia-IIc: 2.25,3.8,9.9,10.24.

b. I-II-IIIb: 11.40.

c. IId-IIIb: 15.40,15.73,15.106,16.43,16.80,16.115.

The a examples occur when a single 5 (on the stobhas hāi or e) follows the sequence to conclude the parvan. Example (from 9.9-10):

(23) 5_{656}

a. I-IIce-IIIb-IIc-IIIb: 6.42,7.62,8.46.

This sequence occurs always on the final syllable of a parvan. The above tonal scheme holds true in all cases. Example (from 6.42):

(24) 1^{1111}_{2345} (utsvarita or svāra)

a. I-IIc-IIIb: 12.274. Example (from 12.274):

(25) 2^{111}_{345} (utsvarita or svāra)

a. IIc-IIIb: 12.53,12.109,12.162,12.215,13.77.

Example (from 12.53):

(26) 3^{1111}_{2345} (<u>utsvarita</u> or <u>svāra</u>)

a. I-IIe-IIIb: 3.36,5.48,9.34.

b. IIc-IIIb: 6.6,7.52,9.22.

Type <u>b</u> is a shortened variant of <u>a</u>. Example (from 5.48):

Duration

The Mātrālakṣaṇa's assertion that short syllables bear 1 <u>mātrā</u> (time unit), long syllables (long vowels with superscribed <u>r</u>) 2 <u>mātrās</u>, and augmented syllables (long vowels without superscribed <u>r</u>) 3 <u>mātrās</u> is so often contradicted by the Kauthumas that a thorough documentation of musical practice concerning duration is required. The author of the treatise may have intended to give only a general guideline and to leave the detailed knowledge of time proportionment to the Sāmavedins themselves. The use of the term <u>mātrā</u>, possibly borrowed from the phonetic treatises, implies a rigid and confining organization which does not exist in actual fact. However, one does hear in the Sāmaveda recitals divisions into specific temporal units, although the chanters do not in any sense "beat time" as they sing.

The singers devote special attention to pratyutkrama (ascent) and atikrama (omission). These terms do not necessarily refer to tones or tone levels but rather to a "rise" of the finger positions (for example, from the second finger to the first) or to the omission of a finger in ascent or descent (for example, the fifth mudrā followed by the third, thus avoiding the fourth finger). This procedure is clarified when we understand the seating posture taken by the Sāmavedī as he chants. We have been given an explanation by Yamunā Prasād Tripāṭhī,[73] who states that the singer should first be seated, facing east or north, on a deerskin or woolen carpet spread over a mat of pure kuśā grass; then he should assume the padmāsana position, a posture frequently employed in meditation, with the hands resting on the knees (therefore with the thumb on top). Hence ascent and descent should be thought of in regard to the fingers; for example, the tonal level signified by touching the fourth finger is often higher than that indicated by touching the third finger. Therefore use of the term pratyutkrama (ascent) for this progression obviously alludes to the finger movement and not to the music resulting from that movement.

It is difficult to formulate a single rule that would apply to durational value for the many sequences. A general principle is that the mudrās are of approximately equal time value (one or two mātrās), except the first, which in most cases is of slightly longer duration. An exception to this rule involves pratyutkrama, where the mudrā to which ascent is made is sometimes prolonged.

The durational laws for pure prakṛti-numbers are more involved. Although all possible number combinations are not present in the sixteen transcribed chants, a number of rules can be presented that apply to the entire *sāman* repertoire. Each maxim is illustrated by a musical example, and reference is made to passages from the first seven chants. One *mātrā* is roughly equivalent to an eighth note of the transcriptions.

(1) Syllables with short (*hrasva*) vowels are ordinarily held for one *mātrā*, unless special rules come into play. Example (3.1-2,5-7):

See also the following: 1.16,1.18,1.20,1.23,1.38,2.7,2.14,4.6, 4.8,4.18,4.23,4.24,5.38,5.44,6.5,6.8,6.11,6.15,6.22,6.23,6.27, 6.28,7.2,7.3,7.6,7.8,7.10,7.21,7.33,7.34,7.37,7.38,71.42,7.43.

(2) Augmented syllables (those having long vowels without the superscribed *r*) are held for three *mātrās*. Example (3.16):

See also the following: 1.4,1.5,1.24,2.4,2.12,2.15,2.17,2.19, 2.26,3.20,3.22,3.33,3.35,5.4,5.5,5.8,5.15,5.16,5.19,5.21,5.23, 5.26,5.27,5.30,5.32,5.34,5.37,5.41,6.1,6.3,6.15,6.20,6.21,6.26, 6.35,7.5,7.30,7.31,7.36,7.40,7.46,7.47,7.49,7.55. Exceptions to the rule are 5-notated augmented syllables final in the *parvan*, which are often held for shorter duration.

(3) In a series of syllables having the same notational numeral, long vowels with the superscribed *r* ordinarily have the same duration as short vowels (one *mātrā*). However, when

two or more consecutive syllables have the *repha*, only the last is treated as a short syllable; the preceding syllables are elongated (two *mātrās*). The *repha*-designated syllables are often ornamented. Example (3.3-4):

See also the following: 1.2,1.17,1.19,2.21,3.14,4.1,4.7,6.2,6.4, 6.7,7.1,7.7,7.9,7.32.

(4) Short and *r*-designated long syllables are held for two *mātrās* when two tone levels are involved. Example (1.1,3):

See also the following: 1.6,1.8,1.21,1.22,1.30,1.32,1.33,1.37, 1.44,2.1,2.16,2.20,3.10,3.17,3.21,3.26,3.32,3.34,4.12,5.9,5.31, 6.14,6.19,6.32,6.33,6.38,7.15,7.17,7.19,7.29,7.45,7.51,7.53,7.58.

(5) Single short l and lr are extended to two and three *mātrās*, respectively, when they follow 2 (*pratyutkrama*). If more than one short l-notated syllable follows 2, then the rule does not apply. Neither does it apply when l follows $l_{\bar{2}}$. Example (1.31):

See also the following: 1.7,1.11,1.29,1.41,1.43,6.34,7.25,7.54.

(6) Short 1 before the sequences $1_{\bar{2}}$, $1S_2$, and 2_1 is extended to three or four mātrās. Example (2.5):

See also the following: 1.9,1.27,3.24.

(7) Single short 1 and 1r before 1_{23} are shortened to approximately one-half and one mātrā, respectively. Example (1.45):

See also the following: 1.35,3.18. An exception is 5.10.

(8) Short 1 and 1r before 2_3, S_3, and 3^{1111}_{2345} are extended to two and three mātrās, respectively. Example (5.47):

See also the following: 4.2,4.19,4.30,5.42.

(9) Short 1 and 1r before 2^ are elongated to two and three mātrās, respectively. Example (6.36):

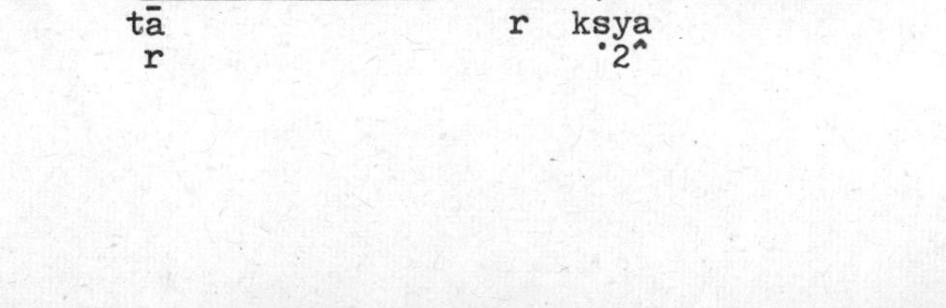

See also the following: 7.56.

(10) The syllable designated 2^ or $1_{\hat{2}}$ is comprised of three <u>mātrās</u>, regardless of the length of its vowel. A pause usually follows. Example (5.13):

See also the following: 1.39,2.2,2.10,3.27,5.2,5.6,5.17,5.24, 5.28,5.35,5.39,6.9,6.18,6.24,6.37,7.28,7.44,7.57.

(11) Short 2 following 3 (<u>pratyutkrama</u>) comprises two <u>mātrās</u>. Example (7.13):

See also the following: 7.24.

(12) Single short 2 before 2_3 is sometimes shortened to one-half <u>mātrā</u>. Example (7.26):

See also the following: 6.16.

(13) Short 2 and 2r sung on tone III alone and occurring before 1 (<u>pratyutkrama</u>) are held for two and three <u>mātrās</u>, respectively. Example (5.20):

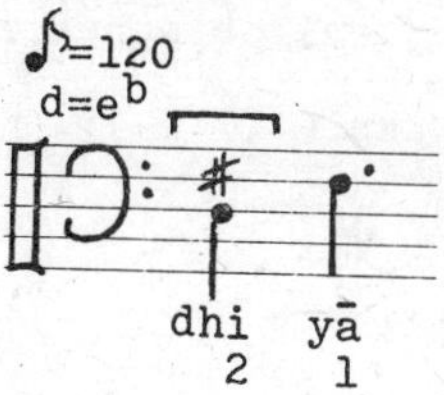

See also the following: 1.34.

(14) A 2r-designated syllable appearing before 2_3 is worth two (or three?) <u>mātrās</u>. Example (4.25):

(15) Single short 2 before 2^ is extended to two <u>mātrās</u>. Example (5.12):

See also the following: 5.1.

(16) Short 3 or 3r following 5 (<u>atikrama</u>, <u>pratyutkrama</u>) are extended to two and three <u>mātrās</u>, respectively. Example (6.13):

See also the following: 7.23.

(17) A 3r-designated syllable before 5 (*atikrama*) comprises two *mātrās*. Example (7.14):

See also the following: 6.31.

(18) Short 4 and 4r following 5 (*pratyutkrama*) are lengthened to two and three *mātrās*, respectively. Example (7.50):

See also the following: 7.18.

(19) Short 5 or 5r prior to 3 (*atikrama*, *pratyutkrama*) are lengthened to two and three *mātrās*, respectively. Example (7.22):

See also the following: 6.12.

(20) The syllables of the *stobha* *au* (5r) *ho* (r) *vā* are worth two, one, and one-half *mātrās*, respectively. Example (3.29-31):

The Gāyatra

The chant par excellence of the soma sacrifices is the gāyatra, the most sacred melody of the Sāmaveda. The prototypical gāyatra is based upon the holy Sāvitrī verse, which is composed in the gāyatrī meter and addressed to the sun god Savitṛ.

```
1   2 3 1   2r  3     1  2  3 1  2
tat savitur vareṇyaṃ bhargo devasya dhīmahi

 2 3  1  2       3 1 2
dhiyo yo naḥ pracodayāt
```

Translation:

That we (would) obtain (dhīmahi) that (tat) splendid (vareṇyam) radiance (bhargaḥ) of the god (devasya) Savitṛ (savituḥ), who (yaḥ) shall propel (pracodayāt) our (naḥ) prayers (dhiyaḥ).

The verse should be repeated daily by members of the twice-born (dvija) castes: Brāhmaṇ, Kṣatriya, Vaiśya. When adapted to melody, the chant takes the following form:

```
              1               r                          r     r
[PRASTĀVA] tat savitur vareṇiyom    [UDGĪTHA] bhārgo devasya

 r              21r  r          2                      1
dhīmāhī2   dhiyo yo naḥ praco1212   [PRATIHĀRA] hum ā2

              1             2111
[UPADRAVA] dāyo    [NIDHANA] ā345
```

In the rituals the five sections (bhaktis) of the chant, given in brackets above, are chanted by three Sāmaveda priests according to the following plan: prastāva by the Prastotṛ, udgītha and upadrava by the Udgātṛ, pratihāra by the Pratihartṛ, and nidhana by the three priests together.

The northern Kauthumas are extremely reluctant to chant this sāman for an outsider. Even my most cooperative informant sent word, in advance of a recording session, that I should not request that the gāyatra be sung.[74] However, the rules

♪=120
ta tsa vi tu rva re ṇi yo m / bhā
1 r
rgo de va sya dhī mā hī /
r r r 1$\bar{2}$
dhi yo yo na ḥpra co
2 lr r 2 1212
/ hum ā /
1 1$\bar{2}$
dā yo / ā
1 2 111 345

presented above for correctly interpreting the notation enable a transcription to be made without recourse to a taped example. The laws governing this musical interpretation are as follows:

(1) Syllables 1-5, 7, 12-13: 1-notated syllables are sung on tone I. Short syllables have a duration of one mātrā.

(2) Syllables 6, 11, 14, 19: Long r-designated syllables in a series of like-notated syllables are treated as short syllables (one mātrā) unless several r-syllables appear in succession--in which case only the last such syllable has one mātrā. The syllables may be treated to some ornamentation.

(3) Syllables 8, 26: Augmented 1-notated syllables final in the parvan have three mātrās and are often sung I-II-I.

(4) Syllables 9, 15, 25: Augmented 1-notated syllables are sung to tone I and are comprised of three mātrās.

(5) Syllables 10, 18: When two or more r-notated syllables appear in succession in a series of syllables with the same notational numeral, all except the last are worth two mātrās. They may be subjected to some ornamentation.

(6) Syllables 16, 24: The sequence vinata (preṅkha) consists of the tone pattern I-II-III.

(7) Syllable 17: An initial 2-notated syllable before a 1-notated syllable falls to tone III.

(8) Syllable 21: A short 1-notated syllable before the sequence 2_1, and hence also before 2_{1212}, is worth three mātrās and comprises the tones I-II-I.

(9) Syllable 22: The sequence 2_{1212} (avanardana), which is actually 2_1 notated twice with 2 added at the end, consists alternately of tones falling to III and rising to I.

(10) Syllable 23: A short 1-notated syllable before the sequence $1_{\bar{2}}$ is held for three mātrās.

(11) Syllable 27: The sequence utsvarita (svāra) is

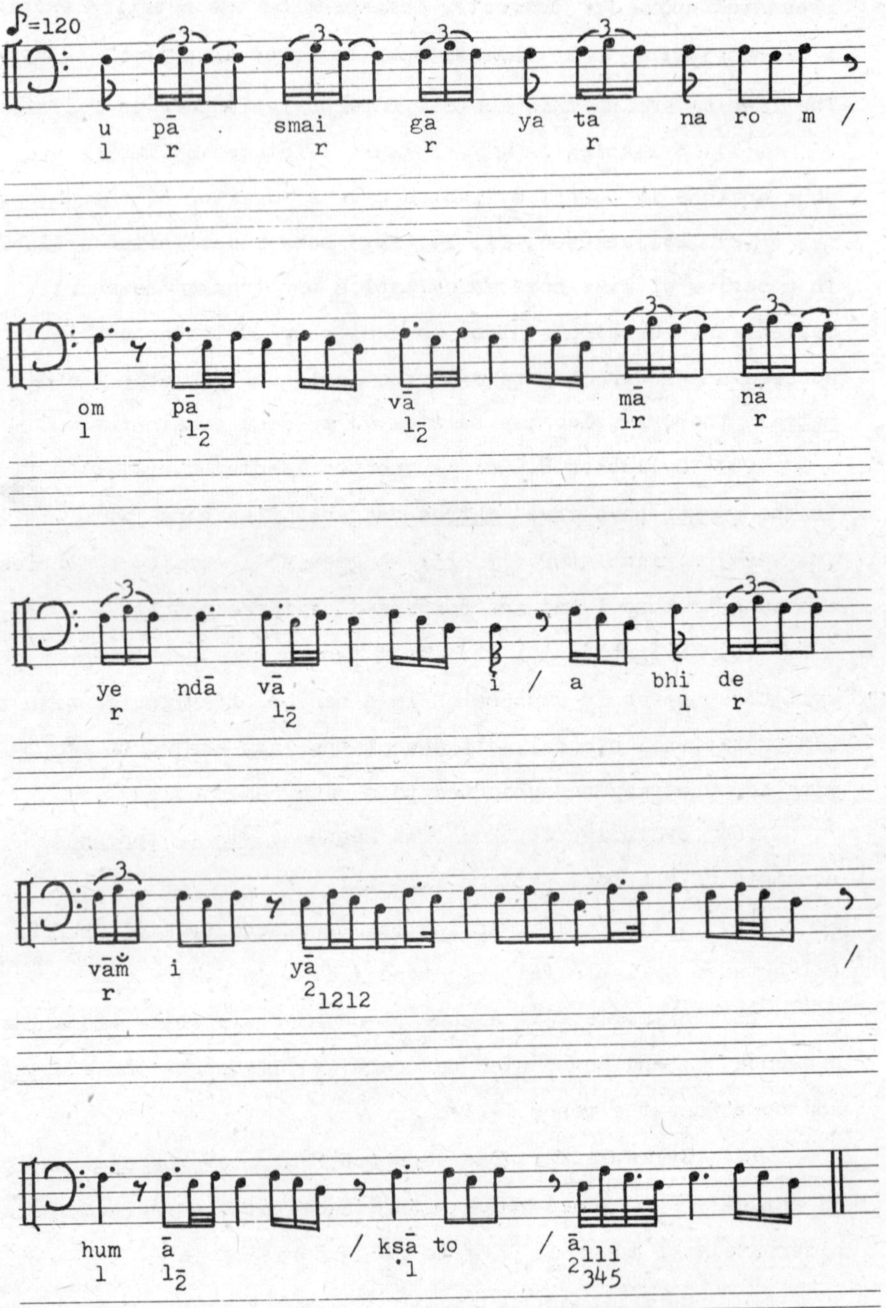
=120
u pā smai gā ya tā na ro m /
l r r r r
om pā vā mā nā
l l2 l2 lr r
ye ndā vā i / a bhi de
r l2 l r
vām̐ i yā /
r 21212
hum ā / ksā to / ā111
l l2 l 2345

comprised of the tone levels II-III.

This version of the gāyatra serves as a model for the gāyatra chants of the soma sacrifices. But in the rituals certain syllables are replaced by the vowel o, and occasionally the basic melody is altered by the imposition of modifications called dhurs.[75] For example, the first ritual chant of the agniṣṭoma sacrifice is the bahiṣpavamānastotra ("out-of-doors pavamāna laud"), which consists of nine statements of the gāyatra set to different texts. The first of these modifies the fundamental melody in the following way: whereas the original setting has the number sequence $1_{\bar{2}}212_{1212}$ in the udgītha, the principal bhakti of the chant, the modified version has the number series $1_{\bar{2}}1_{\bar{2}}1_{\bar{2}}212_{1212}$. This adaptation with the original words of the first verse (the enunciated chant or niruktagāna) reads as follows:

Source Verse:

1 2 3 1 2 3 1 2 3 2 3 1 2r
upāsmai gāyatā naraḥ pavamānāyendave / abhi devāṁ iyakṣate

Translation:

Sing (gāyata) to (upa) him (asmai), O people (naraḥ), to Indu (indave), purified (pavamānāya), desired to offer (iyakṣate) to (abhi) the gods (devān).

It is the unenunciated form of this chant (aniruktagāna) which is used in the sacrifices. This unexpressed chant is obtained by replacing the syllables of the udgītha and upadrava sections by okāras (o-vowels) but retaining the music of the nirukta version. In this particular verse of the bahiṣpavamāna-stotra the pratihāra is omitted. Notice also that the nidhana text is different here.[76]

=120
u pā smai gā ya tā na ro m /
1 r r r r
om o o o
1 1$\bar{2}$ 1$\bar{2}$ 1r
o o o o / o o
r r 1$\bar{2}$ 1
o o o o /
r r 2 1212
o o / sā
1 2 111 345
t

Fig. 2. Śrī Dr. Śrīkṝṣṇa Vāman Dev
(Ṛgvedī)

Fig. 3. Śrī Dr. Viśvanāth Vāman Dev
(Ṛgvedī)

Fig. 4. Śrī Anant Rām Puṇtāmbekar
(Ṛgvedī)

Fig. 5. Śrī S. Śrīnivās Dīkṣit
(Kṛṣṇa Yajurvedī)

Fig. 6. Śrī Rājārām Bhaṭ Nirmale
(Śukla Yajurvedī)

Fig. 7. Śrī Dr. Gajānan Śāstrī
"Musalgāvkar"
(Śukla Yajurvedī)

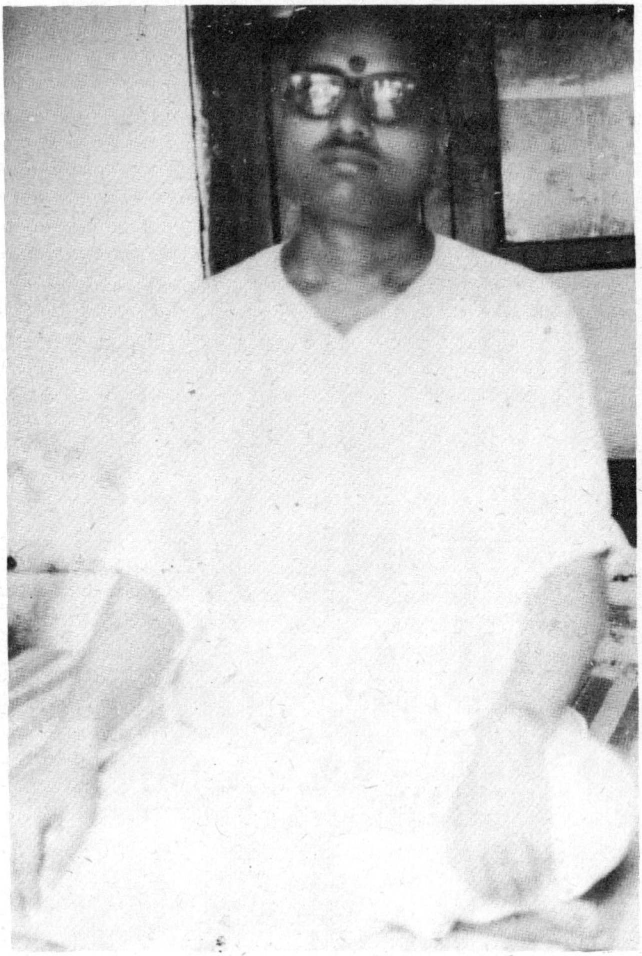

Fig. 8. Śrī Lakṣmīkānt Śāstrī Khaṇaṅg
(Śukla Yajurvedī)

Fig. 9. Śrī Agniṣvātt Śāstrī Agnihotrī
(Sāmavedī)

Fig. 10. Śrī Nārāyaṇ Śaṅkar Tripāṭhī
(Sāmavedī)

Fig. 11. Śrī P. Kṛṣṇamūrti Śrauti
(Sāmavedī)

Fig. 12. Śrī Rāmcandra Śāstri Raṭāṭe
(Atharvavedī, Ṛgvedī)

Fig. 13. Śrī Nārāyaṇ Śāstrī Raṭāṭe
(Atharvavedī, Ṛgvedī)

Bibliography

Allen, W. S. *Phonetics in Ancient India*. London: Oxford University Press, 1953.

Altekar, Anant Sadashiv. *Benares and Sarnath: Past and Present*. 2d ed. Varanasi: Benares Hindu University Culture Publication House, 1947.

Bhātkhaṇḍe, Viṣṇu Nārāyaṇ. *Hindustānī Saṅgīt-Paddhati: Kramik Pustak-Mālikā*. Hindi Edition in 6 vols. Hāthras: Saṅgīt-Kāryālay, 1970-76.

Bhaṭṭ, Viśvaṃbharnāth. *Saṅgīt Arcnā*. 6th ed. Hāthras: Saṅgīt-Kāryālay, 1972.

________. *Saṅgīt Kādambinī*. 5th ed. Hāthras: Saṅgīt-Kāryālay, 1972.

Caland, Willem, ed. *Der Ārṣeyakalpa des Sāmaveda*. Vol. 12:3 of *Abhandlungen für die Kunde des Morgenlandes*. Leipzig, 1908; reprint ed., Nendeln: Kraus Reprint, 1966.

________, trans. *Pañcaviṃśa-Brāhmaṇa: The Brāhmaṇa of Twenty Five Chapters*. Work 255 of *Bibliotheca Indica*. Calcutta: Asiatic Society of Bengal, 1931.

Dev, Viśvanāth Vāman. "Kāśī kī śraut yāg paramparā." *Āj* (Vārāṇasī), 8 May 1966, p. 12.

Dīkṣit, A. M. Rāmnāth, ed. *Ūhagānam--Ūhyagānam*. Vedic Research Series, Banāras Hindu University, vol. 3. Vārāṇasī: Banāras Hindu University Press, 1967.

Dumont, Paul-Émile. *L'Aśvamedha, description du sacrifice solennel du cheval dans le culte védique d'après les textes du Yajurveda blanc*. Paris: P. Geuthner, 1927.

Eggeling, Julius, trans. The Śatapatha-Brāhmaṇa According to the Text of the Mādhyandina School. Vols. 12, 26, 41, 43, 44 of Sacred Books of the East. Oxford, 1900; reprint ed., Delhi: Motilal Banarsidass, 1972.

Geldner, Karl Friedrich. Der Rig-Veda, aus dem Sanskrit ins Deutsche Übersetzt und mit einem laufenden Kommentar versehen. Harvard Oriental Series, vols. 33-35. Cambridge: Harvard University Press, 1951.

The Geographical Encyclopedia of Ancient and Medieval India, Pt. I. Vārāṇasī: Indic Academy, 1967, s.v. "Daśāśvamedha."

Gonda, Jan. Vedic Literature (Saṃhitās and Brāhmaṇas). Vol. 1, fasc. 1 of A History of Indian Literature. Wiesbaden: Otto Harrassowitz, 1975.

Gray, J. E. B. "An Analysis of Nambudiri Ṛgvedic Recitation and the Nature of the Vedic Accent." Bulletin of the School of Oriental and African Studies 22 (1959): 499-530.

________. "An Analysis of Ṛgvedic Recitation." Bulletin of the School of Oriental and African Studies 22 (1959): 86-94.

Haug, M. "Ueber die vedischen Accente." Zeitschrift der Deutschen Morgenländischen Gesellschaft 17 (1863): 799-802.

Havell, E. B. Benares, the Sacred City: Sketches of Hindu Life and Religion. London: Blackie & Son, 1905.

Heesterman, J. C. The Ancient Indian Royal Consecration: The Rājasūya Described According to the Yajus Texts and Annotated. Vol. 2 of Disputationes Rheno-Trajectinae. The Hague: Mouton, 1957.

Herbert, Jean. Banaras: A Guide to Panch-Kroshi Yatra. Calcutta: Saturday Mail Publications, 1957.

Howard, Wayne. "The Music of Nambudiri Unexpressed Chant (Aniruktagāna)." Agni: The Vedic Ritual of the Fire Altar.

Vol. 2. Edited by J. F. Staal. Berkeley: Asian Humanities Press (1982): 311-42.

________. Sāmavedic Chant. New Haven and London: Yale University Press, 1977.

________. "A Yajurveda Festival in Kerala." Music East and West: Essays in Honor of Walter Kaufmann. Edited by Thomas L. Noblitt. New York: Pendragon Press (1981): 1-42.

Kashikar, C. G., et al., eds. Śrautakośa. Vol. 2: Sanskrit Section, Pt. I (Agniṣṭoma with Pravargya). Poona: Vaidika Saṃśodhana Maṇḍala, 1970.

Kashikar, C. G., and Parpola, Asko. "Śrauta Traditions in Recent Times.'' Agni: The Vedic Ritual of the Fire Altar. Vol. 2. Edited by J. F. Staal. Berkeley: Asian Humanities Press (1982): 199-251.

Kaufmann, Walter. The Rāgas of North India. Bloomington: Indiana University Press, 1968.

Keith, A. B., trans. The Veda of the Black Yajus School, Entitled Taittirīya-Saṃhitā. Harvard Oriental Series, vols. 18-19. Cambridge, 1914; reprint ed., Delhi: Motilal Banarsidass, 1967.

Macdonell, Arthur A. Vedic Grammar. Vol. 1:4 of Grundriss der indo-arischen Philologie und Altertumskunde. Strassburg: Verlag von Karl J. Trübner, 1910.

McCrindle, J. W. Ancient India As Described by Megasthenês and Arrian: Being a Translation of the Fragments of the Indika of Megasthenês Collected by Dr. Schwanbeck, and of the First Part of the Indika of Arrian. Calcutta: Chuckervertty, Chatterjee and Co., 1926.

Monier-Williams, M. A Sanskrit-English Dictionary. London, 1899; reprint ed., Delhi: Motilal Banarsidass, 1970.

Müller, Max, ed. Ṛgveda-Saṃhitā. 4 vols. London, 1892; reprint ed., Vārāṇasī: Chowkhamba, 1966.

A Musical Anthology of the Orient: India I (Record Album). Edited by Alain Daniélou. Kassel: Bärenreiter Musicaphon (BM 30 L 2006), n.d.

Nāradīyā Śikṣā. Edited by Śrī Pītāmbarapīṭha-Saṃskṛta-Pariṣad. Jhānsī: Śrī Rām Press, 1964.

Nārāyaṇasvāmī, R., ed. *Grāmageyagāna-Āraṇyakagāna*. Pārḍī: Svādhyāya-Maṇḍala, 1958.

Parpola, Asko. *The Śrautasūtras of Lāṭyāyana and Drāhyāyaṇa and Their Commentaries: An English Translation and Study*. Vols. 42:2 and 43:2 of *Commentationes Humanarum Litterarum*. Helsinki: Societas Scientiarum Fennica, 1968-69.

Raghavan, V. "Present Position of Vedic Chanting and Its Future." *Bulletin of the Institute of Traditional Cultures* 1 (1957): 48-69.

Renou, Louis. *Classical India*. Vol. 3: *Vedic India*. Translated by Philip Spratt. Delhi: Indological Book House, 1971.

———. *Les écoles védiques et la formation du Veda*. Vol. 9 of *Cahiers de la Société Asiatique*. Paris: Imprimerie Nationale, 1947.

———. "La Vājasaneyisaṃhitā des Kāṇva." *Journal Asiatique* 236, series 14 (1948): 21-52.

———. *Vocabulaire du rituel védique*. Paris: Librairie C. Klincksieck, 1954.

Sātvalekar, Dāmodar, ed. *Atharvaveda-Saṃhitā*. Pārḍī: Svādhyāya-Maṇḍala, n.d.

———, ed. *Sāmaveda [-Saṃhitā]*. Pārḍī: Svādhyāya-Maṇḍala, 1956.

Sharma, B. R., ed. *Pañcavidha-Sūtra and Mātrālakṣaṇa, with Commentaries*. Tirupati: Kendriya Sanskrit Vidyapeetha, 1970.

Shastri, Mahamahopadhyaya Haraprasad. "Dakshini Pandits at Benares." The Indian Antiquary 41 (1912): 7-13.

Sherring, M. A. Benares, the Sacred City of the Hindus, in Ancient and Modern Times. London, 1868; reprint ed., Delhi: B. R. Publishing Corp., 1975.

Simon, Richard. "Die Notationen der vedischen Liederbücher." Wiener Zeitschrift für die Kunde des Morgenlandes 27 (1913): 305-46.

Singh, R. L. Banaras: A Study in Urban Geography. Banaras: Nand Kishore & Bros., 1955.

Staal, J. F., ed. Agni: The Vedic Ritual of the Fire Altar, Pt. I (prepublication version). Berkeley, 1977.

________. Nambudiri Veda Recitation. Vol. 5 of Disputationes Rheno-Trajectinae. The Hague: Mouton, 1961.

________. "Notes" to The Four Vedas (Record Album). New York: Asch Mankind Series (AHM 4126), 1969.

________. "Some Vedic Survivals: Report on Research Done in India, Dec. 1970--March 1971, A.I.I.S. Grant." Vārāṇasī, 20 March 1971.

________. ''Vedic Mudras.'' Agni: The Vedic Ritual of the Fire Altar. Vol. 2. Edited by J. F. Staal. Berkeley: Asian Humanities Press, (1982): 359-79.

Sukul, Kuber Nath. Varanasi Down the Ages. Patna: Kameshwar Nath Sukul, 1974.

Tripāṭhī, Ṛṣiśaṅkar, ed. Sāmavedīyarudrajapavidhiḥ. Compiled by Yamunā Prasād Tripāṭhī. Vārāṇasī: Chowkhamba, 1963.

Varma, Siddheshwar. "The Vedic Accent and the Interpreters of Pāṇini." Journal of the Royal Asiatic Society (Bombay Branch) 26 (1950): 1-9.

Vasu, S. C., ed.-trans. The Aṣṭādhyāyī of Pāṇini. 2 vols. 1891; reprint ed., Delhi: Motilal Banarsidass, 1962.

Weber, Albrecht. The History of Indian Literature. London, 1878; reprint ed., Vārāṇasī: Chowkhamba, 1974.

________, ed. The Śatapatha-Brāhmaṇa in the Mādhyandina-Śākhā with Extracts from the Commentaries of Sāyaṇa, Harisvāmin and Dvivedagaṅga. London, 1855; reprint ed., Vārāṇasī: Chowkhamba, 1964.

________, ed.-trans. Das-Vājasaneyi-Prātiśākhyam. Vol. 4 of Indische Studien. Berlin: F. Dümmler's Verlagsbuchhandlung, 1858.

________, ed. The Vājasaneyi-Saṃhitā in the Mādhyandina and the Kāṇva-Śākhā with the Commentary of Mahīdhara. Reprint ed., Vārāṇasī: Chowkhamba, 1972.

Zaehner, R. C., trans. Hindu Scriptures. Vol. 944 of Everyman's Library. London: J. M. Dent & Sons, 1966.

NOTES

Introduction

1. Louis Renou, *Classical India*, vol. 3: *Vedic India*, trans. by Philip Spratt (Delhi: Indological Book House, 1971), p. 108.

2. The above description is from the summary in ibid., pp. 108-9. The rite is described in full in Paul-Émile Dumont, *L'Aśvamedha, description du sacrifice solennel du cheval dans le culte védique d'après les textes du Yajurveda blanc* (Paris: P. Geuthner, 1927).

3. 13.5.4.19-22. See the ed. of Albrecht Weber, *The Śatapatha-Brāhmaṇa in the Mādhyandina-Śākhā with Extracts from the Commentaries of Sāyaṇa, Harisvāmin and Dvivedagaṅga* (London, 1855; reprint ed., Vārāṇasī: Chowkhamba, 1964), p. 996. The pertinent passage is found in English in Julius Eggeling, trans., *The Śatapatha-Brāhmaṇa According to the Text of the Mādhyandina School*, vol. 44 of *Sacred Books of the East* (Oxford, 1900; reprint ed., Delhi: Motilal Banarsidass, 1972), pp. 400-1.

4. See *The Geographical Encyclopedia of Ancient and Medieval India, Pt. I* (Vārāṇasī: Indic Academy, 1967), s.v. "Daśāśvamedha," cit. Jayaswal, *History of India, 150 A.D.-350 A.D.*, p. 5. The *tīrth* is mentioned by the Matsya- and Liṅga-Purāṇas; the Mahābhārata and several Purāṇas locate a Daśāśvamedha *tīrth* also at the following places (see ibid. for further details): at Gayā, on the Narmadā, at Prayāg (Allahābād), at Mathurā, at Kurukṣetra, and on the Godāvarī. J. F. Staal writes that the ten *aśvamedhas* at Vārāṇasī can be traced back to "the Gupta dynasty, in the fourth and fifth century A.D." See his *Agni: The Vedic*

Ritual of the Fire Altar, Pt. I (Berkeley: prepublication copy, 1977), p. 29.

5. Varanasi Down the Ages (Patna: Kameshwar Nath Sukul, 1974), p. 271.

6. This map is reproduced at the end of Sukul's book. The original is preserved at the Bhārat Kalā Bhavan, on the campus of Banāras Hindu University.

7. Ibid.

8. Benares, the Sacred City of the Hindus, in Ancient and Modern Times (London, 1868; reprint ed., Delhi: B.R. Publishing Corp., 1975), pp. 140-43.

9. Moti Chandra, in his Kāśī kā itihās (1962; cit. by Sukul, Varanasi, pp. 172-73), believes the later purāṇas to have assigned new legends to old tīrths.

10. In addition to the Gaṅgā, which brings the Yamunā and Sarasvatī from the West, two subterranean currents, Kiraṇa and Dhūtapāpā, are said to join the river at the same spot. For the legend surrounding these two names, see Sherring, Benares, pp. 107-8.

11. Benares, the Sacred City: Sketches of Hindu Life and Religion (London: Blackie & Son, 1905), pp. 137-38.

12. Other legends are connected with the well, for which see ibid.

13. The six-day pilgrimage (yātrā) is described in Jean Herbert, Banaras: A Guide to Panch-Kroshi Yatra (Calcutta: Saturday Mail Publications, 1957).

14. Varanasi, p. 274.

15. Ibid., pp. 276-77.

16. Banaras: A Study in Urban Geography (Banaras: Nand Kishore & Bros., 1955), passim.

17. See Sukul, Varanasi, p. 90.

18. Benares, p. 347.

19. The Indian Antiquary 41 (1912): 7-13.

20. Ibid., p. 13.

21. Varanasi, pp. 99-100.

22. Ibid., p. 101.

23. See ibid.

24. See ibid., p. 102.

25. "Dakshini Pandits," p. 7.

26. See Sukul, Varanasi, p. 107. In addition to this institution and the Sanskrit University, Anant Sadashiv Altekar refers to seven other establishments set up to promote learning primarily in Sanskrit: Goenka Sanskrit Mahāvidyālaya, Marwari Sanskrit College, Tikamani Sanskrit College, Birla Sanskrit Vidyālaya, Śrī Chandra Mahāvidyālaya, Syādvāda Jain Vidyālaya, Ranvir Sanskrit Pāthashālā--listed in Altekar's Benares and Sarnath: Past and Present, 2d ed. (Varanasi: Benares Hindu University Culture Publication House, 1947), p. 54. Whether all of these colleges impart instruction in Veda recitation, or indeed whether all of them are still in existence, I am unable to say.

27. The ritual is described in detail in Staal's Agni.

28. See Renou, Vedic India, pp. 101-2.

29. "Kāśī kī śraut yāg paramparā," Āj, 8 May 1966, p. 12. A brief summary of the article forms an appendix to Sukul's Varanasi, pp. 327-28. The present writer first met Śrī Viśvanāth Dev on February 7, 1971, during a vedasammelana (Vedic conference) at the Santirām Mandir, Naḍiād, Gujarāt; the acquaintance was renewed in December of the same year. Much of the material in Part I is based upon tape-recordings of his recitation.

30. Benares, pp. 177-78.

31. Viśvanāth Dev makes reference in his article "Kāśī kī śraut yāg paramparā" to a seventeenth-century paṇḍit, Śyāmā

Dīkṣit Pāṭhak (a dakṣiṇī White Yajurvedī residing in Vārāṇasī), who performed the rājasūya ("Royal Consecration") sacrifice for the King of Jaipur, Mān Siṅgh.

32. To be published in Staal's Agni, Vol. 2, pp. 199-251.

Part I

1. Indeed, the only Nambudiri I came across there is Prof. C. P. M. Nambudiri, who teaches in the Philosophy Department at Banāras Hindu University. Although he is extremely knowledgeable in Vedic matters and has close ties to Vaidikas in Kerala, he himself is an ōttillātta Nambudiri, a sub-caste not eligible to recite the Vedas.

2. The Śāṅkhāyana (Kauṣītaki) Sūtra is followed in Kerala by Nambudiri Brāhmaṇs; but, as seen from the foregoing list of agnihotrīs, it has been present in Vārāṇasī in the past.

3. See Louis Renou, Les écoles védiques et la formation du Veda, vol. 9 of Cahiers de la Société Asiatique (Paris: Imprimerie Nationale, 1947), pp. 57-58.

4. "Present Position of Vedic Chanting and Its Future," Bulletin of the Institute of Traditional Cultures 1 (1957): 59-60. The publication of the Poona vedapāṭhaśālā (see ibid., p. 59, n. 8) is the following: Sītārām Viṣṇu Kelkar, ed., Vaidik Vidvānanca Paicaya, Bhāga 1 (Poona: Puṇa Veda Pāṭhaśālā, 1957).

5. Bulletin of the School of Oriental and African Studies 22 (1959): 86-94.

6. Ibid., p. 86.

7. "An Analysis of Nambudiri Ṛgvedic Recitation and the Nature of the Vedic Accent," Bulletin of the School of Oriental and African Studies 22 (1959): 499-530.

8. A thorough description of the types and rules of accentuation is presented in chap. III of A. A. Macdonell, Vedic Grammar, vol. 1, pt. 4 of Grundriss der indo-arischen Philologie und Altertumskunde (Strassburg: Verlag von Karl J. Trübner, 1910), pp. 76-107.

9. This and all Ṛgveda specimens are taken from Max Müller, ed., Ṛgveda-Saṃhitā, 4 vols. (London, 1892; reprint ed., Vārāṇasī: Chowkhamba, 1966).

10. See Macdonell, Vedic Grammar, pp. 81-82, for a fuller discussion of double accent and lack of accent.

11. See the numerous examples in Wayne Howard, "A Yajurveda Festival in Kēraḷa," Music East and West: Essays in Honor of Walter Kaufmann (New York: Pendragon Press, 1981), pp. 1-42.

12. See Wayne Howard, Sāmavedic Chant (New Haven and London: Yale University Press, 1977), pp. 455-500.

13. Der Rig-Veda, aus dem Sanskrit ins Deutsche übersetzt und mit einem laufenden Kommentar versehen, Harvard Oriental Series, vols. 33-35 (Cambridge: Harvard University Press, 1951).

14. See "An Analysis of Ṛgvedic Recitation," pp. 87-88.

15. See ibid., pp. 86-87.

16. The Aṣṭādhyāyī of Pāṇini, vol. 1 (1891; reprint ed., Delhi: Motilal Banarsidass, 1962), pp. 85-87.

17. See "The Vedic Accent and the Interpreters of Pāṇini," Journal of the Royal Asiatic Society (Bombay Branch) 26 (1950): 1-9.

18. See Phonetics in Ancient India (London: Oxford University Press, 1953), pp. 87-93.

19. "Nambudiri Ṛgvedic Recitation," pp. 512-13.

20. Ibid., pp. 519-20.

21. Allen, Phonetics in Ancient India, pp. 89-90.

22. Ibid., p. 89.

23. See Howard, Sāmavedic Chant, pp. 31-38, 120-24, 543-44.

24. "Analysis of Ṛgvedic Recitation," p. 89.

25. "Analysis of Nambudiri Ṛgvedic Recitation," pp. 517-18.

26. kaścit kañcid adhīyānam āha kim uccair rorūyase śanair vartatām iti / tam eva tathādhīyānam apara āha kim antardanta-kenādhīṣe uccair vartatām iti /

27. See Louis Renou, Vocabulaire du Rituel Védique (Paris: Librairie C. Klincksieck, 1954), p. 68.

28. See ibid., p. 87.

29. Well-documented instances of ekaśruti occur in the ōttūṭṭu, the Vedic feast of the Nambudiri Yajurvedīs. It is their practice to go through the entire Taittirīya-Saṃhitā 16 times: 6 in saṃhitā, 6 in pada, 4 in koṭṭu (this last a special type of pada). In saṃhitā and pada, each paññāti (group of fifty words) is normally recited once, with svara, by a single Yajurvedī, then five times ekaśruti by the full assembly (see Howard, "A Yajurveda Festival," p. 9). Koṭṭu takes four words at a time. First they are stated, in ordinary padapāṭha, by a solo reciter, then repeated three times ekaśruti by the full group. Just as they begin their third repetition, the soloist begins singing the next group of four words. When he reaches the fourth word, the assembly begin their threefold repetition. This exchange continues until koṭṭu is concluded (see Howard, "A Yajurveda Festival," pp. 35-37).

30. See Renou, Vocabulaire, p. 165; Howard, Sāmavedic Chant, pp. 540-42.

31. See his Nambudiri Veda Recitation (The Hague: Mouton, 1961), pp. 42-43.

32. Siddheshwar Varma ("The Vedic Accent," p. 2, n. 3) reports the "startling theory" put forth by Śivarāmakrishna

Shastri in the introduction to his edition of the Svarasiddhānta-candrikā (Annamalai University, 1936). Shastri insists, on grounds other than those cited above, that udātta was originally recited at a middle pitch. However, Varma disagrees, adding that "the acceptance of such a theory would upset the whole structure of Indo-European Comparative Philology."

33. "Nambudiri Ṛgvedic Recitation," p. 510.

34. See the photographs in Staal, Nambudiri Veda Recitation, opp. p. 41.

35. See Staal's "Vedic Mudras," Agni: The Vedic Ritual of the Fire Altar ed. J. F. Staal, Vol. 2 (Berkeley: Asian Humanities Press, 1982), 359-79 for exhaustive information on the Ṛgvedic gestures. His account relies to a great extent on an article by Parameśvara Bhāratikal entitled ''Vedamudrakal,'' published in Malayāḷam in 1967 in the Souvenir Volume brought out to celebrate the Golden Jubilee of the Brahmasva Maṭham. The article was translated for Staal by Māḍamp Nārāyaṇan Nambudiri, with complementary material supplied by Dr. K. M. J. Nambudiri.

36. See Gray, "Nambudiri Ṛgvedic Recitation," p. 511.

37. See ibid., p. 512.

38. Allen, Phonetics in Ancient India, p. 91.

39. This Vaidika chants Sāmaveda hymns on the UNESCO record album A Musical Anthology of the Orient: India I, ed. Alain Daniélou (Kassel: Bärenreiter Musicaphon, BM 30 L 2006, n.d.), nos. 9-10.

40. I heard rumors of an Atharvavedī at the Mahārājā's Sanskrit College in Mysore City, but it was impossible to arrange a meeting.

41. Nambudiri Veda Recitation, p. 18.

42. Renou, Écoles védiques, p. 87.

43. See Dāmodar Sātvalekar, ed., Atharvaveda-Saṃhitā

(Pardi: Svādhyāya-Maṇḍala, n.d.), p. 364. The reader is invited to peruse an article by M. Haug (the earliest Western scholar to report on actual Vedic recitations), who deals primarily with Atharvavedic chanting, presumably of the Mahārāṣṭrian type (the article is dated July 8, 1863, from Poona): "Ueber die vedischen Accente," Zeitschrift der Deutschen Morgenländischen Gesellschaft 17 (1863): 799-802.

Part II

1. See Albrecht Weber, *The History of Indian Literature* (London, 1878; reprint ed., Vārāṇasī: Chowkhamba, 1974), pp. 103-4. This is the explanation offered by Dvivedagaṅga in his commentary on the Bṛhad-Āraṇyaka, which forms part of the fourteenth and final book of the Śatapatha-Brāhmaṇa.

2. Ibid., p. 104.

3. See M. Monier-Williams, *A Sanskrit-English Dictionary* (London, 1899; reprint ed., Delhi: Motilal Banarsidass, 1970), pp. 455, col. 1; 938, col. 2 (cit. Viṣṇu-Purāṇa 3.5.1-29). See also Renou, *Écoles védiques*, pp. 158, 205-6; and Weber, *History of Indian Literature*, p. 104, n. 118. However, the name Taittirīya is probably a patronymic and has little or no connection with the purāṇic legend. See Jan Gonda, *Vedic Literature (Saṃhitās and Brāhmaṇas)*, vol. 1, fasc. 1 of *A History of Indian Literature* (Wiesbaden: Otto Harrassowitz, 1975), p. 325 and n. 17.

4. Weber, *History of Indian Literature*, p. 106.

5. J. W. McCrindle, *Ancient India As Described by Megasthenês and Arrian: Being a Translation of the Fragments of the Indika of Megasthenês Collected by Dr. Schwanback, and of the First Part of the Indika of Arrian* (Calcutta: Chuckervertty, Chatterjee and Co., 1926), p. 191.

6. Ibid., n. on p. 195.

7. Ibid., n. on pp. 194-95.

8. *Écoles védiques*, p. 200.

9. *History of Indian Literature*, p. 106, n. 120.

10. Gonda, *Vedic Literature*, pp. 336-37.

11. A. B. Keith, trans., *The Veda of the Black Yajus*

School, Entitled Taittirīya Saṃhitā, vol. 18 of the Harvard Oriental Series (Cambridge, 1914; reprint ed., Delhi: Motilal Banarsidass, 1967), p. xciii. The proclamation of the king during the rājasūya ritual is delivered with the words, "This is your king, O Bharatas." Some texts, among them the Kāṇva recension of the Vājasaneyi-Saṃhitā, have the variants, "O Kurus," "O Pañcālas" (see ibid.). See also J. C. Heesterman, The Ancient Indian Royal Consecration: The Rājasūya Described According to the Yajus Texts and Annotated (The Hague: Mouton, 1967), p. 71. The Bharata tribe was eventually absorbed by the Kurus.

12. Renou, Écoles védiques, p. 199.

13. Eggeling, Śatapatha-Brāhmaṇa trans., I, pp. xlii-xliii. The passage from the Bṛhad-Āraṇyaka-Upaniṣad (Kāṇva recension) reads:

> Driptabālāki was a learned member of the Gārgya clan. He said to Ajātaśatru, [king] of Benares: "Shall I tell you about Brahman?" And Ajātaśatru said: "I will give you a thousand [cows] for your teaching. In fact people do come running [to this place] saying, 'a [second] Janaka is here.'"

The foregoing is from R. C. Zaehner, trans., Hindu Scriptures, vol. 944 of Everyman's Library (London: J. M. Dent & Sons, 1966), p. 41.

14. Renou, Écoles védiques, p. 204. Staal (Nambudiri Veda Recitation, p. 19) writes, "At the present day Mādhyaṃdinas exist as far South as Mysore City . . . ." The present writer met only one Śukla Yajurvedin there, at the Mahārājā's Sanskrit College, but his śākhā is Kāṇva. Raghavan ("Position of Vedic Chanting," p. 52, n. 4a) points to epigraphical references to both Mādhyandinas and Kāṇvas in Orissā.

15. Renou, Écoles védiques, p. 200, n. 1.

16. "Position of Vedic Chanting," pp. 60-62.

17. Ibid., pp. 52, 62.

18. Staal, Nambudiri Veda Recitation, p. 73.

19. This according to the Mahārṇava, cit. Renou, Écoles védiques, p. 200, n. 1.

20. Ibid., p. 204.

21. Ibid.

22. Ibid. Later surveys place the Kāṇva śākhā in Mahārāṣṭra, in Āndhra, at Kānyakubja, at Utkala (Orissā), and in Bengāl (here transmitted by Parāśara Brāhmaṇs): see ibid., p. 200, n. 2, cit. J. Wilson, Ind. Caste, II, pp. 24, 53, 57, 153, 228; and Census 1931, Bengāl, I, p. 462.

23. See "Position of Vedic Chanting," pp. 52, 54, 57, 60, 61, 62.

24. In regard to South India, Raghavan (Ibid., p. 54) refers to "the tradition of the Śuklayajurvedin being impure for a brief duration at noontime according to a curse . . ." and to "a reputation that they, and sometimes their womenfolk too, knew a number of good and bad incantations for helping or harming people."

25. See Nambudiri Veda Recitation, p. 87.

26. See J. F. Staal, "Some Vedic Survivals: Report on Research Done in India, Dec. 1970--March 1971, A.I.I.S. Grant" (Vārāṇasī: 20 March 1971), pp. 10-11.

27. See ibid., p. 12.

28. See Howard, Sāmavedic Chant, p. 487.

29. See his "Analysis of Nambudiri Ṛgvedic Recitation," pp. 507, n. 2; 509-11; 529-30.

30. Ibid., p. 509.

31. Krama is not among the eight, but it is the only vikṛti discussed by the Vājasaneyi-Prātiśākhya (4.179-195). See Albrecht Weber, ed.-trans., Das Vājasaneyi-Prātiśākhyam, vol. 4

of *Indische Studien* (Berlin: F. Dümmler's Verlagsbuchhandlung, 1858), pp. 280-90. Another edition is that of V. Venkatarama Sharma, *Vājasaneyi Prātiśākhya of Kātyāyana, with the Commentaries of Uvaṭa and Anantabhaṭṭa*, Madras University Sanskrit Series, no. 5 (Madras: University of Madras, 1934).

32. Gajānan Śāstrī's explanation, in Hindī, reads as follows (from a letter of October 10, 1978): un vikṛtiyõ ke nām un ke guṇõ ke anurūp hãĩ / jaise bālõ kī 2 laṭāyẽ ek mẽ gūnthne se jaṭā bantī hai, usī prakār mantrõ ke 2 padõ ko gūnthne se jaṭā vikṛti hotī hai / puṣpamālā mẽ phūl kī mālā ke samān phūl gūnth kar ḍorā ulṭā kar punaḥ sīdhā karte hãĩ usī prakār padõ ko kiyā jātā hai / śikhā mẽ bāl bāndh kar chor nikālā jātā hai, usī prakār jaṭā ke bād ek pad āge nikālā jātā hai / rekhā mẽ pãti baddh padõ kā nyās sīdhā kā sīdhā hotā hai / ataḥ use rekhā vikṛti kahte hãĩ / yahī sthiti āge dhvajādi cārõ vikṛtiyõ ke nām kī bhī hai, jo pūrṇ yaugik hai /.

33. "Analysis of Nambudiri Ṛgvedic Recitation," p. 509.

34. See Allen, *Phonetics in Ancient India*, p. 43, n. 7. Kāṇva Vājasaneyīs and Tamil-speaking Kṛṣṇa Yajurvedīs also transmit this feature.

35. See ibid., pp. 55-56. Here Allen states that this pronunciation "is traditional in Yajurvedic recitation."

36. Texts of this and subsequent verses are from Albrecht Weber, ed., *The Vājasaneyi-Saṃhitā in the Mādhyandina and the Kāṇva-Śākhā with the Commentary of Mahīdhara* (Reprint ed., Vārāṇasī: Chowkhamba, 1972).

37. See Part I, under "Forms of Ṛgvedic Recitation."

38. The same type is sung, by a Sāmavedī, on the UNESCO *Musical Anthology* album, no. 14.

39. See J. F. Staal, "Notes" to the record album *The Four Vedas* (New York: Asch Mankind Series, Album AHM 4126), p. 6. The singers here are Ṛgvedīs.

40. The use of this particular verse for the *daṇḍa-vikṛti* is illustrative of the sense of humor which I encountered among several Vedic paṇḍits.

41. To alleviate his job of recitation but to confound the listener, the reciter has chosen a verse in which each *pāda* begins with the words *svasti naḥ* ("prosperity to us").

42. Refer to the Atharvaveda discussion in Part I and to the section on Kāṇva recitation at the end of this Part.

43. See Staal, "Some Vedic Survivals," pp. 10-11. But Renou, referring to criteria other than those cited above, has argued that the Kāṇva recension is the most recent of all Vedic *saṃhitās*. See his "La Vājasaneyisaṃhitā des Kāṇva," *Journal Asiatique* 236, series 14 (1948): 49.

44. See Gray, "Analysis of Nambudiri Ṛgvedic Recitation," p. 508; and Staal, *Nambudiri Veda Recitation*, pp. 21-28.

45. See Howard, *Sāmavedic Chant*, pp. 460-61.

46. *Écoles védiques*, p. 161.

Part III

1. The Ārṣeyakalpa of Maśaka lists chants to be performed at all *soma* rituals. See Willem Caland, ed., *Der Ārṣeyakalpa des Sāmaveda*, vol. 12, no. 3 of *Abhandlungen für die Kunde des Morgenlandes* (Leipzig, 1908; reprint ed., Nendeln: Kraus Reprint, 1966).

2. Chants for expiation and desire are listed in the Kṣudrasūtra, which has been appended to Caland's ed. of the Ārṣeyakalpa.

3. For a description of contents, see Willem Caland, trans., *Pañcaviṃśa-Brāhmaṇa: The Brāhmaṇa of Twenty Five Chapters*, work 255 of *Bibliotheca Indica* (Calcutta: Asiatic Society of Bengal, 1931), pp. ii-vii.

4. *Sāmavedic Chant*, pp. 76-102.

5. Ibid., p. 76.

6. Renou, Écoles védiques, p. 127, cit. Siegling's ed. of the Caraṇavyūha. Mahidāsa lived in the sixteenth century.

7. Ibid., pp. 127-28, cit. Wilson, Ind. Caste, II, pp. 110, 154, 211.

8. Ibid., pp. 128-29.

9. Howard, Sāmavedic Chant, pp. 134-36.

10. Described in ibid., pp. 115-24.

11. See ibid., pp. 114-133. Transcriptions of Muḷḷanṭiram chant are found on pp. 287-88.

12. "Position of Vedic Chanting," p. 55.

13. This is not to say that the Kannaḍiga Sāmagas are without a sacrificial tradition of their own: see Howard, Sāmavedic Chant, pp. 114-15.

14. See Staal, Nambudiri Veda Recitation, p. 19, n. 38; p. 89 (the chanter of tape IV(1)A).

15. See Renou, Écoles védiques, pp. 88-89.

16. Has some confusion arisen in Tamil country because of the similar spellings of Kauthuma and Gautama in the Tamil script? One vowel is all that distinguishes one name from the other.

17. See Asko Parpola, The Śrautasūtras of Lāṭyāyana and Drāhyāyaṇa and Their Commentaries: An English Translation and Study, vol. 42, no. 2 of Commentationes Humanarum Litterarum (Helsinki: Societas Scientiarum Fennica, 1968-69), I:1, p. 29, cit. Weber, Academische Vorlesungen über die indische Literaturgeschichte, 2 Aufl. (Berlin, 1876), p. 83.

18. Ibid., pp. 29-30.

19. Ibid., pp. 40-41.

20. Ibid., p. 41.

21. Ibid., p. 41, n. 2.

22. Ibid., p. 43.

23. Écoles védiques, p. 96.

24. See Howard, Sāmavedic Chant, p. 133.

25. See Parpola, Śrautasūtras of Lāṭyāyana and Drāhyāyaṇa trans., I:1, pp. 45-46.

26. See the transcriptions of Jaiminīya chant in Howard, Sāmavedic Chant, pp. 376-451.

27. C. G. Kashikar, et al., eds. (Poona: Vaidika Saṃśodhana Maṇḍala, 1970).

28. Ibid., Preface, p. 17.

29. Renou, Vedic India, p. 103.

30. Benares, p. 105.

31. Compiled by Yamunā Prasād Tripāṭhī (Vārāṇasī: Chowkhamba, 1963).

32. See ibid., pp. 2-4.

33. Photographs of Ṛṣiśaṅkar Tripāṭhī, Yamunā Prasād Tripāṭhī, Svāmī Sāligrām Dās, and Kṛṣṇa Kumār Goyal are found in ibid., following p. 4.

34. See Howard, Sāmavedic Chant, pp. 540-42.

35. Pañcaviṃśa-Brāhmaṇa 7.7.12. See Caland's trans., p. 150.

36. Published in Howard, Sāmavedic Chant, figs. 3-16.

37. Ibid., pp. 76-102.

38. Ibid., pp. 95-100.

39. This review summarizes material in chap. 1 of ibid., as well as in the earlier article by Richard Simon, "Die Notationen der vedischen Liederbücher," Wiener Zeitschrift für die Kunde des Morgenlandes 27 (1913): 305-46.

40. See the photographs in Howard, Sāmavedic Chant, figs. 3-7, as demonstrated by Gopāl Rām Tripāṭhī.

41. Monier-Williams, Sanskrit-English Dictionary, p. 322, col. 2.

42. This feature has been kept by some Brāhmaṇs in South India (see Howard, *Sāmavedic Chant*, pp. 132-33; 135, n. 3; 138).

43. Monier-Williams, *Sanskrit-English Dictionary*, p. 61, col. 3.

44. Some singers, however, represent 11 in a slightly higher elevation of the thumb (see Howard, *Sāmavedic Chant*, pp. 89-90, 105-8). The use of identical postures for 1 and 11 reflects the fact that *kruṣṭa* is sometimes designated by 1 and that little or no difference exists in the vocal interpretations of the two figures.

45. See ibid., fig. 8.

46. See ibid., fig. 9.

47. See ibid., figs. 10-13.

48. The use of the term *vinata* for this pattern is evidently the practice only of northern Kauthumas. See Tripāṭhī, *Sāmavedīyarudrajapavidhiḥ*, "*Bhūmikā*," p. 15.

49. The term *utsvarita* for these patterns is again the northern usage; elsewhere it refers to the pattern 4_5. See ibid.

50. The paṇḍits maintain that the use of the circumflex or *avagraha* (ऽ) with the number 2 results in long articulation (Hindī: *dīrgh uccāraṇ*). See ibid., p. 16.

51. Ed. B. R. Sharma (Tirupati: Kendriya Sanskrit Vidyapeetha, 1970).

52. The three hundred or so "typical *parvans*" were recorded by the author from two Rāṇāyanīya Sāmavedīs of the North Kannaḍa District, Karṇāṭaka, and transcribed in Howard, *Sāmavedic Chant*, pp. 289-362.

53. This *parvan* is an exception to the general rule that no two *parvans* out of the three hundred present the same sequence of numbers. However, the *stobha* *au*^{5r} *ho*^{r} *vā* is sung in a special

way; therefore the musical interpretation of the preceding "typical parvan" in the list, $\underline{\overset{1}{i}v\bar{a}\hat{2}}$ $\underline{pr\bar{a}\overset{3}{2}34ya\overset{5}{m}}$, is different, even though it has the same number series.

54. The system is described in ibid., pp. 115-120.

55. The source is Manuscript B.89, leaf 2 verso, of the India Office Library, London. This is a palm leaf ms. in the grantha script.

56. See, for example, Raghavan, "Position of Vedic Chanting," p. 67, where it is disclosed that some chanters began to sing the notational syllables as part of the text. However, this old notation has been preserved in the northern Tamil districts, as previously noted.

57. See Howard, Sāmavedic Chant, pp. 120-24.

58. See ibid., pp. 121-22.

59. See ibid., p. 117.

60. Grāmageyagāna--Āraṇyakagāna (Pārḍī: Svādhyāya-Maṇḍala, 1958), pp. 1-2. This edition is represented in the analysis by the letter N.

61. Described in Howard, Sāmavedic Chant, chap. 3.

62. Hindī ed. in 6 vols. (Hāthras: Saṅgīt Kāryālay, 1970-76).

63. Ibid., II, p. 487.

64. For a full description of the rāga see Walter Kaufmann, The Rāgas of North India (Bloomington: Indiana University Press, 1968), pp. 285-89.

65. Based upon Bhātkhaṇḍe's notation in the devanāgarī script, Kramik Pustak-Mālikā IV, p. 814. Many Indian musicologists of the present day base their rāga analyses on Bhātkhaṇḍe, who is rightfully held in the highest esteem by northern musicians as the exemplary music scholar of this century.

They too give lists of svarvistārs and sometimes include the rhythmic element. See, for example, Viśvambharnāth Bhaṭṭ, Saṅgīt Arcnā, 6th ed. (Hāthras: Saṅgīt Kāryālay, 1972), and, by the same author, Saṅgīt Kādambinī, 5th ed. (Hāthras: Saṅgīt Kāryālay, 1972). Rāg Vasant is dealt with on pp. 130-42 of the last-mentioned book.

66. 1.5.1-2. See the ed. of Śrī Pītāmbarapīṭha-Saṃskṛta-Pariṣad (Jhānsī: Śrī Rām Press, 1964), p. 28.

67. Sources of the notated chants are the gāna editions of Nārāyaṇasvāmī (for the Grāmageyagāna and Āraṇyakagāna) and A. M. Rāmnāth Dīkṣit, Ūhagānam--Ūhyagānam, Banāras Hindu University Vedic Research Series, no. 3 (Vārāṇasī: Banāras Hindu University Press, 1967).

68. The source verses are taken from Dāmodar Sātvalekar, ed., Sāmaveda [-Saṃhitā] (Pārḍī: Svādhyāya-Maṇḍala, 1956).

69. Sāmavedic Chant, p. 93, table 7.

70. Ibid., p. 93.

71. Compare these interpretations of the sequences with those transcribed in ibid., pp. 95-100.

72. See, for example, chants 4-6 of the Jaiminīya Grāmageyagāna, Caland Ms. 7 of the University of Utrecht Library. The Jaiminīyas pronounce iḻā instead of iḍā.

73. Sāmavedīyarudrajapavidhiḥ, p. 13.

74. J. E. B. Gray, who also has made recordings among the Vārāṇasī Sāmavedīs, may have succeeded in obtaining the gāyatra on tape. If so, it would be interesting to compare his recording(s) with my theoretical transcription. The South Indians are not as secretive about this chant; I was able to obtain more than two dozen versions among the various Sāmavedic schools of the region. See the catalogue of recordings in Howard, Sāmavedic Chant, pp. 457-500.

75. For a thorough discussion of these elements, see Wayne Howard, "The Music of Nambudiri Unexpressed Chant (Aniruktagāna)," Agni: The Vedic Ritual of the Fire Altar. ed. J. F. Staal, Vol. 2 (Berkeley: Asian Humanities Press, 1982): 311-42.

76. The complete text of the Kauthuma bahiṣpavamānastotra, as edited by Ṛṣiśaṅkar Tripāṭhī, is found in the agniṣṭoma vol. of the Śrautakośa, pp. 279-80.

INDEX

Abhigīta, 216, 323, 327

Abhikrama, 133

Abhiṣeka, 7

Accents, 23-25, 75-87, 163-165, 173, 190, 214, 228-229

Achaval, Son Bhaṭṭ, 9

Adhvaryu, 15, 17

Agni, 11, 31-33, 170, 192, 193, 199, 229

Agnicayana, 11-12; at Rām Kaṭorā and Bauliyā Bāgh, 13; at Reṇukā Devī Mandir, 12

Agnihotra, 11, 13

Agnihotra-vrata-grahaṇa, 13

Agnihotrī, 11, 17, 208, 211, 212, 368 (n. 2)

Agniṣṭoma, 5, 11-15, 208, 211, 345; at Assī Ghāṭ, 15; at Baṅgālī Bāṛā, 12, 14 15; at Bhūlanpur village, 14; at Brahmā Ghāṭ, 13; at Durgā Devī Mandir (Rāmnagar), 14; at Hanumān Ghāṭ, 14; at Rāj Mandir, 13; at Rājā of Kāśī Mandir (Śivālā Ghāṭ), 15; at Sapt Sāgar, 15; at Satī Cabūtarā, 13

Āhavanīya, 11

Ahilyābāī Ghāṭ, 3

Ahīna-parvan, 200, 201

Āhitāgni, 11-12, 17-18, 208, 210-212

Aiyaṅgār Brāhmaṇs, 10

Aiyar, T. K. Rājagopāla, 203

Aiyar Brāhmaṇs, 10

Ajātaśatru, 118 374 (n. 13)

Ālāp, 224

Allāhābād Road, 14

Allen, W. S., 23, 95, 96, 105, 375 (n. 35)

Alpaprāṇa, 96-99

Altekar, Anant Sadashiv, 367 (n. 26)

Amahīyu, 277

Andhomatī River, 116

Āndhra Pradesh, 22, 110, 120, 375 (n. 22); Nellūr, 110 Vizagapatam, 119

Aṅga, 119

Aniruktagāna, 345

Anudātta, 24-25, 93, 95-96, 98 99, 100, 101 104-105, 228-229, ; of Atharvavedic recitation, 113, 114, of Kāṇva Yajurvedic recitation, 193 of Mādhyandina Yajurvedic recitation, 163, of Ṛgvedic recitation, 78-81, 87, 88-92, 103-107 of Taittirīya Yajurvedic recitation, 191-192

Anukrama, 133

Anunāsika, 305

Anusvāra, 29, 123, 162, 216, 305
Āpastamba-Śrauta-Sūtra, 14, 18
Aptoryāma, 11; at Bhairo Bāvṛī, 13; at Rām Kaṭorā and Bauliyā Bāgh, 13
Āraṇyakagāna, 199-201, 203, 260, 263,
Āraṇyaka-Saṃhitā, 199, 201, 263
Ārcika, 199
Arka-parvan, 199, 201
Arrian, 116
Ārṣeya-Brāhmaṇa, 213
Ārṣeyakalpa, 377 (nn. 1, 2)
Aryaman, 233
Āryans, 117-118, 209
Āruṇeya, Śvetaketu, 118
Āśram, 211-212
Assī Ghāṭ, 12, 16
Assī River, 2, 4, 16, 116
Aṣṭādhyāyī of Pāṇini, 93
Aṣṭa-vikṛti, 121-122
Āśvalāyana-Śrauta-Sūtra, 13, 15, 21
Aśvamedha, 1-5, 10, 143-48, 365 (n. 4); of the Bhāraśivas, 2, 4-5, of Brahmā, 3; ; of Śatānīka Sātrājita, 2
Aśvins, 46-47
Atharvaveda, 25, 109-114, 164, 198, 377 (n. 42)
Āṭhvale, Rāmçandra, 109
Atikrama, 314-315, 334, 339-340
Atirātra, 11
Atisvārya, 216
Atyagniṣṭoma, 11; at Rām Kaṭorā and Bauliyā Bāgh, 13
Aurangzeb, 6
Avagraha, 380 (n. 50)
Avanardana, 343
Bādal, Maṅgaleśvar, 17
Bagh 12, 13
Bahiṣpavamānastotra, 345, 345, 383 (n. 76)
Bake, Arnold, 121
Banāras Hindu University, 10, 16, 121, 173, 213, 227, 366 (n. 6), 368 (n. 1)
Baṅgālī Bāṛā, 12, 14, 16
Baṅgladesh, 120; Dacca, 120
Bāpaṭ, Ganeś Bhaṭṭ (Yajurvedī and Sāmavedī), 9, 17, 192, 212
Bāpaṭ, Ganeś Dīkṣit, 17
Bāpaṭ, Kāśīnāth, 17, 212
Bāpaṭ, Rāmcandra, 192
Bāpaṭ, Somnāth, 9
Barṇā. See Varṇā
Bauliyā Bāgh, 13, 16
Bay of Bengal, 119
Bengal, 10, 14, 19, 116, 119, 202, 211, 375 (n. 22);
Bardvān, 116, 202; Barrakpur, 22; Calcutta Sanskrit College, 8; Dinajpur, 202
Bettigiri, Ganeś Śāstrī, 18

Bhadainī Mohalla, 3

Bhairavnāth, 13

Bhairo Bāvṛī, 13, 16

Bhakāra-rathantara, 212

Bhakti, 341, 345

Bharadvāja, 260

Bharadvāja family, 8

Bhāraśiva dynasty, 2, 4-5

Bhārat Kalā Bhavan, 366 (n. 6)

Bharata tribe, 374 (n. 11)

Bharvāśilkar, Ātmārām, 15

Bhātkhande, Viṣṇu Nārāyaṇ, 224-225, 381 (n. 65)

Bhaṭṭ, Pāṇḍuraṅg Dīkṣit 13

Bhaṭṭ, Gāgā (Viśveśvar), 7

Bhaṭṭ, Ganeś Dīkṣit Dāūjī, 17

Bhaṭṭ, Gopālkṛṣṇa 15

Bhaṭṭ, Lakṣmīkānt Dīkṣit Jāvjī, 190

Bhaṭṭ, Mallāri, 7

Bhaṭṭ, Nāgojī, 7

Bhaṭṭ, Nārāyaṇ, 7, 22

Bhaṭṭ, Rāmeśvar, 7, 21

Bhaṭṭ, Sadāśiv Dīkṣit Jāvjī, 13

Bhaṭṭ, Śaṅkar, 7

Bhaṭṭ, Sokhārām Dīkṣit Dāūjī, 17

Bhaṭṭ, Triambak Dīkṣit, 8

Bhavanilāljī, 18

Bhelupur, 10

Bholānāth, 18

Bhūlanpur, 13 16

Bihār, 117, 119. Gayā, 365 (n. 4); Pāṭaliputra, 116; Puraniyā, 116; Tirhut, 116

Bindu, 219

Birla Sanskrit Vidyālaya, 367 (n. 26)

Black Yajurveda. See Kṛṣṇa Yajurveda

Brahmā, 2-3

Brahmā Ghāṭ, 8, 13, 16

Brāhmaṇa, 23, 95, 117, 200, 213

Brahmcārī, Satyadev, 211

Bṛhad-Āraṇyaka-Upaniṣad, 118, 373 (n. 1), 374 (n. 13)

Bṛhaspati, 139, 140, 141, 149-150

Bulānālā, 15-16

Caland, W., 377 (n. 2), 382 (n. 72)

Candragupta Maurya, 116

Caraṇa, 5

Caraṇavyūha, 202, 204, 378 (n. 6)

Cardona, George, 31, 97, 106

Caturdhara. See Caudharī

Cāturmāsya, 109, 209

Caturvidyā-caraṇa, 6

Catuṣpāda, 122, 148-149

Caudharī family, 8

Cauk, 10

Centonization, 220, 224

Chāndogya-Upaniṣad, 213

Chāndosāma school, 204

Chandra, Moti, 366 (n. 9)

Citlai, Sītārām Dīkṣit, 15

Cīz, 224

Dakṣiṇāgni, 11
Dakṣiṇī paṇḍits, 6-10, 12, 13, 14, 368 368 (n. 31)
Daṇḍa: vikṛti, 121, 142-148, 151
vertical line, 219
Daśarātra-parvan, 200, 201
Daśāśvamedh Ghāṭ, 2, 4
Daśāśvamedh Tīrth, 2-5, 365 (n. 4)
Daśāśvamedh ward, 4
Dātār, Nārāyaṇ, 17, 212
Dāve, Cunnī Lāl, 8
Deccan, 119
Delhī, 116
Deoghar, Śrīkṛṣṇa, 9
Dev, Gaṅgādhar, 108
Dev, Śrīkṛṣṇa Vāman, 9, 11, 15, 21 347 (photograph)
Dev, Viśvanāth Vāman, 9 11-12, 15, 21, 30, 107, 348, (photograph), 367, (nn. 29, 31)
Devanāgarī, 206 381 (n. 65)
Devassthale, Mukund, 9
Devatādhyāya-Brāhmaṇa, 213
Devnāth, 18
Dharmadaya River, 116
Dharmādhikārī family, 8
Dhekāre, Morbhaṭṭ, 9
Dhṛtarāṣṭra, 1-2
Dhur, 345
Dhvaja, 121, 141-143, 151, 167
Dīkṣit, A. M. Rāmnāth, 10 213
Dīkṣit, Bhaṭṭoji, 7
Dīkṣit, Lakṣmīkānt, 17
Dīkṣit, Ratanjī, 18
Dīkṣit, S. Śrīnivās, 192, 350 (photograph)
Dīkṣit, Vināyak Rām, 211
Dīrgha vowels, 217
Divodās, 3
Doāb, 117
Doṅgre, Vināyak Bhaṭṭ, 8
Drāhyāyaṇa-Śrauta-Sūtra, 204 206
Draviḍ, Candraśekhar, 9
Draviḍ, Puruṣottam Śāstrī, 14
Draviḍ, Rājeśvar Śāstrī, 9
Draviḍ, Subrahmaṇya Śāstrī, 18
Dravidian Brāhmaṇs, 6 192
Duncan, Jonathan, 9)
Duration of syllables: in Atharvavedic recitation, 113-114; in Kāṇva Yajurvedic recitation, 193 197 198; in Kauthuma Sāmavedic chant, 333-341, 343, 345; in Mādhyandina Yajurvedic recitation, 123-124, 151-162, 173, 189-190; in Ṛgvedic recitation, 75-93, 106-109
Durgā Devī Mandir, 14, 16
Durgā Ghāṭ, 10
Durgā Mandir, 12, 16
Durgākuṇḍ, 12
Dvādaśāha, 200
Dvandva-parvan, 199, 201

Dvija castes, 213, 341
Dvipāda, 122
Dvivedagaṅga, 373 (n. 1)
Dvivedī, Hariśaṅkar Rām Dalpatrām, 18
East India Company, 9
Ekāha-parvan, 200-201
Ekaśruti, 100, 106, 370 (n. 29)
Epigraphy, 22, 110, 120, 202, 207, 374 (n. 14)
Forest Songbook. See Āraṇyakagāna
Gāḍgīl, Vināyak Śāstrī, 13
Gādhi family, 7-8
Gādhivaṃśānucarita, 7
Gāi Ghāṭ, 13, 16
Gāna, 199, 206, 213 See Grāmageya, Āraṇyaka, Ūha, Ūhya
Gaṇḍakī River, 118
Gaṅgā River, 2, 3, 4, 13, 14, 15, 16, 116, 117, 119, 213, 366 (n. 10)
Gaṅgādharjī, 15
Ganges. See Gaṅgā
Gaṇorkar, Lakṣmaṇjī, 15, 17
Gārhapatya, 11
Gati, 206, 300, 329
Gauḍādya Brāhmaṇs, 202
Gaurīvita, 236
Gautama school, 204, 378 (n. 16)
Gavodkar, Raghunāth, 13
Gāyatra, 341-345
Gayatrī, 341
Geldner, Karl Friedrich, 31
Ghana, 26, 64-74, 87, 92, 121-122, 170
Ghanapāṭhī, 26, 120, 190, 192
Ghāṭ, 2, 4 See Ahilyābāī, Assī, Brahmā, Daśāśvamedh, Durgā, Gāi, Ghoṛā, Hanumān, Hariścandra, Kedār, Maṇikarṇikā, Pañcgaṅgā, Prayāg, Rāj, Rājendra Prasād, Rām, Śītalā, Śivālā, Tulsī Dās
Ghoṛā Ghāṭ, 2
Ghum, 123, 154, 155, 161, 165, 168, 189, 191, 198
Giri, Maheśānand, 5, 210
Gobhila-Gṛhya-Sūtra, 204
Godāvarī River, 7, 119, 365 (n. 4)
Godse, Gajānan, 17
Godse, Śrīkṛṣṇa, 17
Goenkā Saṃskṛta Mahāvidyālaya, 208, 367 (n. 26)
Gonda, Jan, 31
Gotra, 21, 30, 211
Government of India, 9
Government Sanskrit College, 9
Govinata, 2
Govindācārya, 15
Grāmageyagāna, 199-201, 203, 219, 221, 229, 233, 236, 249, 257, 260, 297, 382 (n. 72)
Grand Trunk Road, 14
Grantha, 206, 381 (n. 55)
Gray, J. E. B., 23, 88, 89, 95, 97, 98, 99, 103, 121, 123, 382 (n. 74)
Gregorian chant, 209

Gujarāt, 6, 15, 109, 110, 119-120 202, 205, 207-208, 212, 367 (n. 29); Baroda, 119; Bhāvnagar, 109-110; Dvārākā, 7, 110; Naḍiād, 109; Santirām Mandir (Naḍiād), 367, (n. 29)
Gūrjar, Viṣṇupādhye, 8
Gupta dynasty, 5, 365 (n. 4)
Hand postures. See *Mudrā*
Hanumān Ghāṭ, 10, 14, 16
Hardikar, Kāśināth, 9
Hariścandra Ghāṭ, 14
Haryana, 119; Ambāla, 119
Hāthīgalī, 9
Haug, M., 372 (n. 43)
Havell, E. B., 4, 14, 209
Hiatus (*vivṛtti*), 28-29, 153, 155, 157, 158 165-168, 191, 197-198, 206-207
Himālaya Mountains, 117
Hindī, 10, 12
Hindustānī Saṅgīt-Paddhati, 224
Horse sacrifice. See *aśvamedha*
Hotṛ, 13, 15, 21
Hrasva vowels, 217, 335
India Office Library (London), 221 381 (n. 55)
Indika of Arrian, 116
Iṇdra, 33-38, 46-48, 64-65, 149-151, 192-193, 195, 199, 233, 236, 257, 260, 263, 277, 282
Indus River, 116
Jaiminīya school, 202-203, 205-207 214, 224, 326, 379, (n. 26), 382 (n. 72)
Jammu, 119; Raghunāth Temple, 119
Janaka, 117, 374 (n. 13)
Japa, 100
Jaṭā, 26, 101, 103, 121, 122, 124, 132, 136, 151, 170
Jaṭamātrā, 101-103
Jhā, Lābhśaṅkar, 109
Jośī, Bāl Dīkṣit, 18
Jośī, Dinkar Anna, 8, 109
Jośī, Vināyak Dīkṣit, 9
Jumnā. See Yamunā
Kāl Bhairav Mandir, 13, 16
Kāle, Bāl Dīkṣit, 8, 18
Kāle, Har Dīkṣit, 12
Kāle, Somnāth Dīkṣit, 8
Kāle, Son Dīkṣit, 13
Kaliṅga, 120
Kāṇva school, 103, 115, 119-121, 164, 191 192, 197-198, 374 (nn. 11, 13), 375 (nn. 14, 22) 376-377 (nn. 34, 42, 43)
Karatoyā River, 118
Karṇāṭaka, 22 110, 120, 202-203; Bādāmi, 202; Bangalore, 120 Bijāpur, 110 Kannaḍa, 121, 378 (n. 13); Mahārājā's Sanskrit College (Mysore), 120, 371 (n. 40), 374 (n. 14); Mysore City, 120, 371 (n. 40), 374 (n. 14); North Kannaḍa District, 203, 206, 380 (n. 52)

Karṣaṇa, 217, 323-324
Kashikar, C. G., 18
Kāśi, Kingdom of, 1, 118
Kāśī Devī Mandir, 15, 16
Kāśī Gośālā, 13
Kāśī-Khaṇḍa, 2, 4
Kāśī Vyāyāmśālā, 13
Kāśikā, 93
Kāṭhaka school, 117, 198
Kaṭhiāvāṛ, 119
Katre, Sumitra 93-94, 101 104, 106
Kātyāyana, 95, 98-100
Kātyāyana-Śrauta-Sūtra, 15, 120
Kauṣītaki-Upaniṣad, 118
Kauthuma-Saṃhitā, 199-202, 228-229, 233, 236, 249, 257, 260, 263, 277, 281-282
Kauthuma school, 15, 199, 202-207, 208, 210-214, 218-220, 224-225, 227-228, 298, 326, 333, 341 383 (n. 76)
Kavīndra, Vidyānidhi, 7
Kedār Ghāṭ, 10
Kedāreśvar Temple, 10
Kelkar, Bābū Pādhye, 9
Kelkar, Bālkṛṣṇa Śāstrī, 18
Kelkar, Raghunāth Bhaṭṭ, 9
Kelkar, Tatya, 18
Kerala, 21, 101, 120, 207, 368 (nn. 1, 2); Brahmasva Maṭham, 101, 371 (n. 35); Chelakkara, 120 Muṇṭamuka, 101 Palghat District, 101 Trichur, 101 Veṅganellūr, 120
Khanaṅg, Lakṣmīkānt Śāstrī, 120, 192, 353 (photograph)
Khyāl, 224
Kosala, 117-118
Koṭṭu, 370 (n. 29)
Kotvālī, 13
Krama, 26, 55-63 121, 124, 129, 142-143, 375 (n. 31)
Kramadaṇḍa, 142
Kramamālā, 122, 129-130, 151
Kṛṣṇa Yajurveda, 6, 13, 14, 18 22, 27, 115, 164, 191-192, 377 (n. 34)
Kruṣṭa, 216-217, 227, 380 (n. 44)
Kṣatriya caste, 213, 341
Kṣlekar, Rājārām, 9
Kṣudra-parvan, 200-201
Kṣudra-Sūtra, 377 (n. 2)
Kuñj Galī, 13
Kuru tribe, 116-117, 374 (n. 11)
Kurukṣetra, 365 (n. 4)
Kuśā, 334
Lacchī Rām Dharmśālā, 13
Lal, Rājā Muṃśī Mādho, 13, 16
Lāṭa, 204
Lāṭyāyana-Śrauta-Sūtra, 202, 204-206
Lele, Bhiku Dīkṣit, 17-18
Length of syllables. See Duration
Liṅga-Purāṇa, 365 (n. 4)
Lodī, Sikandar, 6
Lolārk Well, 3
Macdonell, A. A., 27
Madhya Pradesh, 119, 202

Baghelkhaṇḍ, 202; Gwālior, 13, 121, Indore, 119; Mālvā, 22, 202 Mandhātā, 22; Ujjain, 119
Madhyadeśa, 116
Mādhyandina school, 12-14, 115-, 116, 118-119, 121-192, 198, 209, 214, 374 (n. 14)
Magadha, 117
Mahābaleśvarkar, Yajñeśvar Dīkṣit, 14
Mahābhārata, 365 (n. 4)
Mahābhāṣya of Patañjali, 95, 211
Mahadkar, Kṛṣṇa Dīkṣit, 15
Mahāprāṇa, 96-99
Mahārājā, 5
Mahārājā of Banāras, 212-213
Mahārāṣṭra, 4-7, 9-10, 21-23, 26, 31, 87, 97, 101, 103, 109-110, 114, 119-121, 164, 198, 202, 372 (n. 43), 375 (n. 22); Bhonsle Sanskrit Mahāvidyālaya (Nāgpur), 119-120; ; Bombay, 22; Brahman Sabhā (Bombay), 22; Mīmāṃsā Kāryālaya (Poona), 22; Nāgpur, 119; 120; Nāsik, 119-120; Poona, 22, 22, 206, 368 (n. 4), 372 (n. 43); Pratiṣṭhāna, 7; Vedaśāstrottejaka Sabhā (Poona), 22
Mahārṇava, 119, 375 (n. 19)
Mahāvārttika of Kātyāyana, 95
Mahidāsa, 202, 378 (n. 6)
Maitrāyaṇī school, 117 198
Mālā, 121-122, 129-133
Mall, The, 14
Mālvīya, Madan Mohan, 10
Maṇikarṇikā Ghāṭ, 4, 209
Maṇikarṇikākuṇḍ, 4,
Mannujī, 18
Mantra-Brāhmaṇa, 213
Marāṭhā, 7, 22
Maruts, 277
Marwari Sanskrit College, 367 (n. 26)
Maśaka, 377 (n. 1)
Māthava, Videgha, 118
Mātrā, 101, 107-109, 217-218, 333, 335-341, 343
Mātrālakṣaṇa, 217, 218, 333
Matsya-Purāṇa, 365 (n. 4)
Maurya dynasty, 116
Megasthenes, 115-116
Mehtā, Vallabharām Sāligrām, 9
Melā, 3
Meters, Vedic, 75, 341
Middle Country. See Madhyadeśa
Mīmāṃsā, 121
Miśra, Kapildev Prasād, 173
Miśra, Vāyunandan, 18
Mitra, 38- 46, 233
Mnemonics, 106
"Monkey Temple," 12
Motives, 295-333
Mudrā, 103-106, 212, 214-221, 227, 298, 323, 327, 334
Musalgāvkar, Gajānan Śāstrī, 121-122, 133, 165, 170, 173, 352 (photograph), 376 (n. 32)
Musalgāvkar, Gaṅgādhar Śāstrī, 121

Muslims, 6

Nāgar Brāhmaṇs, 212

Namana, 326

Namaskāre, 12

Nambudiri, C. P. M., 368 (n. 1)

Nambudiri Brāhmaṇs, 21, 23, 97, 101 103, 207, 368 (nn. 1, 2), 370 (n. 29)

Nanal, Bhik Bhaṭṭ, 9

Nārada, 227

Nāradīya-Śikṣā, 227

Nārāyaṇasvāmī, R., 221, 257

Narmadā River, 365 (n. 4)

Nene, Bālkṛṣṇa, 9

Nepal, 13, 103, 121; Kathmandu, 13

Nepālī, Śiromaṇi Śāstrī, 13

New School of Sāmaveda, 203-204

Nidhana, 341, 345

Nigamāgam Darbhaṅgā Vidyālaya, 109

Nirmale, Babbū, 170

Nirmale, Rājārām Bhaṭ, 170, 173, 351 (photograph)

Niruktagāna, 345

Numeral notation of Sāmaveda, 203, 214-224

Nyuṅkha, 100

Om, 108

Orissā, 120, 202, 374 (n. 14); Gañjām, 202; Kaṭak, 202, Purī, 120 Sanskrit Vidyālaya (Purī), 120 Utkala, 375 (n. 22)

Ōttillātta, 368 (n. 1)

Ōttūṭṭu, 370 (n. 29)

Oudh, 7

Pāda, 25, 122, 148, 377 (n. 41)

Padapāṭha, 25, 103, 124, 130-131, 134-136, 139, 143, 149, 370 (n. 29)

Padma Bhūṣaṇ, 9

Padmāsana, 334

Paippalāda school, 109

Pālande, Cintāmaṇi, 17, 212

Pallava dynasty, 22

Pañcāla tribe, 116-118, 374 (n. 11)

Pañcasandhi, 122, 133-36, 151, 170

Pañcaviṃśa-Brāhmaṇa, 200, 213

Pañcgaṅgā Ghāṭ, 4, 13

Pañcgāvkar, Dattu Dīkṣit, 9

Pañcgāvkar, Śrīdhar Bhaṭṭ, 18

Pañcgāvkar, Vināyak Dīkṣit, 8

Pañc-kos pilgrimage, 4

Pañc-kroś. See Pañc-kos

Pañc-nad, 4

Pañc-tīrth, 3-4

Pāṇḍe Brāhmaṇs, 211

Pāṇḍey, Sītal, 14

Pāṇini, 93-95, 98-104, 106-107

Pāṇinīya-Śikṣā, 104

Pañjāb, 117, 119; Jullundur, 119; Nirmaṇḍa, 110

Paññāti, 370 (n. 29)

Parāśara Brāhmaṇs, 375 (n. 22)

Parigraha, 27, 88, 124, 131, 138, 143, 155, 158, 161, 165, 167-169, 191.

Pariśiṣṭa to the Āraṇyakagāna, 199, 201
Parpola, Asko, 18, 204-206
Parvan: a gāna section, 200-201; a sāman section, 218-223, 305, 309-310, 320-323, 325- 327, 330-332, 335, 343, 380 (n. 53).
Paṣṭhavāt, 233
Patañjali, 95, 99-100, 211
Pāṭhak, Śyāmā Dīkṣit, 368 (n. 31)
Pāṭhak, Vāman Dīkṣit, 12
Paṭvardhan, Anant Rāmjī (Bābāguru), 9, 30
Paṭvardhan, Bhikkam Bhaṭṭ, 8, 30
Paṭvardhan, Rājārām Bhaṭṭ, 8
Pāyaguṇḍe, Vaidyanāth, 8
Pāyaguṇḍe family, 8
Peśvā, 21
Peśvā, Bājī Rāo, 4
Peṭhkar, Bālājī, 192
Phadke, Rām Kṛṣṇa, 8
Pitre, Gaṇapati, 19
Prabhudattjī, 18
Pracaya, 24, 100, 104, 106, 229; of Atharvavedic recitation, 114; of Kāṇva Yajurvedic recitation, 197-198; of Ṛgvedic recitation, 84-86, 90, 92-93, 103-104, 106-108 of Taittirīya Yajurvedic recitation, 192
Prācīna school, 203
Pragraha, 27, 129, 131
Pragṛhya-pada, 27
Prajāpati, 229, 257, 263
Prakṛti: a division of the Kauthuma-Saṃhitā, 201; a primary number, 217, 223, 298-323, 330, 334
Prakṛtigāna, 200
Praṇata, 217, 224, 323, 327
Praṇava, 108
Prastāva, 341
Prastotṛ, 341
Pratihāra, 341, 345
Pratihartṛ, 341
Prātiśākhya, 100, 104, 105
Pratyutkrama, 327, 328, 334, 336, 338, 339, 340
Prayāg Ghāṭ, 2
Prayāg Tīrth, 2
Prāyaścitta-parvan, 200, 201
Prayoga, 11
Preṅkha, 217, 323, 326, 343
Prinsep, James, 2
Pūjā, 209-210
Puṇtāmbekar, Anant Rām, 15, 21, 30, 349 (photograph)
Puṇtāmbekar family, 8
Purāṇa, 109, 365 (n. 4), 366 (n. 9), 373 (n. 3)
Purāṇik, Lakṣmīkāntācārya, 192
Purohit, Āb Dīkṣit, 18
Purohit, Sītārām Dīkṣit, 15
Puruṣa-sūkta, 129, 173-188
Pūrvagāna, 200

Pūrvārcika, 199-201
Pūṣan, 149-151
Puṣpamālā, 122, 131-133, 151, 170
Rāga, 2; 224, 381 (nn. 64, 65)
Raghavan, V., 22-23, 119-120, 203, 374-375, (nn. 14, 24)
Raghunāthjī, 15
Rāj Ghāṭ, 4, 5
Rāj Mandir, 13, 16
Rājā of Kāśī Mandir, 15, 16
Rājā of Pratāpgaṛh, 7
Rājasthān, 22, 23, 120; Jaipur, 120, 368 (n. 1); Jodhpur, 22
Rājasūya, 368 (n. 31), 374 (n. 11)
Rājendra Prasād Ghāṭ, 2
Rājpūtānā, 202
Rām Ghāṭ, 19
Rām Kaṭorā, 13, 16
Rāmnagar, 9, 14, 16, 213
Ranāḍe, Bāl Śāstrī, 13
Rāṇāyanīya-Saṃhitā, 205
Rāṇāyanīya school, 109, 202-206, 213-214, 219-220, 224, 326, 380 (n. 52)
Randohkar, Bābūbhaṭṭ, 8
Randohkar, Vīreśvar Bhaṭṭ, 8
Raṅgappa, Bāl Śāstrī, 18
Ranvir Sanskrit Pāṭhaśālā, 367 (n. 26)
Raṭāṭe, Nārāyaṇ Śāstrī, 109-110, 358 (photograph)
Raṭāṭe, Rāmcandra Bhaṭṭ, 8, 18, 109, 357 (photograph)
Ratha, 121-122, 148-151
Rathantara, 212
Rāvaḷ, Lakṣmīśaṅkar Gaurīśaṅkar, 109-110, 5
Rekhā, 121-122, 138-142, 151
Renou, Louis, 116, 198, 206, 377 (n. 43)
Reṇukā Devī Mandir, 12, 16
Repha, 217, 336
Ṛgveda, 6, 7, 9, 11, 13-15, 18, 21-109, 114, 164, 192, 198, 257, 376 (n. 39)
Ṛk-Prātiśākhya, 96, 99, 104, 218
Ṛk-Saṃhitā, 199
Rudra, 124, 209-210
Rūpakālāp, 229
Rūpāntara, 204
Sadānīrā River, 118
Sādhu, 122, 211
Ṣaḍviṃśa-Brāhmaṇa, 200, 213
Sahasrabuddhe, Ganeś Vyaṅkaṭeśa, 18
Sahasrabuddhe, Vyaṅkaṭeśa, 18
Śākala school, 21-22
Sākamaśva, 233
Sākamedha, 209
Śākhā, 109, 119-121, 164, 191, 198-199, 202-207, 326, 374 (n. 14)
Sāman, 199-200, 212, 214-215, 223, 228, 295, 299, 335, 341
Sāmaveda, 6, 10, 15, 96, 100, 105-106, 109, 164, 199-345
Sāmaveda-Saṃhitā. See Kauthuma-

Saṃhitā

Sāmavedīyarudrajapavidhiḥ of Ṛsiśaṅkar and Yamunā Prasād Tripāṭhī, 210

Sāmavidhāna-Brāhmaṇa, 213

Saṃhitā, 23, 117, 198-199, 377 (n. 43)

Saṃhitāpāṭha, 25, 31, 33, 47, 54, 88, 90, 103, 107, 110-112, 173-176, 178-88, 370 (n. 29)

Saṃhitā-Upaniṣad-Brāhmaṇa, 213

Saṃkrama, 133-134

Saṃnyāsī, 7, 10

Saṃskṛta Mahāvidyālaya (Sanskrit College), Banāras Hindu University, 10, 121, 173, 212

Saṃsthā, 11

Saṃvādī, 224, 225

Saṃvatsara-parvan, 200, 201

Sandhi, 25-30 91, 123, 133, 138, 143, 151, 164-165, 169

Śāṇḍilya, 117

Saṇḍjī Bāgh, 12

Sāṅgaveda Vidyālaya, 9, 109, 212

Saṅkar, Dev, 210

Saṅkarācārya of Dvārākā, 110

Saṅkat Mocan Mandir, 2

Śāṅkhāyana-Śrauta-Sūtra, 18, 368 (n. 2)

Sanskrit College, Banāras Hindu University. See Saṃskṛta Mahāvidyālaya

Sanskrit Commission, 22

Sanskrit Pāṭhaśālā, 9

Sanskrit University. See Vārāṇaseya Saṃskṛta Viśvavidyālaya

Sapre, Bālkṛṣṇa Bhaṭṭ, 9, 30

Sapt Sāgar, 15, 16

Saptarṣi, Lakṣmīnāth Pāṭhak, 15, 17-18

Saptarṣi, Somnāth Pāṭhak, 17

Sārasvata Brāhmaṇs, 15

Sārasvata, Śrīnāthjī, 190

Sarasvatī, 46-48, 54

Sarasvatī River, 117, 366 (n. 10)

Śarmā, Prem Latā 210

Sarvamedha, 131-133

Sarvānudātta, 24-25; of Kāṇva Yajurvedic recitation, 198; of Ṛgvedic recitation, 92; of Taittirīya Yajurvedic recitation, 192

Sarvapṛṣṭha-aptoryāma, 13

Saryūpārīṇ Brāhmaṇs, 14, 210

Śaśibhūṣaṇ, 15

Śāstrī, Agnisvātt, 211-212, 228, 298 310-311, 315, 317-318, 320, 323, 354 (photograph)

Śāstrī, Dāmodar, 8

Śāstrī, Gopāl Candra, 214

Śāstrī, Govind, 8

Śāstrī, Haraprasād, 7, 9

Śāstrī, Kiśor, 214, 228

Śāstrī, Śivarāmakṛṣṇa, 370-371 (n. 32)

Śāstrī, Yugal Kiśor, 214, 228

Śāstrī, Kṛṣṇapant, 19

Śāstrī, M. M. Vaṃśidhar, 19

Śatapatha-Brāhmaṇa, 1, 2, 117-118, 170, 373 (n. 1)

Sāthe, Viṣṇu Śāstrī, 19
Satī Cabūtarā, 13, 16
Satlaj River, 110
Sātrājita, Śatānīka, 2
Sattra-parvan, 200-201
Satyāṣāḍha-Śrauta-Sūtra, 13, 18-19
Satyayajñi, Somaśuṣma, 118
Śāṭyāyana school, 205
Śaunaka school, 109, 164
Śaunakīyā Caturādhyāyikā, 99
Savitṛ, 341
Sāvitrī verse, 341
Seleukus Nikator, 115
Sena dynasty, 22
Sequence, 218-219, 300, 314, 321, 323-333
337, 343, 345
Śeṣ, Bhikojī Pant, 14-15
Śeṣa family, 8
Shāh Jahān, 7
Sherring, M. A., 2, 6
Siddhānta-Kaumudī of Bhaṭṭoji
Dīkṣit, 7
Siddhnāth, 19
Śikhā, 121-122, 136-138, 151
Śikṣā, 104-105
Singh, Chet, 14
Singh, Mān, 368 (n. 31)
Singh, R. L., 5
Singh, Vibhuti Nārāyaṇ, Mahārājā of
Banāras, 212
Śītalā Ghāṭ, 8
Śiva, 2, 3-4, 209
Śivājī, 7
Śivālā Ghāṭ, 15-16
Skanda-Purāṇa, 2
Ṣoḍaśin, 11
Soma Pavamāna, 54-56, 199, 257, 260, 277,
319, 345
Soma rituals, 1, 5, 11, 13, 12-17, 100, 200,
208, 211-212, 341, 345, 377 (n. 1)
Soman, Sadāśiv Śāstrī, 14
Somayāgas. See Soma rituals 11
Śrauta rituals, 10-19 208
Śrautakośa, 208
Śrautasūtra, 200, 202, 205-206
Śrauti, P. Kṛṣṇamūrti, 213, 356
(photograph)
Śrī Chandra Mahāvidyālaya, 367 (n. 26)
Śrīmālī Brāhmaṇs, 15, 18, 202, 208
Śruti, 11
Staal, J. F., 101, 110 120, 365
(n. 4), 371 (n. 35), 374 (n. 14)
Stobha, 199, 322-323, 329, 332, 340, 380
(n. 53)
Stotra, 200
Subrahmaṇyā, 100, 211
Śūdra caste, 208, 227
Sukhlāl Sāhu Phāṭak, 13
Śukla Yajurveda, 12-14, 115-198, 209
214, 368 (n. 31)
Śukriya-parvan, 199 201
Sūkta, 24

Sukul, Kuber Nāth, 2, 4, 8, 366 (n. 6)
Sumer Mandir, 14
Sūrya, 133-138
Svādhyāya, 11, 23, 210
Svara: sound, 96, 99, 370 (n. 29); tone of a rāga, 224
Svāra, 217, 224, 323, 333, 343
Svaravistāra, 224, 225, 382 (n. 65); of Rāg Vasant, 225
Svarita, 24-25, 94-97, 99-101, 104-105, 214, 228-229
of Atharvavedic recitation, 133
114; of Kāṇva Yajurvedic recitation, 197-198; of Ṛgvedic recitation, 81-83, 89-91, 103-108;
of Taittirīya Yajurvedic recitation, 191-192
Svarūpa, 204
Svaśākhā, 109
Syādvāda Jain Vidyālaya, 367 (n. 26)
Syllable notations of Sāmaveda, 203, 214, 219-224
Taittirīya-Saṃhitā, 370 (n. 29)
Taittirīya school, 27, 115, 117, 17 191-192, 198
Tāla, 218
Tamil Brāhmaṇs, 10, 21, 120, 192, 198, 202-204, 207, 213, 378 (n. 34)
Tamilnāḍ, 22, 120, 192, 202-204, 213, 381 (n. 56); Aḍayappalam, 203; Alivam, 120; Anakkāvūr, 204; Iñjikkollai, 120; Kāñcīpuram, 22, 120; Kumbakoṇam, 213; Madras, 213 Maraiturai, 213; Muḷḷanṭiram, 203 377, (n. 4); Nannilam, 120 North Arcot District, 22, 120, 203; Panayūr, 204 Paranūr, 204; Peruhamaṇi, 120; Perumāḷkoil, 204; Śedinipuram, 120; Śermādevi, 120; Śiruhamaṇi, 120; Śrīraṅgam, 120; Tañjāvūr, 22; Tañjāvūr District, 120; 202-204, 213; Tiruccirāppaḷḷi, 120 Tiruccirāppaḷḷi District, 120; Tirunelvēli District, 22, 120; Tiruvārūr, 120; Tiruvidaccheri, 120; Tiruvidaimarudūr, 213, Vaihanallūr, 120; Varadarāja Temple (Kāñcīpuram), 120; Villupuram, 204
Tān, 224
Tārkṣya, 149-150, 236-249
Temples of Vārāṇasī. See Durgā Devī (Rāmnagar), Durgā, Kāl Bhairav, Kedāreśvar, Rāj, Rājā of Kāśī, Reṇukā Devī, Saṅkat Mocan, Sumer (Rāmnagar), Viśvanāth
Thatte, Gaṅgādhar Śāstrī, 19
Ṭhumrī, 224
Ṭikamani Sanskrit College, 367 (n. 26)
Tīrth, 2, 3, 4, 363 (n. 9)
Tivārī Brāhmaṇs, 202
Tones: of Atharvavedic recitation,

110, 113-114of Kāṇva Yajurvedic recitation193, 197-198;of Kauthuma Sāmaveda, 228, 295-334 343-345; of Mādhyandina Yajurvedic recitation, 123, 151-170, 173, 178-191; of North Indian classical music, 225, 227; of Ṛgvedic recitation, 75-93; of Taittirīya Yajurvedic recitation,191
Toro, Bāl Dīkṣit, 19
Town Hall, 15
Traividyā-caraṇa, 6
Tripāda, 122
Tripāṭhī, Devkṛṣṇa, 17, 212
Tripāṭhī, Gopāl Rām, 212, 379 (n. 40)
Tripāṭhī, Maṅgal Datt, 173
Tripāṭhī, Nandkṛṣṇa, 17, 212
Tripāṭhī, Nārāyaṇ Śaṅkar, 212, 228, 355 (photograph)
Tripāṭhī, Ṛṣiśaṅkar, 15, 17, 208-212, 379 (n. 33), 383 (n. 76)
Tripāṭhī, Śiv Datt, 17, 212
Tripāṭhī, Śiv Rām (Yajurvedī), 17
Tripāṭhī, Śiv Rām (Sāmavedī),17 212
Tripāṭhī, Yamunā Prasād, 210-211, 334, 379 (n. 33)
Tristhalī-Setu of Nārāyaṇ Bhaṭṭ, 7
Trivedī, Hari Śaṅkar, 212, 228
Tughlak, Firoz, 6
Tulsī Dās Ghāṭ, 3
Udātta, 24-25, 93-101, 104-105, 214, 228-229, 371 (n. 32); of Atharvavedic recitation, 113-114; of Kāṇva Yajurvedic recitation, 193, 197-198; of Mādhyandina Yajurvedic recitation, 163, of Ṛgvedic recitation, 75, 86-88, 89, 91, 97-99, 103-104, 106-108; of Taittirīya Yajurvedic recitation, 191
Udgātṛ, 15, 17, 209, 212, 341
Udgītha, 341 345
Ūha, 200, 213
Ūhagāna, 200-201, 203, 213, 277, 281
Ūharahasyagāna. See Ūhyagāna
Ūhyagāna, 200-201 203, 213, 282
Ukthya, 11
Upadrava, 341, 345
Upaniṣad, 213-214
Utkrama, 133
Utrecht, University of, 382 (n. 72)
Utsvarita, 217, 331, 332-333, 343, 380 (n. 49)
Uttar Pradesh, 210, 211; Āzamgaṛh, 210 Bādā District, 210; Bharthanā, 211; Dehrādūn, 210; Faizābād, 210; Gorakhpur District, 211; Iṭār, 211; Iṭāvā District, 211; Kānyakubja, 202, 375 (n. 22); Lucknow, 210; Markā, 210; Mathurā, 365 (n. 4); Murādābād, 210; Pratāpgaṛh, 211; Pratāpgaṛh District, 211; Prayāg

(Allāhābād), 3, 7, 210, 365 (n. 4);
Rāmnagar, 9, 14, 16, 213; Saryā, 211
Uttaragāna, 200
Uttarārcika, 200-201
Uvaṭa, 104
Vādī, 224-225
Vaiśampāyana, 113
Vaiṣṇava Brāhmans, 204
Vaiśvadeva, 209
Vaiśya caste, 213, 341
Vājapeya, 11
Vājasaneya, 115
Vājasaneyi-Prātiśākhya, 375 (n. 31)
Vājasaneyi-Saṃhitā, 28-29, 103, 115, 117
121, 124, 129, 131, 133, 136-139, 143, 149, 163,
170, 173, 191-192, 374(n. 11), 376 (n. 34)
Vājasani, 115
Vājikāṇva school, 119
Vāmadeva, 281
Vāmanācārya, 17
Vaṃśa-Brāhmaṇa, 213
Vaṅga, 119
Varaṇā. See Varṇā
Vārāṇaseya Saṃskṛta Viśvavidyālaya (Sanskrit University), 9-11, 13, 16, 109, 214
Varma, Siddheshwar, 95, 370 (n. 32)
Varṇā River, 2, 4, 16, 116
Varuṇa, 33, 38, 46, 233, 277
Varuṇapraghāsa, 209
Vasant, Rāg, 224-225
Vāśīmkar, Ātmārām, 17
Vasiṣṭha, 260, 282
Vasu, S. C., 93-94
Vauṣaṭ, 100
Vāyu, 24, 33, 38
Vāze, Rāmeśvar Bhaṭṭ, 19
Vedādhyayana, 109, 121, 170, 202
Vedapāṭhaśālā, 8-9, 22-23, 109, 119, 368 (n. 4)
Vedasammelana, 109, 367 (n. 29)
Vedavyās, 14
Vedic Grammar of A. A. Macdonell, 27
Vetal, M. M. Vināyak Śāstrī, 19
Videha, 17-118
Vikṛti: a derivative recitation, 26-27
87-91, 107, 121-122, 124, 129-130, 132-134,
136-141, 144, 150-151, 161-162, 164-165, 170;
of the Kauthuma-Saṃhitā, 201; a secondary number, 217, 223, 298, 323
Vikṛtigāna, 200
Village Songbook. See Grāmageyagāna
Vinata, 217, 323, 324, 326, 343, 380 (n. 48)
Vindhya Mountains, 117
Visarga, 30, 88, 91-92, 108, 114, 153-155,
158, 160-161, 163, 165, 167-168, 173, 189,
191, 300, 304, 317
Viṣṇu, 4
Viṣṇu Mahāyajña, 211
Viśvanāth Mandir, 13, 16
Viśve Devāsa, 46-48
Viśveśvar Gañj, 12
Vrata-parvan, 199, 201

<u>Vṛddha</u> vowels, 217

Vyāsa Brāhmaṇs, 202

<u>Vyutkrama</u>, 133

Weber, Albrecht, 115-116

White Yajurveda. See Śukla Yajurveda

Yagyavaru, Bābū Dīkṣit, 9

<u>Yajamāna</u>, 11-12, 17, 208-211

Yājñavalkya-Śikṣā, 104

Yājñavalkya Vājasaneya, 115, 118

Yajurveda, 6, 9, 12-15, 18, 22, 27, 115-118, 120-121 123, 164, 191, 197-198, 209, 214, 368 (n. 31), 370 (n. 29)

Yamunā River, 3 116-117 366 (n. 10)

<u>Yātrā</u>, 366 (n. 13)